Dear reader

*L*ike the city of Paris, The Michelin Guide never stands still. In this, the 2007 edition, we have presented the information in a more practical and appealing manner, in order to make it more accessible to you, the reader. Take your pick from some of the best hotels and restaurants in Paris, which have been carefully selected for this guide.

*O*ur aim in producing the guide of course remains unchanged and our selection (because it is a selection-we do not claim to be exhaustive) is based on the same criteria as always: the quality of the welcome, the service and the cooking. The range of different types of restaurants included in the guide means that the choice should be sufficiently wide to satisfy all tastes. Without abandoning our principles or succumbing to fashion, we have endeavoured to present you with a wide selection of Michelin starred restaurants, gastronomic bistrots, brasseries and a choice of cuisine from all over the globe.

*A*lthough Michelin stars continue to signify establishments serving cuisine of the highest standards, they are not our only award. Restaurants serving good quality food at affordable prices are highlighted with a 'Bib Gourmand'.

*T*he sixty hotels listed are similarly classified; divided into categories reflecting the different prices and levels of comfort that you would expect to find in Paris. From prestigious palaces to more modest - but still charming - establishments, the importance of a friendly welcome and good service is never forgotten.

*W*e hope that this new guide will help you to appreciate the different culinary aspects of Paris, and that your journey through these pages will be one to savour.

Consult the Michelin Guide at www.viamichelin.com
and write to us at : leguidemichelin-france@fr.michelin.com

CONTENTS

Richer X./MICHELIN

Richer X./MICHELIN

WHERE TO STAY

How to use this guide

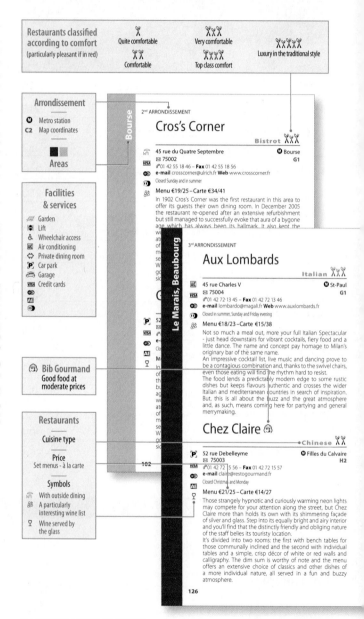

Restaurants classified according to comfort
(particularly pleasant if in red)

X — Quite comfortable
XX — Comfortable
XXX — Very comfortable
XXXX — Top class comfort
XXXXX — Luxury in the traditional style

Arrondissement

Ⓜ Metro station
C2 Map coordinates

Areas

Facilities & services

🌿 Garden
🛗 Lift
♿ Wheelchair access
AC Air conditioning
⟷ Private dining room
P Car park
🚗 Garage
VISA Credit cards

🉐 **Bib Gourmand**
Good food at moderate prices

Restaurants

Cuisine type

Price
Set menus - à la carte

Symbols

🌿 With outside dining
🍷 A particularly interesting wine list
🍷 Wine served by the glass

Bourse

2ND ARRONDISSEMENT

Cros's Corner

Bistrot XX

45 rue du Quatre Septembre — Ⓜ Bourse
✉ 75002 — G1
VISA ☎ 01 42 55 18 46 - **Fax** 01 42 55 18 56
e-mail crosscorner@ulrich.fr **Web** www.crosscorner.fr
Closed Sunday and in summer

Menu €19/25 - Carte €34/41

In 1902 Cros's Corner was the first restaurant in this area to offer its guests their own dining room. In December 2005 the restaurant re-opened after an extensive refurbishment but still managed to successfully evoke that aura of a bygone age which has always been its hallmark. It also kept the...

Le Marais, Beaubourg

3RD ARRONDISSEMENT

Aux Lombards

Italian XXX

45 rue Charles V — Ⓜ St-Paul
VISA ✉ 75004 — G1
☎ 01 42 72 13 45 - **Fax** 01 42 72 13 46
e-mail lombardo@magali.fr **Web** www.auxlombards.fr
Closed in summer, Sunday and Friday evening

Menu €18/23 - Carte €15/38

Not so much a meal out, more your full Italian Spectacular - just head downstairs for vibrant cocktails, fiery food and a little dance. The name and concept pay homage to Milan's originary bar of the same name.
An impressive cocktail list, live music and dancing prove to be a contagious combination and, thanks to the swivel chairs, even those eating will find the rhythm hard to resist.
The food lends a predictably modern edge to some rustic dishes but keeps flavours authentic and crosses the wider Italian and mediterranean countries in search of inspiration. But, this is all about the buzz and the great atmosphere and, as such, means coming here for partying and general merrymaking.

Chez Claire 🉐

Chinese XX

P 52 rue Debelleyme — Ⓜ Filles du Calvaire
✉ 75003 — H2
VISA ☎ 01 42 72 72 56 - **Fax** 01 42 72 15 57
e-mail claire@restogourmand.fr
AE Closed Christmas and Monday
🍷 Menu €21/25 - Carte €14/27

Those strangely hypnotic and curiously warming neon lights may compete for your attention along the street, but Chez Claire more than holds its own with its shimmering façade of silver and glass. Step into its equally bright and airy interior and you'll find that the distinctly friendly and obliging nature of the staff belies its touristy location.
It's divided into two rooms: the first with bench tables for those communally inclined and the second with individual tables and a simple, crisp décor of white or red walls and calligraphy. The dim sum is worthy of note and the menu offers an extensive choice of classics and other dishes of a more individual nature, all served in a fun and buzzy atmosphere.

126

102

Hotels classified according to comfort
(particularly pleasant if in red)

Quite comfortable	Very comfortable
Comfortable	Top class comfort
	Luxury in the traditional style

Hotels

Symbols

39 rm	Number of rooms
	Breakfast included
♦/♦♦	Prices for a single / double room
⁑⃝	With restaurant
⊘/⊘	Quiet hotel / very quiet hotel
▣	Swimming pool
⊛	Spa
⋒	Sauna
⚲	Tennis
𝕴-ᴅ	Exercise room
✆	WIFI
▦	Satellite TV
🖳	Equipped conference room

Plan & Arrondissement

PLAN 6ᵗʰ ARRONDISSEMENT

Le Grand Vesco

26 rue Monsieur Le Prince   **◎ Odéon**
✉75006   **C2**
✆ 01 45 98 63 75 – **Fax** 01 45 98 63 77
e-mail legrandvesco@quiethotels.com
Web www.legrandvesco.com

36 rm ⊡ – **♦**€75/90 **♦♦**€85/112
⁑⃝ **Sous le dôme** (See restaurant listing)

...certainly knew how to build hotels. Le Grand ...ginally called the Great Dome and was one ...the great railway hotels; the façade today still ...hitectural style of that age. Once inside, howe-...y realise you're in the company of an internatio-...oration, where size, comfort and facilities fit the ...dards demanded by your average 21st century

...ing feature of the hotel is the vast glass-roofed ... which the Sous le Dôme restaurant serves ...a French menu at lunch and dinner. Those after ...ttle more traditional should head downstairs to ...elled Cellar Bar, while the Mirror Bar is an alto-...ophisticated spot for cocktail hour.

..., many of which face inwards into the atrium, ...sly proportioned and have every mod con you ...oms are also a good size and the majority have ...ers and double washbasins. Those looking for ...vels of relaxation will be more than happy with ...ped Health Club.

WHERE TO STAY **397**

Right margin: St-Germain des Prés, Quartier Latin, Luxembourg

---

3ᵣᵈ ARRONDISSEMENT

La Table de Marie ✿

Contemporary XX

33 rue Amelot   **◎ St-Sébastien Froissart**
✉ 75011   **H1**
✆01 42 63 18 86 – **Fax** 01 42 63 18 87
e-mail tabledemarie@resto.com **Web** www.tabledemarie.com
Closed Monday and Sunday evening
Menu 24/45€ (lunch) – **Carte** 18/27€

Mary's table is a handsome four storey 18th century building in the heart of Paris. To gain entry, you ring the doorbell and you'll then be ushered into one of the two dining rooms. Regulars may have their favourite but there's little to choose between them – they're both warm and welcoming, although the first floor room is slightly larger than the ground floor.

There is something about being cosseted in a characterful house that makes dining here such a pleasure and it provides the perfect antidote for those feeling bruised and buffeted by the bigger, more boisterous places.

The cooking is modern in its approach and presentation but flavours are far more vigorous and full bodied than one expects and the marriages of various ingredients bear testament to real talent. Evidence of Marie's South-East roots pops up here and there. Tasting and Garden menus are available for those making it an occasion and there are some interesting small producers featured on the wine list.

Left margin: Le Marais, Beaubourg

À LA CARTE		
FIRST COURSES	**MAIN COURSES**	**DESSERT**
• Millefeuille de thon rouge mariné et coulis de tomates vertes	• Bar de ligne grillé au safran et chutney de courgettes	• Soufflé au chocolat noir et son croustillant de noix de coco
• Pâté chaud de colvert en croûte de pain d'épices	• Pigeonneau rôti à la cannelle et ses échalotes confites	• Macarons aux fruits rouges et aux mirabelles

127

Stars for good cooking :
from ✿✿✿ to ✿

...and the sample menu.

Practical information

Should you want to get to the airport, book a taxi or buy theatre tickets in between two gourmet treats, we have provided a short practical information section to make Paris life easier.

ARRIVAL/DEPARTURE

By air

www.aeroportsdeparis.fr
Information on flights of the day: ℘ 0033 (0) 892 68 15 15
Roissy-Charles-de-Gaulle Airport, ℘ 0033 (0) 1 48 62 12 12.
By taxi, allow between 30 min and 1hr for the trip to/from Paris.
By RER B (Châtelet): 30mn.
By Roissybus (Opéra): 50-60 mn.
Noctiliens (night bus): N°120/121 (Châtelet) and N°140 (Gare de l'Est): allow 1hr.
Autocars Air France: N°2 (Porte Maillot, Étoile): 45 min and N°4 (Gare de Lyon, Gare Montparnasse): 50 min
Orly Airport, ℘ 0033 (0) 1 49 75 15 15.
By taxi, allow 20 to 30 min.
Orlybus (Denfert-Rochereau): 30 min.

Noctiliens (night bus): N°31 (Gare de Lyon) or N°120 (Châtelet): 30 min.
Autocars Air France: N°1 (Invalides, Gare Montparnasse): 35 min.

Useful to know, Navette Roissy (℘ 0033 (0) 1 48 42 29 51 or www.navetteroissy.com) provides collective taxi-type transport from your home (Paris and suburbs) to the airports and SNCF railway stations. Other companies also operate out of **Beauvais-Tillé Airport;** shuttles are also in service to and from Porte Maillot (75 min).

By train

www.sncf.fr
Gare de Lyon: trains from southeast France, Italy and Switzerland.
Gare d'Austerlitz: southwest France and Spain.
Gare du Nord: northern France, United Kingdom, Belgium, the Netherlands.
Gare de l'Est: eastern France and Germany.
Gare Montparnasse: west of France.

WHEN TO COME TO PARIS

All year round! We do however strongly recommend booking well ahead of time if you plan on coming during the peak tourist season, Christmas period or

Blackwell K./MICHELIN

school holidays. You should also know that in August Paris is more or less deserted by its inhabitants and some establishments are closed (check beforehand). Some events also require early booking (see the list of fairs and shows). Be forewarned: from 7 September to 20 October 2007, the Stade de France (northern Paris) and Parc des Princes stadiums will be hosting the **Rugby World Cup.**

GETTING ROUND PARIS

Inner and outer Paris have an excellent and inexpensive public transport system (Transilien) combining the metro and buses **(RATP)** and railway networks **(SNCF)** which operates 7 days a week. The first section of the new **tramline** has been operating in the south of Paris since January 2007. At night time, a network of Noctilien buses takes over. Times, tickets and itineraries can be found on **www.ratp.fr** and **www.transilien.com** (both in English).

Taxi!

Taxis can be hailed in the street – unoccupied taxis have a white light on the roof – or called from a taxi rank. A surcharge of around 10% is applied from 7pm (night rate).
Taxis Bleus, ✆ 0 891 701 010 (€0.23/min)
Alpha Taxis, ✆ 01 45 85 85 85
Taxis G7, ✆ 01 47 39 47 39
Taxis G-Space, ✆ 01 47 39 01 39

By car

Does the prospect of driving in Paris appeal? Why not, providing you

Fairs and Shows

Salon International de l'Agriculture, Porte de Versailles, 3 to 11 March.
Foire de Paris, Porte de Versailles, 27 April to 8 May.
Salon du Livre, Porte de Versailles, 23 to 27 March.
Mondial du Deux Roues, Porte de Versailles, 29 September to 7 October.

are patient and take a few basic precautions, such as avoiding peak hours and consulting **traffic** sites: www.viamichelin.fr, www.sytadin.tm.fr. **On your mobile phone:** http://wap.sytadin.gouv.fr, www.bison-fute.equipement.gouv.fr or www.infotrafic.com.
You will also need to buy a **Paris-Carte** which is practically the only way to pay the parking meters. They can be bought from tobacconists and some newspaper stalls (€10 or €30).
Car parks: www.infoparking.com (public car parks) or www.parkingsdeparis.com (hard copy version also available).
If you break down: SOS Dépannage 24hr service, ✆ 01 47 07 99 99 (66 bd Auguste-Blanqui, 13th).
If you get towed away: Pré-Fourrière, Préfecture de Police, ✆ 01 53 71 53 71.

By bicycle

An extremely pleasant way of exploring Paris, all the more so as Paris has more and more cycling paths. Bicycles can be rented from the RATP via **Maison Roue Libre,** ✆ 0 810 441 534 or www.rouelibre.fr

Living in Paris

News

Newspaper stalls: in addition to the national dailies and magazines, a number of other titles provide news on cultural events in Paris: *l'Officiel des Spectacles, Pariscope* and the Nouvel Observateur's *Paris-Île-de-France* and Télérama's *Sortir* supplements.

Radio: in addition to nationwide radios, several local radio stations broadcast in the capital, such as FIP (105.1 FM with traffic updates every 15-30 min).

Television: in addition to the Hertzian and cable stations, **Paris Première** broadcasts several programmes devoted to life in Paris including *Paris Dernière,* which is ideal for finding out which are the "in" places of the moment.

Museums and monuments

As a general rule, national museums are closed on Tuesdays and those of the City of Paris on Mondays. In addition, most of the major museums stay open until 9.30pm at least once a week (every day except Tuesday in the case of the Centre Georges-Pompidou).

A **Museum and Monument Pass** (1, 3 or 5 days) makes it possible to jump the queue; it is also possible to book tickets for the Louvre and many other museums (TicketNet, Fnac, department stores, etc.). The RATP-Louvre combined ticket (on sale in tourist offices and the Eiffel tower) offers priority access to permanent collections.

Office du Tourisme et des Congrès de Paris, ℰ 0 892 68 30 00 or www.parisinfo.com

Office du Tourisme de Paris-Île-de-France, ℰ 01 56 89 38 00 or www.pidf.com

Sight-seeing

Open Tour (double-decker bus), ℰ 01 42 66 56 56 or www.paris-opentour.com

Balabus (main sights of the capital), ℰ 08 92 68 77 14 or www.ratp.fr

Batobus (Compagnie des Bateaux-Mouches; you can get off and on at each halt), ℰ 01 42 25 96 10.

Bateaux parisiens, ℰ 0 825 01 01 01.

Entertainment

In terms of entertainment, Paris offers a range that is as dense as it is eclectic from the most mythical of stages to the tiniest of halls and every evening the "city of light" raises the curtain on a dizzying array of drama, ballet and concert performances. Among the more

Discount tickets!

www.ticketac.com covers all the shows on in Paris at discount prices. There are also ticket stands at Madeleine and the Montparnasse Tower Esplanade where you can buy theatre tickets for the same day at half price (mainly privately run theatres).

To smoke... or not to smoke?

Since February 1 2007, all public places in France have been non-smoking. Cafés, tobacconists, restaurants and nightclubs will not have to apply this rule until January 1 2008.

well-known are Opéra-Bastille, Opéra national de Paris Palais Garnier, Salle Pleyel, Casino de Paris, Cigale, Bataclan, Palais des Congrès de Paris, New Morning, Élysée-Montmartre, Zenith de Paris, Olympia, Crazy-Horse, Folies Bergère, Lido, Moulin Rouge, etc.

Shopping

Paris shops are generally open from Monday to Saturday and from 9am to 7pm (and on Sundays in some tourist districts). **Gourmet shops** are often closed on Mondays, but are open on Sunday mornings. Most of the big department stores close late (9.30pm) once a week.

Every week, nearly 70 street and covered markets add life and colour to Paris. Days and times on www.paris.fr, the web sites of the arrondissement town halls or from the **Bureau du Commerce** (✆ 01 42 76 70 14).

Eating

While the traditional brasserie remains the emblematic icon of Parisian restaurants (see the list at the end of the guide), the capital teems with establishments of every level of comfort and every type of cuisine. In this guide we provide a list of the best restaurants in each price category.

Late night dining: consult the list of restaurants at the end of the guide.

Health

Police, ✆ 17
Fire brigade, ✆ 18
Medical emergencies - Samu, ✆ 15
SOS Doctors, ✆ 01 47 07 77 77.
Anti-poison centre (Fernand-Widal Hospital), ✆ 01 40 05 48 48
Dental emergencies,
✆ 01 43 37 51 00
24 hour chemists:
84 av. des Champs-Élysées (Galerie les Champs), 8th, ✆ 01 45 62 02 41
6 pl. Clichy, 9th, ✆ 01 48 74 65 18
6 pl. Félix-Eboué, 12th,
✆ 01 43 43 19 03

Other useful telephone numbers

Lost and found, ✆ 0821 00 25 25
Loss/theft Visa bank card
(7 days a week, 24 hours),
✆ 0 892 705 705
Loss/theft American Express card (7 days a week, 24 hours),
✆ 01 47 77 72 00
24 hour baby-sitting:
Baybichou, ✆ 01 43 13 33 23
Louvre Post Office:
2 rue du Louvre, 75001
(open 24 hrs a day),
✆ 01 40 28 76 00

Where to eat

Alphabetical index of restaurants

E

F

G

H

I

J

K

L

the **MICHELIN** guide

a collection to savour !

Belgique & Luxembourg
Deutschland
España & Portugal
France
Great Britain & Ireland
Italia
Nederland
Österreich
Portugal
Suisse

Also :

Paris
London
New York City
San Francisco
Main Cities of Europe

Starred establishments...

'A good restaurant in its category'- *'Excellent cooking, worth a detour'* – *'Exceptional cuisine, worth a special journey'*: the mere definition of one, two and three stars says it all. Or nearly all. This has been the case ever since Michelin decided, several decades ago, to mark out the best restaurants by attributing stars - known to some as macaroons because of their resemblance - for quality cuisine.

If we accept the principle that "only one type of cooking exists: good cooking," restaurants with a range of culinary styles can strive to obtain the awards given by Michelin inspectors; those anonymous explorers with oft-used cutlery and finely-tuned taste buds. What criteria are used? It is always about the quality of the ingredients, the mastery of the cooking and the flavours, the consistency, and the personal touches that make up the presentation.

It's important to remember, too, that the number of stars visible in the Michelin sky varies from one year to the next, and that some of the chefs who are at this moment approaching our constellation - known as the 'Rising Stars'- may at some time in the future, if they continue on the same trajectory, shine just as brightly.

Given the number of varied and ever-changing gourmet temptations one will find here, Paris occupies a special place among the gastronomic capitals. Have you appreciated a great restaurant or discovered a new talent? Do you agree with our choices or are you sceptical of our judgements? Do not hesitate to let us know: our readers' letters are always very much appreciated.

Lastly, remember that it is all about the food; nothing but the food. Any opinions we might hold about the quality of comfort or service do not influence our ultimate judgements.

Exceptional cuisine :
worth a special journey !

One always eats extremely well here, sometimes superbly

Alain Ducasse au Plaza Athénée (8ᵉ)	XxXxX	176
L'Ambroisie (4ᵉ)	XxXX	92
Arpège (7ᵉ)	XxX	140
Astrance (16ᵉ)	XxX	317
Le Grand Véfour (1ᵉʳ)	XxXX	54
Guy Savoy (17ᵉ)	XxXX	336
Ledoyen (8ᵉ)	XxXxX	178
Meurice (le) (Rest.) (1ᵉʳ)	XxXxX	52
Pierre Gagnaire (8ᵉ)	XxXX	183
Pré Catelan (16ᵉ)	XxXX	310

Excellent cooking :
worth a detour

Les Ambassadeurs (8ᵉ)	XxXxX	175
Apicius (8ᵉ)	XxXxX	180
Le Bristol (Rest.) (8ᵉ)	XxXxX	177
Carré des Feuillants (1ᵉʳ)	XxX	55
Le "Cinq" (8ᵉ)	XxXxX	174
Les Élysées (8ᵉ)	XxX	185
Hélène Darroze-La Salle à Manger (6ᵉ)	XxX	123
Lasserre (8ᵉ)	XxXxX	181
Michel Rostang (17ᵉ)	XxXX	337
Relais Louis XIII (6ᵉ)	XxX	122
Senderens (8ᵉ)	XxX	188
La Table de Joël Robuchon (16ᵉ)	XxX	314
Taillevent (8ᵉ)	XxXxX	179

A very good restaurant in its category

L'Angle du
  Faubourg (8e)   XX   203

L'Atelier de
  Joël Robuchon (7e)   X   155

Auguste (7e)   XX   152

Au Trou Gascon (12e)   XX   255

Bath's (17e)   X   344

Benoît (4e)   XX   93

Braisière (La) (17e)   XX   339

Le Carpaccio (8e)   XXX   191

Le Céladon (2e)   XXX   72

Le Chamarré (7e)   XX   143

Le Chiberta (8e)   XXX   190

Copenhague (8e)   XXX   189

Dominique
  Bouchet (8e)   X   206

Le Duc (14e)   XXX   275

L'Espadon (1er)   XXXXX 53

Les Fables de
  La Fontaine (7e)   X   157

Gaya Rive Gauche par
  Pierre Gagnaire (7e)   X   156

Gérard Besson (1er)   XXX   57

Goumard (1er)   XXX   56

Grande
  Cascade (16e)   XXXX 311

Hiramatsu (16e)   XXXX 312

Jacques Cagna (6e)   XXX   121

Le Jardin (8e)   XXXX 184

Jean (9e)   XX   223

Laurent (8e)   XXX   182

Le Divellec (7e)   XXX   141

Maison Courtine (14e)   XX   277

Mont-
  parnasse'25 (14e)   XXXX 274

Les Muses (9e)   XXX   220

Les Ormes (7e)   XX   145

Paris (6e)   XXX   120

Passiflore (16e)   XXX   319

Le Pergolèse (16e)   XXX   316

Relais d'Auteuil (16e)   XXX   313

Le Relais du Parc (16e) XX   321

Stella Maris (8e)   XX   199

La Table du
  Baltimore (16e)   XXX   315

La Table du
  Lancaster (8e)   XXX   186

Tour d'Argent (5e)   XXXXX 104

Vin sur Vin (7e)   XX   147

Violon d'Ingres (7e)   XX   144

Rising Stars

For ✿✿✿

Les Ambas-
  sadeurs (8e)   XXXXX 175

For ✿✿

L'Atelier de
  Joël Robuchon (7e)   X   155

Bib Gourmand

Restaurants offering good-quality cooking for less than 35€ (excluding drinks)

L'Affriolé *(7ᵉ)*	𝕏	166
Les Allobroges *(20ᵉ)*	𝕏𝕏	370
Ambassade d'Auvergne *(3ᵉ)*	𝕏𝕏	84
Auberge Pyrénées Cévennes *(11ᵉ)*	𝕏	247
Au Bon Accueil *(7ᵉ)*	𝕏	158
Aux Lyonnais *(2ᵉ)*	𝕏	76
Azabu *(6ᵉ)*	𝕏	133
Le Bélisaire *(15ᵉ)*	𝕏	303
Beurre Noisette *(15ᵉ)*	𝕏	298
Bistro de l'Olivier *(8ᵉ)*	𝕏	207
Buisson Ardent *(5ᵉ)*	𝕏	110
Caroubier *(15ᵉ)*	𝕏𝕏	293
Carte Blanche *(9ᵉ)*	𝕏𝕏	224
La Cave Gourmande *(19ᵉ)*	𝕏	364
Caves Petrissans *(17ᵉ)*	𝕏	348
Chez Cécile la Ferme des Mathurins *(8ᵉ)*	𝕏	207
La Cerisaie *(14ᵉ)*	𝕏	282
Chez Géraud *(16ᵉ)*	𝕏𝕏	328
Chez l'Ami Jean *(7ᵉ)*	𝕏	166
Chez Léon *(17ᵉ)*	𝕏𝕏	343
Chez les Anges *(7ᵉ)*	𝕏𝕏	149
Clos des Gourmets *(7ᵉ)*	𝕏	161

L'Entredgeu *(17ᵉ)*	𝕏	350
L'Épi Dupin *(6ᵉ)*	𝕏	129
Fish La Boissonnerie *(6ᵉ)*	𝕏	133
Florimond *(7ᵉ)*	𝕏	162
Graindorge *(17ᵉ)*	𝕏𝕏	341
Jean-Pierre Frelet *(12ᵉ)*	𝕏	257
Mansouria *(11ᵉ)*	𝕏𝕏	245
Mellifère *(2ᵉ)*	𝕏	77
Oscar *(16ᵉ)*	𝕏	331
Paris XVII *(17ᵉ)*	𝕏	349
La Petite Sirène de Copenhague *(9ᵉ)*	𝕏	225
Les Petites Sorcières *(14ᵉ)*	𝕏	280
Le Pré Cadet *(9ᵉ)*	𝕏	227
P'tit Troquet *(7ᵉ)*	𝕏	165
La Régalade *(14ᵉ)*	𝕏	281
Ribouldingue *(5ᵉ)*	𝕏	111
La Rotonde *(6ᵉ)*	𝕏	128
Severo *(14ᵉ)*	𝕏	284
La Soupière *(17ᵉ)*	𝕏	346
Spring *(9ᵉ)*	𝕏	230
Stéphane Martin *(15ᵉ)*	𝕏	296
Le Temps au Temps *(11ᵉ)*	𝕏	246
Thierry Burlot *(15ᵉ)*	𝕏𝕏	293
Le Troquet *(15ᵉ)*	𝕏	299

Moderately priced

Set priced menu for less than 33€ (lunch and dinner)

A et M Restaurant (16ᵉ) ⚔ 329
L'Affriolé (7ᵉ) ⚔ 166
L'Aiguière (11ᵉ) ⚔⚔⚔ 244
A La Bonne Table (14ᵉ) ⚔ 283
Al Ajami (8ᵉ) ⚔⚔ 205
Alcazar (6ᵉ) ⚔⚔ 126
L 'Alchimie (15ᵉ) ⚔ 302
Allard (6ᵉ) ⚔ 132
Les Allobroges (20ᵉ) ⚔⚔ 370
Ambassade
d'Auvergne (3ᵉ) ⚔⚔ 84
L'Ami Marcel (15ᵉ) ⚔ 298
L'Amuse Bouche (14ᵉ) ⚔ 282
L'Appart' (8ᵉ) ⚔ 209
Astier (11ᵉ) ⚔ 248
L'Atelier des
Compères (8ᵉ) ⚔ 211
Atelier Maître
Albert (5ᵉ) ⚔⚔ 106
L'Auberge
Aveyronnaise (12ᵉ) ⚔ 260
Auberge Etchegorry (13ᵉ) ⚔ 267
Auberge Pyrénées
Cévennes (11ᵉ) ⚔ 247
Au Bon Accueil (7ᵉ) ⚔ 158
Au Clair de
la Lune (18ᵉ) ⚔⚔ 357
Au Petit Riche (9ᵉ) ⚔⚔ 222
Au Pied de
Cochon (1ᵉʳ) ⚔⚔ 59
Aux Lyonnais (2ᵉ) ⚔ 76
L'Avant Goût (13ᵉ) ⚔ 267
Azabu (6ᵉ) ⚔ 133
Baan Boran (1ᵉʳ) ⚔ 64
Bastide Odéon (6ᵉ) ⚔⚔ 125
Bath's (17ᵉ) ⚔ 344
Beato (7ᵉ) ⚔⚔ 150
Le Bélisaire (15ᵉ) ⚔ 303
Benkay (15ᵉ) ⚔⚔⚔ 290
Beurre Noisette (15ᵉ) ⚔ 298
La Biche au Bois (12ᵉ) ⚔ 258

Bistrot de
l'Étoile Niel (17ᵉ) ⚔ 347
Bistrot Papillon (9ᵉ) ⚔⚔ 222
Bistrot St-Honoré (1ᵉʳ) ⚔ 64
Bofinger (4ᵉ) ⚔⚔ 94
Les Bouquinistes (6ᵉ) ⚔⚔ 127
Braisière (La) (17ᵉ) ⚔⚔ 339
Brasserie Flo (10ᵉ) ⚔⚔ 236
Buisson Ardent (5ᵉ) ⚔ 110
La Butte Chaillot (16ᵉ) ⚔⚔ 328
Café Constant (7ᵉ) ⚔ 169
Le Café d'Angel (17ᵉ) ⚔ 347
Caroubier (15ᵉ) ⚔⚔ 293
Carte Blanche (9ᵉ) ⚔⚔ 224
Chez Cécile la Ferme des
Mathurins (8ᵉ) ⚔ 207
La Cerisaie (14ᵉ) ⚔ 282
Le Chateaubriand (11ᵉ) ⚔ 245
Château Poivre (14ᵉ) ⚔ 285
Chez Casimir (10ᵉ) ⚔ 237
Chez Géraud (16ᵉ) ⚔⚔ 328
Chez l'Ami Jean (7ᵉ) ⚔ 166
Chez La Vieille
"Adrienne" (1ᵉʳ) ⚔ 65
Chez Léon (17ᵉ) ⚔⚔ 343
Chez Michel (10ᵉ) ⚔ 237
Christophe (5ᵉ) ⚔ 114
Clos des Gourmets (7ᵉ) ⚔ 161
Clos Morillons (15ᵉ) ⚔ 299
Le Clou (17ᵉ) ⚔ 348
Cô Ba Saigon (8ᵉ) ⚔ 214
Coco de Mer (5ᵉ) ⚔ 109
Coconnas (4ᵉ) ⚔⚔ 94
Conti (16ᵉ) ⚔⚔ 325
Le Copreaux (15ᵉ) ⚔ 297
Le Cou de la Girafe (8ᵉ) ⚔ 208
La Coupole (14ᵉ) ⚔⚔ 278
La Cuisine (7ᵉ) ⚔⚔ 151
Le Dirigeable (15ᵉ) ⚔ 303
Le Dôme du Marais (4ᵉ) ⚔⚔ 95
Du Marché (15ᵉ) ⚔ 301

Outside

For business

Business menu at lunchtime

A Beauvilliers (18e)	✗✗✗	356
L'Affriolé (7e)	✗	166
A La Bonne Table (14e)	✗	283
L'Appart' (8e)	✗	209
Arpège (7e)	✗✗✗	140
Astrance (16e)	✗✗✗	317
L'Atelier des Compères (8e)	✗	211
Au Bon Accueil (7e)	✗	158
Auguste (7e)	✗✗	152
Au Petit Monsieur (11e)	✗	246
Au Trou Gascon (12e)	✗✗	255
Baan Boran (1er)	✗	64
Bastide Odéon (6e)	✗✗	125
Bath's (17e)	✗	344
Benkay (15e)	✗✗✗	290
Benoît (4e)	✗✗	93
Le Bistrot des Soupirs "Chez les On" (20e)	✗	370
Bistrot du Sommelier (8e)	✗✗	202
Les Bouquinistes (6e)	✗✗	127
Braisière (La) (17e)	✗✗	339
Le Bristol (Rest.) (8e)	✗✗✗✗	177
Café de la Paix (9e)	✗✗✗	221
Carré des Feuillants (1er)	✗✗✗✗	55
Chez Cécile la Ferme des Mathurins (8e)	✗	207
Le Céladon (2e)	✗✗✗	72
Le Chamarré (7e)	✗✗	143
Le Chateaubriand (11e)	✗	245
Chez Catherine (8e)	✗✗	196
Chez La Vieille "Adrienne" (1er)	✗	65
Christophe (5e)	✗	114
Le "Cinq" (8e)	✗✗✗✗	174
Coconnas (4e)	✗✗	94
Conti (16e)	✗✗	325
Copenhague (8e)	✗✗✗	189
Le Cou de la Girafe (8e)	✗	208
Daru (8e)	✗	213
Delizie d'Uggiano (1er)	✗✗	60
Le Duc (14e)	✗✗✗	275
Les Élysées (8e)	✗✗✗	185
L'Espadon (1er)	✗✗✗✗	53
Et dans mon coeur il y a... (10e)	✗	238
Les Fables de La Fontaine (7e)	✗	157
Ferme St-Simon (7e)	✗✗	148
Le Fin Gourmet (4e)	✗	96
Florimond (7e)	✗	162
La Fontaine Gaillon (2e)	✗✗✗	73
Gastroquet (15e)	✗	300
Gérard Besson (1er)	✗✗✗	57
Le Grand Véfour (1er)	✗✗✗✗	54
Hélène Darroze - La Salle à Manger (6e)	✗✗✗	123
Hiramatsu (16e)	✗✗✗	312
Indra (8e)	✗✗✗	193
Jacques Cagna (6e)	✗✗✗	121
Le Jardin (8e)	✗✗✗	184
Lapérouse (6e)	✗✗✗	124
Lasserre (8e)	✗✗✗✗	181
Le Divellec (7e)	✗✗✗	141
Ledoyen (8e)	✗✗✗✗	178
Marius et Janette (8e)	✗✗	198
Market (8e)	✗✗	204
Mellifère (2e)	✗	77
le Meurice (1er)	✗✗✗✗	52
Michel Rostang (17e)	✗✗✗✗	337
Le Mûrier (15e)	✗	302
Les Muses (9e)	✗✗	220
L'O à la Bouche (14e)	✗	281
Les Ombres (7e)	✗✗	146

Paris *(6ᵉ)*	❌❌❌	120	Stella Maris *(8ᵉ)*	❌❌ 199
Passiflore *(16ᵉ)*	❌❌❌	319	La Table de	
Le Pergolèse *(16ᵉ)*	❌❌❌	316	Babette *(16ᵉ)*	❌❌ 322
La Petite Sirène de			La Table de	
Copenhague *(9ᵉ)*	❌	225	Joël Robuchon *(16ᵉ)*	❌❌❌ 314
Petit Marguery *(13ᵉ)*	❌❌	266	La Table d'Erica *(6ᵉ)*	❌ 134
Port Alma *(16ᵉ)*	❌❌❌	320	La Table du	
Relais d'Auteuil *(16ᵉ)*	❌❌❌	313	Baltimore *(16ᵉ)*	❌❌❌ 315
Relais Louis XIII *(6ᵉ)*	❌❌❌	122	Taillevent *(8ᵉ)*	❌❌❌❌ 179
Rôtisserie d'en Face *(6ᵉ)*	❌	132	Tante Louise *(8ᵉ)*	❌❌ 195
Sa Mi In *(7ᵉ)*	❌	169	Tante Marguerite *(7ᵉ)*	❌❌ 148
Sensing *(6ᵉ)*	❌❌	124	Tour d'Argent *(5ᵉ)*	❌❌❌❌ 104
Sormani *(17ᵉ)*	❌❌❌	338	Villaret *(11ᵉ)*	❌ 249
Spoon (Le) *(8ᵉ)*	❌❌	193	Willi's Wine Bar *(1ᵉʳ)*	❌ 63

Restaurants with private dining rooms

A Beauvilliers *(18ᵉ)*	❌❌❌	356	Le Céladon *(2ᵉ)*	❌❌❌ 72
Aida *(7ᵉ)*	❌	165	Chen-Soleil d'Est *(15ᵉ)*	❌❌❌ 290
L'Aiguière *(11ᵉ)*	❌❌❌	244	Chez Léon *(17ᵉ)*	❌❌ 343
Alcazar *(6ᵉ)*	❌❌	126	Chez les Anges *(7ᵉ)*	❌❌ 149
Ambassade			Le Chiberta *(8ᵉ)*	❌❌❌ 190
d'Auvergne *(3ᵉ)*	❌❌	84	Le "Cinq" *(8ᵉ)*	❌❌❌❌ 174
Les Ambas-			Delizie d'Uggiano *(1ᵉʳ)*	❌❌ 60
sadeurs *(8ᵉ)*	❌❌❌❌	175	Dominique Bouchet *(8ᵉ)*	❌ 206
L'Ambroisie *(4ᵉ)*	❌❌❌❌	92	Drouant *(2ᵉ)*	❌❌❌ 73
Apicius *(8ᵉ)*	❌❌❌❌❌	180	Du Marché *(15ᵉ)*	❌ 301
Arpège *(7ᵉ)*	❌❌❌	140	L'Espadon *(1ᵉʳ)*	❌❌❌❌❌ 53
L'Atelier Berger *(1ᵉʳ)*	❌	63	La Fontaine	
L'Atelier Gourmand *(17ᵉ)*	❌❌	342	Gaillon *(2ᵉ)*	❌❌❌ 73
Auberge Etchegorry *(13ᵉ)*	❌	267	Fouquet's *(8ᵉ)*	❌❌❌ 187
Au Petit Riche *(9ᵉ)*	❌❌	222	Gallopin *(2ᵉ)*	❌❌ 74
Ballon des Ternes *(17ᵉ)*	❌❌	342	La Gauloise *(15ᵉ)*	❌❌ 292
Benkay *(15ᵉ)*	❌❌❌	290	Gaya Rive Gauche par	
Benoît *(4ᵉ)*	❌❌	93	Pierre Gagnaire *(7ᵉ)*	❌ 156
Bistrot de Paris *(7ᵉ)*	❌	159	Goumard *(1ᵉʳ)*	❌❌❌ 56
Bistrot du			Grande Cascade *(16ᵉ)*	❌❌❌❌ 311
Sommelier *(8ᵉ)*	❌❌	202	Le Grand Véfour *(1ᵉʳ)*	❌❌❌❌ 54
Bofinger *(4ᵉ)*	❌❌	94	Guy Savoy *(17ᵉ)*	❌❌❌❌ 336
Café de la Paix *(9ᵉ)*	❌❌❌	221	Kinugawa *(1ᵉʳ)*	❌❌ 62
Café Lenôtre -			Lapérouse *(6ᵉ)*	❌❌❌ 124
Pavillon Elysée *(8ᵉ)*	❌	208	Lasserre *(8ᵉ)*	❌❌❌❌❌ 181
Le Carpaccio *(8ᵉ)*	❌❌❌	191	Laurent *(8ᵉ)*	❌❌❌❌ 182
Carré des			Ledoyen *(8ᵉ)*	❌❌❌❌❌ 178
Feuillants *(1ᵉʳ)*	❌❌❌	55	Macéo *(1ᵉʳ)*	❌❌❌ 58

La Maison des Polytechniciens (7ᵉ)	ⅩⅩⅩ	142
Marty (5ᵉ)	ⅩⅩ	106
Mavrommatis (5ᵉ)	ⅩⅩ	105
Maxan (8ᵉ)	ⅩⅩ	204
Méditerranée (6ᵉ)	ⅩⅩ	125
Meurice (le) (Rest.) (1ᵉʳ)	ⅩⅩⅩⅩⅩ	52
Michel Rostang (17ᵉ)	ⅩⅩⅩⅩ	337
Papilles (5ᵉ)	Ⅹ	113
Paris (6ᵉ)	ⅩⅩⅩ	120
Pétrus (17ᵉ)	ⅩⅩⅩ	338
Relais Louis XIII (6ᵉ)	ⅩⅩⅩ	122
Rue Balzac (8ᵉ)	ⅩⅩ	202
Senderens (8ᵉ)	ⅩⅩⅩ	188

Sormani (17ᵉ)	ⅩⅩⅩ	338
La Table de Babette (16ᵉ)	ⅩⅩ	322
Table des Oliviers (17ᵉ)	Ⅹ	346
La Table du Lancaster (8ᵉ)	ⅩⅩⅩ	186
Taillevent (8ᵉ)	ⅩⅩⅩⅩⅩ	179
Tante Louise (8ᵉ)	ⅩⅩ	195
Tante Marguerite (7ᵉ)	ⅩⅩ	148
Terminus Nord (10ᵉ)	ⅩⅩ	236
Thoumieux (7ᵉ)	Ⅹ	160
Tour d'Argent (5ᵉ)	ⅩⅩⅩⅩⅩ	104
35 ° Ouest (7ᵉ)	Ⅹ	164
Tsé Yang (16ᵉ)	ⅩⅩ	322
La Violette (19ᵉ)	Ⅹ	365

Brasseries

Au Pied de Cochon (1ᵉʳ)	ⅩⅩ	59
Ballon des Ternes (17ᵉ)	ⅩⅩ	342
Balzar (5ᵉ)	Ⅹ	111
Bofinger (4ᵉ)	ⅩⅩ	94
Brasserie Flo (10ᵉ)	ⅩⅩ	236
La Coupole (14ᵉ)	ⅩⅩ	278
Le Dôme (14ᵉ)	ⅩⅩⅩ	276
Gallopin (2ᵉ)	ⅩⅩ	74
La Gauloise (15ᵉ)	ⅩⅩ	292
Marty (5ᵉ)	ⅩⅩ	106
La Rotonde (6ᵉ)	Ⅹ	128
Terminus Nord (10ᵉ)	ⅩⅩ	236
Thoumieux (7ᵉ)	Ⅹ	160
Vaudeville (2ᵉ)	ⅩⅩ	74

Bistros

Allard *(6e)*	⚒	132
L'Ami Marcel *(15e)*	⚒	298
Astier *(11e)*	⚒	248
Au Bascou *(3e)*	⚒	85
Au Moulin à Vent *(5e)*	⚒	109
Aux Lyonnais *(2e)*	⚒	76
L'Avant Goût *(13e)*	⚒	267
Le Bélisaire *(15e)*	⚒	303
Benoît *(4e)*	⚒⚒	93
Bistrot de Paris *(7e)*	⚒	159
Le Bistrot des Soupirs "Chez les On" *(20e)*	⚒	370
Bistrot St-Honoré *(1er)*	⚒	64
Buisson Ardent *(5e)*	⚒	110
Caves Petrissans *(17e)*	⚒	348
Chez Cécile la Ferme des Mathurins *(8e)*	⚒	207
Chez Casimir *(10e)*	⚒	237
Chez Georges *(2e)*	⚒	75
Chez Léon *(17e)*	⚒⚒	343
Le Clou *(17e)*	⚒	348
Le Comptoir *(6e)*	⚒	130
Du Marché *(15e)*	⚒	301
Fontaine de Mars *(7e)*	⚒	163
Joséphine "Chez Dumonet" *(6e)*	⚒	131
Léo Le Lion *(7e)*	⚒	168
Louis Vins *(5e)*	⚒	110
Mellifère *(2e)*	⚒	77
Moissonnier *(5e)*	⚒	108
Oscar *(16e)*	⚒	331
Oudino *(7e)*	⚒	167
Pierrot *(2e)*	⚒	78
P'tit Troquet *(7e)*	⚒	165
Quincy *(12e)*	⚒	258
La Régalade *(14e)*	⚒	281
Relais Beaujolais *(9e)*	⚒	229
Reminet *(5e)*	⚒	112
Villaret *(11e)*	⚒	249

Viennaslide/Stockfood/Studio X

Cuisine from France...

Classic French specialities: where to try each dish

Andouillette

La Biche au Bois (12e)	✗	258
Bistrot de l'Étoile Niel (17e)	✗	347
Bistrot de Paris (7e)	✗	159
Le Bistrot des Soupirs "Chez les On" (20e)	✗	370
Bistrot St-Honoré (1er)	✗	64
Château Poivre (14e)	✗	285
Joséphine "Chez Dumonet" (6e)	✗	131
La Marlotte (6e)	✗	128
Mellifère (2e)	✗	77
Moissonnier (5e)	✗	108
L'Oenothèque (9e)	✗	226
Relais Beaujolais (9e)	✗	229

Boudin

L'Auberge Aveyronnaise (12e)	✗	260
Aux Lyonnais (2e)	✗	76
Bistro d'Hubert (15e)	✗	297
Fontaine de Mars (7e)	✗	163

Bouillabaisse

Bistro de l'Olivier (8e)	✗	207
Le Dôme (14e)	✗✗✗	276
Goumard (1er)	✗✗✗✗	56
Marius (16e)	✗✗	326

Cassoulet

Gastroquet (15^e)	✗	300

Choucroute

Ballon des Ternes (17e)	✗✗	342
Balzar (5e)	✗	111

Confit

Au Bascou (3e)	✗	85
Au Clair de la Lune (18e)	✗✗	357
Au Trou Gascon (12e)	✗✗	255
Chez Jacky (13e)	✗✗	266
D'Chez Eux (7e)	✗✗	153
Lescure (1er)	✗	66
Paul Chêne (16e)	✗✗	324
Pierrot (2e)	✗	78
Le Sarladais (8e)	✗✗	197

Coq au vin

Au Moulin à Vent (5e)	✗	109

Coquillages, crustacés, poissons

Au Pied de Cochon (1er)	✗✗	59
Le Bistrot de Marius (8e)	✗	213
Bistrot du Dôme (4e)	✗	96
Bistrot du Dôme (14e)	✗	283
Bofinger (4e)	✗✗	94

Cap Vernet (8ᵉ)	✗	209
Dessirier (17ᵉ)	✗✗	340
Le Duc (14ᵉ)	✗✗✗	275
L'Ecaille de		
la Fontaine (2ᵉ)	✗	79
L'Espadon Bleu (6ᵉ)	✗	129
Gallopin (2ᵉ)	✗✗	74
Gaya Rive Gauche par		
Pierre Gagnaire (7ᵉ)	✗	156
L'Huîtrier (17ᵉ)	✗	349
Le Divellec (7ᵉ)	✗✗✗	141
La Luna (8ᵉ)	✗✗	194
Marius et Janette (8ᵉ)	✗✗	198
Marty (5ᵉ)	✗✗	106
Méditerranée (6ᵉ)	✗✗	125
Pétrus (17ᵉ)	✗✗✗	338
Port Alma (16ᵉ)	✗✗✗	320
Vin et Marée (7ᵉ)	✗	159
Vin et Marée (1ᵉʳ)	✗✗	61
Vin et Marée (14ᵉ)	✗✗	279
Vin et Marée (11ᵉ)	✗✗	244

Escargots

Chez Georges (2ᵉ)	✗	75
Chez Géraud (16ᵉ)	✗✗	328
Le Pré Cadet (9ᵉ)	✗	227
La Rotonde (6ᵉ)	✗	128

Fromages

| Grande Cascade (16ᵉ) | ✗✗✗✗ | 311 |
| Montparnasse'25 (14ᵉ) | ✗✗✗✗ | 274 |

Grillade

| Brasserie Flo (10ᵉ) | ✗✗ | 236 |

La Coupole (14ᵉ)	✗✗	278
Fermette		
Marbeuf 1900 (8ᵉ)	✗✗	198
La Maison de		
L'Aubrac (8ᵉ)	✗	211
Quincy (12ᵉ)	✗	258
Rôtisserie d'en Face (6ᵉ)	✗	132
Terminus Nord (10ᵉ)	✗✗	236

Tête de veau

Apicius (8ᵉ)	✗✗✗✗✗	180
Astier (11ᵉ)	✗	248
Au Petit Riche (9ᵉ)	✗✗	222
Benoît (4ᵉ)	✗✗	93
Palais Royal (1ᵉʳ)	✗✗	58
La Petite Tour (16ᵉ)	✗✗	324
Stella Maris (8ᵉ)	✗✗	199
Vaudeville (2ᵉ)	✗✗	74

Paëlla

| Auberge Etchegorry (13ᵉ) | ✗ | 267 |
| Rosimar (16ᵉ) | ✗ | 331 |

Soufflés

L'Amuse Bouche (14ᵉ)	✗	282
Cigale Récamier (7ᵉ)	✗✗	146
Le Soufflé (1ᵉʳ)	✗✗	60

Tripes

Allard (6ᵉ)	✗	132
Auberge Pyrénées		
Cévennes (11ᵉ)	✗	247
Chez La Vieille		
"Adrienne" (1ᵉʳ)	✗	65
Thoumieux (7ᵉ)	✗	160

...and from around the world

Belgian

Graindorge (17ᵉ)	☓☓	341

Chinese, Thai, Vietnamese

Baan Boran (1ᵉʳ)	☓	64
Banyan (15ᵉ)	☓	304
Chen-Soleil d'Est (15ᵉ)	☓☓☓	290
Cô Ba Saigon (8ᵉ)	☓	214
Erawan (15ᵉ)	☓☓	295
Kim Anh (15ᵉ)	☓	296
Mme Shawn (10ᵉ)	☓	238
Sukhothaï (13ᵉ)	☓	268
Tang (16ᵉ)	☓☓	323
Thiou (7ᵉ)	☓☓	150
Tsé Yang (16ᵉ)	☓☓	322
Village d'Ung et Li Lam (8ᵉ)	☓☓	205

Franco-Mauritian

Le Chamarré (7ᵉ)	☓☓	143

French West Indies

Coco de Mer (5ᵉ)	☓	109
La Table de Babette (16ᵉ)	☓☓	322
La Table d'Erica (6ᵉ)	☓	134

Greek

Cristina's Tapas by Mavrommatis (1ᵉʳ)	☓	65
Les Délices d'Aphrodite (5ᵉ)	☓	107
Mavrommatis (5ᵉ)	☓☓	105

Hungarian

Le Paprika (9ᵉ)	☓	228

Indian

Indra (8ᵉ)	☓☓☓	193
Jodhpur Palace (12ᵉ)	☓	260
New Jawad (7ᵉ)	☓☓	149
Ratn (8ᵉ)	☓☓	201
Yugaraj (6ᵉ)	☓☓	126

Italian

Beato (7ᵉ)	☓☓	150
Caffé Minotti (7ᵉ)	☓☓	151
Le Carpaccio (8ᵉ)	☓☓☓	191
Conti (16ᵉ)	☓☓	325
Da Claudio (9ᵉ)	☓	228
Delizie d'Uggiano (1ᵉʳ)	☓☓	60
Dell Orto (9ᵉ)	☓	227
Emporio Armani Caffé (6ᵉ)	☓	130
L'Enoteca (4ᵉ)	☓	97
Fontanarosa (15ᵉ)	☓☓	294
Giulio Rebellato (16ᵉ)	☓☓	323
I Golosi (9ᵉ)	☓	226
Montefiori (17ᵉ)	☓	345
L'Osteria (4ᵉ)	☓	97

Le Perron *(7ᵉ)* ⅋ 161

Romain *(9ᵉ)* ⅋⅋ 224

Sormani *(17ᵉ)* ⅋⅋⅋ 338

Le Stresa *(8ᵉ)* ⅋⅋ 201

Le Vinci *(16ᵉ)* ⅋⅋ 327

Japanese

Azabu *(6ᵉ)* ⅋ 133

Benkay *(15ᵉ)* ⅋⅋⅋ 290

Isami *(4ᵉ)* ⅋ 98

Kinugawa *(1ᵉʳ)* ⅋⅋ 62

Miyako *(7ᵉ)* ⅋ 167

Yen *(6ᵉ)* ⅋ 127

Korean

Sa Mi In *(7ᵉ)* ⅋ 169

Shin Jung *(8ᵉ)* ⅋ 214

Tcham *(15ᵉ)* ⅋ 304

Lebanese

Al Ajami *(8ᵉ)* ⅋⅋ 205

Fleurs de Thym *(4ᵉ)* ⅋ 98

Pavillon Noura *(16ᵉ)* ⅋⅋⅋ 318

North-African

Caroubier *(15ᵉ)* ⅋⅋ 293

El Mansour *(8ᵉ)* ⅋⅋⅋ 192

Essaouira *(16ᵉ)* ⅋⅋ 327

La Maison de
Charly *(17ᵉ)* ⅋⅋ 343

Mansouria *(11ᵉ)* ⅋⅋ 245

L'Oriental *(18ᵉ)* ⅋ 358

404 *(3ᵉ)* ⅋ 86

La Table de Fès *(6ᵉ)* ⅋ 134

Timgad *(17ᵉ)* ⅋⅋ 340

Portuguese

Saudade *(1ᵉʳ)* ⅋⅋ 61

Russian

Daru *(8ᵉ)* ⅋ 213

Scandinavian

Copenhague *(8ᵉ)* ⅋⅋⅋ 189

La Petite Sirène de
Copenhague *(9ᵉ)* ⅋ 225

Spanish

Rosimar *(16ᵉ)* ⅋ 331

Tibetan

Lhassa *(5ᵉ)* ⅋ 114

Turkish

Le Janissaire *(12ᵉ)* ⅋⅋ 256

Sizin *(9ᵉ)* ⅋ 230

It's open!

Restaurants open on Sunday

Al Ajami*(8ᵉ)*	✗✗	205
Alcazar*(6ᵉ)*	✗✗	126
Allard*(6ᵉ)*	✗	132
Ambassade d'Auvergne*(3ᵉ)*	✗✗	84
Astier*(11ᵉ)*	✗	248
L'Atelier de Joël Robuchon*(7ᵉ)*	✗	155
L'Auberge Aveyronnaise*(12ᵉ)*	✗	260
Au Pied de Cochon*(1ᵉʳ)*	✗✗	59
Ballon des Ternes*(17ᵉ)*	✗✗	342
Balzar*(5ᵉ)*	✗	111
Benkay*(15ᵉ)*	✗✗✗	290
Benoît*(4ᵉ)*	✗✗	93
Le Bistrot de Marius*(8ᵉ)*	✗	213
Bistrot du Dôme*(4ᵉ)*	✗	96
Bofinger*(4ᵉ)*	✗✗	94
Brasserie Flo*(10ᵉ)*	✗✗	236
Le Bristol (Rest.)*(8ᵉ)*	✗✗✗✗✗	177
La Butte Chaillot*(16ᵉ)*	✗✗	328
Café de l'Alma*(7ᵉ)*	✗	163
Café de la Paix*(9ᵉ)*	✗✗✗	221
Caïus*(17ᵉ)*	✗	345
Caroubier*(15ᵉ)*	✗✗	293
Le Carpaccio*(8ᵉ)*	✗✗✗	191
Christophe*(5ᵉ)*	✗	114
Le "Cinq"*(8ᵉ)*	✗✗✗✗✗	174
Le Comptoir*(6ᵉ)*	✗	130
La Coupole*(14ᵉ)*	✗✗	278

Les Délices d'Aphrodite*(5ᵉ)*	✗	107
Dessirier*(17ᵉ)*	✗✗	340
Devez*(8ᵉ)*	✗	210
Drouant*(2ᵉ)*	✗✗✗	73
L'Enoteca*(4ᵉ)*	✗	97
L'Équitable*(5ᵉ)*	✗✗	107
L'Espadon*(1ᵉʳ)*	✗✗✗✗✗	53
L'Esplanade*(7ᵉ)*	✗✗	154
Les Fables de La Fontaine*(7ᵉ)*	✗	157
Fermette Marbeuf 1900*(8ᵉ)*	✗✗	198
Le Fin Gourmet*(4ᵉ)*	✗	96
Fontaine de Mars*(7ᵉ)*	✗	163
Fontanarosa*(15ᵉ)*	✗✗	294
Fouquet's*(8ᵉ)*	✗✗✗	187
Gallopin*(2ᵉ)*	✗✗	74
La Gauloise*(15ᵉ)*	✗✗	292
Ginger*(8ᵉ)*	✗✗	200
Giulio Rebellato*(16ᵉ)*	✗✗	323
Goumard*(1ᵉʳ)*	✗✗✗	56
Grande Cascade*(16ᵉ)*	✗✗✗	311
Jodhpur Palace*(12ᵉ)*	✗	260
Kim Anh*(15ᵉ)*	✗	296
Lhassa*(5ᵉ)*	✗	114
Louis Vins*(5ᵉ)*	✗	110
Le Lys d'Or*(12ᵉ)*	✗	259
La Maison de Charly*(17ᵉ)*	✗✗	343
La Maison de L'Aubrac*(8ᵉ)*	✗	211

Marius et Janette(8e)	XX	198
Market(8e)	XX	204
Marty(5e)	XX	106
Meating(17e)	XX	341
Méditerranée(6e)	XX	125
Millésimes 62(14e)	X	285
Mme Shawn(10e)	X	238
Le Moulin de la Galette(18e)	XX	357
New Jawad(7e)	XX	149
Les Ombres(7e)	XX	146
L'Oriental(18e)	X	358
Le Paprika(9e)	X	228
Pasco(7e)	X	162
Pavillon Noura(16e)	XXX	318
Le Père Claude(15e)	XX	295
Petit Pontoise(5e)	X	113
Pétrossian(7e)	XXX	142
Pétrus(17e)	XXX	338
Pinxo(1er)	XX	62
404(3e)	X	86
Ratn(8e)	XX	201
Le Relais Plaza(8e)	XX	194
Reminet(5e)	X	112
Repaire de Cartouche(11e)	X	247
La Rotonde(6e)	X	128
Sizin(9e)	X	230
La Table de Joël Robuchon(16e)	XXX	314
La Table du Lancaster(8e)	XXX	186
Terminus Nord(10e)	XX	236
Thoumieux(7e)	X	160
Timgad(17e)	XX	340
Toi(8e)	X	210

Tour d'Argent(5e)	XXXX	104
Tsé Yang(16e)	XX	322
Vaudeville(2e)	XX	74
Mon Vieil Ami(4e)	X	95
Village d'Ung et Li Lam(8e)	XX	205
Vin et Marée(7e)	X	159
Vin et Marée(1er)	XX	61
Vin et Marée(14e)	XX	279
Vin et Marée(11e)	XX	244
Yugaraj(6e)	XX	126

Restaurants open in July and August

A Beauvilliers(18e)	XXX	356
L'Aiguière(11e)	XXX	244
Al Ajami(8e)	XX	205
Alcazar(6e)	XX	126
Ambassade d'Auvergne(3e)	XX	84
L'Appart'(8e)	X	209
Arpège(7e)	XXX	140
Astier(11e)	X	248
L'Atelier Berger(1er)	X	63
L'Atelier de Joël Robuchon(7e)	X	155
Au Petit Riche(9e)	XX	222
Au Pied de Cochon(1er)	XX	59
L'Avant Goût(13e)	X	267
Azabu(6e)	X	133
Baan Boran(1er)	X	64
Balzar(5e)	X	111
Benkay(15e)	XXX	290
Bistro d'Hubert(15e)	X	297

Marty(5ᵉ)	✗✗	106
Meating(17ᵉ)	✗✗	341
Méditerranée(6ᵉ)	✗✗	125
Mellifère(2ᵉ)	✗	77
Le Mesturet(2ᵉ)	✗	77
Mme Shawn(10ᵉ)	✗	238
Le Moulin de la Galette(18ᵉ)	✗✗	357
New Jawad(7ᵉ)	✗✗	149
Les Ombres(7ᵉ)	✗✗	146
L'Oriental(18ᵉ)	✗	358
L'Oulette(12ᵉ)	✗✗✗	254
L'Ourcine(13ᵉ)	✗	268
Palais Royal(1ᵉʳ)	✗✗	58
Le Paprika(9ᵉ)	✗	228
Pasco(7ᵉ)	✗	162
Pataquès(12ᵉ)	✗	257
Pavillon Montsouris(14ᵉ)	✗✗	278
Pavillon Noura(16ᵉ)	✗✗✗	318
Le Père Claude(15ᵉ)	✗✗	295
Petit Pontoise(5ᵉ)	✗	113
Port Alma(16ᵉ)	✗✗✗	320
Pré Catelan(16ᵉ)	✗✗✗✗	310
404(3ᵉ)	✗	86
Ratn(8ᵉ)	✗✗	201
Rôtisserie d'en Face(6ᵉ)	✗	132
La Rotonde(6ᵉ)	✗	128
Sa Mi In(7ᵉ)	✗	169
Saudade(1ᵉʳ)	✗✗	61
Senderens(8ᵉ)	✗✗✗	188
Shin Jung(8ᵉ)	✗	214
La Table de Joël Robuchon(16ᵉ)	✗✗✗	314
Tcham(15ᵉ)	✗	304
Terminus Nord(10ᵉ)	✗✗	236
Thierry Burlot(15ᵉ)	✗✗	293
Thoumieux(7ᵉ)	✗	160
Timgad(17ᵉ)	✗✗	340
Toi(8ᵉ)	✗	210
La Truffière(5ᵉ)	✗✗✗	105
Tsé Yang(16ᵉ)	✗✗	322
Vaudeville(2ᵉ)	✗✗	74
Villa Corse(15ᵉ)	✗	300
Village d'Ung et Li Lam(8ᵉ)	✗✗	205
Vin et Marée(7ᵉ)	✗	159
Vin et Marée(1ᵉʳ)	✗✗	61
Vin et Marée(14ᵉ)	✗✗	279
Vin et Marée(11ᵉ)	✗✗	244
Yen(6ᵉ)	✗	127
Ze Kitchen Galerie(6ᵉ)	✗	131

Restaurants serving after midnight

Atelier Maître Albert(5ᵉ)	✗✗	106
Au Petit Riche(9ᵉ)	✗✗	222
Au Pied de Cochon(1ᵉʳ)	✗✗	59
Bofinger(4ᵉ)	✗✗	94
La Coupole(14ᵉ)	✗✗	278
Devez(8ᵉ)	✗	210
Le Dôme(14ᵉ)	✗✗✗	276
L'Esplanade(7ᵉ)	✗✗	154
La Maison de L'Aubrac(8ᵉ)	✗	211
Terminus Nord(10ᵉ)	✗✗	236
Vaudeville(2ᵉ)	✗✗	74
Vin et Marée(1ᵉʳ)	✗✗	61

Glossary

This section provides translations and explanations of many terms commonly found on French menus. It will also give visitors some idea of the specialities listed under the "starred" restaurants which we have recommended for fine food. Far be it from us, however, to spoil the fun of making your own inquiries to the waiter, as, indeed, the French do when confronted with a mysterious but intriguing dish !

A

Agneau – Lamb
Aiguillette (caneton or canard) – Thin, tender slice of duckling, cut lengthwise
Ail – Garlic
Andouillette – Sausage made of pork or veal tripe
Artichaut – Artichoke
Avocat – Avocado pear

B

Ballotine – A variety of galantine (white meat moulded in aspic)
Bar – Sea bass (see Loup au Fenouil)
Barbue – Brill
Baudroie – Monkfish
Béarnaise – Sauce made of butter, eggs, tarragon, vinegar served with steaks and some fish dishes
Belons – Variety of flat oyster with a delicate flavor
Beurre blanc – "White butter", a sauce made of butter whisked with vinegar and shallots, served with pike and other fish
Boeuf bourguignon – Beef stewed in red wine
Bordelaise (à la) – Red wine sauce with shallots and bone marrow
Boudin grillé – Grilled pork blood-sausage
Bouillabaisse – A soup of fish and, sometimes, shellfish, cooked with garlic, parsley, tomatoes, olive oil, spices, onions and saffron. The fish and the soup are served separately. A Marseilles speciality
Bourride – Fish chowder prepared with white fish, garlic, spices, herbs and white wine, served with aïoli
Brochette (en) – Skewered

Caille – Quail

Calamar – Squid

Canard à la rouennaise – Roast or fried duck, stuffed with its liver

Canard à l'orange – Roast duck with oranges

Canard aux olives – Roast duck with olives

Carré d'agneau – Rack of lamb (loin chops)

Cassoulet – Casserole dish made of white beans, condiments, served (depending on the recipe) with sausage, pork, mutton, goose or duck

Cèpes – Variety of mushroom

Cerfeuil – Chervil

Champignons – Mushrooms

Charcuterie d'Auvergne – A region of central France, Auvergne is reputed to produce the best country-prepared pork-meat specialities, served cold as a first course

Charlotte – A moulded sponge cake although sometimes made with vegetables

Chartreuse de perdreau – Young partridge cooked with cabbage

Châtaigne – Chestnuts

Châteaubriand – Thick, tender cut of steak from the heart of the fillet or tenderloin

Chevreuil – Venison

Chou farci – Stuffed cabbage

Choucroute garnie – Sauerkraut, an Alsacian speciality, served hot and "garnished" with ham, frankfurters, bacon, smoked pork, sausage and boiled potatoes. A good dish to order in a brasserie

Ciboulette – Chives

Civet de gibier – Game stew with wine and onions (civet de lièvre = jugged hare)

Colvert – Wild duck

Confit de canard or d'oie – Preserved duck or goose cooked in its own fat, sometimes served with cassoulet

Coq au vin – Chicken (literally, "rooster") cooked in red wine sauce with onions, mushrooms and bits of bacon

Coques – Cockles

Coquilles St-Jacques – Scallops

Cou d'oie farci – Stuffed goose neck

Coulis – Fruit or vegetable-based sauce

Couscous – North African dish of semolina (crushed wheat grain) steamed and served with a broth of chick-peas and other vegetables, a spicy sauce, accompanied by chicken, roast lamb and sausage.

Crêpes – Thin, light pancakes

Crevettes – Shrimps

Croustades – Small moulded pastry (puff pastry)

Crustacés – Shellfish

D

Daube (Bœuf en) – Beef braised with carrots and onions in red wine sauce

Daurade – Sea bream

E

Écrevisses – Freshwater crayfish

Entrecôte marchand de vin – Rib steak in a red wine sauce with shallots

Escalope de veau – (Thin) veal steak, sometimes served panée, breaded, as with Wiener Schnitzel

Escargot – Snails, usually prepared with butter, garlic and parsley

Estragon – Tarragon

F

Faisan – Pheasant

Fenouil – Fennel

Feuillantine – See feuilleté

Feuilleté – Flaky puff pastry used for making pies or tarts

Filet de bœuf – Fillet (tenderloin) of beef

Filet mignon – Small, round, very choice cut of meat

Flambé(e) – "Flamed", i.e., bathed in brandy, rum, etc., which is then ignited

Flan – Baked custard

Foie gras au caramel poivré – Peppered caramelized goose or duck liver

Foie gras d'oie or de canard – Liver of fatted geese or ducks, served fresh (frais) or in pâté

Foie de veau – Calf's liver

Fruits de mer – Seafood

G

Gambas – Prawns

Gibier – Game

Gigot d'agneau – Roast leg of lamb

Gingembre – Ginger

Goujon or goujonnette de sole – Small fillets of fried sole

Gratin (au) – Dish baked in the oven to produce thin crust on surface

Gratinée – See : onion soup under soupe à l'oignon

Grenadin de veau – Veal tournedos

Grenouilles (cuisses de) – Frogs' legs, often served à la provençale

Grillades – Grilled meats, mostly steaks

H

Homard – Lobster

Homard à l'américaine or à l'armoricaine – Lobster sautéed in butter and olive oil, served with a sauce of tomatoes, garlic, spices, white wine and cognac

Huîtres – Oysters

J

Jambon – Ham (raw or cooked)

Jambonnette de barbarie – Stuffed leg of Barbary duck

Joue de boeuf – Ox cheek

Julienne – Vegetables, fruit, meat or fish cut up in small sticks

L

Lamproie – Lamprey, often served à la bordelaise

Langoustines – Dublin Bay prawns

Lapereau – Young rabbit

Livre – Hare

Lotte – Monkfish

Loup au fenouil – In the south of France, sea bass with fennel (same as bar)

M

Magret – Duck steak

Marcassin – Young wild boar

Mariné – Marinated

Marjolaine – A pastry of different flavors often with a chocolate base

Marmite dieppoise – Fish soup from Dieppe

Matelote d'anguilles or de lotte – Eel or monkfish stew with red wine, onions and herbs

Méchoui – A whole roasted lamb

Merlan – Whiting

Millefeuille – Puff pastry slice

Moelle (à la) – With bone marrow

Morilles – Morel mushrooms

Morue fraîche – Fresh cod

Mouclade – Mussels prepared without shells, in white wine and shallots with cream sauce and spices

Moules farcies – Stuffed mussels (usually filled with butter, garlic and parsley)

Moules marinières – Mussels steamed in white wine, onions and parsley

N

Nage (à la) – A court-bouillon with vegetables and white wine

Nantua – Sauce made with freshwater crayfish tails and served with fish quenelles, seafood, etc.

Navarin – Lamb stew with small onions, carrots, turnips and potatoes

Noisettes d'agneau – Small, round, choice morsels of lamb

O

Œufs brouillés – Scrambled eggs

Œufs en meurette – Poached eggs in red wine sauce with bits of bacon

Œufs sur le plat – Fried eggs, sunnyside up

Omble chevalier – Fish : Char

Omelette soufflée – Souffléed omelette

Oseille – Sorrel

Oursin – Sea urchin

P

Paëlla – A saffron-flavored rice dish made with a mixture of seafood, sausage, chicken and vegetables

Palourdes – Clams

Panaché de poissons – A selection of different kinds of fish

Pannequet – Stuffed crêpe

Pâté – Also called terrine. A common French hors-d'oeuvre, a kind of cold, sliced meat loaf which is made from pork, veal, liver, fowl, rabbit or game and seasoned appropriately with spices. Also served hot in a pastry crust (en croûte)

Paupiette – Usually, a slice of veal wrapped around pork or sausage meat

Perdreau – Young partridge

Petit salé – Salt pork tenderloin, usually served with lentils or cabbage

Petits-gris – Literally, "small greys" ; a variety of snail with brownish, pebbled shell

Pétoncles – Small scallops

Pieds de mouton Poulette – Sheep's feet in cream sauce

Pigeonneau – Young pigeon

Pintade – Guinea fowl

Piperade – A Basque dish of scrambled eggs and cooked tomato, green pepper and Bayonne ham

Plateau de fromages – Tray with a selection of cheeses made from cow's or goat's milk (see cheeses)

Poireaux – Leek

Poivron – Red or green pepper

Pot-au-feu – Beef soup which is served first and followed by a joint of beef cooked in the soup, garnished with vegetables

Potiron – Pumpkin

Poule au pot – Boiled chicken and vegetables served with a hot broth

Poulet à l'estragon – Chicken with tarragon

Poulet au vinaigre – Chicken cooked in vinegar

Poulet aux écrevisses – Chicken with crayfish

Poulet de Bresse – Finest breed of chicken in France, grain-fed

Pré-salé – A particularly fine variety of lamb raised on salt marshes near the sea

Provençale (à la) – With tomato, garlic and parsley

Q

Quenelles de brochet – Fish-balls made of pike ; quenelles are also made of veal or chicken forcemeat

Queue de bœuf – Oxtail

Quiche lorraine – Hot egg-custard tart flavoured with chopped bacon and baked in an unsweetened pastry shell

R

Ragoût – Stew

Raie aux câpres – Skate fried in butter garnished with capers

Ris de veau – Sweetbreads

Rognons de veau – Veal kidneys

Rouget – Red mullet

S

St-Jacques – Scallops, as coquilles St-Jacques

St-Pierre – Fish : John Dory

Salade niçoise – A first course made of lettuce, tomatoes, celery, olives, green pepper, cucumber, anchovy and tuna, seasoned to taste. A favourite hors-d'oeuvre

Sandre – Pike perch

Saucisson chaud – Pork sausage, served hot with potato salad, or sometimes in pastry shell (en croûte)

Saumon fumé – Smoked salmon

Scampi fritti – French-fried shrimp

Selle d'agneau – Saddle of lamb

Soufflé – A light, fluffy baked dish made of eggs yolks and whites beaten separately and combined with cheese or fish, for example, to make a first course, or with fruit or liqueur as a dessert

Soupe à l'oignon – Onion soup with grated cheese and croûtons (small crisp pieces of toasted bread)

Soupe de poissons – Fish soup

Steak au poivre – Pepper steak, often served flamed

Suprême – Usually refers to a fillet of poultry or fish

T

Tagine – A stew with either chicken, lamb, pigeon or vegetables

Tartare – Raw meat or fish minced up and then mixed with eggs, herbs and other condiments before being shaped into a patty

Terrine – See pâté

Tête de veau – Calf's head

Thon – Tuna

Tournedos – Small, round tenderloin steak

Tourteaux – Large crab (from Atlantic)

Tripe à la mode de Caen – Beef tripe with white wine and carrots

Truffe – Truffle

Truite – Trout

V

Volaille – Fowl

Vol-au-Vent – Puff pastry shell filled with chicken, meat, fish, fish-balls (quenelles) usually in cream sauce with mushrooms

Desserts

Baba au rhum – Sponge cake soaked in rum, sometimes served with whipped cream

Beignets de pommes – Apple fritters

Clafoutis – Dessert of apples (cherries, or other fruit) baked in batter

Glace – Ice cream

Gourmandises – Selection of desserts

Nougat glacé – Iced nougat

Pâtisseries – Pastry, cakes

Profiteroles – Small round pastry puffs filled with cream or ice cream and covered with chocolate sauce

St-Honoré – Cake made of two kinds of pastry and whipped cream, named after the patron saint of pastry cooks

Sorbet – Sherbet

Soupe de pêches – Peaches in syrup or in wine

Tarte aux pommes – Open apple tart

Tarte Tatin – Apple upside-down tart, caramelized and served warm

Vacherin – Meringue with ice-cream and whipped cream

Fromages - Cheese

Cow's milk – Bleu d'Auvergne, Brie, Camembert, Cantal, Comté, Gruyère, Munster, Pont-l'Évêque, Tomme de Savoie

Goat's milk – Chabichou, Crottin de Chavignol, Ste-Maure, Selles-sur-Cher, Valençay

Sheep's milk – Roquefort

Fruits

Airelles – Cranberries **Pamplemousse** – Grapefruit

Cassis – Blackcurrant **Pêches** – Peaches

Cerises – Cherries **Poires** – Pears

Citron – Lemon **Pomme** – Apple

Fraises – Strawberries **Pruneaux** – Prunes

Framboises – Raspberries **Raisins** – Grapes

Palais Royal, Louvre, Tuileries, Châtelet

Palais Royal, Louvre, Tuileries, Châtelet

Blackwell K./MICHELIN

The 1st arrondissement, a narrow rectangle that hugs the right bank of the Seine, reveals two aspects of Paris: to the east, the Halles district, the former "Belly of Paris" that was home to the capital's wholesale market but is still a busy shopping and working-class area, and the Louvre to the west, once the seat of power and still one of the smartest districts of the capital.

A ROYAL STROLL

Who can remain insensitive to the majesty of the perspective that runs from the Cour Carrée of the **Louvre** to the Arc de Triomphe on the **Place de l'Étoile**, especially at night when the city's illuminations light up the Champs-Élysées? The obelisk, straight as a gold-tipped pencil, marks the centre. To the east, it is bordered by the green Tuileries gardens, dotted with sculptures by Maillol and Rodin, which lead to the Louvre museum. An outstanding cultural and tourist attraction, the former palace never empties and patience is required before you can see the Mona Lisa's smile for yourself.

However the Café Marly, set in the museum itself and popular with the Parisian jet-set and tourists alike, is perfect for a break. Take a seat under the arcades and enjoy the view of the glass pyramid.

Alternatively, make your way to the peaceful walled gardens of the **Palais Royal,** another favourite with Parisians. Gourmets also flock here because beneath the arcades, in between two top fashion designers, is the **Grand Véfour,** a historic and starred establishment popular with Cocteau, Colette and Sartre.

48

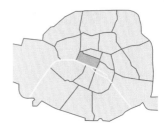

JEWELS AND GADGETS

As they make their way towards the Comédie Française, visitors to the Louvre gradually mingle with the man in the street and then with wealthy foreign tourists on shopping sprees in the capital's luxury shops. Along **rue Saint-Honoré** elite fashion designers rub shoulders with the "haute couture" of chocolate and further on, **place Vendôme** is the exclusive bastion of the top jewellery houses and luxury hotels. The contrast with **rue de Rivoli**'s arcades, more focused on plastic replicas of the Eiffel tower, is striking. However the street is also home to Angelina's, a chic tea-room reputed to serve the best Mont-Blanc and the most delicious hot chocolate in Paris.

Further north, the lovely glass and steel edifice on **Marché Saint-Honoré** stands in the heart of a small business district rich in good restaurants. Alternatively, head for the mythical Hemingway bar of the **Ritz,** a much-loved haunt of the author and sample one of his favourite pure malt whiskies in the lap of luxury… for just the price of a glass!

AROUND MIDNIGHT

Eastbound, the scenery changes with the impressive **Forum des Halles,** built on the site of the massive iron halls designed by Baltard that used to house the main marketplace of Paris. Now the realm of retail chain stores, the area resembles an immense human ant-hive, constantly fed by arrivals from the gigantic underground metro and RER station, **Châtelet-les Halles.** At peak hours, it is almost impracticable and even a tad disreputable in the evenings. However jazz lovers are not put off as they make their way to the vaulted cellars along **rue des Lombards** and **rue de la Ferronnerie,** guided by familiar trumpet, piano and saxophone melodies. If in need of sustenance, head for the Pied de Cochon that has been catering to hungry night-birds 24 hours a day since 1946.

Sauvignier S./MICHELIN

Palais Royal, Louvre, Tuileries, Châtelet

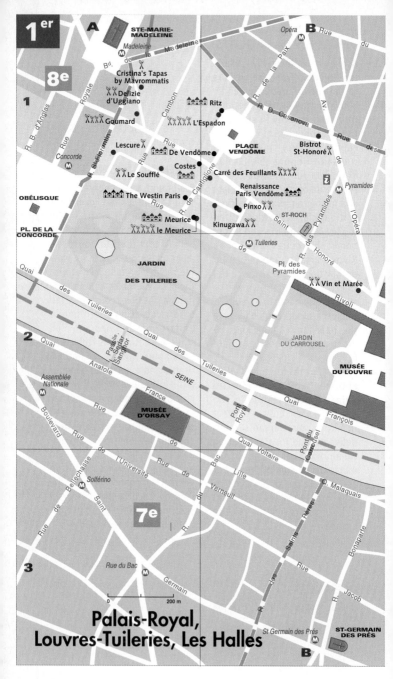

Palais-Royal,
Louvres-Tuileries, Les Halles

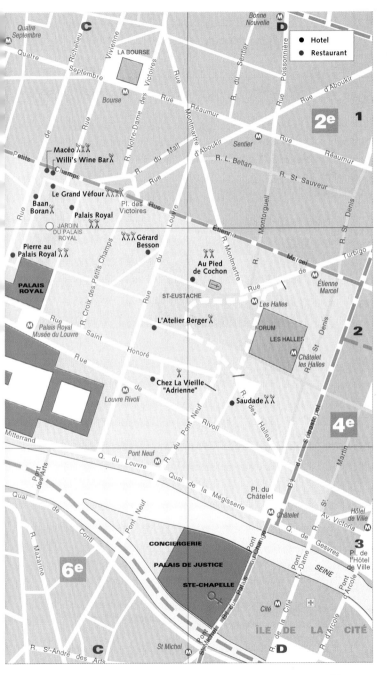

le Meurice ✿✿✿

Innovative ✗✗✗✗✗

A/C
VISA
MC
AE
①

Hôtel Le Meurice,
228 r. Rivoli ✉ 75001
✆ 0144581055 – **Fax** 0144581076
e-mail restaurant@lemeurice.com **Web** www.lemeurice.com
closed 28 July-26 August, February half-term holidays, Saturday and Sunday

Ⓜ Tuileries
A1

Menu €75 (lunch)/€190 – Carte €164/262

le Meurice

Yannick Alleno was already acquainted with the kitchens of le Meurice from his time as chef de partie in 1992. When he returned in September 2003 as executive chef, it was with a single ambition: to restore the glory of this grand hotel dining room. Today, this has been achieved!

At 38, this youthful talent, who trained under Roland Durand and Louis Grondard, states quite simply: "I'm very attached to French cuisine"… And we can believe him.

Here, French classics are re-invented and made sublime by following two golden rules: a constantly renewed interpretation of flavours and a fierce respect for seasonality. A perfectionist yet not averse to taking risks, he has given himself the challenge of revealing the very essence of the ingredient, not hesitating, for example, to submit a sole to the chaud-froid treatment... with stunning results!

Refined and authentic, his recipes express all the facets of his character. Trained in the same "school", his kitchen brigade and the entire team accompany him with an irreproachable savoir-faire in a setting inspired by the Château de Versailles, often described as "the most beautiful dining room in Paris".

A LA CARTE

FIRST COURSE	MAIN COURSE	DESSERT
• Vapeur de Saint-Jacques aux truffes, nage au corail de homard (autumn-winter).	• Noix de ris de veau rôtie (autumn-winter).	• Fraises soufflées, crème normande vanillée au "caviar" de fruits (summer).
• Foie gras de canard simplement poché au vin de Chambertin.	• Tronçon de turbot rôti à l'arête.	• Tuile croustillante fourrée d'une ganache tendre, quenelles glacées à la menthe.

Palais-Royal, Louvre-Tuileries, Les Halles

L'Espadon

Traditional XXXXX

Hôtel Ritz,
15 pl. Vendôme ✉ 75001
✆ 01 43 16 30 80 – **Fax** 01 43 16 33 75
e-mail food-bev@ritzparis.com **Web** www.ritzparis.com

Ⓜ Opéra
B1

Menu €75 (lunch)/€265 wine included –
Carte €121/221

Ⓐ/Ⓒ
VISA
Ⓜ③
ⒶⒺ
Ⴤ

L'Espadon

"Good cooking is the basis for true happiness", said Auguste Escoffier, the first chef in the kitchen at the Ritz in Paris and a friend of César Ritz, who created the hotel. The inventor of the famous Peach Melba (dedicated to an Australian singer) was too early to have known L'Espadon, created in 1956 at the initiative of Charles Ritz, son of the founder and an avid fisherman. Its prestige is evident in the luxurious decor of the dining room with its trompe l'œil ceiling and profusion of plants and flowers. The food is equally impressive. For twenty years this gastronomic restaurant has been the perfect creative environment for Michel Roth, the only French chef to have been awarded the title of Meilleur Ouvrier de France as well as winning the two most outstanding culinary prizes, the Prix Culinaire Pierre Taittinger and the Bocuse d'Or. Besides a short interlude at Lasserre, he has spent most of his professional life at the Ritz, where his classic and contemporary cuisine is highly appealing.

A LA CARTE

FIRST COURSE
• Araignée de mer, riviera de mangue au jus d'agrumes.

• Moelleux de volaille et foie gras, cèpes, bouquet de mâche, chutney de fruits.

MAIN COURSE
• Turbot en tronçon rôti à la fleur de sel.

• Rosette d'agneau en écrin d'herbes, pommes soufflées.

DESSERT
• Millefeuille tradition Ritz.

• Chocolat soufflé, crème glacée à la pistache de Sicile.

Palais-Royal, Louvre-Tuileries, Les Halles

1ST ARRONDISSEMENT

Le Grand Véfour ✿✿✿

Innovative XXXX

17 r. Beaujolais

✉ 75001

☎ 0142965627 – **Fax** 0142868071

e-mail grand.vefour@wanadoo.fr **Web** www.grand-vefour.com

closed 14-22 April, 30 July-27 August, 24 December-1st January, Friday dinner, Saturday and Sunday

Menu €78 (lunch)/€256 – Carte €177/207

Ⓜ Palais Royal

C1

Le Grand Véfour

Romantic and revolutionary meetings marked the beginnings of this historic place. Located in the Palais Royal gardens, and formerly called the Café de Chartres, it has been well-known since 1782. It took off during the Restoration period under Jean Véfour, a famous chef who gave his name to the restaurant, which closed in 1905. When Louis Vaudable, who found it in ruins, decided to sell it to Raymond Oliver after the war, the Grand Véfour regained its former lustre and the Michelin stars arrived soon thereafter. Guy Martin has run the establishment and its kitchen since 1991. He who dreamt of becoming a rock star never trained in any of the great restaurants; but that hasn't stopped him from reaching great heights! The place has remained magical, and while the Directoire decor seems to defy time, the menu juggles between modernity and tradition, displaying the chef's creativity. The service is exactly what you would expect in such a top establishment.

A LA CARTE

FIRST COURSE

· Ravioles de foie gras à l'émulsion de crème truffée.

· Thon et légumes, avocat assaisonné au wasabi, jeunes poireaux en salade.

MAIN COURSE

· Pigeon Prince Rainier III.

· Daurade poêlée, jus persil-gingembre, champignons et tofu.

DESSERT

· Palet noisette et chocolat au lait, glace au caramel brun et sel de Guérande.

· Pêche pochée à la verveine, en fine gelée et en sorbet.

Carré des Feuillants ✿✿

Traditional XXXX

14 r. Castiglione
✉ 75001
✆ 01 42 86 82 82 – **Fax** 01 42 86 07 71
e-mail carre.des.feuillants@wanadoo.fr
Web www.carredesfeuillants.fr
closed August, Saturday and Sunday

Menu € 65 (lunch)/€ 165 – Carte € 127/158

Ⓜ Tuileries
B1

Carré des Feuillants

Alain Dutournier dreamed of having a place where the cuisine and setting would be in perfect harmony, and painter and sculptor Alberto Bali fulfilled that dream by renovating the restaurant, once a convent. Located between place Vendôme and The Tuileries gardens, this contemporary venue combines precision and experimentation with a restful aesthetic, creating a total osmosis with the very up-to-date cuisine from a chef who knows how to bring the best out of his ingredients. His food has deep flavours and real tastes, with an amazing generosity and elegance which evoke the great *maisons bourgeoises* in the Southwest - in the Landes region, as the chef would immediately specify, since he has no intention of forgetting the place from which he draws his inspiration. The remarkable cellar contains some real treasures, including wines from his *terroir* which are a must. The attentive and precise service gives an added note of charm to the experience.

A LA CARTE

FIRST COURSE
• Homard bleu en feuille de riz (autumn-winter).

• Cuisses de grenouilles épicées, pousses de roquette, girolles en tempura.

MAIN COURSE
• Tendron de veau de lait dans son jus truffé (spring-summer).

• Carré d'agneau des Pyrénées au four, gigot cuit à l'étouffée dans l'argile.

DESSERT
• Ravioles de mangue aux fruits de la passion.

• Framboises, parfait chocolat noir "conception", verveine glacée et en gelée.

Palais-Royal, Louvre-Tuileries, Les Halles

Goumard ✿

Seafood 🗙🗙🗙🗙

A/C	9 r. Duphot	**Ⓜ** Madeleine
	✉ 75001	**A1**
	☎ 0142603607 – **Fax** 0142600454	
VISA	**e-mail** goumard.philippe@wanadoo.fr **Web** www.goumard.com	
MC	Menu €46/€60 (lunch) wine included – Carte €67/142	

A/C · 🛗 · VISA · MC · AE · ◑ · ✿ · ♀

Youpi la création

Fish and seafood are a constant at this unique establishment. The former Maison Prunier has remained a Parisian institution, uniting the names Prunier and Goumard. In 1872, Alfred and Catherine Prunier opened a modest restaurant with a dozen tables, specializing in oysters. Business thrived, and in 1904 their son Émile commissioned the painter Louis Majorelle to redecorate the entire place in the Art Nouveau style that was so popular at the time. In 1992 the restaurant was saved by Jean-Claude Goumard who added his name to the Pruniers. Years later, what exactly has remained of Goumard besides the name? Part of Majorelle's decor, the elegant atmosphere, and the extremely well-prepared food. Not to mention the concern with quality that is typical of Philippe Dubois, who has breathed new life into this fine establishment.

À LA CARTE

FIRST COURSE
- Tranches de tomate, balsamique blanc et crevettes tigrées au romarin (June to October).
- Thon rouge en ceviché, fruits croquants au naturel.

MAIN COURSE
- Aiguillettes de Saint-Pierre doré (June to September).
- Bourride et poissons de petite pêche servis façon bouillabaisse.

DESSERT
- Moelleux d'amandes, marmelade de cassis, fin craquant sucré aux framboises, onctueux aux citrons (summer).
- Feuillé de chocolat craquant, mousseline passion.

Gérard Besson ✿

Traditional 🗙🗙🗙

5 r. Coq Héron
✉ 75001
✆ 0142331474 – **Fax** 0142338571
e-mail gerard.besson4@libertysurf.fr **Web** www.gerardbesson.com

closed 13 July-19 August, Monday lunch, Saturday lunch and Sunday

M Louvre Rivoli
C2

Menu €56 (lunch)/€125 – Carte €100/157

Gérard Besson

Since 1978 this timeless restaurant has remained at the same address a stone's throw from the old Les Halles market. The warm dining room setting is cosy and elegant, featuring *toile de Jouy* wallpaper with Oriental motifs, and nooks illuminated by a collection of decanters. Gérard Besson comes from the Ain region, where people know how to eat well, and there is no chance of his giving in to fleeting fashions or forgetting his Bressan roots. His remarkably consistent cooking has remained generous and masterful, cleverly navigating between tradition and modernity. The restaurant offers some seasonal classics that are hard to find elsewhere. Try it in the autumn for a peak experience. The chef is an avid hunter and connoisseur who will delight you with the game he has bagged, matched with a perfect wine.

A LA CARTE

FIRST COURSE	MAIN COURSE	DESSERT
• Fricassée de homard "Georges Garin". • Pâté en croûte au foie gras de canard.	• Gibier (end of September to end of December). • Entrecôte de Salers vigneronne, purée de céleri.	• Fenouil confit, glace à la vanille de Tahiti, épices et agrumes. • Prélat d'Alexandre Dumaine, sauce et glace au café.

Palais-Royal, Louvre-Tuileries, Les Halles

Palais-Royal, Louvre-Tuileries, Les Halles

Macéo

Innovative XXX

15 r. Petits-Champs
✉ 75001
☎ 0142975385 – **Fax** 0147033693
e-mail info@maceorestaurant.com
Web www.maceorestaurant.com
closed in August, Saturday lunch and Sunday

Ⓜ Bourse
C1

Menu €30/€36 – Carte €46/61

When he took over this restaurant founded in 1880, Mark Williamson treated himself to a superb place full of history – both in its Second Empire decor redesigned with a chic contemporary spirit and in the personalities who have frequented it such as Colette and Eisenhower. Renamed Macéo, the place has remained a favourite of celebrities. Thierry Bourdonnais' cuisine reinvents the classics using seasonal ingredients in dishes such as saddle of hare with raisins, lentil and foie gras vinaigrette, gingerbread macaroons and pepper sorbet. There is also an asparagus menu (in season), a 100% vegetarian "green menu" and an incomparable cellar – a passion of the proprietor's, who also owns Willi's Wine Bar – featuring 250 wines from around the world.

Palais Royal

Traditional XX

110 Galerie de Valois
– Jardin du Palais Royal
✉ 75001
☎ 0140200027 – **Fax** 0140200082
e-mail palaisrest@aol.com **Web** www.restaurantdupalaisroyal.com
closed 20 December-10 January and Sunday

Ⓜ Bourse
C1

Carte €36/64

A dream location in the Palais-Royal with its arcades and beautiful garden. In summer the terrace is set up there - an idyllic spot. In winter there is a lovely view from the large picture window in the dining room. The atmosphere is intimate, with an Art Deco look, mirrors, modern paintings, photographs of Colette (who lived just above here), candlelight dinners, and enthusiastic service. Bruno Hees' cuisine oscillates between tradition and seasonal dishes, including lobster and porcini mushroom cappuccino, *buisson d'escargots*, raw sea bass with olive oil and Parmesan, chestnut *millefeuille* and "*Paris-Brest et retour*".

Pierre au Palais Royal

Contemporary ✗✗

A/C
VISA
MC
DC
🍷

10 r. Richelieu
✉ 75001
☏ 0142960917 – **Fax** 0142962640
e-mail pierreaupalaisroyal@wanadoo.fr
Closed 5-26 August, Saturday lunch, Sunday and public holidays

Ⓜ Palais Royal
C2

Menu €38

They take care over the little things at Pierre au Palais Royal – flowers in the entrance, contemporary lines and aubergine tones to stay up with the times. This establishment taken over by chef David Frémondière has shown itself equal to its refined setting. Your taste buds will be thrilled by the straightforward southern-based flavours and magnificent ingredients on the fixed menu, renewed every two months. Sample this: *dos de cabillaud* (fresh cod) *à la plancha, piquillos farcis à la brandade de morue* with a shellfish coulis and carrot purée, *pressé de cailles* (quail) with foie gras, and homemade sorbet. Everything is delicious! As an added bonus, it's open late for after-theatre meals (the Comédie Française is not far).

Au Pied de Cochon

Brasserie ✗✗

A/C
VISA
MC
AE
DC
🍷

6 r. Coquillière
✉ 75001
☏ 0140137700 – **Fax** 0140137709
e-mail de.pied-de-cochon@blanc.net
Web www.pieddecochon.com

Ⓜ Châtelet-Les Halles
D2

Menu €24 – Carte €30/65

This is truly a historic monument. Need we introduce the Blanc Brothers' indispensable brasserie, a bastion in Les Halles where diners can feast cheerfully day and night? Tourists and night owls know it well. The former admire its typically Parisian Belle Epoque decor, while the latter enjoy a good bowl of onion soup before going home to bed. "*Canaille*" dishes are featured here, exemplified by the "Tentation Saint-Antoine", a gargantuan ode to pork (grilled trotters, ears, snout and tails or braised ribs). Shellfish platters are another speciality. Attractive new formulas and menus await you at lunchtime and after midnight.

1st ARRONDISSEMENT

Le Soufflé

Soufflés ✕✕

[A/C]
[VISA]
[MC]
[AE]
[Y]

36 r. Mont-Thabor
⊠ 75001
✆ 0142602719 – **Fax** 0142605498
e-mail c_rigaud@club-internet.fr
Closed 29 July-19 August, 10-24 February, Sunday and public holidays

Ⓜ Tuileries
A1

Menu €30/€33 – **Carte** €34/54

This restaurant devoted to soufflés ought to be puffed up with pride! Especially since this French speciality is becoming rather scarce. Here, it is made in many forms and for all tastes: savoury (cheese, tomato, avocado, morels, roquefort and walnuts, foie gras, chicken) or sweet (coffee, Grand Marnier, red berries). We recommend the set menu for the single-minded; others may opt for more traditional dishes as an alternative. This unique establishment, over thirty years old, is not just a curiosity; it is also a charming and stylish place which delights a large clientele ranging from businessmen to Japanese tourists on a spree near Place de la Concorde. Remember to book.

Delizie d'Uggiano

Italian ✕✕

[↻]
[VISA]
[MC]
[AE]
[O]
[Y]

18 r. Duphot
⊠ 75001
✆ 0140150669 – **Fax** 0140150390
e-mail losapiog@wanadoo.fr **Web** www.delizieduggiano.com
closed 10-20 August, Saturday lunch and Sunday

Ⓜ Madeleine
A1

Menu €42 (lunch) – **Carte** €55/85

This very Italian establishment celebrates its Tuscan origins, paying a loving tribute to the Uggiano estate. You can see that it was originally a wine and olive oil shop from the gold-ochre decor – in the style of a deluxe trattoria – with a personal touch in the form of ceramics and bottles on display in the window. The shop is still there, sandwiched between the restaurant upstairs and the vaulted 16C cellar (tastings and meals are held for groups). The cuisine pulls out all the stops, using only the best ingredients in dishes such as antipasti, risotto, veal Milanese, pasta, and a few truffle specialities in season. The prices tend to be rather high, but the service is perfect. Think of it as a place for special occasions.

Saudade

Portuguese 🗡🗡

|AC|
|VISA|
|⓿⓿|
|AE|
|🍷|

34 r. Bourdonnais   Ⓜ Pont Neuf
✉ 75001   **D2**
✆ 0142363071 – **Fax** 0142363071
Web www.restaurantsaudade.com
closed Sunday

Menu €20 (weekday lunch) – Carte €27/52

There's nothing sad about this Saudade! But it is a powerful remedy against homesickness, with fado music playing in the background and large gulps of old Port. For three generations – Fernando Moura took over in 1979 – this "embassy" of Portugal has confirmed its reputation for authenticity and local flavour, all with great modesty in the discreet façade and dining rooms tastefully decorated with azulejos tiles. Maria de Fatima, the guardian of tradition, has no equal in preparing pork with clams, *caldo verde* (cabbage soup), and *arroz doce* (rice pudding with cinnamon), not to mention salt-cod, the national dish, grilled, pan-fried, au gratin, breaded, and deep-fried. Music-lovers will enjoy the live music on the first Tuesday of every month.

Vin et Marée

Fish and shellfish 🗡🗡

|VISA|
|⓿⓿|
|AE|
|🍷|

165 r. St-Honoré   Ⓜ Palais Royal
✉ 75001   **B2**
✆ 0142860696 – **Fax** 0142860697
Web www.vinetmareesainthonore.com

Menu €40/€59

Vin et Marée attracts your attention with its pavement stand of oysters (delivered daily from Brittany). Inside, the crew is ready to treat the numerous seafood and shellfish fans to a great meal – with friends or business colleagues. The marine brasserie setting is appropriate for any kind of date, but book a table in the upstairs dining room for a view of the Comédie Française. The food reflects the simple Vin et Marée formula. The excellent catch includes grilled sardines, scallops *à la plancha*, sea bass with fennel, and pan-fried shrimp. To top it off, try the generous *baba de Zanzibar* – a name that conjures up voyages to far-off places!

Pinxo

Innovative 🍴🍴

A/C Hôtel Renaissance Paris Vendôme,
9 r. Alger ✉ 75001   Ⓜ Tuileries
VISA 🖋 0140207200 – **Fax** 0140207202   **B1**
Ⓜ© **Web** www.pinxo.fr
closed Aug.
AE
🍷 **Menu** €32 (weekday lunch) wine included – Carte
€37/58

The kitchen is on display in the centre of the room – bordered by a fine granite bar – in this highly fashionable, black-and-white minimalist decor (the least you expect for a restaurant at the Hôtel Renaissance Paris Vendôme). The menu features succulent tapas-style sweet and savoury creations which the chic clientele has fun eating with their fingers or picking off their neighbour's plate. This is the latest concept from Alain Dutournier, a new form of gourmet sharing! Under the impulse of this Landais and lover of Spain, the friendly staff at Pinxo propose sautéed *chipirons*, royal crab in a vegetable roll, *blidas* of chocolate, coconut and pistachio tiramisu, perfectly presented in three portions for you to mix to your heart's content.

Kinugawa

Japanese 🍴🍴

A/C 9 r. Mont Thabor
✉ 75001   Ⓜ Tuileries
🛋 🖋 0142606507 – **Fax** 0142605736   **B1**
VISA **e-mail** higashiuchi.kinugawa@free.fr **Web** http://kinugawa.free.fr
Ⓜ© Closed 24 December-8 January, Sunday and public holidays
Ⓓ **Menu** €30 (weekday lunch)/€125 – Carte €35/85
🍷
The art of making sushi holds no secrets for the *sushiya* here, who has mastered the ingredients and is uncompromising about their quality and freshness. But these divine mouthfuls – prepared before your very eyes at the ground floor bar – are only a glimpse of his talent. Tempura, soba, *suimonos* (soups and egg dishes) and *nikoutoris* (meat and poultry), each one more delicious than the last, round out the choices at this establishment, a worthy ambassador of Japan in the capital. Regulars – businessmen and celebrities – are fond of the two upstairs dining rooms, as serene, delicate and refined as a Hokusai print.

L'Atelier Berger

Contemporary

49 r. Berger
✉ 75001
☎ 01 40 28 00 00 – **Fax** 01 40 28 10 65
e-mail atelierberger@wanadoo.fr
Web www.restaurant-atelierberger.com

Ⓜ Louvre Rivoli
C2

closed Saturday lunchtime and Sunday

Menu €36 – Carte €36/49

Three places in one! To diversify the gourmet experience, L'Atelier Berger has multiplied the number of spaces and kinds of ambiance. The trail starts at the infinitely cosy bar, where you can snack on cold meats, cheese and bistro dishes. Then there's the English club-style smoking lounge, where you can enjoy fine cigars and spirits (well-stocked cellar). Lastly, the warm contemporary restaurant upstairs, where you can taste the creations of Franco-Norwegian chef Jean Christiansen, who trained in some great establishments. The cuisine with Nordic and sunny southern influences features some fine specialities, including herring "from back home" marinated with spices, red tuna tartare with ginger, and recipes using Havana tobacco leaves.

Willi's Wine Bar

Bistro

13 r. Petits-Champs
✉ 75001
☎ 01 42 61 05 09 – **Fax** 01 47 03 36 93
e-mail info@williswinebar.com **Web** www.williswinebar.com

Ⓜ Bourse
C1

closed in August and Sunday

Menu €25 (lunch)/€34 – Carte €28/42

More than a wine bar, this is an exceptional cellar which also has an art gallery! Born out of Englishman Mark Williamson's passion for œnology, Willi's Wine Bar has been a model since 1980. Behind its cask-shaped façade, three hundred vintages (with a clear preference for Côtes du Rhône) are available on the – almost encyclopedic – wine list, or by the glass. Other "collectors" bottles are on display in this very British décor. Chef François Yon cooks up simple Mediterranean-style dishes, served with no fuss at the bar or in the dining room, to accompany this worship of Bacchus. Have a look at the Bottle Art Collection, a series of posters commissioned every year from a contemporary artist, illustrating the remarkable nature of the place.

Palais-Royal, Louvre-Tuileries, Les Halles

Bistrot St-Honoré

Bistro ✗

VISA
MC

10 r. Gomboust
✉ 75001
📞 0142617778 – **Fax** 0142617410

🅜 Pyramides
B1

AE

closed 10-20 August, 24 December-2 January, Saturday and Sunday

Menu €28 – Carte €32/72

Fresh frogs' legs, snails, *œufs en meurette* (poached eggs in red wine sauce) and *veau sauce vigneronne en cocotte* (veal cooked in a red wine reduction) – all these great Burgundy specialities await you at this establishment next to the Place du Marché-St-Honoré. These authentic and invigorating dishes share the limelight with the daily specials on the blackboard. The carefully selected wines in the cellar pay tribute to the region's vineyards. With its ham and *rosette* sausages hanging from the ceiling, and quintessentially old Paris decor (zinc bar, wooden chairs and tables), this convivial bistro oozes charm. Detective novel writer Frédéric Dard was a regular here and wrote about its fun-loving spirit in several of his books.

Baan Boran

Thai ✗

A/C

43 r. Montpensier
✉ 75001
📞 0140159045 – **Fax** 0140159045
Web www.baan-boran.com

🅜 Palais Royal
C1

VISA
MC

AE

closed Saturday lunchtime and Sunday

Menu €14,50 (lunch)/€45 (dinner) – Carte €26/48

With its naive paintings and orchids, the yellow and red exotic contemporary decor at Baan Boran is neither overdone nor trendy. The Thai cuisine is prepared by two women, from central and northern Thailand, busy cooking in their woks. The more or less spicy (depending on your taste), light and vegetarian dishes are made with age-old *savoir-faire*. Soup, *tom yam khung* (shrimp with lemon grass), sautéed chicken in sesame oil and basil, beef curry with coconut milk, sticky rice, mango soup, etc. Enticing aromas waft into the dining room. At last the dishes are served on bamboo place settings by the charming staff in traditional dress. The journey is about to commence.

Chez La Vieille "Adrienne"

Traditional

1 r. Bailleul   **Ⓜ** Louvre Rivoli
✉ 75001   **C2**
✆ 0142601578 – **Fax** 0142338571

Closed 30 July-19 August, Saturday, Sunday and dinner except Thursday and Friday – pre-book

Menu €27 (lunch)/€56

Adrienne has left the kitchen but her "old" establishment – housed in a 16C residence – is still favoured by longstanding fans. Yannick Guepin (formerly with Gérard Besson) has just taken over under the watchful gaze of the ex-proprietress (the tiny room is dotted with black-and-white photographs of her). The good old-fashioned cooking has lightened up, but the "basics" still get high marks, including calf's liver, kidneys, beef with carrots, stew, *blanquette de veau à l'ancienne*, baba au rhum and *crème caramel*, sprinkled with a few Corsican dishes. The polished bistro, lace curtains and counter top with dishes of the day haven't changed a bit. This is tradition with a capital "T"!

Cristina's Tapas by Mavrommatis

Mediterranean

18 r.Duphot   **Ⓜ** Madeleine
✉ 75001   **A1**
✆ 0142975304
Web www.mavrommatis.com

closed Monday dinner, Tuesday dinner and Sunday

Carte €22/40

First there was the book, with its reassuring title "Ma cuisine pour femmes au bord de la crise de nerfs" (Cooking for Women on the Verge of a Nervous Breakdown). After its success, author Cristina Egal decided to open a tapas bar – a live demonstration of her clever cooking skills – and the grilled sardines, *pimientos del piquillo, tortillas* and other spirited snacks made her reputation. The news is that the Mavrommatis Brothers have joined in to flesh out the 100% Spanish menu with Greek, Provençal, Italian and North African specialities. In short, this is a blend of Mediterranean flavours to be sampled as quick snacks – at the bar on the ground floor or in the spotless *venta*-style room upstairs brightened with photographs.

Lescure

7 r. Mondovi
✉ 75001
✆ 0142601891

Ⓜ Concorde
A1

closed 2-29 August, 21 December-2 January, Saturday and Sunday

Menu €23 – Carte €21/33

Lescure, located on a street behind the American Embassy, is the kind of place that improves with age, like a good wine. It has been handed down from father to son since it was first opened in 1919, and the owners, from the Corrèze region, have a faithful following of friends who have passed the word on. The old country inn look is a great draw with its rustic tables – and no more than thirty place settings. Cured meats and braids of onion and garlic hang from the ceiling. Copious, mouth-watering dishes from the Limousin region are featured, as well as beef bourguignon, stuffed *poule au pot* (boiled stuffed chicken with vegetables), and for dessert, *fondant aux trois chocolats*. Exceptionally friendly staff.

Bourse

Legac H./MICHELIN

Wedged in between the Palais Royal, Opéra and boulevard de Sébastopol, the second arrondissement is both the smallest and least populated of Paris. However don't be mistaken: deeply rooted in the heart of the capital, it is home to a genuine hive of commercial activity around which an often surprising mosaic of atmospheres and décors has grown up.

From financial marketplaces...

The Bourse district owes its name to the famous Palais Brogniard, a pompous neo-classical edifice, home, until only a short time ago, to the Paris Stock Exchange. Now closed, the temple of French finance has nonetheless retained a faithful network of devotees and the ostentatious marks of its industrious and merchant traditions are still visible in the corporate headquarters of the many banks and financial and credit institutions in the neighbourhood as well as in the streets that teem with executives and luxury cars during working hours.

A few steps away, the Sentier district – the manufacturing face of this "economic forum" – reveals the same thriving entrepreneurial spirit and its narrow streets are often blocked by delivery vans and wholesale goods. Even though the clothing workshops, the core of Parisian fashion, are gradually giving way to young IT start-ups, the neighbourhood continues to overflow with little establishments that are perfect for a quick meal between two appointments.

... to vegetable markets

The former effervescence is in striking contrast to the almost provincial charm of the Montor-

gueil district. Its largely pedestrian streets are lined in traditional fruit and vegetable stalls and subtly old-fashioned cafés where the locals plonk down their basket between shops for a cup of coffee.

The neighbourhood also hides countless covered galleries whose high glass and metal roofs are typical of the 19C. In between rue d'Aboukir and rue Saint-Denis in particular, don't miss the Passage du Caire (1798) whose original décor is still intact and which is home to dozens of tiny shops selling lithographs and to a highly singular population of models for shop windows, intended for the textile trade just next door in the Sentier.

Legac H./MICHELIN

HIGH-CLASS ELEGANCE

The setting and the class moves markedly upmarket between rue de la Paix, headquarters of international calibre jewellers and place des Victoires, a stylish royal square encircled by high fashion designers. The atmosphere is decidedly plush, if not luxurious. An impression further reinforced by the refined architecture of the buildings, a succession of elegant façades of all styles and all periods. From the medieval tower of Jean sans Peur on rue Etienne Marcel to the lofty glass and steel merchant buildings on rue Réaumur, every era of Parisian history is represented.

BISTROS!

Few Parisians actually live in the second arrondissement, so bound up as it is in the world of trade and industry, but the traffic is nonetheless often at a standstill due to its central location and the appeal of its shops. So take your time and stop at one of the many traditional old bistros and admire their zinc-covered counters, walls lined in mirrors and comfortable upholstered bench seating as you sample a menu devoted for the most part to good wholesome fare.

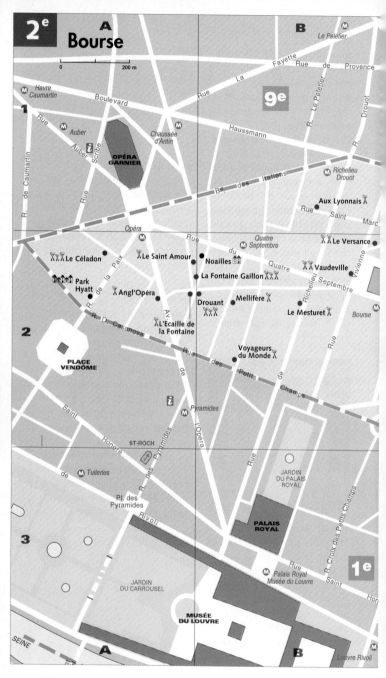

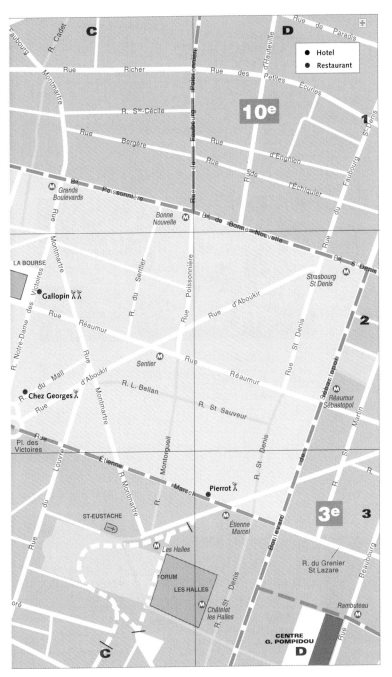

Le Céladon ✿

A/C
VISA
MC
AE
D
Y

Hôtel Westminster,
15 r. Daunou ✉ 75002
✆ 0147034042 – **Fax** 0142613378
e-mail christophemoisand@leceladon.com
Web www.leceladon.com

closed August, Saturday and Sunday

Menu €48 (lunch)/€110 – Carte €82/111

M Opéra
A2

Le Céladon

If you find yourself dreaming in front of the window displays on Place Vendôme, keep walking. At n° 13 rue de la Paix, you could open the door and enter the Hotel Westminster. But if you walk another ten yards you will reach 15 rue Daunou where the Céladon awaits you with its menu by Christophe Moisand, formerly of the Relais de Sèvres and the Meurice. The culinary philosophy of this chef, intent on continuing in the great French tradition, can be summed up in a few words: gastronomy is a celebration of service and presentation as well as flavour. Not to mention the decor designed by Pierre-Yves Rochon, with its discreet ambience highlighted by damask wall hangings and "celadon" green Chinese porcelain vases that blend in well with the colour of the walls. The subtle and masterful cuisine combines classicism and modernity, with well-balanced dishes and a selection of wines chosen by sommelier Richard Rahard. The recipe is a success.

A LA CARTE

FIRST COURSE
· Pâté froid de lapin de garenne (15 September to 15 January).

· Crabe royal à la crème d'avocat, eau de tomate à la verveine.

MAIN COURSE
· Langoustines bretonnes en tempura au carry.

· Saint-Pierre de petit bateau masqué de pousses de moutarde, "cru et cuit" de légumes niçois aux olives.

DESSERT
· Soufflé chaud au chocolat guanaja, glace au pain d'épice.

· Ananas effeuillé au sorbet de pamplemousse, "rocher coco" et miel basilic.

La Fontaine Gaillon

Seafood ✕✕✕

pl. Gaillon
✉ 75002
☎ 0147426322 – **Fax** 0147428284
Web www.la-fontaine-gaillon.com

closed 4-26 August, Saturday and Sunday

Ⓜ Quatre Septembre
A-B2

Menu € 38 (lunch) – Carte € 47/66

Everyone has been talking about this restaurant ever since Gérard Depardieu took over. But that isn't the most convincing asset possessed by this fine townhouse built in 1672 by Jules Hardouin-Mansart. The main event is the well-prepared cuisine by Laurent Audiot, formerly of Marius et Jeannette, featuring seafood, classics of French gastronomy with a twist, and daily inspirations based on market produce. Then there is the cellar, which takes an interest in small-scale producers and wines from sunny places (Morocco, Sicily, etc.). Lastly, there are the stylish, intimate dining rooms with their wood panelling, period furniture and fine paintings, not to mention the extremely pleasant "Provençal" terrace coiled around the fountain.

Drouant

Traditional ✕✕✕

16 pl. Gaillon
✉ 75002
☎ 0142651516 – **Fax** 0149240215
e-mail reservations@drouant.com **Web** www.drouant.com

Ⓜ Quatre Septembre
B2

Menu € 42 (weekday lunch)/€ 52 – Carte € 65/75

Antoine Westermann has breathed new life into Drouant, the restaurant on Place Gaillon where the Goncourt Academy awards its yearly prize. His ambition is to turn this legendary place into the next chic brasserie where people meet to exchange ideas over a festive meal. The sleek new decor is muted yet luminous, with well-balanced proportions. The dark furniture offsets the light walls decorated with photographs; the Ruhlmann staircase leads up to a pleasant loft space; the bar area is adorned with gold; and the private dining rooms have retained their classic style. A fine setting for the expressive cuisine that blends traditions and features top-quality seasonal ingredients (vegetables, truffles, foie gras, oysters, etc.).

Gallopin

Brasserie 🍴🍴

A/C	40 r. N.-D.-des-Victoires	Ⓜ Bourse
	✉ 75002	**C2**
VISA	✆ 0142364538 – **Fax** 0142361032	
	e-mail administration@brasseriegallopin.com	
	Web www.brasseriegallopin.com	

Menu €28/€34 wine included – Carte €28/73

The name comes from a certain Monsieur Gallopin, who opened his first business here in 1876 and invented the famous silver-plated beer mugs of the same name. Since then, many *gallopins* (urchins) have stood at its bar. Arletty and Raimu were once regulars; nowadays many businessmen come to enjoy the lovely decor with its venerable bar, wood panelling, gleaming copper-ware, mirrors, mouldings and, above all, its superb 1900s glass roof (in the Belle Epoque room). The menu features simple but reliable brasserie fare such as *foie gras de canard* (duck foie gras), *andouillette* sausages, seafood platters, sole (grilled or meunière), and *pièce de bœuf*. With the relaxed service and atmosphere here you'll enjoy every sip of beer – and the rest too!

Vaudeville

Brasserie 🍴🍴

VISA	29 r. Vivienne	Ⓜ Bourse
	✉ 75002	**B2**
	✆ 0140200462 – **Fax** 0140201435	
AE	**Web** www.vaudevilleparis.com	

Menu €24/€31 – Carte €30/64

Businessmen and journalists come here for lunch (the Stock Exchange and Agence France Presse are nearby). But in the evenings it is filled with the lively theatre crowd. Art Deco furnishings begin to sparkle, decibels rise and ever-smiling wait-ers slalom from table to table. No doubt about it, the Vaude-ville knows its part by heart – that of a true Parisian brasserie! Featured "On the Boards" are all the classics of the genre, highlighted by house specialities such as *Tranche de morue grillée* (grilled slice of cod) and *purée de pommes de terre au jus de truffe* (mashed potatoes with truffle juice). You can order from a set menu or à la carte, and there is even a late supper for theatre-goers. The terrace is a nice bonus in fine weather.

Le Versance

Contemporary ✗✗

🅰🅒 16 r. Feydeau   ⓜ Bourse
VISA ✉ 75002   **B2**
   ✆ 0145080008 – **Fax** 0145084799
ⓜⓒ **e-mail** contact@leversance.fr **Web** www.leversance.fr

closed August, Saturday lunch, Sunday and Monday

🅐🅔 Menu €38 wine included – Carte €40/71

🍷

Luxe, calme et volupté (comfort, calm and bliss) – the expression is rather hackneyed; but in this case it corresponds to reality. Le Versance is truly a gem – tasteful and elegant, classic and modern with its clean lines and grey-and-white tones. Period beams and stained glass, tables dressed to the nines, prim and proper professional waiters, smoking lounge, and serene ambiance. This is a masterstroke for Samuel Cavagnis, and his first restaurant. In the kitchen this young globe-trotter sticks with French flavours. This return to his roots is illustrated by the nicely named dishes, such as *raviole de potiron au sirop d'érable* (pumpkin ravioli with maple syrup), and *poire coing aux épices et châtaignes* (quince pear with spices and chestnuts).

Chez Georges

Traditional ✗

🅰🅒 1 r. Mail   ⓜ Bourse
VISA ✉ 75002   **C2**
   ✆ 0142600711
ⓜⓒ closed August, Saturday and Sunday

🅐🅔 Carte €42/65

🍷

A real institution in the Sentier district, near the Place des Victoires, this authentic Parisian bistrot has preserved its 1900s decor, with zinc bar, banquettes, stucco and mirrors, and its warm, friendly atmosphere. The owner loves to pamper diners; the purely traditional dishes are generous and designed to please food-lovers: *terrines de foie de volaille* (chicken liver terrine), *harengs-pommes à l'huile* (herring cured in oil with potatoes), *entrecôte grillée* (grilled steak), *profiteroles au chocolat*, etc. Regulars have been coming to this place for a century (despite slightly high prices) with its top-quality produce – special praise going to meat dishes such as the famous *pavé de bœuf* –, perfect cooking and well-chosen French wines.

Aux Lyonnais 😊

A/C
VISA
MC
AE
Y

32 r. St-Marc
⊠ 75002
☏ 01 42 96 65 04 – **Fax** 01 42 97 42 95
e-mail auxlyonnais@online.fr

closed 22 July-21 August, 23 December-2 January, Saturday lunch, Sunday and Monday
– pre-book

Ⓜ Richelieu Drouot
B1

Menu €30 – Carte €40/52

This deliciously retro bistrot, open since 1890 and a member of the Alain Ducasse group, is very stylish with its mirrors, mouldings, tiling, paintings and old zinc bar. Sitting comfortably on one of the banquettes, you are all set to read the menu (despite the tables being a bit too close). Explore the tasty Lyon recipes made with the best regional products: *cervelle de Canut, quenelles* and crayfish, *cochonnailles* (pork delicacies), *cervelas pistaché* (cured pork sausage and pistachios), *tarte aux pralines roses* etc. The cellar features wines from the Rhône and Burgundy regions. The attentive service, ambiance and good value for money (the wines, however, are a bit expensive) make this a true *bouchon lyonnais* in Paris.

Voyageurs du Monde

A/C
VISA
MC
⸛
Y

51 bis r. Ste-Anne
⊠ 75002
☏ 01 42 86 17 17 – **Fax** 01 42 86 17 88
e-mail restaurant@vdm.com **Web** http://restaurant.vdm.com

Closed Easter holidays, August, Christmas holidays, Saturday and Sunday

Ⓜ Pyramides
B2

Menu €23 (lunch)/€70

This book shop/restaurant is well-known to globe-trotters, who come to find information for their next trip, pick up a good guidebook or an exotic knick-knack. But have you tried the food? It's a world tour. Since settling in here, after the Grand Véfour and Les Trois Marches, chef Patrick Charvet has done a brilliant job putting together a creative blend of food from five continents. The result is a festival of flavours subtly blending local products with exotic spices and tastes, enhanced by a fine international wine list. The menu honours a different country every day at lunchtime, and the dinner/talks on Monday and Tuesday evenings in the cosy ethnic decor (reservations required) are a delightful journey for the mind and taste buds.

Mellifère ⑬

Traditional Ⅹ

VISA

MC

AE

Ⴤ

8 r. Monsigny   Ⓜ Quatre Septembre
✉ 75002   **B2**
℘ 01 42 61 21 71 – **Fax** 01 42 61 31 71
e-mail mellifère@free.fr

closed Monday evening, Saturday lunchtime and Sunday

Menu €30 (lunch)/€34

Regulars at the Théâtre des Bouffes Parisiens are certainly familiar with this "local restaurant" just next to the theatre. A few tables on the sidewalk serving as a terrace, a typical bistro interior with wood panelling, old knick-knacks, lithographs and bullfighting posters set the tone. Welcome to Basque country, the homeland of chef Alain Atibard! The menu features regional and market produce, with some "house" specials: *œuf cocotte au foie gras* (eggs with foie gras), *boudin basque rôti* (roasted Basque sausage) with mashed potatoes and butter, and for dessert, *profiteroles au chocolat chaud* or – a must – the famous Basque cake. And the plates are nice and big too.

Le Mesturet

Traditional Ⅹ

A/C

VISA

MC

AE

①

Ⴤ

77 r. de Richelieu   Ⓜ Bourse
✉ 75002   **B2**
℘ 01 42 97 40 68 – **Fax** 01 42 97 40 68
e-mail lemesturet@wanadoo.fr **Web** www.lemesturet.com

Closed Saturday lunch, Sunday and public holidays

Menu €26 – Carte €27/37

People crowd in to sit shoulder-to-shoulder in the keyed-up atmosphere at Le Mesturet! The passionate chef at this old-style bistro champions "homemade" food and real regional produce. The meat, *charcuterie*, fruits, vegetables and cheese all come from small-scale producers whose names appear on the menu. You can enjoy the food here at any hour of the day, from old-fashioned dishes to more creative recipes, express menus for those in a hurry ("at the bar"), breakfasts, brunches and aperitifs. It also boasts a judicious selection of wines, a warm welcome and an authentic setting (stone and wood work, bottle drainers, bric-a-brac and banquettes). The price of success: the restaurant is full until closing time!

Pierrot

Traditional 🍴

18 r. Étienne Marcel   Ⓜ Etienne Marcel
⊠ 75002   **D3**
☏ 01 45 08 00 10 – **Fax** 01 42 77 35 92

closed 30 July-19 August and Sunday

Menu €40/€50 – Carte €33/50

A typical bistrot (banquettes, zinc bar, mirrors) with a warm and
friendly atmosphere in the heart of Les Halles. Sound appealing?
The flavours and fine products from the Aveyron region are
another (really good) reason to try it. Farm-raised meat from
Aubrac, confit de canard (preserved duck), homemade foie gras,
etc. All these well-made, plain and simple, generous dishes are
written up on the slate menu, complemented by the latest
additions. The service is attentive, friendly and fast. In good
weather you can eat on the sidewalk terrace and enjoy people-
watching on busy rue Étienne-Marcel.

Angl' Opéra

Innovative 🍴

Hôtel Edouard VII,   Ⓜ Opéra
39 av. Opéra ⊠ 75002   **A2**
☏ 01 42 61 86 25 – **Fax** 01 42 61 47 73
e-mail resto@anglopera.com

closed 12-22 August, Saturday and Sunday

Carte €43/47

On the ground floor of the very chic Edouard VII, a fashionable
restaurant managed by Gilles Choukroun, a young, talented chef
with a taste for the avant-garde and a passion for inventing and
blending flavours both sweet and savoury, getting his inspiration from the four corners of the globe. The result is a succinct
menu that associates playful, sometimes bold associations, all
of which are delicious. "Crème brûlée, radish, soya sauce, coffee
and foie gras", "grapefruit, green tea, spinach leaves and rump
steak" and for dessert "petits farcis, salted caramel, ginger, maple
and chocolate". Give your taste buds a surprise! Snacks, quick
lunches and pastries are sold at the bar.

L'Ecaille de la Fontaine

Fish and shellfish 🍴

VISA
MC
AE
Y

15 r. Gaillon
✉ 75002
✆ 0147420299 – **Fax** 0147428284
closed 4-26 August, 23-30 December, Saturday and Sunday – number of covers limited, pre-book

🔵 Quatre Septembre
A2

Menu €29 – Carte €31

This is another restaurant run by Gérard Depardieu and Laurent Audiot, located almost across the street from Fontaine Gaillon, specialising in shellfish obtained from small oyster-farmers and fish merchants from Quiberon, Marennes, Oléron, etc. A small slate menu also features appetizing seafood recipes to go or to enjoy at the bar. Or, if you feel like taking your time, try the little upstairs dining room which is cosy and intimate. Have a look in any case. Depardieu has created an impressive "study" with photographs evoking his life as an artist. Note that this national star also supervises the wine list.

Le Saint Amour

Seafood 🍴

VISA
AE
🔵
Y

8 r. Port Mahon
✉ 75002
✆ 0147426382 – **Fax** 0147426382
e-mail hervbrun@hotmail.fr
Closed 1st-15 August, Saturday and Sunday

🔵 Quatre Septembre
A2

Menu €34

The Saint Amour is a welcome haven of peace and quiet amidst the hustle and bustle of this central district of Paris, home to the Opéra and the big department stores. On a small side street, it features two different styles of decor on two levels – one with banquettes and exotic wood tables on the ground floor, and another with an old sideboard and country atmosphere on the first floor (with smoking area). But the generous traditional cuisine is the main focus of attention here, featuring fresh fish and shellfish from Brittany. And the chef's mother extends a warm welcome at this friendly and hospitable "pocket" restaurant.

Le Marais, Beaubourg

Blackwell K/MICHELIN

Adjoining the working-class Halles district, the 3ʳᵈ arrondissement displays an equal vitality with its countless shops and boutiques and the highly popular Beaubourg museum. However it differs in one notable respect, the soul of historic Paris can still be felt in the Marais, proud of its hectic, multicultural past and still a haven for differences of every nature…

GAY PARIS

The Marais owes its name to the marshes that used to border the Seine, turned into cottage gardens in the Middle Ages. Since then, the district has never ceased to prosper, changing personality with every era: aristocratic in the 17C, laboriously toiling in the 19C, it then floundered for a while, abandoned in indifference before being brought back to life again in

the early 1980s with the arrival of the gay community.

The neighbourhood is frequently accused of being a museum-district because of its many cultural and historic sites (**Picasso, Carnavalet museums,** etc.). However for its inhabitants, the Marais is first and foremost a "village" such is its resemblance with a microcosm where everyone knows everyone. It has above all remained human in size because of its narrow streets that were typical of Paris prior to the Hausmannian revolution. A walk in the Marais is like embarking on a journey through time, past the half-timbered medieval houses and elegant town mansions in **rue des Archives** and **rue François-Miron.** Don't miss **place des Vosges,** lined in identical arcaded buildings, home to antique dealers and good restaurants, in the centre

of which stands the majestic and very chic Louis XIII square. Just behind lies the **rue des Francs-Bourgeois** dotted with fashion boutiques located in old bakers and butchers shops that have retained their original façades. The street is always packed with fashionistas, even on Sundays when the whole neighbourhood stays open for shopping addicts! Two steps away the picturesque **rue des Rosiers** abounds in tempting kosher shops, a throwback to its Jewish traditions. It is here that you can sample the best falafels and eastern European Jewish pastries of the capital.

Rue Vieille-du-Temple and the aptly named **rue du Trésor** swarm for their part with cafés and are ideal to start the evening. On **rue Ste-Croix-de-la-Bretonnerie** the rhythm increases a notch in the gay bars that have taken up residence here.

Legac H./MICHELIN

ART AND TECHNOLOGY

To the west, modern-day Paris once again rears its head in one of its best-known icons, the **Centre Georges Pompidou**,

referred to as Beaubourg and known as much for its modern art museum as for its amazing (at the time) architecture. The "piazza" in front of the museum is undoubtedly the most popular location in the whole arrondissement and is frequented by an improbable mixture from students and tourists to street performers and portrait painters. If you're in the area, particularly at sunset, go up to the rooftop terrace of the restaurant and admire the stunning view of the roofs of Paris.

To the north, between the **Arts et Métiers Museum** (don't miss its surprising metro station) and République, you are in a "designer" land of confidential and more than trendy fashion addresses, art galleries and café-restaurants belonging to an amazing hotchpotch of registers from organic and world fusion. However let's not forget two institutions, the venerable **marché des Enfants Rouges** (1615), ideal for a quick bite between shops and the **carreau du Temple,** devoted to second-hand clothes and built out of glass and iron in tribute to the old Baltard pavilions of Les Halles.

81

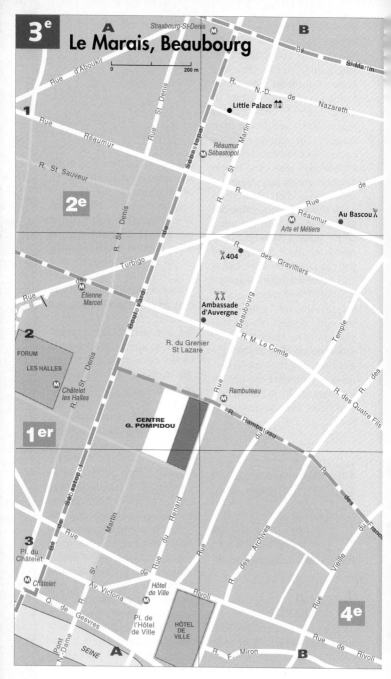

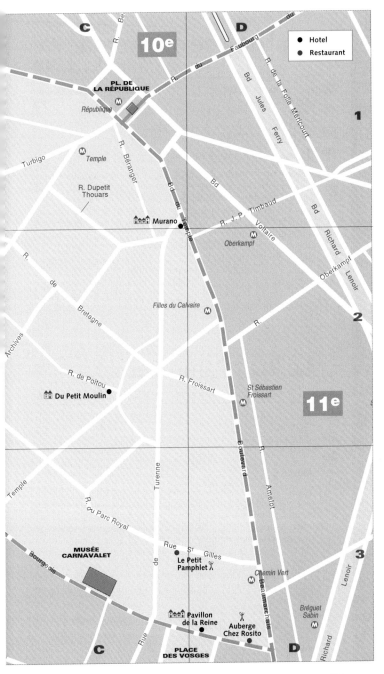

Ambassade d'Auvergne 😊

Traditional 🍴🍴

A/C	22 r. Grenier St-Lazare	Ⓜ Rambuteau
	✉ 75003	**B2**
VISA	✆ 0142723122 – **Fax** 0142788547	
	e-mail info@ambassade-auvergne.com	
	Web www.ambassade-auvergne.com	
Ⓜⓒ	Menu €28 – Carte €30/45	

Where can you get the best *aligot* (mashed potatoes with cheese) in Paris? At the Ambassade d'Auvergne, of course, where it is whipped in a copper pot before your very eyes. Other regional specialities include pork delicacies, green lentils and *potée de porc fermier aux choux braisés* (pork and cabbage hotpot), and only the best ingredients are used in preparing these authentic, generous recipes. The establishment has a bountiful selection of local cheeses and wines (the Auvergne region also features prominently on the cheese platter). Here you can enjoy a copious culinary adventure from a province with rich traditions and flavours in one of the four elegant themed dining rooms – Auberge, Artisans, Peintres, and Rotonde.

Le Petit Pamphlet

South-West of France 🍴

A/C	15 r. St Gilles	Ⓜ Chemin Vert
	✉ 75003	**C3**
VISA	✆ 0142712221	
Ⓜⓒ	closed 5-25 August, 1st-10 January, Monday lunch, Saturday lunch and Sunday	
	Menu €31	

This discreet annexe of Le Pamphlet, in a street near the rue des Franc-Bourgeois and its trendy boutiques, is a warm neighbourhood bistrot – just contemporary enough – that has plenty of character and a fun collection of little posters and engravings. The convivial atmosphere is another plus at this charming establishment with its tiny tables. And let's not forget the most important thing of all – the delicious bistro dishes on the short menu and the blackboard suggestions renewed every week. Regulars like to take time to enjoy their meals here, at lunch and dinner.

Le Marais, Beaubourg

Au Bascou

 South-West of France 🍴

VISA   38 r. Réaumur (3rd)   Ⓜ Arts et Métiers

✉ 75003   **B1**

Ⓜ❡   ☎ 01 42 72 69 25 – **Fax** 01 42 72 69 25

Ⓐ🄴   closed 1 - 29 Aug., 24 Dec. - 2 Jan., Saturday and Sunday

♉   Menu €16 (lunch) – Carte €30/35

Aficionados of this charming place should rest assured – there is a new chef-owner in charge, but the staff is the same. And Basque specialities are still featured on the menu, including *piperades* (spicy omelelet), *pimientos del piquillo* (stuffed pimentos), *chipirons sautés au piment d'Espelette* (baby squid), *axoa de veau* (ground veal with onions and Basque peppers) and for dessert, the famous *béret*. Indeed, why would Bertrand Guéneron change the formula here, which has guaranteed the success of Le Bascou for so many years? Diners always come back – for the atmosphere as well as the dishes made with fine ingredients fresh from the Basque country, the authentic recipes and warm welcome.

Auberge Chez Rosito

 Corsican 🍴

VISA   4 r. Pas de la Mule   Ⓜ Bastille

✉ 75003   **D3**

Ⓜ❡   ☎ 01 42 76 04 44 – **Fax** 01 42 76 04 44

♉   closed 7-18 August, Saturday lunch and Sunday

Carte €32/51

The Corsican flag floats above this genuine ambassador of the Isle of Beauty. The proprietors extend a warm welcome, in a spirit of simple generosity. The retro dining room has been carefully decorated with frying pans, herbs, peppers, old posters and other objects from the island. Regulars – whether from Corsica or not – enjoy the homely feeling of this establishment serving the island's treasured gastronomy (game, fish and pork) and wine. You'll feel like you've taken a one-way trip to Ajaccio in the heart of this neighbourhood full of antique and design shops.

404

Moroccan

69 r. des Gravilliers
✉ 75003
☎ 0142745781 – **Fax** 0142740341
e-mail 404resto@wanadoo.fr

Ⓜ Arts et Métiers
B2

Menu €30/77

Two of the specialities on the menu at this North African restaurant – its famous homemade couscous and tajine dishes – have gained it a solid reputation. Carefully prepared with high-quality ingredients, they attract a clientele that enjoys the exotic decor in this small establishment with its low wooden tables, superb moucharabiehs, finely worked lanterns and painted tableware from Morocco, Syria and Egypt. The menu has something for everyone, and while the atmosphere is rather trendy in the evening, the place is filled with neighbourhood regulars at lunchtime. Tables can be hard to come by in this pleasant Thousand and One Nights decor with its delightful patio-terrace, so be sure to book!

Le Marais, Beaubourg

SALADE CHARBON
~~~~~

* QUICHE JAMBON -
  EMMENTAL

* BEIGNETS DE CREVETTES
  SAUCE AIGRE - DOUCE

* CAVIAR D'AUBERGINE

10,5 €

Île de la Cité, Île St-Louis, Hôtel-de-Ville, St-Paul

Richer X/MICHELIN

The seat of religious and political power since Antiquity, the islands of St-Louis and the Cité mark the heart of Paris. The home of some of the most emblematic (and tourist) monuments of the capital, they stand like timeless jewels cut off from the rest of Paris by the Seine. The unassuming village of St-Paul, just nearby, for its part is endowed with an almost provincial art de vivre…

FROM ISLAND TO ISLAND

Is it their isolation by the Seine that gives these islands such a special character in the Parisian landscape? Despite the affluence of tourists, nothing seems to trouble the serenity of their ancient facades, so sensibly aligned behind the trees.

Île de la Cité remains singularly impressive, as it is home all on its own to the law courts, police headquarters (the "Quai des Orfèvres" of Clouzot and Jouvet), the medieval turrets of the Conciergerie (first prison of Paris), the court of trade and Hôtel-Dieu Hospital, a fact that explains the surplus of robed lawyers and policemen… You may also see many passers-by, nose up in the air desperately seeking the entrance to the Sainte-Chapelle, tucked away behind the law courts.

The island is also home to another gothic masterpiece, **Notre-Dame Cathedral,** as popular today as it was in past times. Once you've made your way across the esplanade, sidestepping the snap-shotters, souvenir vendors and roller bladers, venture indoors and enjoy the classical concerts that take place beneath its ribbed vaults – don't miss the evening organ concerts.

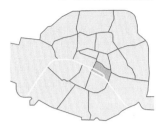

In contrast to these grandiose sites, you may want to take a breather at **place Dauphine**, the **flower market** or **square du Vert-galant,** as you head down towards **Pont Neuf** – in fact the oldest bridge of Paris. Beneath you boats of tourists and barges make their way up and down the Seine.

Walk over to **Île Saint-Louis** across the bridge of the same name – the only link between the two islands. The atmosphere here is much quieter and more peaceful. A throwback perhaps to when the island was little more than a field given over to cows, duels and washerwomen! A residential district since the 17C, its noble edifices are also

Richer X./MICHELIN

reminders of the artists and poets who found refuge here in the 19C. In short it is a haven for romantic strolls. In the evening, walk up **rue Saint-Louis-en-l'Île,** the backbone of the island and the location of shops, galleries and restaurants, and also of the famous ice-cream maker, **Berthillon**.

Town and village

A parenthesis in time, **village Saint-Paul** is an unexpected enclave with its tiny maze of lanes

and ancient houses, now home to high-class antique dealers and also popular with strollers. Almost a medieval miniature, it is only a few steps from the modern traffic and bustle of **rue Saint-Antoine** and **rue de Rivoli.** The basement of the hundred-year-old Bazar de l'Hôtel de Ville (BHV) is heaven for do-it-yourself fans who, once their bolt found, can take a break at the café Boulon. Finally **place de l'Hôtel de Ville** resonates to the capital's major cultural, sporting and political events, while place Baudoyer, just behind, is where the only market in the 4th is held.

Bastille on one side and **Châtelet** on the other, the symbolic frontiers of this arrondissement, are high places of opera and theatre in the capital. Surrounded by brasseries and cafés that are open until early in the morning, they embody the personality of the city of light and revolution.

Richer X./MICHELIN

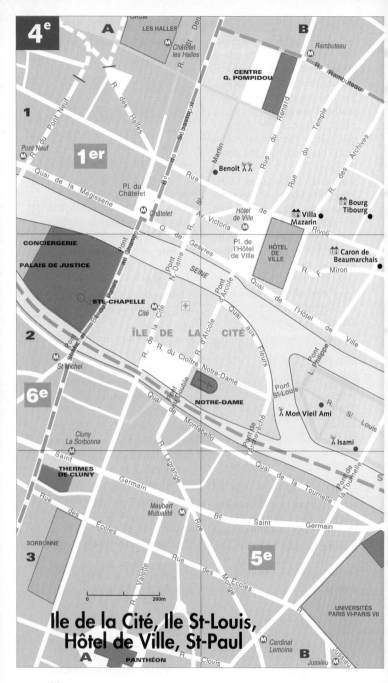

Ile de la Cité, Ile St-Louis,
Hôtel de Ville, St-Paul

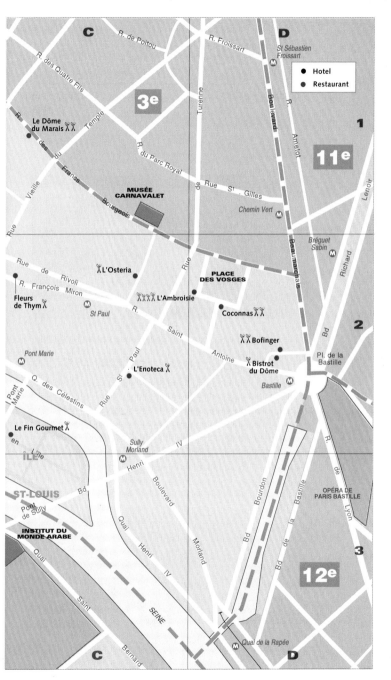

L'Ambroisie ✿✿✿

Classic 🍴🍴🍴🍴

9 pl. des Vosges
☒ 75004
✆ 0142785145

Ⓜ St-Paul
D2

Closed 31 July-26 August, February half-term holidays, Sunday and Monday

Carte € 185/272

A/C

VISA
MC
AE
♀

Owen Franken

The dictionary gives the following definition for "ambrosia", the name chosen by Bernard Pacaud for his establishment: "food of the gods of Olympus, a source of immortality"; thus, by extension, food that is exquisite. The restaurant was established in 1986 under the arcades of the Place des Vosges near a little garden far from the hustle and bustle of the city. The antique mirrors and tapestries give the dining room the look of a Florentine palace where you may catch yourself whispering to fit in with the calm and peaceful atmosphere. Smooth service and superb wine list. The cuisine is an elegant reinterpretation of tradition - classic dishes featuring carefully selected ingredients, precision cooking and infallible blends of flavours. In short, everything is impeccable.

A LA CARTE

FIRST COURSE
• Feuillantine de langoustines aux graines de sésame, sauce curry.
• Marbré de foie gras, céleri rave et truffe en gelée.

MAIN COURSE
• Navarin de homard et pommes de terre fondantes au romarin.
• Poulette de Bresse rôtie au beurre de truffe, salsifis au jus.

DESSERT
• Tarte fine sablée au chocolat, glace vanille.
• Parfait praliné aux marrons glacés.

Benoît

Traditional ✗✗

20 r. St-Martin ⊠ 75004

Ⓜ Châtelet-Les Halles **B1**

☎ 01 42 72 25 76 – **Fax** 01 42 72 45 68

e-mail restaurant.benoit@wanadoo.fr **Web** www.alain-ducasse.com

closed 21 July-20 August and 22 December-1st January

Menu € 38 (lunch) – Carte € 54/83

Marie Hennechart

In 1912, it was a true bouchon lyonnais, with its clientele of shopkeepers from the artistic and picturesque Paris quarter of Les Halles close by. Benoît Matray, a butcher by profession, bought the restaurant and gave it his name and spirit. A half century later, his grandson Michel Petit gave up the idea of becoming a veterinarian and followed his grandfather's spirit of conviviality and sharing that have made the restaurant a success. Regulars here have been known to assert that "At Benoît's, you can eat, drink and be merry." In April 2005, the business went out of the family's hands and became part of the Alain Ducasse group, which is keen on continuing its bistro tradition, while adding a touch of modernity by putting David Rathgeber in the kitchen. And the food? It is "authentic, and a tribute to the traditional dishes that have made French cooking what it is today", featuring dishes that everyone knows but hardly ever eats – except here.

A LA CARTE

FIRST COURSE
- Tête de veau sauce ravigote.
- Escargots en coquille aux fines herbes.

MAIN COURSE
- Cassoulet maison.
- Vol-au-vent de cuisine bourgeoise.

DESSERT
- Vacherin aux marrons glacés.
- Tarte tatin.

Île de la Cité, Île St-Louis, St-Paul

Coconnas

Traditional 🍴🍴

 2 bis pl. des Vosges   Ⓜ Chemin Vert
✉ 75004   **D2**
☏ 0142785816 – **Fax** 0142781628
Closed February half-term holidays, Monday and Tuesday

Menu €27 (lunch) – Carte €42/69

Going into this restaurant is a bit like opening a French history book. Annibal de Coconas was condemned by Queen Margot for having taken part in the Vincennes plot designed to bring about the death of Charles IX. Apart from the history lesson, the elegant decor of medieval inspiration – imitation red leather chairs, darkwood furniture, old stone walls – seems to be straight out of the 16th century. It really is an astonishing journey to the very heart of a chic and comfortable medieval inn. Although tourists flock to this original establishment, the quality of the menu (traditional cuisine) and the prestigious location under the arcades of the Place des Vosges also attract local gourmets.

Bofinger

Brasserie 🍴🍴

A/C   5 r. Bastille   Ⓜ Bastille
 ✉ 75004   **D2**
 ☏ 0142728782 – **Fax** 0142729768
e-mail eberne@groupeflo.fr **Web** www.bofingerparis.com

Menu €24 (weekday lunch)/€31 – Carte €28/68

When Frédéric Bofinger opened this brasserie in 1864, it was almost an immediate success. Parisians came to sample the draught beer on sale. The greatest craftsmen of art (Royer, Panzani, Spindler...) then shaped the capital's gourmet memorial. Of special note is the superb upstairs room (6-8 places) where the woodwork painted by Hansi represents kougelhopf, bretzel, storks, ladybirds and Alsatian ladies in local dress. The splendid decor is still just as fascinating today, with its magnificent glass dome with floral patterns, its stained glass windows, marquetry, vases and paintings. And the vistor's book is practically a 20th century Who's Who!

Le Dôme du Marais

Contemporary XX

53 bis r. Francs-Bourgeois   🅜 Rambuteau
✉ 75004   **C1**
☏ 0142745417 – **Fax** 0142777817
e-mail ledomedumarais@hotmail.com

closed 1st-4 May, 8-31 August, Sunday and Monday

Menu €23 (weekday lunch)/€100 wine included– Carte €42/56

The two major attractions of this charming restaurant are in the name itself. First of all, the light emanating from the majestic dome, a legacy from the "Mont-de-Piété" once housed here, bathes the former auction room, where one may sample the chef's modern-day specialities. The pleasant glass-roofed court-yard room has been decorated in a winter garden style. Secondly, the location in the Marais, in the rue de Franc-Bourgeois, is another advantage of this venue much appreciated by tourists and Parisians alike.

Mon Vieil Ami

Contemporary

69 r. St-Louis-en-l'Ile   🅜 Pont Marie
✉ 75004   **B2**
☏ 0140460135 – **Fax** 0140460135
e-mail mon.vieil.ami@wanadoo.fr **Web** www.mon-vieil-ami.com

closed 1st-20 August, 1st-20 January, Monday and Tuesday

Menu €40

This old friend will do you no harm, according to Antoine Westermann! Foreign customers and Parisian gourmets flock to his rather chic bistrot, proof that the talented Alsatian chef knows how to add the "French touch" that may, or may not, bring universal success to these "new generation" establish-ments. Below the lofty ceilings of the former stables (almost 5 metres high!) the decor is resolutely modern. Black and brown tones harmonise with the frosted glass walls. A long table to the left, and small, nicely set tables to the right give the restau-rant the appearance of a trendy inn where the chef will delight you with savoury, traditional recipes with more modern touches and hints of Alsace.

Le Fin Gourmet

Contemporary

VISA
MO
AE
O

42 r. Saint-Louis en l'Ile · ✉ 75004
✆ 01 43 26 79 27 – **Fax** 01 43 26 96 08
Web www.lefingourmet.fr
closed Tuesday lunch and Monday

M Pont-Marie
C2

Menu € 20 (lunch)/€ 35 (dinner) wine included

Two young associates, both enthusiastic and friendly, run this fine little restaurant on the Ile Saint-Louis. With it their childhood dream came true. Yohann Gerbout is in charge of the kitchen. He loves to prepare delicious, carefully presented dishes in keeping with current tastes, and then hear the acclaim from the customers when they arrive on the tables. David Magniez takes care of the dining area, where he seats the guests in one of the charming rooms, part-rustic (freestone, exposed beams, antique furniture) and part-contemporary (designer lamps, paintings by young artists). The ground floor is reserved for non-smokers.

Bistrot du Dôme

Seafood

A/C
VISA
MO
AE
♀

2 r. Bastille · ✉ 75004
✆ 01 48 04 88 44 – **Fax** 01 48 04 00 59
closed 1st-21 August

M Bastille
D2

Carte € 36/46

Painted earthenware decorating the façade tells it all. You are about to enter a bistrot truly dedicated to seafood. The décor inside confirms the restaurant's vocation, with marine-inspired paintings that enliven the two rather sober dining rooms. A bistrot-like atmosphere reigns on the ground floor, with lighting provided by artificial bunches of grapes on a vine arbour. Upstairs there's a brighter and more comfortable area. The menu offers fish, shellfish, crabs, all carefully chosen and prepared by the chef. All in all, it's a much appreciated business venue a stone's throw from the Bastille.

L'Enoteca

Italian ✗

VISA

25 r. Charles V   Ⓜ St-Paul
✉ 75004   **C2**
✆ 0142789144 – **Fax** 0144593172
e-mail enoteca@enoteca.fr

closed 11-20 August – pre-book

Carte € 26/46

What's the secret of this trattoria? Of course, the 500 or so Italian wines, from a wine cellar of over 30,000 bottles! This would be enough to attract Italian gourmets and lovers of antipasti (buffet available on the ground floor) and other "pasta del giorno". But the Enoteca's charm doesn't stop there. Behind its 16th century walls, in the heart of the Marais, original exposed beams and Murano chandeliers provide a more than welcoming atmosphere, which is also lively to say the least, especially in the evenings. This is for a quick trip to Rome with friends rather than a romantic escapade to Venice!

L'Osteria

Italian ✗

[AC]
VISA

10 r. Sévigné   Ⓜ St-Paul
✉ 75004   **C2**
✆ 0142713708
e-mail osteria@noos.fr

closed August, Monday lunch, Saturday and Sunday – pre-book

Carte € 33/92

The management may have changed but not the rest! No name or menu on the façade, as the Osteria prefers a private club atmosphere dear to a loyal clientele. Celebrities who have made the venue their favourite trattoria have left their mark with all kinds of drawings, paintings and autographs. But be reassured in the fact that, for what are nevertheless Parisian prices, one may enjoy fine Italian cuisine prepared and served by the chef himself. And when you see the risotto, you'll know he's made it just for you!

Île de la Cité, Île St-Louis, St-Paul

4ᵗʰ ARRONDISSEMENT

Isami

Japanese 🍴

A/C	4 quai Orléans
VISA	✉ 75004
	✆ 01 40 46 06 97

Ⓜ Pont-Marie
B2

♀ Closed 5-27 August, Christmas holidays, Sunday and Monday – number of covers limited, pre-book

Carte € 40/80

The restaurant's renown among the Japanese, who all know where to go to eat as they would back home, is proof that this is where you will find probably the best raw fish in Paris. Local and international customers are not mistaken either. Behind his bar Katsuo Nakamura performs wonders with sushi and shirashi. With fresh products of exceptional quality, and remarkable dexterity with his knives the sushi expert has risen to the top ranks among Japanese restaurants in Paris. There's no outdated folklore in the decoration (except for a few calligraphies) and advance booking is obviously needed in the small dining room where the sign "Isami" (ardour, exaltation) is carved on a wooden panel.

Fleurs de Thym

Lebanese 🍴

VISA	19 r. François Miron
Ⓜ◎	✉ 75004
AE	✆ 01 48 87 01 02
⓪	closed Sunday

Ⓜ St-Paul
C2

Menu € 17 (weekday lunch) – Carte € 24/30

♀ Three Lebanese brothers run this family concern where you will find a simple and warm welcome. Small tables huddled together, bare stone and a few oil lamps make for a no-frills décor, but what pleasure awaits you on your plate! Authentic mezze, grills and pastries, deliciously prepared and full of the flavours of the Lebanon are accompanied by delightfully fresh wines, and all this for very reasonable prices in view of the location. With oriental background music, the restaurant is a haven in the middle of this largely touristic part of Paris.

Panthéon, Jardin des Plantes, Mouffetard

Richer X./MICHELIN

An amphitheatre 2000 years old, a "mountain" of resistance, a garden of rare and exotic plants, a hi-tech museum and picturesque markets – the appeals of this surprising and rebellious district are countless.

KNOWLEDGE IN CAPITAL LETTERS

The district is home to the **Sorbonne**, Jussieu, Censier, **Collège de France** and to top secondary and prestigious business schools. Marked by a long history of idealistic combats, the neighbourhood between **St-Michel** and **Port-Royal** has been marked by legendary personalities such as Saint Geneviève – patron saint of Paris who defended the city on her hill when the town was still Lutèce, the "great freedom fighters" honoured for eternity under the cupola of the

Pantheon, dissident theologians (Abélard, Sorbon), thinkers and the heroes of May 1968.

The **fountain** where Saint Michael slays the dragon remains a popular meeting-point to this day. From morning to night, the square never empties and is literally packed during Parisian rituals such as the Music Festival. It leads to a string of high-street chain stores along the wide **Boul'Mich** or to the delightful lanes of the old **St-Séverin** district. Students and tourists mingle on **quai de Montbello** and **quai de la Tournelle,** overflowing from the friendly bars and tightly-packed café terraces.

In terms of cuisine, the 5th displays a marked taste for exotic flavours, particularly those of the Mediterranean and Asia. The nights are equally lively from the laid-back Irish pubs and cosy cellars playing acoustic jazz to the cafés that stay open until dawn of **rue du Petit-Pont.**

PHILOSOPHY AND CARTOONS

In terms of culture, the area is proud of its traditions! Ionesco's plays have been playing at the Théâtre de la Huchette since 1957, arthouse retrospectives abound, Shakespeare & Co, a mythical English bookshop, stays open until midnight with beds available upstairs for bohemian globe-trotters and the debates are always heated in the "cafés philo". However more up-to-date leisure activities are also available for today's online youth as the cyber cafés and cartoon-strip bookstores prove. The fifth arrondissement, despite its solemn, bourgeois air, has nonetheless retained its teenage spirit.

TRAVEL THROUGH TIME

Architecture in the 5th crosses the centuries and styles from gothic and neo-classical to contemporary, all of which creates a stunning cultural shock: the

Richer X/MICHELIN

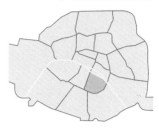

Gallo-Roman ruins of the **Arènes de Lutèce** and the **Thermes de Cluny** beneath the **Museum of the Middle Ages,** the classical **Val de Grâce** Hospital and modern **Institute of the Arab World.** From the rooftop of this glass and steel structure, the café commands a view of the Seine and **quai St-Bernard,** where improvised riverside performances of tango, salsa and capoeira take place in the summer evenings. For a taste of the orient, head for the **Paris Mosque!** You have a choice between a Turkish bath, mint tea and pastries in a unique setting.

Opposite, the **Jardin des Plantes** takes us back to our childhood. It is a traditional hit with families with a rose garden, zoo and the immense gallery of evolution of the **Natural History Museum.**

Finally take the time to savour the atmosphere of the district's many outdoor markets **(Maubert, Monge)** and busy shopping streets. If we were to recommend only one, it would be that of **rue Mouffetard** – a string of old-fashioned boutiques and handsome attic facades that stretch out between place de la Contrescarpe (lively cafés and hip intellectual atmosphere) and square St-Médard.

Panthéon, Jardin des Plantes, Mouffetard

101

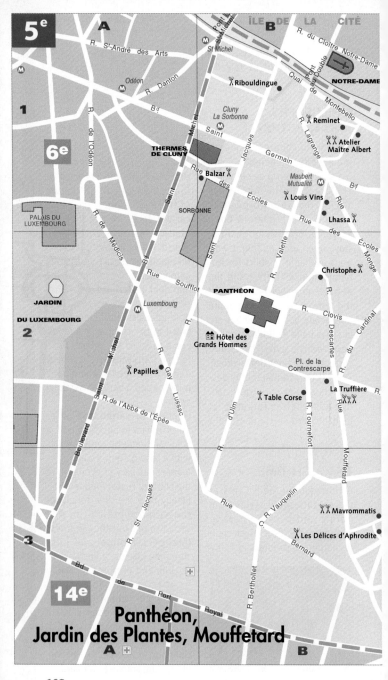

5e

A

B

ÎLE DE LA CITÉ

R. St-André des Arts

St Michel

R. du Cloître Notre-Dame

1

Odéon

R. Danton

Bd

6e

R. de l'Odéon

Cluny
La Sorbonne

✗ Ribouldingue

Quai

Pont au Double

NOTRE-DAME

Pont de Montebello

R. Lagrange

✗ Reminet

✗✗ Atelier
Maître Albert

THERMES
DE CLUNY

Germain

Saint

R. des

✗ Balzar

Maubert
Mutualité

Bd

✗ Louis Vins

Écoles

SORBONNE

Rue

Lhassa ✗

R. des Écoles

PALAIS DU
LUXEMBOURG

Rue Soufflot

R. Valette

Christophe ✗

Monge

R. de Médicis

PANTHÉON

R. Clovis

Cardinal

JARDIN

Luxembourg

R.

Descartes

DU LUXEMBOURG

2

Saint

🏨 Hôtel des
Grands Hommes

R. Gay Lussac

✗ Papilles

R. d'Ulm

Pl. de la
Contrescarpe

R. Tournefort

La Truffière
✗✗✗

Rue

Michel

R. de l'Abbé de l'Épée

✗ Table Corse

Mouffetard

Boulevard

R. St Jacques

Rue

R. Vauquelin

✗✗ Mavrommatis

3

Bd

de

Port

Royal

R. Berthollet

C.

✗ Les Délices d'Aphrodite

Bernard

14e

Panthéon,
Jardin des Plantes, Mouffetard

A ✚

B

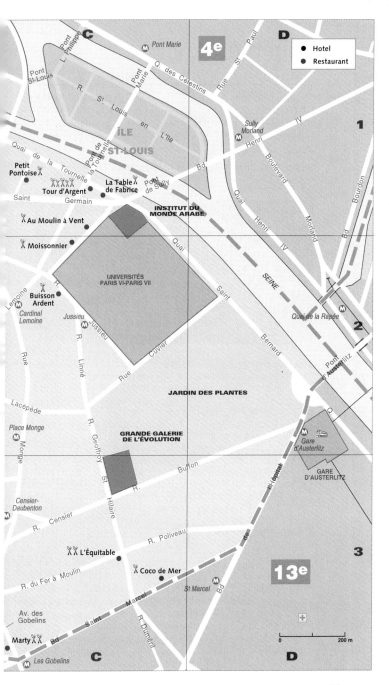

Hotel ●
Restaurant ●

4e

1

2

3

13e

Pont Marie
Pont St-Louis
Pont L. Philippe
Pont St-Louis
Q. des Célestins
Rue St. Paul
Rue
Pont Marie
R. St. Louis en L'Île
ÎLE ST-LOUIS
Quai de la Tournelle
Sully Morland
Rue Henri
Boulevard Morland
Bd Bourdon
Petit Pontoise
Tour d'Argent
La Table de Fabrice
Pont de Sully
Pont de la Tournelle
Saint Germain
INSTITUT DU MONDE ARABE
Quai Henri IV
Au Moulin à Vent
Moissonnier
Quai Saint
SEINE
Quai de la Rapée
UNIVERSITÉS PARIS VI-PARIS VII
Buisson Ardent
Rue Lemoine
Cardinal Lemoine
Jussieu
R. Jussieu
R. Linné
Rue Cuvier
Rue Bernard
Pont d'Austerlitz
Lacépède
Rue
JARDIN DES PLANTES
Place Monge
Monge
GRANDE GALERIE DE L'ÉVOLUTION
R. Geoffroy St Hilaire
Buffon
Gare d'Austerlitz
GARE D'AUSTERLITZ
Censier-Daubenton
R. Censier
R. Poliveau
L'Équitable
R. du Fer à Moulin
Coco de Mer
St Marcel
Bd
Av. des Gobelins
Marty
Bd Saint Marcel
R. Duméril
Les Gobelins

0   200 m

Panthéon, Jardin des Plantes, Mouffetard

Tour d'Argent ✿

Traditional XXXXX

⇜ 15 quai Tournelle   ⓜ Maubert Mutualité
A/C ✉ 75005   **C1**
✆ 0143542331 – **Fax** 0144071204
e-mail resa@latourdargent.com **Web** www.latourdargent.com
Closed 31 July-4 September and Monday

VISA
MC Menu €70 (lunch)/€230 wine included – Carte
AE €132/427
①
✿
♟

Tour d'Argent

This historic restaurant will be linked forever to the Terrail name. First there was André, the grandfather who founded the dynasty, then his son Claude who dreamed of working in the theatre and found expression through the restaurant. Another André is now in charge of the establishment, founded in 1582. The small lift takes you up to a panoramic dining room offering a spectacular view of Paris and Notre-Dame. The food is in line with the great classic tradition and the service is excellent. The famous Challans duck is one of the "musts" on the menu. The cellar, with a direct lift, is exceptional, estimated at 500,000 bottles. This living museum is carefully protected by sommelier David Ridgway, who occasionally allows a few lucky diners to have a peek. Who knows – the next one could be you!

A LA CARTE

FIRST COURSE
• Quenelles de brochet "André Terrail".
• Foie gras des Trois Empereurs.

MAIN COURSE
• Noisette d'agneau des Tournelles.
• Caneton "Tour d'Argent".

DESSERT
• Poire "Vie Parisienne".
• Crêpes "Belle Epoque".

La Truffière

Traditional XXX

AC
VISA
MC
AE
D
器
Y

4 r. Blainville · **M** Place Monge
✉ 75005 · **B2**
✆ 0146332982 – **Fax** 0146336474
e-mail restaurant.latruffiere@wanadoo.fr **Web** www.latruffiere.com
closed 23-30 December, Sunday and Monday

Menu €20 (weekday lunch)/€92 – Carte €70/132

Where can you find an authentic establishment that smacks of tradition? Answer: at La Truffière. Christian Sainsard's restaurant enjoys the discreetly luxurious environment of a well-preserved 17C house. With its stonework, beams and vaulted rooms, the setting exudes a pleasant rustic refinement. The menu features truffle dishes and southwestern specialities, including *magret au miel* (magret with honey), *confit, foie gras, cassoulet* and seasonal game. The impressive cellar has over 2,500 bottles (châteaux petrus, lafitte, mouton, yquem, etc.). There's nothing like an after-dinner liqueur to round off such a fine meal. And why not enjoy a cigar in the lounge?

Mavrommatis

Greek XX

AC
VISA
MC
AE
Y

42 r. Daubenton · **M** Censier Daubenton
✉ 75005 · **B3**
✆ 0143311717 – **Fax** 0143361308
e-mail info@mavrommatis.fr **Web** www.mavrommatis.fr
closed 15 August-15 September, Sunday and Monday

Menu €35/48 – Carte €41/57

If souvlaki, tzatziki and moussaka are all you know of Greek cuisine, then it's time you headed to Andreas and Evagoras Mavrommatis' restaurant for some delicious special education classes. Their establishment is, quite simply, the height of Hellenic cuisine in Paris. Instead of folklore, it features tradition (the dining room is very understated, evoking a 19C Athenian villa) and impeccably fresh ingredients. As a result, the dishes are refined and, as tradition dictates in Greece, tables are laden with the wonderful flavours of *tarama*, grilled octopus, swordfish with pickled peppers, quail roasted in honeyed vine leaves and thyme. To top it off, enjoy a glass of ouzo on the terrace lined with olive trees.

Marty

Brasserie ✗✗

A/C

VISA

MC

20 av. Gobelins
🖂 75005
☎ 0143313951 – **Fax** 0143376370
e-mail restaurant.marty@wanadoo.fr

Ⓜ Les Gobelins
C3

Menu €33 – Carte €36/58

This venerable Parisian brasserie, run by the same family since 1913, has entered the 21C with a new decor that has preserved its essence and soul, as evidenced by the mahogany wood panelling, chandeliers, stained glass, old furniture and paintings. Everything here evokes the retro atmosphere of the 1930s, from the bar and mezzanines to the veranda and terrace. Traditional dishes – huge seafood platters, *andouillette* sausages, *choucroute*, grilled chateaubriand with béarnaise sauce, etc. – share the billing with more up-to-date selections. Save room for the *profiteroles au chocolat* – a classic, like this establishment!

Atelier Maître Albert

Traditional ✗✗

A/C

VISA

MC

AE

1 r. Maître Albert
🖂 75005
☎ 0156813001 – **Fax** 0153108323
e-mail ateliermaitrealbert@guysavoy.com
Web www.ateliermaitrealbert.com

Ⓜ Maubert Mutualité
B1

closed 1st-15 August, Christmas holidays, Saturday lunchtime and Sunday lunchtime

Menu €28 (weekday lunch) – Carte €39/51

When chef Guy Savoy and architect Jean-Michel Wilmotte unite their talents to revive an old establishment across from Notre-Dame, the result is a chic contemporary restaurant-rotisserie which is full of tourists and regulars. Charcoal-grey tones, beams and stonework are featured in three different rooms: the lounge which looks like a New York bar, the dining room with its great medieval fireplace matching the rotisserie and open kitchen, and finally the more intimate wine-tasting area. The menu includes chilled oysters, roasted free-range chicken, spit-roasted veal shanks, and grapefruit terrine with tea sauce. This place has it all – from the ingredients and precision cooking to the presentation of the dishes and professional service.

L' Équitable

Traditional ✕✕

Panthéon, Jardin des Plantes, Mouffetard

VISA

MC

AE

🍷

47bis r. Poliveau
✉ 75005
☎ 0143316920 – **Fax** 0143378552
e-mail equitable.restaurant@wanadoo.fr

closed August, Tuesday lunchtime and Monday

Ⓜ St-Marcel
C3

Menu €21 (weekday lunch)/€32

And equitable it is indeed – both in price and in the generous menus which fulfill all their promises with dishes such as *Œuf-cocotte* with cream of mushrooms, fillet of sea bass with olive paste, caramel duck and semolina scented with orange, *douceur au chocolat* and crème brûlée with saffron. You can sense the hand of Yves Mutin – formerly at Le Jules Verne, Le Vert Galant and l'Ambassade d'Auvergne – whose taste for spices gives unusual flavours to traditional recipes and makes something special out of seasonal dishes. The setting is attractive, like a perfect country inn with its stonework, beams, checked tablecloths, rustic counter and collection of scales. Not to mention the charming service.

Les Délices d'Aphrodite

Greek ✕

A/C

VISA

MC

AE

🍷

4 r. Candolle
✉ 75005
☎ 0143314039 – **Fax** 0143361308
e-mail info@mavrommatis.fr **Web** www.mavrommatis.fr

Ⓜ Censier Daubenton
B3

Carte €29/44

Although many people think this is an annexe of the Mavrommatis brothers' other restaurant, it is actually their first establishment, opened in 1981. At this convivial tavern, more laid-back than the gourmet restaurant on the rue Daubenton, you can enjoy fresh Greek Cypriot specialities full of sunny flavours. The puff pastry with sheep's-milk cheese, vine leaves stuffed with rice and pine nuts, cold meats marinated in red wine, aubergine purée and *mahalepi* (creamy pudding with orange-blossom water) are served with typical Hellenic generosity and friendliness. The blue-and-white setting straight from the Cyclades, ivy on the ceiling and vibrant rebetiko music in the background will make you feel like you're really there.

La Table de Fabrice

Traditional 🍴

A/C

13 quai de la Tournelle
VISA ✉ 75005
✆ 01 44 07 17 57 – **Fax** 01 77 10 25 78

MC closed 15-30 August, Saturday lunch and Sunday

AE

🍴 Menu € 40

Ⓜ Pont-Marie
C1

After his solid training at Lasserre, Senderens and Robuchon, Fabrice Deverly decided to strike out on his own. The 17C house he found on the Quai de la Tournelle, across from the Île Saint-Louis, was the ideal spot for his restaurant, which opened in late 2005. Book a table upstairs for a wonderful view of the Seine and its barges. With its country look and original stonework, the long vaulted room is full of charm. As for the food, you have a choice between a set menu and the blackboard offerings, which change daily according to the chef's inspiration. His signature dishes include sweetbreads, *foie gras mi-cuit*, truffle risotto, crab *millefeuille* and raspberry tiramisu.

Moissonnier

Lyonnais cuisine 🍴

VISA 28 r. Fossés-St-Bernard
✉ 75005
MC ✆ 01 43 29 87 65 – **Fax** 01 43 29 87 65

AE closed August, Sunday and Monday

Ⓓ **Menu € 24 (weekday lunch) – Carte € 27/44**

Ⓜ Jussieu
C2

🍴 This establishment, a typical *bouchon lyonnais* across from the Institut du Monde Arabe, is not new, nor is the decor. This is a true bistro, where you feel at home surrounded by the shiny zinc bar, large moleskin banquettes, wooden tables and –an original touch – the mushroom-shaped lights and wine-harvester's basket and casks. Conviviality and good humour reign here. *Queue de bœuf en terrine* (ox tail terrine), *tablier de sapeur sauce gribiche, rognon de veau* (veal kidneys), *gras double* (tripe), *museau* (headcheese): rather than reinvent these traditional Lyon dishes, Philippe Mayet simply prepares them with delightful generosity, and serves them up with jugs of Beaujolais and Franche-Comté wines. Save a little room for dessert!.

Coco de Mer

Creole cuisine ✕

VISA
MC
AE
DC
♇

34 bd St-Marcel
✉ 75005
℘ 0147070664 – **Fax** 0143314575
e-mail resto@pierre-frichot.com **Web** www.cocomer.fr
closed in August, one week in January, Monday lunchtime and Sunday

Ⓜ St-Marcel
C3

Menu €15 (weekday lunch) wine included/€30

The holidays are over? As a consolation, book a table at Coco de Mer, where you will be whisked off to the Seychelles. Sitting comfortably with your bare feet in the sand (the terrace has been done up like a beach!) between marine frescoes and coconut trees, it's easy to dive into this exotic paradise. The authentic island food is half-Indian, half-African. The fish is imported directly from the Indian Ocean and delicately smoked, marinated, grilled or poached. After tasting the fresh tuna tartare with ginger, *bourgeois* (fish) with green mango chutney, octopus curried in cream with bananas, you'll be ready to hop on the first plane to Mahé!

Au Moulin à Vent

Bistro ✕

VISA
MC
♇

20 r. Fossés-St-Bernard
✉ 75005
℘ 0143549937 – **Fax** 0140469223
e-mail alexandra.damas@au-moulinavent.fr
Web www.au-moulinavent.com
closed 6-27 August, 1st-7 January, Saturday lunch, Sunday and Monday

Ⓜ Jussieu
C1

Carte €42/59

Don't judge the place by its modest façade. This very atmospheric bistro has a very pretty little eggshell-coloured dining room which hasn't changed since it opened in 1948. This is the Moulin à Vent, prized by both Parisians and tourists in search of a typically French spot. The long row of tables is simply set. On the left, a group of regulars savours a *boeuf ficelle*, calf's liver or *magret de canard* (breast of duck); on the right, an American couple enjoys delicious Burgundy snails and frog's legs *à la provençale*. Why not try one of these timeless, down-to-earth dishes yourself? And don't forget the *viandes de Salers*, a house speciality. Desserts and wines are in keeping with the rest. Classically good!

Panthéon, Jardin des Plantes, Mouffetard

Buisson Ardent

Traditional 🍴

A/C	25 r. Jussieu
VISA	✉ 75005
	✆ 0143549302 – **Fax** 0146333477
🅜🅒	**e-mail** info@lebuissonardent.fr **Web** www.lebuissonardent.fr
♈	closed August, Saturday lunch and Sunday

Ⓜ Jussieu

C2

Menu € 29/45

This bistro close to the Jussieu towers is a favourite spot for students at the university. The atmosphere in this former (18C) post house evokes the sparkling days of the Roaring Twenties, particularly in the first dining room with its bar, mirrors, tiles and magnificent original frescoes. The second room, also quite charming, has a more contemporary look. The terrace is another option, weather permitting. The dishes are titillating: asparagus and mozzarella *croustillant* with citrus, calamari risotto with parmesan, peaches with basil and frozen yoghurt. Stéphane Mauduit has worked with some of the great chefs (including Rostang) and it shows in his fine cooking!

Louis Vins

Bistro 🍴

A/C	9 r. Montagne-Ste-Geneviève
🎐	✉ 75005
	✆ 0143291212
♈	**Web** www.fifi.fr

Ⓜ Maubert Mutualité

B1

Menu € 27

The recently opened Louis Vins – done up like an old bistro – is a happy addition to the capital's little family of wine bars. It has a crimson façade and 1900s brasserie-style interior decor with a walnut bar, mirrors, chandeliers and frescoes, as well as a glass cellar to delight the eye. That sets the tone for this establishment, run by a restaurateur who has been collecting fine bottles for thirty years. 280 wines, to be exact, which you can taste by the glass or *à la ficelle* (you pay for however much you drink). The menu features ingredients from the *terroir*, with generous blackboard recipes such as poached eggs with foie gras, monkfish cheeks in white sauce, and house desserts. Success is well-deserved given the reasonable prices.

Balzar

Brasserie ✗

A/C
VISA
M©
AE
①
♉

49 r. Écoles
✉ 75005
✆ 01 43 54 13 67 – **Fax** 01 44 07 14 91

Ⓜ Cluny la Sorbonne
B1

Carte € 26/64

When Amédée Balzar left Picardy in 1890 to open a tavern in the capital, he had no idea of the future in store for his little establishment. This brasserie (now part of the Flo group), bought in 1931 by the Cazes family who turned it into their "second Lipp", is a wonderful example of the Parisian look. With wood panelling, dark walls, large mirrors and banquettes, the Art Deco setting hasn't aged a bit. Nor has the menu, which features calf's liver and *millefeuilles*. "Speed, simplicity and quality", the motto of the house, has drawn students, professors and intellectuals for over a century. What better place than here, a stone's throw from the Sorbonne, to have a meal, reinvent the world and run into the Sartres and Camus of tomorrow?

Ribouldingue 😊

Bistro ✗

VISA
M©
♉

10 r. St-Julien le Pauvre
✉ 75005
✆ 01 46 33 98 80

Ⓜ Maubert Mutualité
B1

closed August, Sunday and Monday

Menu € 27

Tripe is in fashion! Go and see for yourself at Ribouldingue, a friendly neo-bistro that has replaced the former Fogon. The chef, Claver Dosseh, ex-second for Camdeborde, has taken up the bold challenge of reconciling diners with offal. And he has more than succeeded. To start off, try the fine Brittany artichokes, served with a smile by Nadège. Then come the melt-in-your-mouth dishes – classic or reinvented – including snouts, teats, brains, tongue and cheeks. The menu also has items for more delicate diners, such as asparagus, *foie gras* or *endives au gratin*. And everyone enjoys the desserts: *caillé de brebis* with chestnut honey and rice pudding with orange marmalade. A real favourite, at an affordable price.

Reminet

Traditional ✗

VISA
_MC_
♀

3 r. Grands Degrés
✉ 75005
✆ 01 44 07 04 24

Ⓜ Maubert Mutualité
B1

closed 11 August-1st September, Tuesday and Wednesday

Carte € 35/44

Walking into the Reminet, an exquisite bistro off the Quai de Montebello, almost feels like entering a private club. It isn't, but there are two reasons for that impression – the hushed and intimate narrow dining rooms with stone walls, and the rather Baroque decor with its theatrical use of reflected lighting (with chandeliers and mirrors). And given the international clientele and attentive service, it seems to be very popular with a wide following of gourmet diners. So you don't have to be a tourist or a businessman to enjoy the slightly exotic food here which blends regional ingredients and faraway spices with great panache.

Table Corse

Corsican ✗

VISA
_MC_
_AE_
♀

8 r. Tournefort
✉ 75005
✆ 01 43 31 15 00 – **Fax** 01 43 31 12 51

Ⓜ Place Monge
B2

closed August, 24 December-1st January and Sunday – dinner only

Carte € 34/51

The discreet establishment's yellow awning is like a ray of sunshine on this peaceful street in the Contrescarpe area, and the sign says right away that the focus here is on Corsican cuisine. The decor is understated (paintings of the Isle of Beauty), but the food is bold, and the talented chef creates interesting dishes using ingredients from the island. The _quenelles de brocciu au confit de tomates_ (cheese dumplings with preserved tomatoes), _langoustines croustillantes à la mélisse_ (crispy langoustines with lemon balm), _cochon noir aux châtaignes rôties_ (black pork with roasted chestnuts), and _poires pochées au vin de myrte_ (poached pears in myrtle wine) are examples of his talent. Wide choice of Corsican wines, and a few kinds of beer.

Petit Pontoise

Bistro 🍴

A|C
VISA
💳
AE
◑
🍷

9 r. Pontoise
✉ 75005
☎ 01 43 29 25 20

🅜 **Maubert Mutualité**
C1

Carte €29/47

There are very few restaurants where you really feel at home, but the Petit Pontoise is one of them. Yes it's small, yet so charming with its pure 50s decor, appetizing blackboard suggestions and cheerful ambiance. The regulars here like to take their time and know the establishment's golden rule – patience! – which can be slightly disconcerting for newcomers. The service is in keeping with the dishes, "made to order" as the sign in the restaurant says. Philippe Tondetta's bistro is still full for lunch and dinner. And when the dishes arrive, they are well worth it, including foie gras with figs, roasted sea bass with vanilla, and pan fried *girolle* mushrooms with chopped parsley and garlic. Subtle and genuine traditional cuisine.

Papilles

South-West of France 🍴

🎲
VISA
💳
🥂
🍷

30 r. Gay Lussac
✉ 75005
☎ 01 43 25 20 79 – **Fax** 01 43 25 24 35
closed 1st-21 August, 1st-8 January and Sunday

🅜 **Luxembourg**
A2

Menu €29 – Carte €31/35

Is it to eat here, or to go? Not to worry. Papilles, Bertrand Bluy's restaurant-cellar-deli, is no fast food joint – far from it! On one side are the wine racks where you help yourself; on the other side, the shelves of terrines, foie gras and jam for sale in addition to the fine bottles; and, in the middle, the tables (there's another room in the cellar with a television screen where you can watch football matches). Monotony has been banned from the kitchen. Every day at lunchtime, the blackboard features different market-based dishes with a southwest flavour; for dinner, there is a fixed surprise menu. If you book the night before, you can find out what they'll be serving; but that takes all the fun out of it!

Christophe

Contemporary ✗

VISA
8 r. Descartes
✉ 75005
Ⓜ🄾 ℰ 0143267249 – **Fax** 0146339341
♀ closed 15 August-1st September and Monday

Ⓜ Maubert Mutualité
B2

Menu € 19 (lunch) – Carte € 31/53

Although the Pantheon is a major sightseeing spot, this little gourmet bistro is anything but a tourist-trap. The tasteful decor, part minimalist, part Japanese-inspired, features spotless – and discreet – orange walls, and old black-and-white photographs of Paris. People come here for the "brainstorming" cuisine by Christophe Philippe, who trained with Eric Briffard. Alone in the kitchen, he invents new versions of bistro classics. In addition to *langoustines* with basil, try one of his unbeatable dishes such as the pork trilogy (pig's foot and ear ragout, and roasted loin and boudin sausage) or the crunchy Guanaja chocolate mousse with pralines. Attractive prices.

Lhassa

Tibetan ✗

VISA
13 r. Montagne Ste-Geneviève
✉ 75005
Ⓜ🄾 ℰ 0143262219 – **Fax** 0142170008
♀ closed Mon.

Ⓜ Maubert Mutualité
B1

Menu € 11 (weekday lunch)/€ 21 – Carte € 17/25

If you want to breathe in the air of the Himalayas without getting dizzy, just climb up the rue de la Montagne-Sainte-Geneviève. There lies Lhassa, one of the rare good Tibetan restaurants in Paris. Intimate lighting, antique rugs, embroidery, dolls, religious objects, a photograph of the Dalai Lama, and tourist brochures about the country and its culture. The peaceful atmosphere and soft background music have a calming effect, like entering a sacred temple. The kind welcome prolongs the immediate feeling of well-being. The food is full of foreign flavours, featuring steamed dishes, soup made with barley flour, spinach and meat, beef ravioli, balls of hot rice and raisins in yoghurt, and salted butter tea! Are you ready for the journey?

Panthéon, Jardin des Plantes, Mouffetard

St-Germain-des-Prés, Quartier Latin, Luxembourg

Richer X./MICHELIN

Has the sixth arrondissement become a model of chic urbane life? Such is the idea put forward by those nostalgic for their lost intellectual district, now a luxury shop window. From one legend to another, it is only a short step. True the left bank has changed but only to keep pace with its era and it remains a pleasure to walk the streets of this glossy part of Paris.

ST-GERMAIN:
THE ART OF FASHION

The headquarters of culture in Paris where one just has to be seen, St-Germain is dotted with mythical cafés, the famous meeting places of the French intelligentsia: **Deux Magots**, the (flawlessly classical) **Flore** and the **Brasserie Lipp**, said to be the canteen of politicians. They continue to attract a mixture of writers, dandies and tourists by surfing on their existentialist post-War hour of glory (Sartre, cellars, jazz, etc.). Some even award their own literary prizes.

Never one to be caught wrong-footed in terms of trend, St-Germain is a must for art, design and fashion. The arrival of top fashion houses may have upset the muted world of letters, ousting the publishing houses, but the neighbouring Académie française has yet to be disturbed. While it may still be distinguished to leaf the pages of the latest publications at **La Hune** bookshop (open until midnight), the world of fashion reigns undisputed on **rue de Rennes**, creating a closed circle with the antique shops and art galleries on **rue de Seine** and the design shops of **Bd St-Germain.** Heaven on earth for fashion addicts from the world over.

Traditional bistros line the street of **rue des Cannettes.** Afterwards make a detour to **place de Furstenberg,** in the shadow of the church, or to the romantic and very trendy **Pont des Arts.** In the evening, the cafés on **rue Mazarine** vibrate to "electro-funk". To complete your hedonist experience, stop at one of the master chocolate makers, **Hermé, Mulot** or **Hévin,** and sample their delicious wares.

ODÉON:
THEATRE AND CINEMA

Recognisable by its lovely rotunda theatre, Odéon attracts students and tourists night and day. Lined in crêperies (pancake bars), pubs, sushi bars and independent cinemas, **rue St-André-des-Arts** and **rue Monsieur-le-Prince** are constantly lively and busy. The same is true of the handsome brasseries on **Carrefour de l'Odéon** and of the lively market stalls of **Carrefour Buci. Passage du Commerce St-André** is both peaceful and picturesque and fiercely attached to its past. It leads to **cour de Rohan** and the rear of the **Procope,** the oldest café in Paris, frequented by Voltaire and revolutionaries in their time. This is also the location of modern-day gastronomic restaurants, French and further afield, that make the headlines.

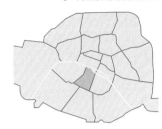

BUCOLIC PLEASURES

The vast Italian-style Luxembourg gardens are ideal to rest and relax. At all hours of the day, its flowerbeds, balustrades, ornamental pools and statues are popular with Parisians who move the green chairs about to catch the sun's rays. Lovers hand in hand wander past, joggers sprint along and whole families flock to the little boats on the pools, the swings, the tennis courts and the temporary photo exhibitions put up around the garden's railings.

To the southwest, **Notre Dame-des-Champs** changes register: it is a bourgeois "refuge" of stars and jet-setters, who you will run into at **Café de la Mairie** on **place St-Sulpice,** or as you go shopping around **Sèvres…**

Richer X./MICHELIN

St-Germain-des-Prés, Quartier Latin, Luxembourg

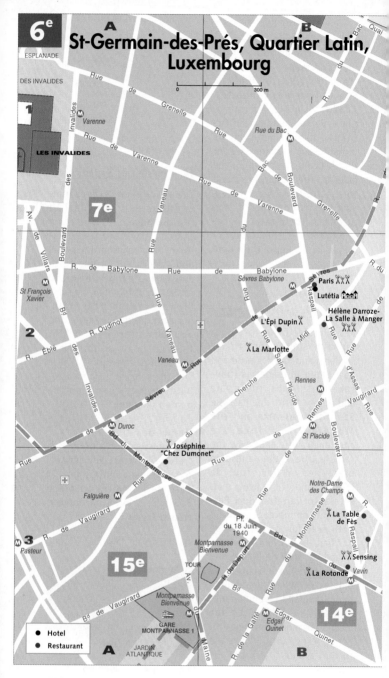

6e

St-Germain-des-Prés, Quartier Latin, Luxembourg

0   300 m

ESPLANADE

DES INVALIDES

1

LES INVALIDES

Varenne

Rue

de

Grenelle

Rue

de

Varenne

Rue

du Bac

Rue

de

Varenne

Boulevard

Grenelle

7e

Av.

de

Villars

Boulevard

des

Invalides

St François
Xavier

Bd

R. de Babylone

Rue

de

Babylone

Sèvres Babylone

Sèvres

Paris

Lutétia

**Hélène Darroze-
La Salle à Manger**

2

R. Oudinot

R.

Éblé

Vaneau

Rue

de

Sèvres

de

L'Épi Dupin

Saint

Placide

Midi

La Marlotte

Vaneau

Cherche

Rennes

Rennes

d'Assas

Rue

Vaugirard

Duroc

Bd

de

Montparnasse

St Placide

Boulevard

**Joséphine
"Chez Dumonet"**

Falguière

Rue

de

Vaugirard

Rue

Montparnasse

Notre-Dame
des Champs

Raspail

**La Table
de Fès**

3

Pasteur

R.

de

Vaugirard

15e

Pl.
du 18 Juin
1940

Montparnasse
Bienvenue

TOUR

R. du Départ

Bd

Montparnasse

du

Vavin

Sensing

La Rotonde

Bd

de

Vaugirard

Montparnasse
Bienvenue

GARE
MONTPARNASSE 1

JARDIN
ATLANTIQUE

Av.

R. du Départ

Maine

Bd

Rue

de la Gaîté

Edgar
Quinet

Edgar

Quinet

14e

| ● | Hotel |
| ● | Restaurant |

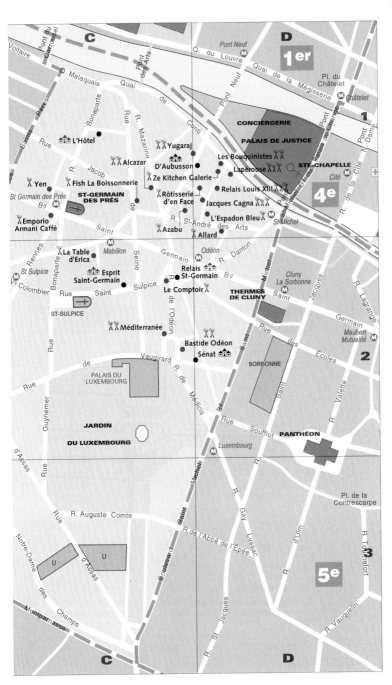

Paris ✿

Traditional 🗙🗙🗙

Hôtel Lutetia,
45 bd Raspail ✉ 75006
📞 01 49 54 46 90 – **Fax** 01 49 54 46 00
e-mail lutetia-paris@lutetia-paris.com **Web** www.lutetia-paris.com

Closed August, Saturday, Sunday and public holidays

Menu €55 (lunch)/€135 – Carte €94/107

Ⓜ Sèvres Babylone
B2

G.Corbic/MICHELIN

It is no coincidence that the Lutetia is so close to the Bon Marché department store. In 1910 the hotel management, eager for its customers to find lodgings nearby, commissioned the same architect to build a hotel. From the street, the large bay window of the hotel's gourmet restaurant tempts you to step inside. In pure Art Deco style – thankfully preserved in Sonia Rykiel's renovations – the dining room is an exact replica of that on the cruise ship Normandie, the pride of the Compagnie Trans-atlantique before it was destroyed in a fire in New York harbour in 1942. The same discreet luxury is evident in the tasteful decor with its antique furnishings. The service is efficient and low-key. The peace and quiet here – almost like being on a ship at sea – contrasts with the hustle and bustle outside. To preserve this fine ambiance, the chef has deliberately limited the number of diners at each sitting. His classical cuisine is clearly appreciated by the well-heeled local clientele.

A LA CARTE

FIRST COURSE
• Saint-Jacques marinées au caviar d'esturgeon blanc (October to April).

• Araignée de mer au pamplemousse rose et avocat, jus parfumé de colombo.

MAIN COURSE
• Homard cuit en carapace (June to November).

• Agneau de lait des Pyrénées (January to May).

DESSERT
• Clafoutis du Limousin aux cerises entières, crème épaisse.

• Tout chocolat d'un gourmand de cacao.

Jacques Cagna ✿

Traditional 🗙🗙🗙

[A/C]
[VISA]
[MC]
[AE]
[①]
[Ⴏ]

14 r. Grands Augustins
✉ 75006
☎ 0143264939 – **Fax** 0143545448
e-mail jacquescagna@hotmail.com **Web** www.jacques-cagna.com
closed 27 July-24 August, Monday lunch, Saturday lunch and Sunday

Ⓜ St-Michel
D1

Menu €45 (lunch)/€100 – Carte €81/199

Jacques Cagna

This restaurant in a historic 17th century building in the heart of Paris' Left Bank is a wonderful place to relax and enjoy a great meal. With its exposed oak beams, pale wood panelling and Flemish paintings, it has weathered the years without a wrinkle. The soft lighting further enhances the warm and intimate atmosphere. This is a traditional establishment, like the cuisine prepared by Jacques Cagna, who has made this his "lair" for many years now. He knows the meaning of the word classical, and his generous cuisine with strong but harmonious flavours has passed the test of time and fashions. The wine list has some rare bottles (with corresponding prices). For dessert, diners have been known to sell their soul for one of his amazing Paris-Brest pastries! A slightly old-fashioned – but eminently reassuring – restaurant with a whole range of appealing features designed to delight its refined clientele.

St-Germain-des-Prés, Quartier Latin, Luxembourg

A LA CARTE

FIRST COURSE
• Foie gras de canard poêlé aux fruits de saison caramélisés.

• Homard breton en salade, roquette, mousse de chou-fleur, champignon de Paris et sauce gaspacho.

MAIN COURSE
• Noix de ris de veau en croûte de sel.

• Gibier (season).

DESSERT
• Fondant glacé au praliné, biscuit dacquoise crème anglaise parfumée au café.

• Paris-Brest au praliné à l'ancienne.

St-Germain-des-Prés, Quartier Latin, Luxembourg

Relais Louis XIII ✿✿

Traditional XXX

A/C

8 r. Grands Augustins
⊠ 75006

Ⓜ Odéon
D1

✆ 01 43 26 75 96 – **Fax** 01 44 07 07 80

VISA

e-mail contact@relaislouis13.com **Web** www.relaislouis13.com

closed 1st-10 May, 29 July-20 August, 22 December-3 January, Sunday and Monday

MC

AE

Ⓓ

Menu €50 (lunch)/€100 – Carte €110/126

Relais Louis XIII

On 14 May 1610, on rue de la Ferronnerie, François Ravaillac changed the course of French history. In broad daylight this religious fanatic assassinated King Henri IV, a tireless campaigner for "a chicken in every pot". What's the connection between this drama and the restaurant where Manuel Martinez learned the cooking trade in the early eighties before becoming the owner in 1996? It was here, Saint-Augustin Convent at the time, that Louis XIII, crowned in Reims in 1614, learned that he was about to begin his reign as king of France. This is quite a historical place therefore. With its exposed beams, wood panelling and wall hangings, it evokes the comfortable Parisian inns of a bygone era. So does the food. The chef-owner, who won the Meilleur Ouvrier de France award and worked at Ledoyen, the Crillon and the Tour d'Argent, features tasteful traditional cuisine in complete harmony with the venue.

A LA CARTE

FIRST COURSE

• Ravioli de homard, foie gras et crème de cèpes.

• Quenelle de poularde de Bresse, bouillon léger au coco de Paimpol.

MAIN COURSE

• Coffre de canard rôti entier, cuisse confite.

• Epaisse côte de veau rôtie au beurre demi-sel, gratin d'oignon doux au Parmesan et roquette.

DESSERT

• Millefeuille, crème légère à la vanille bourbon.

• Assiette dégustation chocolat, sauce au vin de Maury.

Hélène Darroze-
La Salle à Manger

South-West of France

4 r. d'Assas
✉ 75006
☎ 0142220011 – **Fax** 0142222540
e-mail reservation@helenedarroze.com

Ⓜ Sèvres Babylone
B2

Menu €72 (lunch)/€235 – Carte €92/192

Hélène Darroze

This enclave of the Southwest is only a stone's throw from the Bon Marché department store. The restaurant is run by chef Hélène Darroze, who packs a lot of feeling into her food. The Salle à Manger is the elegant and discreetly deluxe upstairs dining room, with a contemporary decor in red and gold. Hélène Darroze is guided by her feelings as she reinvents dishes from the *terroir*, with well-paired wines. An unflagging ambassador of her native region, she is intent on proving her equally keen grasp of current trends. That's where the Salon part of the restaurant comes in – serving tapas and rustic regional dishes and the Boudoir for sampling gastronomic finger food. Three styles in the same place, three types of cuisine, and three reasons to enjoy a meal here. Actually, there is even a fourth reason – the pleasure of tasting one of the venerable and lovingly produced armagnacs.

A LA CARTE

FIRST COURSE
• Tarte fondante aux oignons doux des Cévennes et cèpes de Bordeaux, écrevisses "Pattes rouges".
• Foie gras de canard des Landes grillé au feu de bois.

MAIN COURSE
• Cochon de lait de race basque sous toutes ses formes (May to October).
• Suprême de poularde jaune des Landes aux champignons des bois, rôti à la gousse d'ail.

DESSERT
• Chocolat, coriandre, chicorée et vanille bourbon.
• Pinacolada, crème glacée à la vanille, gelée citron et curry, ananas Victoria, croustillant noix de coco.

St-Germain-des-Prés, Quartier Latin, Luxembourg

Lapérouse

Traditional ✕✕✕

[A/C] 51 quai Grands Augustins   Ⓜ St-Michel
⌂   ✉ 75006   **D1**
[VISA]   ✆ 01 43 26 68 04 – **Fax** 01 43 26 99 39
e-mail restaurantlaperouse@wanadoo.fr

closed August, Saturday lunch and Sunday

Menu €45 (lunch) wine included/€120 – Carte €72/97

This renowned address of Parisian gastronomy, once presided over by Auguste Escoffier, seems to have regained some of its past glory of late|The elegant wood façade conceals plush and intimate dining rooms which give onto the Seine, as well as discreet private rooms once frequented by Victor Hugo and Emile Zola. A set lunch menu features classical cuisine, while the à la carte menu is more contemporary. Ingredients are high-quality, and the poultry and game in particular are subtly prepared. Although the wine list is very well-stocked, it's rather on the steep side. Lapérouse is a historic establishment, and history comes at a price.

Sensing

Innovative ✕✕

[♿] 19 r.de Bréa   Ⓜ Vavin
✉ 75006   **B3**
[A/C]   ✆ 01 43 27 08 80 – **Fax** 01 43 26 99 27
[VISA]   **e-mail** sensing@orange.fr

closed 29 July-27 August, Monday lunch and Sunday

Menu €55 (lunch)/€140

Behind the opaque smoked glass façade of Guy Martin's most recent branch, located on a small street near the Boulevard du Montparnasse, lies a haven of chic design. The interior by Malherbe and Faillant Dumas features clean, noble materials – white marble floor and natural wooden furniture. Everything is deliberately modern here, including the images projected onto the walls. The food is up to par, with its highly contemporary short menu created by a chef who is fond of cutting-edge techniques such as vacuum-cooking, low- temperature or induction cooking using carefully chosen and prepared ingredients.

Bastide Odéon

Contemporary XX

A/C
VISA
MC
AE
Y

7 r. Corneille   M Odéon
⊠ 75006   C2
℘ 01 43 26 03 65 – **Fax** 01 44 07 28 93
e-mail bastide.odeon@wanadoo.fr **Web** www.bastide.odeon.com
closed 4 August-3 September, Sunday and Monday

Menu €26 (lunch)/€38

Southern scents and flavours reign at this friendly establishment located near the Luxembourg Gardens and the Théâtre de l'Europe. Decorated in warm colours, its red floor tiles and ochre tones evoke a Provençal bastide. The main dining room is spacious and light, while the snug wooden tables set with white porcelain, and diffused lighting from wall lamps complete the convivial atmosphere. You'll sample food inspired by contemporary Mediterranean cuisine with a personal touch and fresh market-based ingredients. The kitchen, with its young and highly motivated staff, can be seen from the restaurant entrance.

Méditerranée

Seafood XX

A/C
VISA
MC
AE
Y

2 pl. Odéon   M Odéon
⊠ 75006   C2
℘ 01 43 26 02 30 – **Fax** 01 43 26 18 44
e-mail la.mediterranee@wanadoo.fr
Web www.la-mediterranee.com

Menu €32 – Carte €38/61

This restaurant on an elegant little square across from the Théâtre de l'Europe is proud to display its marine heritage. The midnight blue façade with its lovely Cocteau drawing subtly evokes the mysterious depths of the sea. Three dining rooms form a pleasant decor which is very Parisian and boasts a pleasant veranda. Not surprisingly, the menu features seafood, prepared with talent by the experienced staff. The carefully cooked bisques, fish and shellfish are extremely fresh, prepared Mediterranean-style with olive oil marinades, fragrant herbs and saffron flavours. All that is missing is the deep blue sea and the lapping of the waves!

Yugaraj

Indian ✗✗

A/C
VISA
MC
AE
O
Y

14 r. Dauphine
✉ 75006
✆ 01 43 26 44 91 – **Fax** 01 46 33 50 77
e-mail contact@yugaraj.com

closed August, Thursday lunch and Monday

Ⓜ Odéon
C-D1

Menu €30 – Carte €37/60

The setting is exceptional at this well-known venue for of Indian gastronomy specialising in cuisine from the northern part of the country. Hidden behind the discreet sculpted wood façade lies a true museum of Hindu art, with precious silks, decorative wood panelling, ancient statues and bronze animals. The change of scenery is striking. The menu features all the great classics, including various curries and tandooris with their usual, more or less spicy sauces; but it is the quality of the ingredients which makes all the difference here, such as in the first-rate farm-raised Bresse hens and milk-fed lamb. The menu is thorough and informative, inviting you on a journey of discovery.

Alcazar

Contemporary ✗✗

♿
A/C
▨
VISA
MC
AE
O
Y

62 r. Mazarine
✉ 75006
✆ 01 53 10 19 99 – **Fax** 01 53 10 23 23
e-mail contact@alcazar.fr **Web** www.alcazar.fr

Ⓜ Odéon
C1

Menu €30 (weekday lunch) wine included/€40 – Carte €36/59

J.-M. Rivière's famous cabaret, located in a busy little street near Odéon in the heart of Saint-Germain-des-Prés, now houses a trendy restaurant with a contemporary decor. The rather austere façade conceals a spacious interior with a sumptuous glass-topped mezzanine. Wooden tables, a polished zinc bar and soft lighting create a highly attractive dining room. The contemporary and very well-prepared food oscillates between traditional and more innovative dishes and the service is pleasant and competent. Some of tables have a view of the kitchen. Large selection of foreign wines.

Les Bouquinistes

Contemporary

53 quai Grands Augustins   **M** St-Michel

✉ 75006   **D1**

✆ 01 43 25 45 94 – **Fax** 01 43 25 23 07

e-mail bouquinistes@guysavoy.com **Web** www.guysavoy.com

closed August, 23 December-3 January, Saturday lunch and Sunday

Menu €28 (lunch) wine included/€100 – Carte €51/60

With its contemporary banquettes, abstract paintings, large mirrors and colourful lighting, this "trendy" restaurant, designed by Daniel Humair and the most recent addition to the Guy Savoy empire, boldly blends a hip modern setting with Art Deco and even Baroque influences. Located by the Seine, a stone's throw from the famous book-sellers' stands, the establishment opens onto the street through a wide picture window. The food is simple and sometimes inventive. Favourites include the *marinière de moules* (mussels cooked in their own juice with onions) with curried herb gnocchi, and the pig's cheeks simmered in *verjus* with Noirmoutier potatoes. The service is quick and efficient.

Yen

Japanese X

22 r. St-Benoît   **M** St-Germain des Prés

✉ 75006   **C1**

✆ 01 45 44 11 18 – **Fax** 01 45 44 19 48

e-mail restau.yen@wanadoo.fr

closed Sunday

Menu €55 (dinner) – Carte €39/59

The outside of this typically Japanese restaurant is extremely discreet, with a modest side door and pale wood façade exemplifying Asian restraint. The same ambiance reigns inside, in the two dining rooms with carefully aligned teak tables and minimalist "zen" atmosphere. Thinly sliced buckwheat *soba* noodles cut in thin strips and seasoned in different ways are the chef's speciality here. Sushi fans will also find their share of raw fish on the menu. This place attracts a large Japanese clientele who enjoy the authenticity and fine service.

St-Germain-des-Prés, Quartier Latin, Luxembourg

La Rotonde ☺

Brasserie ✗

A/C
VISA
MC
AE
Ƥ

105 bd Montparnasse
✉ 75006
☎ 0143266884 – **Fax** 0146345240

Ⓜ Vavin
B3

Menu €35 – **Carte** €35/67

This is a real institution! Right in the heart of Montparnasse, and a stone's throw from the theatres on the rue de la Gaîté, La Rotonde has been the quintessential Parisian brasserie for nearly a century. The classic decor has a 1930s look with brass everywhere and red velvet banquettes where Picasso, Matisse and then Trotsky once sat. The menu is a happy blend of true classics and more traditional dishes, like the Salers beef and oyster platters, two of their classics. The service goes until 2am, making this establishment a favourite with theatre-goers.

La Marlotte

Traditional ✗

A/C
VISA
MC
AE
①
Ƥ

55 r. Cherche-Midi
✉ 75006
☎ 0145488679 – **Fax** 0145443480
e-mail info@lamarlotte.com **Web** www.lamarlotte.com

Ⓜ St-Placide
B2

closed 1st-21 August and Sunday

Carte €33/50

Behind its rustic inn appearance, this friendly neighbourhood bistro a stone's throw from the Bon Marché conceals a long, pleasant dining room in varnished wood. The ambiance is warm and convivial, with soft lighting, snug tables and an amusing collection of old plates and keys. The fine seasonal ingredients chosen by the owner here are used to produce tasty and varied traditional food, and only the freshest fish and meat are used to prepare the dishes. Although a favourite with publishers, gallery owners and politicians in the area, this fine establishment has managed to retain a rather unassuming side.

L'Épi Dupin

Innovative ✗

VISA

MO

♀

11 r. Dupin
☒ 75006
☎ 0142226456 – **Fax** 0142223042
e-mail lepidupin@wanadoo.fr

Ⓜ Sèvres Babylone
B2

closed August, Monday lunch, Saturday and Sunday – number of covers limited, pre-book

Menu €32

Good value for money at this pocket restaurant in the Bon Marché area. Refined cuisine which is well worth a visit lies behind its rustic little bistro look. The charming decor is unusual for Paris, with quarried-stone walls and a massive wooden frame with exposed beams. The snug room exudes conviviality and the simple and tasty dishes are prepared with impeccably fresh ingredients in the best country tradition: honey duck, *tête de veau*, oxtail and pig's cheeks are all prepared flawlessly. No smoking allowed.

L'Espadon Bleu

Seafood ✗

AC

VISA

MO

AE

①

♀

25 r. Grands Augustins
☒ 75006
☎ 0146330085 – **Fax** 0143545448
e-mail jacquescagna@hotmail.com **Web** www.jacques-cagna.com

Ⓜ St-Michel
D1

closed August, Monday lunch, Saturday lunch and Sunday

Menu €30 – Carte €42/74

Is this another annexe of the Jacques Cagna culinary empire? Or, rather, a pleasant variation on the theme of seafood? This brightly coloured bistro plays the ocean card to the hilt, featuring life-size swordfish on the walls, beams painted in the style of a St.-Malo inn, mosaic tables and blue-and-white striped banquettes colourfully evoking a meeting of the Mediterranean and the Atlantic. The sea bream-shaped blackboard lists some of specialities – including brill fillet *à la plancha* (grilled on a hot, dry griddle) and line-caught whiting in Isigny butter – mainly created with the freshest of fish caught in the Finistère region. The service and cellar are of the same calibre.

St-Germain-des-Prés, Quartier Latin, Luxembourg

Le Comptoir

Traditional

Hôtel Relais-St-Germain,
9 carrefour de l'Odéon ⊠ 75006
℘ 0144270797 – **Fax** 0146334530

Ⓜ Odéon
C2

number of covers limited, pre-book

Menu € 42 (dinner) – Carte € 30/50 (lunch)

This new bistro run by Yves Camdeborde and his wife – adjoining their famous hotel, the Relais Saint-Germain – is a huge success. The setting has an intimate Art Deco look with its 1930s décor, snug tables and large windows overlooking a huge sunny terrace. The cuisine alternates between two complementary concepts: brasserie-style food with simple and well-prepared dishes at lunchtime, and more elaborate gourmet meals for dinner. Daily changes are made to the set menu according to the market and the chef's inclination, but the quality of the dishes and the ingredients are always outstanding. Tasty specialities from southwestern France.

Emporio Armani Caffé

Italian

149 bd St-Germain
⊠ 75006
℘ 0145486215 – **Fax** 0145485317
e-mail contact@emporioarmanicaffe.fr
Web www.emporioarmanicaffe.fr

Ⓜ St-Germain des Prés
C1

closed Sunday

Carte € 47/80

A surprising Italian restaurant located in an unusual spot on the first floor of the Emporio Armani, across from the church in Saint-Germain-des-Prés. To reach the restaurant, you must walk through the famous clothing boutique with its cutting-edge menswear collections. The setting is rather "trendy" – a minimalist dining room decorated with small coloured lamps providing pleasant indirect lighting – and the effect quite "zen". The Italian-inspired cuisine, made with the freshest ingredients, produces tasty and well-prepared dishes. The carpaccio, gnocchis and risotto are good bets, and the desserts are often excellent. The service is quick and efficient.

Joséphine "Chez Dumonet"

Traditional ✗

VISA

117 r. Cherche-Midi
⊠ 75006
MC ✆ 0145485240 – **Fax** 0142840683
AE closed Saturday and Sunday

Ⓜ Duroc
A3

Carte € 29/89

A neighbourhood institution founded in 1898 and named after the wife of the first owner, today this establishment is run by Jean-Christian Dumonet, and has preserved all its original charm. A lustrous zinc bar, venerable banquettes, molten glass chandeliers and period mirrors give this very Parisian bistro a slightly old-fashioned "Roaring Twenties" air. But the kitchen is a serious affair and the traditional dishes – beef bourguignon, leg or noisette of lamb, and cassoulet – are copious and carefully prepared. In addition to the friendly owner and efficient service, it also has a spectacular wine list which, however, does not incline one toward moderation.

Ze Kitchen Galerie

Fusion ✗

A/C

4 r. Grands Augustins
⊠ 75006
VISA ✆ 0144320032 – **Fax** 0144320033
e-mail zekitchen.galerie@wanadoo.fr **Web** www.zekitchengalerie.fr
MC
AE closed Saturday lunchtime and Sunday

Ⓜ St-Michel
D1

Menu € 34 (lunch)/€ 70 – Carte € 52/55

This trendy Left Bank establishment with minimalist decor is both a restaurant and an art gallery. With its experimental culinary bent, it comes out with some of the most creative Franco-Asian fusion cuisine around. The dining room immediately sets the tone with its clean lines, galvanized black steel furniture, designer cutlery and conceptual art work on the walls. The dishes are convincingly rich in flavour, although the portions are sometimes as minimalist as the decor. A window separates the kitchen from the dining room, allowing you to watch the chef in action. The young and efficient waiters makes the experience all the more pleasant.

Allard

Traditional ☓

AC
VISA
MC
AE
DC
♀

1 r. l'Eperon
✉ 75006
✆ 0143264823 – **Fax** 0146330402

closed 29 July-20 August

Ⓜ St-Michel
D1

Menu €32 – Carte €35/78

Allard has had top billing since 1931 and has won over many hearts, including that of President Pompidou's wife and Alain Delon, who were faithful clients. While the dishes are simpler nowadays, the setting has retained its incomparable charm, and the venerable zinc bar, leather banquettes full of history, tiles and period engravings give the place the look of a genuine old bistro. The traditional food is quite invigorating, and the old-fashioned atmosphere highly convivial. The menu, made with fresh ingredients, changes daily based on the market. The service is efficient, and the wine list well-chosen.

Rôtisserie d'en Face

Traditional ☓

AC
VISA
MC
AE
DC
♀

2 r. Christine
✉ 75006
✆ 0143264098 – **Fax** 0143542271
e-mail rotisface@aol.com **Web** www.jacques-cagna.com

closed Saturday lunchtime and Sunday

Ⓜ Odéon
D1

Menu €28 (lunch)/€42 – Carte €39/68

This traditional rotisserie is just across from the main establishment – a listed building – in a small street in old Saint Germain. This is a kind of bistro for Jacques Cagna, where you can taste the recipes invented by him and prepared by a talented colleague, all at friendly prices. The ambiance is both elegant and relaxed in the ochre-toned dining room with soft lighting and long rows of tastefully set tables. Expect simple and tasty market-based cuisine which reinvents the great bistro classics with carefully selected ingredients: *côte de bœuf* (rib of beef), roast chicken, foie gras and terrine of hare are prepared in the traditional way and served by an efficient wait staff. The wine cellar is of the same standard.

Fish La Boissonnerie

Bistro ✗

A/C	69 r. de Seine
VISA	✉ 75006
	✆ 0143543469

🌀 closed 13-20 August, 22-28 December and Monday

🎗 **Menu €22 (lunch)/€33 (dinner)**

Ⓜ Odéon
C1

Could this be the best of two worlds – combining the pleasures of an authentic gastropub with that of a wine bar? This establishment, in a former fish shop with a charming façade covered in coloured mosaics, proposes straightforward quality food at attractive prices. The relaxed setting evokes both the former fish shop and a Parisian bar with its old zinc counter polished by the years, and dining room with exposed beams and decorated with sculptures and drawings of marine fauna. The menu naturally features seafood, but doesn't neglect meat-lovers. Wines include vintner's reserves and grand cru vintages.

Azabu

Japanese ✗

A/C	3 r. A. Mazet
VISA	✉ 75006
	✆ 0146337205 – **Fax** 0177110619

🌀 closed 10-25 June, 18-28 November, Sunday lunch and Monday

Menu €14,50 (weekday lunch)/€59 – Carte €34/52

Ⓜ Odéon
C1

This restaurant near the Carrefour de l'Odéon has a discreet light wood façade and minimalist aesthetic. Named after an area of Tokyo known for its gastronomy, Azabu embodies the essence of Japanese culinary culture: a restrained look and virtuoso cooking. The chef, while remaining faithful to tradition, is open to Western influences and displays his speed and skill at the *teppan-yaki* (cooking table). The menu, which has no raw fish, features reinvented Japanese classics such as sautéed tofu with chicken sauce and grilled *magret de canard*. You can eat at the counter while admiring the chef in action.

St-Germain-des-Prés, Quartier Latin, Luxembourg

La Table de Fès

Moroccan ✗

A/C
VISA
MC

5 r. Ste-Beuve
✉ 75006
☎ 01 45 48 07 22

Ⓜ Notre Dame des Champs
B3

closed 21 July-27 August and Sunday – dinner only

Ⓓ

Carte €47/68

This little gem of North African cuisine (from Morocco to be exact) is hidden behind a modest stucco façade between Raspail and Notre-Dame-des-Champs. The atmosphere is convivial, the decor warm, in a dining room which evokes both the desert and a verdant oasis. The very short menu focuses on couscous, masterfully prepared here. The cook, clearly an expert in Moroccan cuisine, knows the subject by heart. The dishes are full of flavour, the food abundant and the service pleasantly simple. The restaurant is entirely non-smoking and doesn't open in the evening until 8:30pm.

La Table d'Erica

Creole ✗

VISA
MC
AE
Ⓓ
♀

6 r. Mabillon
✉ 75006
☎ 01 43 54 87 61

Ⓜ Mabillon
C2

e-mail table-erica@proximedia.fr **Web** www.tablederica.com

closed August, Monday lunch and Sunday

Menu €13 (lunch)/€45 wine included – Carte €27/49

This nearly invisible little place in a discreet street in the Mabillon area has earned itself an excellent reputation among the many lovers of Creole food in Paris. The cuisine here is a family affair rooted in tradition. The ingredients, full of flavour and aromas, come directly from the Caribbean. The dining room evokes all the richness of the islands, with fruits and vegetables hanging from the beams and paintings of island landscapes to complete the decor. After tasting the obligatory punch, try one of the tasty and unusual dishes such as the *chiquetaille de morue* (cod) or the famous *poulet boucané à l'ancienne* (chicken).

Tour Eiffel, École Militaire, Invalides

Legac H./MICHELIN

The quiet and very green 7th arrondissement is no doubt the one that best personifies the Parisian upper class and bourgeois discretion. Wide avenues lined by century-old trees, listed buildings with flawless stone façades and luxurious private mansions hidden by cascades of greenery adorn this district, renowned for its genteel lifestyle, charming lanes and spectacular vistas. Avenue de Breteuil, whose manicured lawns lead to the Hôtel des Invalides where Napoleon is buried, is the main thoroughfare of this immense fan-shaped district that stretches as far as the Seine.

To the west, the district revolves around the Champ de Mars, an elongated stretch of greenery that runs from the Ecole Militaire to the Tour Eiffel. This emblematic neighbourhood is packed with tourists from all over the world, but as soon as you leave the immediate vicinity of the "Iron Lady", one is surprised by the almost timeless quality of the luxury flats, among the most sought-after of the capital. Two minutes away from the crowded grassy banks of the Champ de Mars, take the time to walk along the pedestrian rue Cler and the rue de l'Université, where you will find some of the finest grocery shops in Paris: bread (Poujaran), wine and cheese (Barthélémy) and even caviar (Pétrossian).

CUISINE AND POLITICS

Further east, the vast esplanades are replaced by the narrow criss-crossing of the opulent streets of rue de **Bourgogne**, rue de **Varenne** and rue de

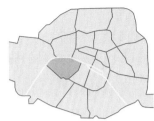

Grenelle. An uninterrupted succession of mansions hidden by high walls, this district concentrates practically all the headquarters of the country's political and administrative activity. The **Assemblée Nationale,** rising on the banks of the Seine, **Hôtel Matignon,** the **Quai d'Orsay** and the national headquarters of countless political parties keep company in edifices, whose well-worn façades have witnessed the legislative history of France.

However the country's political life also takes place in the many bistros tucked away behind the **Palais Bourbon,** to such an extent that the area is sometimes referred to as a second parliament. As a result, you won't be surprised to learn that these establishments serve dishes capable of satisfying the demanding palates of France's elected representatives.

de l'Armée and Napoleon 1's tomb, the arrondissement is rich in other museums. First and foremost, the **Musée d'Orsay,** located in the former railway station of the same name. Under its spectacular metal and glass roof, its collections of sculpture and paintings offer a magnificent insight into the artistic effervescence of the 19C and early 20C. On rue de Varenne, the Musée Rodin exhibits some of the best-known works of the sculptor, while those with a weakness for further-flung destinations will adore the recently inaugurated **Musée des Arts Premiers** on Quai Branly that features sumptuous collections of African, pre-Columbian and Oceanic art.

But if you're more of a shopping-type person, make sure you pay a visit to the **Bon Marché** department store, the temple of "left bank" good taste.

Legac H./MICHELIN

ART AND CULTURE

Finally, it would be unthinkable to speak of the 7th arrondissement without referring to its outstanding cultural and artistic wealth. In addition to the **Invalides,** already mentioned, which are home to the **Musée**

Tour Eiffel, École Militaire, Invalides

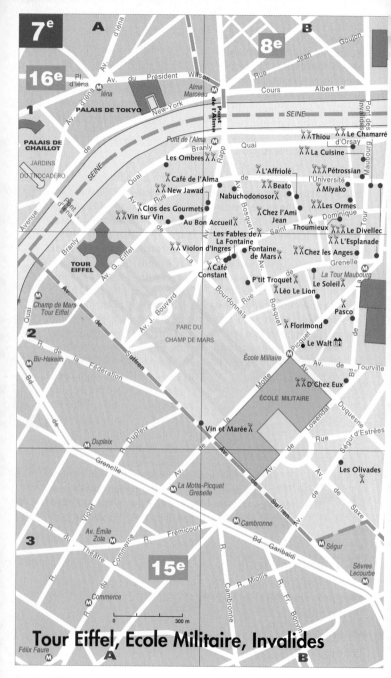

Tour Eiffel, Ecole Militaire, Invalides

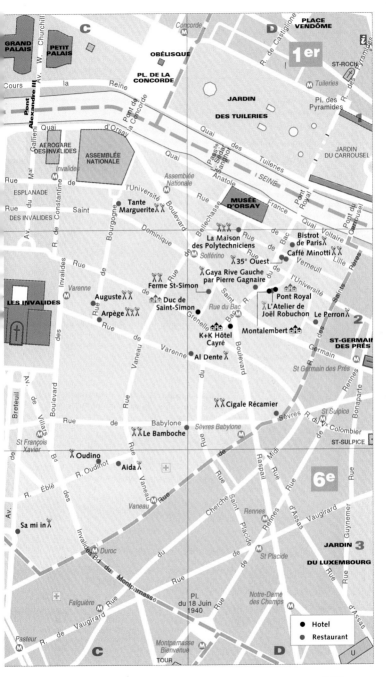

GRAND PALAIS

PETIT PALAIS

Cours

Av. W. Churchill

Pont Alexandre III

AÉROGARE DES INVALIDES

Gallieni

Quai

d'Orsay

Rue

ESPLANADE

Rue

DES INVALIDES

Av. de Constantine

Av. du Mal

ASSEMBLÉE NATIONALE

Concorde

OBÉLISQUE

PL. DE LA CONCORDE

la Reine

Pont de la Concorde

Quai

Assemblée Nationale

Rue de l'Université

Saint

Dominique

Bourgogne

Boulevard

Tante Marguerite ✗✗

La Maison des Polytechniciens ✗

Solférino

✗ 35° Ouest

Gaya Rive Gauche par Pierre Gagnaire

R. de Castiglione

PLACE VENDÔME

1er

ST-ROCH

M Tuileries

Pl. des Pyramides

JARDIN DES TUILERIES

JARDIN DU CARROUSEL

Quai des Tuileries

Passerelle Solférino

SEINE

MUSÉE D'ORSAY

Anatole France

Rue de

Bellechasse

Rue de

Rue de

Bac

de

Bistrot de Paris ✗

Caffé Minotti ✗✗

Verneuil

Lille

LES INVALIDES

Varenne

M

Rue de

Invalides

Rue de

Auguste ✗✗

Arpège ✗✗✗

Ferme St-Simon ✗✗

Duc de Saint-Simon

Rue de

Grenelle

Rue du Bac

K+K Hôtel Cayré

Al Dente ✗

Varenne

Boulevard

Rue de l'Université

Pont Royal

L'Atelier de Joël Robuchon

Montalembert

du

ST-GERMAIN DES PRÉS

M

St Germain des Prés

Le Perron ✗

Quai Voltaire

Pont Royal

Quai du Carrousel

Pont du Carrousel

Rue des Saints Pères

2

Germain

Bd

Breteuil

Av. de

Boulevard de

Villars

St François Xavier

Rue

de

Vaneau

Rue de

Babylone

✗✗ Cigale Récamier

Sèvres Babylone

Sèvres

R. du Vx Colombier

St Sulpice

M

ST-SULPICE

Bonaparte

Rennes

✗✗ Le Bamboche

✗ Oudino

R. Oudinot

Aida ✗

Vaneau

Rue

Rue de

Raspail

Rue de

Cherche Midi

6e

Rue

R. Éblé

Sa mi in ✗

Av. de

Vaneau

Invalides Bd. du

M Duroc

Montparnasse

Falguière

M Rue

Pasteur

R. de Vaguirard

Montparnasse Bienvenüe

TOUR

C

Rennes

Rennes

de

St Placide

M St Placide

Pl. du 18 Juin 1940

Rue

Notre-Dame des Champs

M

D

Saint Placide

d'Assas

Rue

Vaugirard

Guynemer

JARDIN DU LUXEMBOURG

3

Rue

d'Assas

U

● Hotel

● Restaurant

139

Tour Eiffel, École Militaire, Invalides

Arpège ✿✿✿

Innovative 🍴🍴🍴

A|C
📷
📠
VISA
💳
AE
🔵
🍷

84 r. Varenne
🏠 75007
📞 01 45 51 47 33 – **Fax** 01 44 18 98 39
e-mail arpege.passard@wanadoo.fr **Web** www.alain-passard.com
closed Saturday and Sunday

Ⓜ Varenne
C2

Menu € 130 (lunch)/€ 340 (dinner) – Carte € 122/294

Aurore Deligny

Alain Passard has had his headquarters near the Musée Rodin for twenty years. In fact, he has been in the area even longer than that, ever since he worked with Alain Senderens when it was known as L'Archestrate. The ground-floor restaurant, barely noticeable from the rue de Varenne, runs lengthwise all the way to the kitchen, tucked away at the back. With its Lalique glass sculptures, the decor has a tasteful, understated look highlighted by a more contemporary touch in the pear wood adorning the walls. The space is snug here, and in the cellar too, where there is just room for twelve diners. The cuisine is classic, refined, straightforward and accomplished. The chef is a "master of fire" who enjoys playing with different intensities of heat in his cooking. He admits to starting a "whole new professional life" when the focus of his menus turned to vegetables, which this incomparable chef grows on his farm in the Sarthe region.

A LA CARTE

FIRST COURSE
- Légumes du potager.
- Fines ravioles fleuries aux herbes, consommé végétal.

MAIN COURSE
- Aiguillettes de homard des îles Chausey au savagnin.
- Pigeonneau du pays de Racan à la carotte, chocolat chaud "Araguani".

DESSERT
- Millefeuille au miel du jardin.
- Avocat soufflé à la vanille de Tahiti, pointe de pistache.

Le Divellec

Seafood 🍴🍴🍴

|AC| 107 r. Université   Ⓜ Invalides
VISA ✉ 75007   **B1**
📞 01 45 51 91 96 – **Fax** 01 45 51 31 75
e-mail ledivellec@noos.fr
closed 27 July-27 August, Saturday and Sunday

Menu €55 (lunch)/€70 (lunch) – Carte €105/175

Nicolas Leser

It has been nearly a quarter of a century since Jacques Le Divellec left his native town of La Rochelle and headed for Paris, where he opened the most famous "seafood restaurant" in the capital. Having kept in touch with his best suppliers, he has shellfish in the tank and fresh fish arriving daily. Decorated in blue and white, the establishment has the feeling of a yacht, with bay windows overlooking the Esplanade des Invalides. Although a bit dated, it is still quite charming. Longstanding regulars include figures from the worlds of politics, the arts, the media and business. The well-to-do clientele comes for the simply prepared seafood. This "ambassador of the sea"– his self-styled nickname – may not be present at every meal, but the restaurant is in good hands with his solid crew, and the ship is on a steady course!

A LA CARTE

FIRST COURSE	**MAIN COURSE**	**DESSERT**
• Soupe de poisson et sa rouille.	• Blanc de turbot braisé aux truffes.	• La table du pâtissier.
• Assortiment royal de fruits de mer.	• Homard bleu à la presse avec son corail.	• Fondant chocolat noir au caramel à la fleur de sel.

Tour Eiffel, École Militaire, Invalides

Pétrossian

Innovative XXX

A/C	144 r. Université
VISA	✉ 75007
	✆ 0144113232 – **Fax** 0144113235
MC	closed in August, Sunday and Monday
AE	**Menu** €35 (weekday lunch)/€250 – **Carte** €56/149
⑩	
♟	

Ⓜ Invalides
B1

With her dancer's posture, graceful bearing and iron will, Rougui Dia is the high priestess of the Parisian temple of caviar. After the ideal apprenticeship, Pétrossian's "black pearl" has quite naturally rewritten the rule book at this legendary establishment, a symbol of *haute* Russian and Armenian gastronomy since 1920. Her innate and personal approach to fish – learned from her Peul culture – and her taste for spices has imbued the menu at 144 with a promising modern touch. Henceforth, the classic repertoire (Alexandre III caviar tartare, Kyscielli, etc.) has opened up to Senegalese, Indian and Caribbean influences. The decor, also remodelled, is luminous, contemporary and refined.

La Maison des Polytechniciens

Traditional XXX

⊡	12 r. Poitiers
VISA	✉ 75007
	✆ 0149547454 – **Fax** 0149547484
MC	**e-mail** info@maisondesx.com **Web** www.maisondesx.com
AE	Closed 27 July-27 August, 22 December-2 January, Saturday, Sunday and public holidays – number of covers limited, pre-book
⑩	**Menu** €36 – **Carte** €43/66
♟	

Ⓜ Solférino
D1-2

Despite its name, the Maison des Polytechniciens is not the exclusive preserve of Polytechnique students, and you'll run into more businessmen here than mortar boards. That is quite fortunate, given its prestigious historic setting in the delightful Hôtel de Poulpry, an early 18C townhouse with an ancient chandelier which creates a wonderful effect. It is impossible not to succumb to its charms, between the Napoleonic room, the hushed lounges (including one decorated by Watteau), the vaulted cellars, inner garden and idyllic terrace. Particularly with Pascal Chanteloup subtly playing with tradition in the kitchen. His contemporary cuisine is combined with a more classic wine list designed with Les Caves Taillevent.

Le Chamarré

French-Mauritian ✗✗

A/C	13 bd La Tour-Maubourg	Ⓜ Invalides
VISA	✉ 75007	B1
ⓜⓒ	✆ 0147055018 – **Fax** 0147059121	
AE	**e-mail** chantallaval@wanadoo.fr **Web** www.lechamarre.com	
Ⓓ	closed Saturday lunch and Sunday	
♀	Menu €40 (lunch)/€150 – Carte €75/89	

Le Chamarré

Despite its verandah, this restaurant off the beaten track, on the Boulevard de La Tour-Maubourg, doesn't stand out from its neighbours. La Boule d'Or became Le Chamarré, run by a talented French-Mauritian duo. Antoine Heerah and Jérôme Boldereau met while working with Alain Passard at Arpège, where they also rubbed shoulders with Pascal Barbot and Christophe Rohat, partners at Astrance.

This is a very pleasant place, with its mellow-toned contemporary decor and comfortably spaced tables. In their gastronomic world, these two friends, now associates, strive to offer diners a culinary exchange between products from the Mascarene Islands – fruits and vegetables, as well as fish and shellfish – and French cooking traditions. Rather than "fusion", these chefs allude to a desire to blend an array of flavours. "I start with the produce, which then tells me what to do", says Antoine Heerah.

A LA CARTE

FIRST COURSE
• Poulpe aux deux saveurs.
• Sardines marinées aux épices créoles, jus de betterave et légumes croquants.

MAIN COURSE
• Cochon de lait fermier.
• Vapeur de lieu jaune et moules au fenugrec, légumes nouveaux croquants avec anchoïade.

DESSERT
• Savarin punché au rhum.
• Myrtilles au coulis de fruits rouges, glace à la rose.

Violon d'Ingres ❀

Contemporary ✗✗

A/C
VISA
MC
AE
◑
♀

135 r. St-Dominique
✉ 75007
✆ 0145551505 – **Fax** 0145554842
e-mail violondingres@wanadoo.fr **Web** www.leviolondingres.com
closed 30 July-22 August, 1st-7 January, Sunday and Monday

Ⓜ Ecole Militaire
B2

Menu €45/€60

Violon d'Ingres

Pun intended? Violon d'Ingres, the French word for hobby, could mean that the chef's passion for cooking is his favourite pastime. Or it might refer to the fact that he comes from Montauban, like the painter Ingres. One day Christian Constant decided to forget about the posh establishments and their large kitchen brigades. Now he prefers simplicity and a small staff. He has been keeping things going for ten years at this warm restaurant on the rue Saint-Dominique, where recently, he had the decor redone as a chic bistro with tables in careful rows and white tablecloths. No concessions are made in terms of the quality of the traditional French cuisine. The chef has even lowered his prices. This is all good news for diners, who will also enjoy Constant's two other establishments in the area: Les Fables de la Fontaine and Café Constant, both featuring a friendly ambiance.

A LA CARTE

FIRST COURSE
· Millefeuille de langue et foie gras façon Lucullus.
· Pithiviers de gibier à plume (season).

MAIN COURSE
· Volaille des Landes rôtie à la broche.
· Véritable cassoulet montalbanais.

DESSERT
· Tarte chocolat de Christian Constant.
· Soufflé chaud à la vanille, caramel au beurre salé.

Nespresso. What else ?

Coffee, body and soul.

Les Ormes 🕸

Contemporary ✗✗

VISA
🅼🅾
AE
🅾
🍷

22 r. Surcouf
✉ 75007
✆ 0145514693 – **Fax** 0145503011
e-mail molestephane@noos.fr

🅜 La Tour Maubourg
B1

closed 1st-15 August, 7-14 January, Sunday and Monday

Menu €38 (weekday lunch)/€65

Les Ormes

There was once a tiny restaurant of the same name in a small street in the 16th arrondissement, where the chef and his wife won their first star in 2002. Since the spring of 2004, Stéphane and Régina Molé have moved to the heart of the 7th. The couple took over the Bellecour, for thirty years a temple of lyonnaiseries (specialities from Lyon). The tranquil setting and the neither trendy nor fashion-conscious decor have remained unchanged, with the same carpets and light tablecloths, cane chairs and checked blinds, and the personality of the new owners is evident only in the paintings, porcelain and glassware. The real change is in the food. The chef, who favours traditional cooking that is rather discreet and refined, has completely redone the menu, which takes its inspiration from the best of classical cuisine. And, of course, the proper wines to accompany it.

A LA CARTE

FIRST COURSE
• Foie gras d'oie en brioche.

• Gelée de tomate sur caviar d'aubergine et émietté de crabe, langoustines de casier rôties.

MAIN COURSE
• Jarret de veau, gnocchi de pomme de terre.

• Lièvre à la royale (Mid-October to mid-December).

DESSERT
• Café gourmand autour de trois petites bouchées.

• Mirliton aux reines-Claude et raisins, glace au nougat.

Tour Eiffel, École Militaire, Invalides

Les Ombres

Contemporary 🍴🍴

27 quai Branly
✉ 75007
☏ 0147536800 – **Fax** 0147536818
Web www.lesombres.fr

Ⓜ Alma Marceau
A1

Menu € 35 (lunch)/€ 95 – Carte € 57/95

With its futuristic architecture, colourful cubes and vertical gardens, the Musée du Quai Branly, designed by Jean Nouvel, is a striking edifice. The restaurant perched on its rooftop terrace is no less so. Airy and contemporary glass design makes it a unique spot up in the clouds. At lunch, enjoy the breathtaking view of the Eiffel Tower and its majestic play of shadows – thus the restaurant's name – and light. It's enough to dazzle tourists and beautiful people alike. The appealing up-to-date menu, composed by a chef who has worked at a series of fine establishments, features such diverse dishes as aubergine purée, *suprême de volaille grillé,* chocolate-pistachio-ice cream cake with *orgeat* (barley syrup), and red berry tiramisu.

Cigale Récamier

Traditional 🍴🍴

4 r. Récamier
✉ 75007
☏ 0145488658

Ⓜ Sèvres Babylone
D2

closed Sun

Carte € 38/48

In both summer and winter, the Cigale Récamier will treat you to its songs. Sweet and savoury soufflés (its speciality, with an original menu renewed every month), foie gras terrines, grilled lamb chops with thyme, fillet of sea bream, etc. The bistro-style cuisine is elaborated by Gérard Idoux, owner of the establishment. Members of the smart Paris literary set are fond of meeting here to enjoy the calm, contemplative atmosphere. The setting lends itself to this. A haven of peace and quiet, it is nestled in a cul-de-sac which gives onto a garden, and a very appealing flowery terrace. Inside, the dining room has the clean lines of the contemporary look, imparting an air of modernity and conviviality.

Vin sur Vin

Traditional ✗✗

 20 r. de Monttessuy
 ⊠ 75007
✆ 01 47 05 14 20

⊕ Pont de l'Alma
A1

Closed 29 April-8 May, 28 July-27 August, 22 December-6 January, Monday except dinner from mid September to end March, Saturday lunch and Sunday – number of covers limited, pre-book

Carte €65/89

G.Corbic/MICHELIN

With its seven tables and maximum fifteen table settings per service, this is no ordinary restaurant. It is more like a dining room where the owners, Patrice and Sylvie Vidal, extend a warm welcome to their guests. "It's rather like a private place that we open to the public," explains Patrice, who is inexhaustible on the subject of the wines on the menu – several hundred, unearthed with great zeal – which he allows to age properly.

In the wings, chef Pascal Toulza, a native of the Southwest, and his assistant Mustapha Rednaoui, who was trained in Marrakech, are busy in the kitchen. These four people make up the entire staff!

"We're out of the loop," says the owner, who has been established in this little street for twenty years. It's clearly working. The message on the answering machine is unequivocal too: "the restaurant where people go with an appetite because they know the food will be delicious." That says it all!

A LA CARTE

FIRST COURSE	MAIN COURSE	DESSERT
• Saint-Jacques d'Erquy (October to March).	• Canard sauvage (season).	• Millefeuille tout chocolat.
• Ravioles à l'oeuf et aux truffes.	• Pigeon laqué au jus.	• Imparfait à la nougatine.

(side margin) Tour Eiffel, École Militaire, Invalides

Tante Marguerite

Traditional ✕✕

AC	5 r. Bourgogne — Ⓜ Assemblée Nationale
	⊠ 75007 — **C1**

AC
⟨⟩
VISA
ⓂⒸ
ΑΞ
⓪
Ⴤ

5 r. Bourgogne   Ⓜ Assemblée Nationale
⊠ 75007   **C1**
℘ 0145517942 – **Fax** 0147537956
e-mail tante.marguerite@bernard-loiseau.com
Closed August, Saturday, Sunday and public holidays

Menu €34 (lunch)/€65 – Carte €45/63

By a funny coincidence, Tante Marguerite, a well-known restaurant specialising in cuisine from Burgundy, is located on the rue de Bourgogne. The good news is that this institution in the Bernard Loiseau group has had a face lift, with a new bronze-grey contemporary decor – an ode to the Morvan forests – and a new chef, Jean-François Robert (who worked with Savoy, Dutournier and Darroze). The menu features Loiseau-style recipes from the *terroir* and more modern dishes like the *mosaïque de raie aux aromates* (mosaic of skate) or the goat cheese *croustillant* with dates. Political figures love this place for its elegant cuisine, intimacy and soft lighting for hushed conversations. A place worth (re)discovering.

Ferme St-Simon

Traditional ✕✕

AC
VISA
ⓂⒸ
ΑΞ
⓪
Ⴤ

6 r. St-Simon   Ⓜ Rue du Bac
⊠ 75007   **D2**
℘ 0145483574 – **Fax** 0140490731
e-mail fermestsimon@wanadoo.fr
closed 30 July-19 August, Saturday lunch and Sunday

Menu €32 (lunch)/€35 – Carte €50/68

The Ferme St-Simon prefers "provincial" fashions to the kind of trendy atmosphere which makes a splash and then fades out. That doesn't mean this restaurant is out of the Parisian loop. "Everyone has either been here before or is going to come", says Denise Fabre, the owner's wife. For the past 25 years there has been a constant flow of celebrities – from show-biz stars to heads of state! They probably feel a special kind of spirit within these warm walls, like being with your own family. As for the food, the chef prepares updated traditional dishes according to market and season, including tuna carpaccio, cod with sauerkraut, sea bream with grains, and *fondant au chocolat*. There's no doubt about it – life on the farm can be very good indeed.

Tour Eiffel, École Militaire, Invalides

Chez les Anges 😳

Traditional ✕✕

A/C	54 bd de la Tour Maubourg
🖂 75007	Ⓜ La Tour Maubourg **B2**

✆ 0147058986 – **Fax** 0147054556
e-mail mail@chezlesanges.com **Web** www.chezlesanges.com

closed Saturday and Sunday

Menu €34 – Carte €34/65

Tempted by the idea of dining in paradise? In this pure and unembellished contemporary decor by Alberto Bali, the dining room enjoys full daylight thanks to the wide picture windows, and also has a large central bar counter and lithographs of angels on the walls lasting several decades. The tone is set. After a decades-long hiatus, this restaurant won back its name (and spirit) in 2005, under the leadership of Jacques Lacipière. The dishes are well-prepared and genuine, and the up-to-date menu changes according to the market. The cellar is stocked exclusively with Burgundies (and the occasional Bordeaux). Friendly reception, good value for money and service that is – angelic.

New Jawad

Indian-Pakistani ✕✕

A/C	12 av. Rapp
🖂 75007	Ⓜ Ecole Militaire **B1**

✆ 0147059137 – **Fax** 0145503127

Menu €16/€40 (dinner) – Carte €21/42

Enjoy the flavours of northern India in a peaceful atmosphere near the Eiffel Tower. Far from the effervescent local places in Paris' Indiatown, the New Jawad offers a cosy, hushed setting worthy of a private townhouse. The extremely chic 7th arrondissement has clearly left its mark on this Indo-Pakistani establishment, which has done away with all outer signs of exoticism apart from a few precious engravings. The voyage is all in the food. Try a classic menu of assorted starters (*samosas, pakoras, bahjis*), curries and *biryanis*, light-tasting *nans*, and *lassi* or wine – more conventional, and pricier – to experience a delightful gourmet pause in the land of Maharajas.

Tour Eiffel, École Militaire, Invalides

(sidebar) Tour Eiffel, École Militaire, Invalides

Beato

Italian ✗✗

A/C   8 r. Malar   Ⓜ Invalides
⌧ 75007   **B1**
VISA   ☏ 01 47 05 94 27 – **Fax** 01 45 55 64 41
       e-mail beato.rest@wanadoo.fr
Ⓜ©
       closed 15 July-15 August, 24 December-1st January and Sunday
AE
♈   **Menu €27 (lunch) – Carte €40/65**

This restaurant has a true flavour of Italy. From the Porto Fino salad with *langoustines* and shrimp and the *tagliatelle al pesto* (homemade, like all the pasta) to the beef fillet with balsamic vinegar or the *tiramisu all'amaretto,* all the dishes are prepared in the language of chef Ivano Giordani. They are traditional, softly surprising and well-balanced. The comfortable dining room evokes the discreet charm of the Italian bourgeoisie (frescoes, Pompeian columns and neo-Classical chairs). The friendly reception is genuine. Businessmen, local regulars and tourists, glad to receive this kind of attention, treat themselves to a delicious voyage to Milan, Rome and *tutti quanti.*

Thiou

Thai ✗✗

A/C   49 quai d'Orsay   Ⓜ Invalides
⌧ 75007   **B1**
VISA   ☏ 01 40 62 96 50 – **Fax** 01 40 62 97 30
Ⓜ©   closed August, Saturday lunch and Sunday
AE
♈   **Carte €44/84**

V.I.P. – three letters which sum up the "glitter and gloss" ambiance, prized by the in-crowd on the lookout for chic venues. The proprietress – nicknamed Thiou – is also quite media-conscious. The many talents of this self-taught woman from China, already spotted when she was chef at the Bains Douches, come out in her refined exotic touch. Witness the discreetly ethnic dining room (bamboo and warm tones ranging from brass to chocolate), and above all the cuisine. Celebrities have a change of scenery without fear of jet-lag while enjoying the well-prepared Thai and vegetarian dishes. The Crying Tiger (grilled marinated beef) – the house speciality – is a real crowd-pleaser, and no one seems worried about the bill (lots of euros).

La Cuisine

Traditional ✗✗

[A/C]
[VISA]
[MC]
[AE]
[DC]
[glass]

14 bd La Tour-Maubourg
✉ 75007
☏ 0144183632 – **Fax** 0144183042
e-mail lacuisine@lesrestos.com **Web** www.lacuisine.lesrestos.com
closed Saturday lunch

Ⓜ Invalides
B1

Menu €31 (weekday lunch)/€42 – Carte €42/72

Located near the Quai d'Orsay, this cuisine is well worth the detour. Created in 2000 by the Selles-Duboscq duo (seasoned restaurateurs formerly at the Georges V), it has been quietly gaining ground, confident of the excellent reputation it has earned with its clientele of gourmets who care about quality above all. They are rewarded with a selection of top ingredients brilliantly prepared by the chef in the finest tradition: langoustines served in bisque in a *chaud-froid,* John Dory on a bed of spinach, and cannellonis with a white chocolate garnish. Delicious! The contemporary dining room features modern paintings, mirrors and comfortable banquettes. Enjoy the veranda in the daytime, and the soft lighting from the little lamps in the evening.

Caffé Minotti

Italian ✗✗

[VISA]
[MC]
[AE]
[glass]

33 r. Verneuil
✉ 75007
☏ 0142600404 – **Fax** 0142600405
e-mail caffeminotti@wanadoo.fr
closed 29 July-22 August, 23 December-2 January, Sunday and Monday

Ⓜ Rue du Bac
D2

Menu €39 – Carte €43/69

The minute you walk through the door of the Caffé Minotti, you are struck by its elaborate design, like a stage set with a modern bent. Pompei red dominates on the walls, curtains and Murano glass chandelier. Each of the three dining areas has a different atmosphere – minimalist, Baroque and intimate. A mural frieze with a quotation praising the art of fusion sums up the spirit of this establishment inspired by Italian flavours. The cuisine by Nicolas Vernier (he has an Italian mother and was formerly the chef at Il Cortile) features creations such as vegetable antipasti and rabbit *bocconcini.* His favourite dish, risotto, changes daily. This goes beyond temptation, and could soon become a real addiction!

Tour Eiffel, École Militaire, Invalides

Tour Eiffel, École Militaire, Invalides

Auguste ✿

Contemporary ✗✗

A/C
MC
AE
DC
Ψ

54 r. Bourgogne
✉ 75007
✆ 0145516109 – **Fax** 0145512734
Web www.restaurantauguste.fr
closed August, Saturday and Sunday
Menu € 35 (lunch) – Carte € 49/67

Ⓜ Varenne
C2

Auguste

If you're looking for some peace and quiet on "ministry row", this is the place! The decor in this small establishment – with only thirty place settings – is elegant, understated and comfortable, the atmosphere calm and relaxing. When Gaël Orieux opened it in the heart of Paris's political district, he had at least two good reasons for giving it someone else's name. First, because of its proximity to the Musée Rodin, dedicated to the famous sculptor whose first name was Auguste. Secondly, after working for Paul Bocuse, he became an avid reader of the principles of Auguste Escoffier, "king of chefs and chef of kings". Hence his flawless classic cooking which has nonetheless kept up with the times. The short menu changes frequently and is delightfully varied. The wine list has some interesting finds at competitive prices.

A LA CARTE

FIRST COURSE
- Fine gelée iodée aux huîtres creuses et bulots.
- Grenouilles croustillantes, sot-l'y-laisse et crêtes de coq.

MAIN COURSE
- Noix de ris de veau au vin jaune.
- Côte de porc fermière épaisse, parfumée au tandoori.

DESSERT
- Soufflé au chocolat pur Caraïbes.
- Caillé de brebis au poivre long, parfait au caramel.

Le Bamboche

Innovative ✕✕

A/C
VISA
MC
♀

15 r. Babylone
✉ 75007
✆ 01 45 49 14 40 – **Fax** 01 45 49 14 44
e-mail lebamboche@aol.com **Web** www.labamboche.com

Ⓜ Sèvres Babylone
C2

closed 23 July-6 August and Sunday lunch

Menu € 35 – Carte € 58/70

They definitely live it up at this little restaurant hidden behind the Bon Marché. The contemporary setting is resolutely "Left Bank", with glamourous red armchairs where prospective diners can cool their heels while waiting for the mouth-watering food. The place appears to be rather tame. The boldness is in the cuisine, created by the high-powered duo, Serge Arce and Philippe Fabert. Worthy of their predecessors, they have made their mark with tasty ingredients which are prepared in an original way. Their inventions – caviar sorbet, smoked trout and baby spinach, tomatoes and sorbets from the garden (basil, olive oil, tomatoes), grilled sea bass with a delicate compote of fennel and *lardons* – have great appeal and have reassured regulars that Claude Colliot's former establishment has continued in the same vein.

D'Chez Eux

Terroir ✕✕

A/C
VISA
MC
AE
DC

2 av. Lowendal
✉ 75007
✆ 01 47 05 52 55 – **Fax** 01 45 55 60 74
e-mail contact@chezeux.com **Web** www.chezeux.com

Ⓜ Ecole Militaire
B2

closed 29 July-27 August and Sunday

Carte € 46/73

The name refers to Jean-Pierre Court (the owner) and François Casteleyn (the chef). *Chez eux* ("their homeland") is the land of the Southwest and Auvergne featured in their charming inn-like restaurant. The dining room looks right out of a post card with its rustic furniture and checked tablecloths. Tradition is everywhere, in the regional ingredients, generous plates, extensive cellar – focusing partly on Bordeaux and Burgundies – and smocked waiters. It's not surprising that this formula has been a hit for over 40 years! Try the *panier de cochonnailles* (assortment of sausages and pâtés), frog's legs, scallops with preserved shallots, duck breast, and of course the powerful *cassoulet* – all irresistible.

Tour Eiffel, École Militaire, Invalides

L'Esplanade

Brasserie

A/C	52 r. Fabert
VISA	✉ 75007
	✆ 01 47 05 38 80 – **Fax** 01 47 05 23 75

Ⓜ La Tour Maubourg
B2

Carte €37/78

The Costes Brothers can boast that everything they touch turns to gold. Including hip places like the Esplanade, a successful blend of venue, ambiance and decidedly trendy cuisine. It can be proved in four ways. First, the superb view over the Invalides, especially on the terrace. Secondly, the Jacques Garcia label – a "lounge and military" atmosphere evoking Napoleon III, with comfortable armchairs and| canons. Then there's the menu that reinvents brasserie classics in an "urban terroir" genre (tartare, organic *œuf coque "bio"*, etc.) or fusion-style with prawn risotto, or coconut caramel duck. Stylish waiters and valet parking, catering to a clientele of celebrities and politicians. Verdict: rush over to see and be seen – after booking.

Tour Eiffel, École Militaire, Invalides

L'Atelier de Joël Robuchon ✿

Innovative

A/C
VISA
MC
✿✿
♀

Hôtel Pont Royal,
5 r. Montalembert ✉ 75007
✆ 0142225656 – **Fax** 0142229791
e-mail latelierdejoelrobuchon@wanadoo.fr

Reception from 11.30 am to 3.30 pm and from 6.30 pm to midnight. Reservations only for certain services: please inquire

Menu €110 – Carte €52/93

Ⓜ Rue du Bac
D2

L'Atelier de Joël Robuchon

The subdued lighting with subtle red notes plays off the black lacquered furniture, dark granite floors, and jars of spices and vegetables. Diners can watch the chefs cooking away right in front of them.

This Atelier, where the decor was designed by Pierre-Yves Rochon, is the first example of an original concept created by Joël Robuchon who has since opened branches all over the world. With its large bar counter, high red leather stools and "tapas-style" cuisine in sampling dishes, this "chic eatery" has that special feeling of Japanese teppanyakis and sushi bars. Good selection of wines by the glass.

From the moment it opened, this establishment has been all the rage, despite its "first-come, first served" policy (no reservations taken except for the 11:30am and 6:30pm seatings), forcing you to be patient before getting a taste of the chef's creations.

A LA CARTE

FIRST COURSE	MAIN COURSE	DESSERT
• Langoustine en papillote croustillante au basilic.	• Merlan frit colbert, beurre aux herbes.	• Le fameux soufflé chartreuse verte.
• Morilles aux asperges et au cerfeuil.	• Caille farcie de foie gras et caramélisée, pomme-purée truffée.	• Tartes de tradition.

Tour Eiffel, École Militaire, Invalides

Gaya Rive Gauche par Pierre Gagnaire ✲

Contemporary ✗

A/C	44 r. Bac	**Ⓜ** Rue du Bac
	✉ 75007	**D2**
	✆ 01 45 44 73 73 – **Fax** 01 45 44 73 73	
VISA	**e-mail** p.gagnaire@wanadoo.fr **Web** www.pierre-gagnaire.com	
M©Ⓒ	closed 21 July-20 August, 22 December-6 January, Saturday lunch and Sunday	
AE		
♀	Carte €58/97	

Gaya Rive Gauche par Pierre Gagnaire

"This place allows me to express my work in Paris at more affordable prices. This is an everyday restaurant where the food is good and slightly amusing." In those few words, Pierre Gagnaire nearly says it all.

While the "main branch" is still firmly established on the rue Balzac, he opted for expansion by opening Sketch in London, another branch in Tokyo and since September 2005, after three months of construction work, Gaya on the Left Bank in Paris. Architect Christian Ghion designed the decor in a simple, contemporary style with grey and blue tones. The food enjoyed in this relaxed and friendly atmosphere is clever, with a focus on unadulterated seafood. The delicate and creative dishes feature a variety of fresh fish, from the more "noble" ones such as sole, wild bass and red mullet, to the more "modest" like hake and whiting.

A LA CARTE

FIRST COURSE
• Chantilly Slace : velouté d'étrille, riz basmati, crème fouettée au raifort.

• Chiffonnade d'épinard "Thaï", sardine fraîche à l'huile d'olive piquante.

MAIN COURSE
• Barbue en gros dominos poêlée au citron vert, fine tranche d'aubergine.

• Rouget de roche au salers, badigeonné d'un caramel de maïs frais, topinambour.

DESSERT
• Macaron au citron de Menton, bombe glacée vanille.

• Chocolat glacé à l'huile d'olive ardente, coulis d'abricot.

Les Fables de La Fontaine ✿

Seafood ⚔

131 r. Saint-Dominique
✉ 75007
✆ 01 44 18 37 55

Ⓜ Ecole Militaire
B2

Menu €32 (lunch)/€42

Les Fables de La Fontaine

Fish is the main theme here. With his three adjoining restaurants, Christian Constant has made his mark on this section of the rue Saint-Dominique. His bistro is tastefully minimalist with its bar counter near the entrance, sparse tables in a row and miniature kitchen where you can watch the chef at work. The establishment belongs in the "pocket handkerchief" category, with twenty place settings and a small terrace where the tables are snatched up the minute the sun comes out.

Dishes of the day are written on the blackboard. They are appealingly simple, with ingredients of impeccable quality. Prices are reasonable for both food and wine (with an interesting selection of white wines, a fitting choice given the focus on fish) – another reason to pay them a visit.

A LA CARTE

FIRST COURSE
• Brouillade d'oeufs aux champignons, émulsion et copeaux de parmesan.

• Tartare d'huîtres de Marennes.

MAIN COURSE
• Pavé de lieu à la plancha, lasagne d'épaule d'agneau confite aux péquillos.

• Bouillabaissse.

DESSERT
• Gâteau basque maison.

• Figues rôties au porto, crème vanille.

Tour Eiffel, École Militaire, Invalides

Au Bon Accueil

Bistro 🍴

A/C
VISA
MC
AE
🍷

14 r. Monttessuy
✉ 75007
☏ 0147054611 – **Fax** 0145561580

🚇 Pont de l'Alma
A1

closed 4-19 August, Saturday and Sunday

Menu €27 (lunch)/€31 – Carte €34/69

This gourmet bistro has more than one trick up its sleeve to win the hearts of its diners. First, there is the lovely terrace ideally located a stone's throw from the Champ de Mars, with the Eiffel Tower in the background. When the weather is less inviting, you can happily take refuge in the dining room and lounge, offering a contemporary setting which is rather hip in its own 7th arrondissement way. The daily blackboard selections are created according to the market and quality ingredients. The up-to-date dishes and seasonal game have clear and simple flavours, enhanced by vintage Rhône and Burgundy wines. As for the welcome and service, all you have to do is read the sign to know it will be friendly, efficient and spirited.

Nabuchodonosor

Traditional 🍴

A/C
VISA
MC
🍷

6 av. Bosquet
✉ 75007
☏ 0145569726 – **Fax** 0145569844
e-mail rousseau.e@wanadoo.fr **Web** www.nabuchodonosor.net

🚇 Alma Marceau
B1

closed 28 July-21 August, Saturday lunch and Sunday

Menu €28 (weekday lunch)/€45 (dinner) – Carte €39/62

The name refers to the largest sized champagne bottle, an apt metaphor for the aspirations of this elegant restaurant near the Place de l'Alma. The dishes are first rate here, and everything possible is done to make sure you enjoy a great meal. The Nebuchadnezzars sit majestically on the bar, if not on your table. The plush and comfortable setting delights the refined clientele, with its sienna-coloured walls and oak panelling, its spacious and well-laid tables and soft lighting. The chef prepares subtle market-based dishes using various seasonal ingredients from the *terroir*.

Bistrot de Paris

Bistro 🍴

33 r. Lille ⓜ Musée d'Orsay
✉ 75007 **D2**
☏ 0142611683 – **Fax** 0149270609

closed August, 24 December-1st January, Saturday lunchtime, Monday evening and Sunday

Carte € 22/62

This former *bouillon* – once honoured by the presence of André Gide – is a historic Parisian establishment and the kind of timeless place which never loses its appeal. From the street, the view of the kitchen is already an invitation in itself. Inside, the 1900s decor remodelled by Slavik possesses the true, emblematic charm of a certain Parisian art of living with its chandeliers, brass and mirrors, red and gold tones and snug tables appreciated by a large clientele. Naturally it is often packed, but the attentive service is up to the job. The bistro cuisine, accompanied by a hundred or so wines, is brilliantly simple and on the mark. A real godsend in this antique shop district.

Vin et Marée

Seafood 🍴

71 av. Suffren ⓜ La Motte Picquet Grenelle
✉ 75007 **A-B2**
☏ 0142723123 – **Fax** 0140240023
e-mail vin-et-maree@orange.fr **Web** www.vin-et-maree.com

Menu € 24 – Carte € 33/51

Failing a trip to the seaside, you can always take refuge in the welcoming dining room of this first of the Vin et Marée restaurants in the capital. This is a safe bet, which has maintained a steady course ever since it opened. Its formula for success is simple, consisting in only the freshest of ingredients – bought at the morning fish auction – in flawless appetising dishes. Their smoothly running operation is most convincing. The blackboard selections change with daily deliveries, featuring all manner of fish and shellfish. In addition to the tasty food, this establishment is also a delight to the eye with its tailor-made decor including an ultramarine façade and plush sunny interior.

Tour Eiffel, École Militaire, Invalides

Tour Eiffel, École Militaire, Invalides

Les Olivades

A/C   41 av. Ségur   Ⓜ Ségur
VISA   ✉ 75007   **B3**
     ✆ 0147837009 – **Fax** 0142730475

ⓂⒸ   closed August, Saturday lunch, Monday lunch, Sunday and public holidays

AE   Menu €25 (weekday lunch)/€60 – Carte €40/67

The sunny south is present everywhere here, in the discreetly Provençal setting brightened up with modern paintings, and more importantly, in the olive-oil-based recipes. This restaurant is an ardent defender of the flavours and aromas of southern France, as its name attests. The proof is in the menu, featuring creamy courgette soup with ratatouille, *Pain bagnat*-style tuna, gambas with papaya, pepper, lemon and coriander *brunoise*, apple tart with *calissons d'Aix* ice cream, etc. The man behind all these appetising creations is Bruno Deligne, a chef who has worked in some top restaurants (Pic, Maximin, Fauchon, Copenhague, Ritz). The friendly reception afforded by his charming wife, Chantal, will get your meal off to the perfect start.

Thoumieux

   79 r. St-Dominique   Ⓜ La Tour Maubourg
   ✉ 75007   **B1**
     ✆ 0147054975 – **Fax** 0147053696
VISA   **e-mail** thoumieux@thoumieux.com **Web** www.thoumieux.com

ⓂⒸ   Menu €15 (weekday lunch)/€30 (week) – Carte €26/62

Where did you have your last Corrèze-style meal in Paris? Probably here in this authentic brasserie, which opened in 1923. Run by the Bassalert family, it still has the same genuine charm. The cuisine, like the place, is traditional, generous and simple. While the Corrèze region is well-represented, there are also many dishes from the southwest. Fine house specialities simmering in the chef's pot include the *Cassoulet au confit de canard Thoumieux* (preserved duck casserole) which is masterfully prepared, as are the *gigot flageolet* (leg of lamb with white beans) and the *colin du Guilvinec* (hake) exotically spiced with ginger and lime. The flawless meal – somewhere between classic and cutting edge – will no doubt leave you feeling sated and happy!

Clos des Gourmets 🍴

Contemporary ✗

VISA
🔘

16 av. Rapp
✉ 75007
✆ 0145517561 – **Fax** 0147057420
Web www.closdesgourmets.fr

Ⓜ Alma Marceau
B1

closed 10-25 August, Sunday and Monday

Menu €29 (weekday lunch)/€35

The Clos des Gourmets has a very fitting name! This restaurant, which opens onto a veranda and a terrace, is on the lips of many a food-lover. The well-deserved success is due to the talented chef, Arnaud Pitrois, who hasn't forgotten the lessons learned from his teachers (Guy Savoy, Christian Constant, Éric Fréchon). He skilfully prepares food with a personal touch where old-time specialities (stuffed cabbage, duck breast with blueberries) are on a par with more inventive recipes - avocado in puff pastry and preserved lemons with aged rum, reinette apples with salty caramel sauce and thyme ice cream. The wines come from France and all around the world. Do we need to add that the prices are low to convince you to rush over here?

Le Perron

Italian ✗

VISA
🔘
AE
♀

6 r. Perronet
✉ 75007
✆ 0145447151 – **Fax** 0145447151

Ⓜ St-Germain des Prés
D2

closed 1st-20 August and Sunday

Menu €25 (weekday lunch) – Carte €31/43

The cuisine shares one thing at least with film – beyond one's own borders, it should only be experienced in the original version! Such is the case at Le Perron, this friendly Italian restaurant which makes no compromises about its origins. 100% *tradizionalissima*! That could be the motto of the chef here, who cooks up traditional recipes from Italy, in particular from the southern regions of Sardinia, Sicily, Venice and the Abruzzi. In addition to the antipasti, fresh pasta and homemade desserts, we also liked the truly "custom-made" risotti (prepared upon request). As a backdrop, the dining room is both rustic (stonework, exposed beams), and intellectual, with its own bookcase – a nod to the publishers and writers who are regulars here.

Tour Eiffel, École Militaire, Invalides

Florimond 😊

Traditional 🍴

VISA
MC
♈

19 av. La Motte-Picquet
✉ 75007
☎ 0145554038 – **Fax** 0145554038

Ⓜ Ecole Militaire
B2

closed 30 April-5 May, 30 July-18 August, 23 December-6 January, Saturday and Sunday

Menu €21 (lunch)/€36 – Carte €36/53

Although Florimond takes its name from the gardener at Monet's estate in Giverny, that doesn't mean the cuisine here is impressionistic or fussy. On the contrary, this little establishment is known for its generous market-based food and reasonable prices. The chef is skilful at decompartmentalizing genres, proposing dishes which oscillate between bistro, terroir, *canaille* and gourmet food. He is fond of reinventing classics, serving up both specialities that no longer hold any secrets for him (stuffed cabbage, duck breast with blueberries) and more up-to-date dishes. The cellar has a fine selection of proprietor's reserves to accompany them. A sunny and peaceful setting which is strictly non-smoking.

Pasco

Traditional 🍴

---

hh
A/C
VISA
MC
AE
♈

74 bd La Tour Maubourg
✉ 75007
☎ 0144183326 – **Fax** 0144183406
e-mail restaurant.pasco@wanadoo.fr

Ⓜ La Tour Maubourg
B2

closed Mon.

Menu €24 – Carte €27/54

Pasco is run by two Pascals! This resolutely Mediterranean restaurant was born of the solid friendship between Pascal Mousset and Pascal Vignes, two professionals who trained in some of the finest establishments. They created this place together in 2003, and it is just like them – convivial and sincere. Success came instantly to this friendly place with a host of assets, ranging from the wood and brick Provençal setting – refined without being stiff –, the terrace with a view of the Invalides dome, and an olive oil-based southern French menu featuring vegetables and fish. Not to mention the warm welcome, valet parking and – a rarity in this neighbourhood – very reasonable prices. This is definitely a place with a bright future.

Fontaine de Mars

Traditional

129 r. St-Dominique
✉ 75007
☎ 0147054644 – **Fax** 0147051113
e-mail cafedelalma@wanadoo.fr

Ⓜ Ecole Militaire
B2

Menu €23 (weekday lunch)/€66 – Carte €32/66

Test it out for yourself. If you still haven't been to this bistro, try to resist its charming terrace across from the Fontaine de Mars, dedicated to the god of war. It is virtually impossible, because this place, sheltered by an arcade, is a precious haven of peace – so welcome in Paris. Inside there are two small deliciously Art Deco rooms with red-and-white checked tablecloths. The atmosphere is relaxed, and the proprietors' friendly attitude is a joy to behold. The traditional, seasonal dishes are a treat enjoyed without ceremony, including fricasee of rabbit with mustard, black pudding with apples, *cassoulet*, preserved duck, *cochonnailles, tourtière landaise.* Choice wines.

Café de l'Alma

Innovative

5 av. Rapp
✉ 75007
☎ 0145515674 – **Fax** 0145511008
e-mail cafedelalma@wanadoo.fr

Ⓜ Alma Marceau
B1

Carte €34/69

With its plum, anise green and beige colours and wenge wood, the Café de l'Alma stylishly disproves the idealized picture of a Parisian brasserie. There is no zinc counter worn by the years, no moleskin or bistro furniture here. The decor by architect François Champsaur, designed in a highly contemporary spirit just made for cocooning, features cosy nooks upstairs, banquettes for lounging comfortably from morning until night. The food is also up-to-date, with its reinvented classics such as coconut shrimp tempura, fish and chips with tartar and Sherry sauce, *hachis parmentier de pot-au-feu* (spepherd's pie made with stew), caramel tart, etc. The wines are of the same calibre, with a wide selection of bottles from around the world.

Tour Eiffel, École Militaire, Invalides

Tour Eiffel, École Militaire, Invalides

35 ° Ouest

Seafood ✗

A/C 35 r. Verneuil
⌂ ✉ 75007
VISA ✆ 01 42 86 98 88 – **Fax** 01 42 86 00 65
e-mail 35degresouest@orange.fr

Ⓜ Rue du Bac
D2

closed August, Sunday and Monday

ⓂⒸ

AE **Carte** €53/77

♀ They specialise in fine seafood at this elegant restaurant, opened by the former director of the Gaya Rive Gauche. The decor is in the current style (tasteful and refined zen look, in a range of grey tones) and the wooden counter complementing the contemporary tables appeals to the 7th arrondissement suit-and-tie clientele – sometimes rather pressed for time. In the kitchen, the chef prepares some original dishes. Examples from the short menu include foie gras and smoked eel sushi wrapped in thin slices of green apple, pan-fried langoustines and pumpkin with a ginger mousse. In short, the meals are well-executed and the service is polished; the only fly in the ointment is the rather steep bill.

Le Soleil

Traditional ✗

VISA 153 r. Grenelle
✉ 75007
ⓂⒸ ✆ 01 45 51 54 12

Ⓜ La Tour Maubourg
B2

AE Closed August, Christmas holidays, Sunday and Monday

♀ **Carte** €37/79

Le Soleil, owned by Jacques-Louis Vannucci, the proprietor of the restaurant of the same name in St-Ouen, is doing brilliantly at its location in the heart of the distinguished 7th arrondissement. The sunny south and the sea are the main theme in the cuisine and in the decor evoking Mediterranean lands. And while it is an extremely convivial establishment, the fine, flavoursome traditional food is the real focus here. A treat from start to finish: superb bread, porcini mushrooms pan-fried in garlic and parsley, Sisteron lamb fillet with thyme and *cébettes*, cannoli filled with creamy ricotta and oranges. You may run into some of the owner's friends – other talented chefs who have the right idea in coming here. Cheerful atmosphere guaranteed!

Aida

Japanese 🍴

 1 r. Pierre Leroux
✉ 75007
 ☎ 01 43 06 14 18 – **Fax** 01 43 06 14 18

Ⓜ Vaneau
C3

Closed 2 weeks in August, 2 weeks in February, Saturday lunch, Sunday lunch, Tuesday lunch and Monday

Menu €35 (weekday lunch)/€140

The white façade of this small Japanese restaurant blends in so well with the urban landscape that you could easily walk right by without even noticing it. But don't! Hidden inside is a secret which is jealously kept by informed gourmets – a delicious Japanese establishment. The ultra-zen, subdued interior is a chic, welcome change of scenery. You can choose between the red lacquer counter (to be in the first row, across from the huge hot plates) or in the private room. The menu features refined cutting-edge cuisine, a blend of Japanese and French. A lovely marriage of lobster, chateaubriand and calf sweetbreads with teppan-yaki – which gets the better of sushi here – and Burgundies passionately chosen by the chef, an expert œnologist.

P'tit Troquet 🎭

Traditional 🍴

28 r. L'Exposition
✉ 75007
☎ 01 47 05 80 39 – **Fax** 01 47 05 80 39

Ⓜ Ecole Militaire
B2

closed 1st-28 August, Saturday lunchtime, Monday lunchtime and Sunday – number of covers limited, pre-book

Menu €30

It is indeed a small place. But what atmosphere inside! The highly unusual decor, filled with nostalgia, is composed of objects picked up over the years - old advertisements here, siphons and coffee pots there, all remnants of another era, the 1920s. Not to mention the original zinc counter, wood panelling and snug tables. This charming little "museum" – sure to please the tourists – is bubbling with life at mealtimes. Regulars enjoy the traditional recipes such as marinated sardine lasagna, fillet mignon of pork in lemon and honey, and stuffed rabbit. And the staff takes good care of them too, with its fast and friendly service and completely non-smoking dining room.

L'Affriolé 😳

Contemporary 🍴

A/C	17 r. Malar	Ⓜ Invalides
VISA	✉ 75007	**B1**
	☎ 0144183133	
Ⓜ©	closed 30 July-20 August, Sunday and Monday	
♀	**Menu €29 (lunch)/€34**	

With its bits-and-pieces bistro decor (knick-knacks, stucco, mosaic tables), Thierry Vérola's restaurant has some nice gastronomic surprises up its sleeve among the daily blackboard suggestions. And it doesn't take the easy way out, changing its menu by the month. Following the market and his own inclinations, the chef composes generous dishes with a modern touch, such as ham hock croquettes with lentils, swordfish hamburger with fennel, *nonnette* (tart) made with salted butter. People come here for the relaxed yet well-prepared meals, the warm and friendly reception, and attentive service (appetizers with radishes, pots of cream) – all at reasonable prices. Tempting, isn't it?

Chez l'Ami Jean 😳

Terroir 🍴

A/C	27 r. Malar	Ⓜ La Tour Maubourg
VISA	✉ 75007	**B1**
	☎ 0147058689 – **Fax** 0145554182	
Ⓜ©	closed August, 23 December-2 January, Sunday and Monday	
♀	**Menu €30/€50**	

Wood furniture, blackboard specialities of the day, *piments d'Espelette*, *chistera*, old rugby posters and photographs make up the "regionalist" decor of this authentic bistro, quite up-to-date despite its 70 years. Stéphane Jégo, the chef here since 2002, has been given high marks from the gourmets, who enjoy spending time with friends in the open and convivial atmosphere. The market-based cuisine is generous and tasty, alternately featuring seafood – the chef is from Brittany – and Basque-Béarnais dishes (he was the assistant to Camdeborde at La Régalade). A big success, it is always packed, lively and fun.

Miyako

Japanese ✗

A/C

VISA

MC

AE

♀

121 r. Université
✉ 75007
✆ 0147054183 – **Fax** 0145551318
closed 4 August-3 September, Saturday lunch and Sunday

Ⓜ Invalides
B1

Menu €13 (weekday lunch)/€35 – Carte €15/32

On one wall of the dining room is a fresco of the Eiffel Tower and the Esplanade des Invalides, while plants and porcelain dolls on the other wall evoke the Land of the Rising Sun. Welcome to Miyako ("heart" in Japanese), a restaurant which pleasantly cultivates French and Japanese culture in its decor. The food, however, is rooted in the traditions of the archipelago. The menu has a large variety of typical dishes, enjoyed to the sound of classical music. Sushi, sashimi, maki, vegetable ravioli, chicken meatballs and red bean paste are all carefully prepared by Julie Shen, busy at work behind the large bar. The welcome is warm, and as they say over there before a meal, *Itadakimasu!*

Oudino

Bistro ✗

A/C

VISA

MC

Ⓓ

♀

17 r. Oudinot
✉ 75007
✆ 0145660509 – **Fax** 0145665335
Web www.oudino.com
closed 6-19 August, 24 December-2 January, Saturday lunch and Sunday

Ⓜ Vaneau
C3

Carte €24/45

The Oudino, an elegant establishment in the government ministry district, has everything it takes to please its regular clientele. The ambiance is smart yet relaxed and the dining room understated – a streamlined modern replica of an Art Deco bistro (with mirrors, chandeliers, dark wood furniture and ivory walls creating a deeply soothing "yin-yang" effect). The food consists of fine ingredients in keeping with current trends, including cream of pumpkin soup, swordfish steak and fresh fruit salad in coconut milk. Dishes follow the seasons, the market and ideas from here and elsewhere. As a bonus, there are fine wines listed on the blackboard and a friendly welcome that goes with the restaurant's motto: "may diners feel at home here".

Tour Eiffel, École Militaire, Invalides

Al Dente

Italian ✗

VISA
⊠ 38 r. Varenne
75007
✆ 0145487964

Ⓜ Rue du Bac
D2

☽ closed August, Sunday and Monday

𝟀 Carte €27/48

All roads lead to Rome, as everyone knows. And perchance to Italian cuisine, judging from this recent neighbourhood trattoria run by Sylvain Lindon (Vincent's brother), who traded in his job as a television adman for that of a restaurateur. Lacking all pretension – but not lacking in quality – his establishment welcomes you just like at home. The setting remains simple, with red banquettes, dark wood furniture, and sienna and ochre tones for that touch of sun. You could almost imagine yourself in Tuscany. The dishes speak for themselves: fettucine with courgettes and pecorino, three-cheese rigatoni, papardelle with aubergines, tomatoes and mozzarella, pizza with rocket and bresaola. Simple, modern, and *al dente*.

Léo Le Lion

Seafood ✗

VISA
⊠ 23 r. Duvivier
75007
✆ 0145514177 – **Fax** 0145514177

Ⓜ Ecole Militaire
B2

𝟀 closed August, 25 December-1st January, Sunday and Monday

Carte €36/46

This bistro has resisted the sirens of fashion and appeals to people precisely because of its delicious retro setting and atmosphere still plunged into the days of the 1930s. The fine counter, wood-fired grill and velvet banquettes compose the warm and rustic spirit of the establishment, with its friendly service. Fish are featured on the menu year round – chef Didier Méry is an expert after his long turn at the famous seafood restaurant Le Divellec – and game shows up in season. Good catches include the crayfish in raspberry vinegar, snail *cassolette* in champagne, and the fillet of sea bass. For dessert, the crème brûlée with honey is an offer you can't refuse.

Sa Mi In

Korean ✗

VISA
74 av. Breteuil
✉ **75007**
📞 01 47 34 58 96 – **Fax** 01 47 34 58 96
e-mail han@samiin.com

🅜❍ Sèvres-Lecourbe
C3

closed Saturday lunch and Sunday lunch

Menu €14 (lunch)/€49 – Carte €30/71

This authentic little Korean establishment with its atmosphere of Asian serenity is discreet and refined. The dining room is "zen" without being overly minimalist, with flowers and watercolours creating a delicate aesthetic, contemporary lighting in keeping with the clean lines of the furniture, and beige-moka tones for an intimate feeling, enhanced by the background music. Everything is made to calm the mind. But not the appetite! The menu proposes authentic, original and flavoursome dishes that are little known to Western palates, such as *bulgogi, gyoza, bibimbap*, as well as a vegetarian menu. This charming, friendly place is well worth a visit. You'll have every reason to dream of the sweet land of morning calm – and to believe in it.

Café Constant

Bistro ✗

VISA
139 r. Saint-Dominique
✉ **75007**
📞 01 47 53 73 34 – **Fax** 01 45 55 48 42

🅜❍ Ecole Militaire
B2

closed Sunday and Monday

Menu €27

Slowly but surely, Christian Constant, the former chef at the Crillon, is turning the rue Saint-Dominique into a real gourmet haven. This annexe a stone's throw from the Violon d'Ingres, his gastronomic restaurant, is in an unassuming little corner bistro – with no reservations! Simplicity is the watchword here. There is nothing showy about the basic decor. The food shows a keen understanding of ingredients, preserving some of the spirit of the great restaurants (without the affectedness and high prices). The blackboard features tasty market-based bistro dishes such as *œuf mimosa*, cream of pumpkin soup, fillet of beef with pepper sauce, and profiteroles. The service is friendly and the ambiance feisty. A constant source of amazement!

Tour Eiffel, École Militaire, Invalides

Champs-Élysées, Concorde, Madeleine

Richer X./MICHELIN

It is rare to come across a Parisian who actually lives in the 8th, as the arrondissement seems almost entirely the preserve of embassies, luxury boutiques and tourism. Bordered by the 9th, the Seine and place de l'Étoile, the district is home to no less than 40 embassies and general consulates, including those of the United States and the People's Republic of China, as well as the Palais de l'Elysée, permanent residence of the president of the French republic. Understandably, business and commerce play an important role in this district which is the location of a record number of corporate headquarters.

To such an extent, that the streets of the 8th, while they might not be the most congested of the city, can boast the highest concentration of luxury cars. No other part of the capital gives such an impression of being a "global metropolis" and the international diplomatic, political and economic vocation of Paris is expressed here visibly, sometimes to excess. The area also boasts a cultural vocation due to monuments that modelled its history: the obelisk of the Concorde, brought back by Napoleon from Egypt and erected on the former place Louis XV, the Grand Palais and its recently restored glass and steel dome roof, and the Arc de Triomphe, of course, built in honour of Napoleon's military victories.

FICTION AND REALITY

It is difficult to do otherwise than start with the Champs-Elysées, the central artery of this arrondissement and claimed by some to be the most beau-

tiful avenue in the world. Real Parisians, not fooled, know that the avenue is also the scene of some of the capital's most unpleasant aspects. It is nonetheless known the world over for its vast quantity of shops and spectacular perspective and it would be ungracious not to admit that the "Triumphal Way" imagined by Le Nôtre under Louis XIV that links the Louvre to the Arche de la Défense today, continues to offer a vista of rare majesty.

Another myth, according to which the entire 8th is a soulless arrondissement devoted to mass tourism and traffic jams, reveals an ignorance of the many authentic Parisian bastions that continue to hold out, hidden between the showy avenues and legions of chain stores. Rue Marbeuf and rue La Boétie, like the tiny alleys around the church of La Madeleine, are home to a plethora of establishments of character that make good food in Paris a genuine way of life.

8TH GASTRONOMIC MARVEL

The gourmet, keen to imprint his or her taste buds with a

Blackwell K./MICHELIN

Parisian experience could do no better than choose this district due to its quantity of legendary restaurants. The 8th is home to nearly 25 starred establishments, including a few of the capital's most prestigious three-star restaurants; however a culinary portrait of the 8th would not be complete without a reference to its innumerable luxury hotels and gourmet grocery stores.

Blackwell K./MICHELIN

To be brief, anyone interested in tasting the best of French cuisine will want to come here. However those who prefer simpler fare should head for the outskirts of the arrondissement and explore its markets: the one in avenue des Batignolles is specialised in organic produce in particular, and the delightful flower market around la Madeleine provides a colourful picture in all seasons.

Champs-Élysées, Concorde, Madeleine

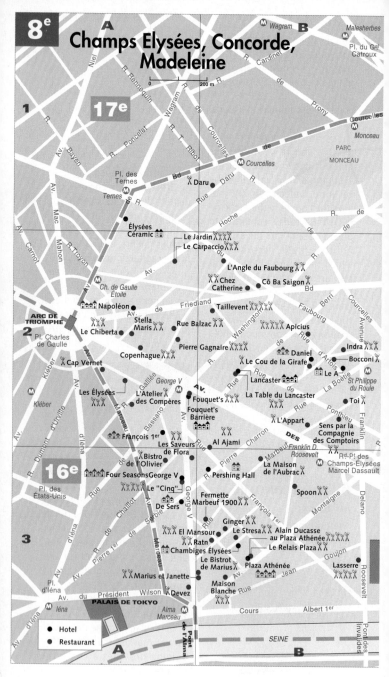

0   200 m

Maleherbes

Pl. du Gal Catroux

Wagram

Courcelles

Monceau

PARC MONCEAU

Pl. des Ternes

Daru

Ternes

Hoche

Élysées Céramic

Le Jardin

Le Carpaccio

L'Angle du Faubourg

Chez Catherine

Cô Ba Saigon

Ch. de Gaulle Étoile

Friedland

Napoléon

Taillevent

Faubourg

ARC DE TRIOMPHE

Stella Maris

Rue Balzac

Washington

Apicius

Le Chiberta

Pl. Charles de Gaulle

Copenhague

Pierre Gagnaire

Daniel

Indra

Le Cou de la Girafe

Bocconi

Le A

Cap Vernet

Lancaster

St Philippe du Roule

Les Élysées

L'Atelier des Compères

Fouquet's

La Table du Lancaster

Toi

Kléber

Fouquet's Barrière

L'Appart

Sens par la Compagnie des Comptoirs

François 1er

Al Ajami

Les Saveurs de Flora

Bistro de l'Olivier

La Maison de l'Aubrac

Rd-Pt des Champs-Élysées Marcel Dassault

16e

Four Seasons George V

Pershing Hall

Pl. des États-Unis

Le "Cinq"

Spoon

De Sers

Fermette Marbeuf 1900

Ginger

El Mansour

Le Stresa

Alain Ducasse au Plaza Athénée

Ratn

Chambiges Élysées

Le Relais Plaza

Lasserre

Le Bistrot de Marius

Plaza Athénée

3

Marius et Janette

Maison Blanche

Devez

Pl. d'Iéna

Av. du Président Wilson

PALAIS DE TOKYO

Iéna

Alma Marceau

Cours Albert 1er

● Hotel
● Restaurant

SEINE

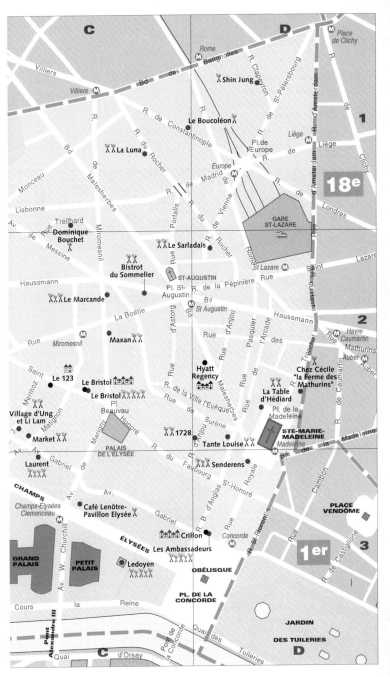

Champs-Élysées, Concorde, Madeleine

Le "Cinq" ❀ ❀

Classic 🍴🍴🍴🍴🍴

A|C

VISA

M|C

AE

D

Hôtel Four Seasons George V,
31 av. George V ✉ 75008
✆ 0149527154 – **Fax** 0149527181
e-mail par.lecinq@fourseasons.com **Web** www.fourseasons.com
Menu €75 (lunch)/€220 – Carte €130/288

Ⓜ George V
A3

Le "Cinq"

The renovations lasted three years and were carried out by architect Pierre-Yves Rochon. The owner, Saudi prince Al Waleed, had asked him to "restore this luxury hotel to its rightful place". That included the restaurant, where the team is headed by Eric Beaumard, considered one of the best *directeurs de salle* in France. When the hotel reopened, an inaugural meal in the superb and completely restored Louis XVI dining room at Le Cinq was imperative.

This is French elegance at its finest: lofty columns, high sprays of flowers and comfortably spaced tables in a deliciously intimate atmosphere created by the lighting coming from the courtyard garden.

The dishes also reflect the same sense of refinement. The classic cuisine uses only the best ingredients, featuring full-bodied and well-paired flavours enhanced by a sumptuous wine cellar. This is what luxury is all about.

A LA CARTE

FIRST COURSE	MAIN COURSE	DESSERT
• Tarte d'artichaut et de truffe noire.	• Fricassée de langoustines, lasagne au vieux parmesan.	• Véritable opéra et fruits secs caramélisés, glace café.
• Pâté de pigeon et gibier en croûte.	• Côte de veau de lait fermier aux câpres de Pantelleria.	• Soufflé au chocolat Caraïbes parfumé au basilic, au coulis de poivron.

Les Ambassadeurs ✿✿

Innovative 🍴🍴🍴🍴

A/C
⟲
VISA
MC
AE
D
⚜
🍷

Hôtel Crillon,
10 pl. Concorde ⊠ 75008
☎ 01 44 71 16 16 – **Fax** 01 44 71 15 02
e-mail restaurants@crillon.com **Web** www.crillon.com

closed August, 1st-8 January, Sunday and Monday

Ⓜ Concorde
D3

Menu € 75 (weekday lunch)/€ 200 – Carte € 154/255

Philippe Forestier

This renowned address in the world of fine cuisine is in the heart of Paris. When Jean-François Piège took over in 2004, he wanted a suitable setting for his culinary creations, so the decor at Les Ambassadeurs, a former 18th century ballroom, was redesigned. The new dining room, combining tradition and modernity, has a contemporary feeling that is a subtle blend of simplicity and elegance. The focus is on the diversity of materials and colours, and new shapes enhanced by clever lighting at dinnertime. The chef, who as a child dreamed of being a gardener, confesses his love of fine ingredients. His cooking is refined and in perpetual motion, and can also be quite playful, handling flavours with flawless technique on his short but well-designed menu. The impeccable service and well-stocked wine list are the establishment's other great assets.

A LA CARTE

FIRST COURSE
• Blanc à manger d'oeuf, truffe noire (January to March).

• Caviar d'Aquitaine, nage corsée, langoustines.

MAIN COURSE
• Pigeonneau désossé, foie gras, jus à l'olive.

• Turbot, galette de Bretagne, cèpes.

DESSERT
• Comme un vacherin, au parfum de saison.

• Choco-café grillé en chaud et froid.

175

Champs-Élysées, Concorde, Madeleine

Alain Ducasse au Plaza Athénée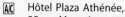

Innovative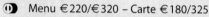

A/C
VISA
M/C
AE
D
⊗
♀

Hôtel Plaza Athénée,
25 av. Montaigne ✉ 75008
✆ 0153676500 – **Fax** 0153676512
e-mail adpa@alain-ducasse.com **Web** www.alain-ducasse.com
closed 13 July-21 August, 21-31 December, Monday lunch, Tuesday lunch, Wednesday lunch,
Saturday and Sunday

Menu €220/€320 – Carte €180/325

🄜 Alma Marceau
B3

Alain Ducasse au Plaza Athénée

The Plaza has dominated the prestigious avenue Montaigne since 1911, exactly eighty-nine years before the arrival of Alain Ducasse in the kitchen of this legendary luxury hotel. As soon as he took over, the chef, who wanted his cuisine to have a fitting decor, commissioned Patrick Jouin to create a "magical and poetic" interior design. The result lived up to his expectations, with its Regency-style furniture made from contemporary materials, chandeliers with thousands of luminous pendants, and elegant lamps giving each table its own private space; not to mention the totem at the entrance inscribed with pithy culinary expressions. The cuisine, now the work of Christophe Moret, is clear, contemporary, reassuring, generous and authentic, superbly highlighting the flawless ingredients. The cellar and service are of the same calibre as the rest of the establishment.

A LA CARTE

FIRST COURSE
• Caviar osciètre d'Iran, langoustines rafraîchies, nage réduite, bouillon parfumé.

• Foie gras de canard des Landes en gelée de thé noir.

MAIN COURSE
• Volaille de Bresse, sauce albuféra aux truffes d'Alba (15 October to 31 December).

• Sole de petit bateau au Château-Chalon, crevettes "bouquet".

DESSERT
• Fraises des bois en coupe glacée, sablé coco.

• Poire Belle-Hélène en chaud et froid.

Le Bristol ⌘ ⌘

Innovative 𝕏𝕏𝕏𝕏𝕏

Hôtel Bristol,
112 r. Fg St-Honoré ✉ 75008
✆ 0153434300 – **Fax** 0153434301
e-mail resa@lebristolparis.com **Web** www.lebristolparis.com

Reopening scheduled for 22 March on completion of work

Ⓜ Miromesnil
C2

Menu €90 (lunch)/€190 – Carte €118/207

Le Bristol

The dining room is located in a former market garden which adjoined the Pépinières Royales dating from the 18C. In the next century, Jules de Castellane had a private theatre built there, of which only the unusual oval form remains. Passing through the white marble lobby, you enter the luxurious winter restaurant with its Regency oak panelling, gold leaf ceiling, paintings by Gustave-Louis Jaulmes, tapestries from the Manufacture de Lille and Baccarat crystal chandeliers. The summer restaurant is in a garden with tables set up by a lawn, chairs with pale fabrics, canopies and striped draperies, in a range of beige, green and red shades. In this unique environment, Éric Fréchon expresses the essence of his cuisine. This winner of the Meilleur Ouvrier de France award – and accomplished saucier – makes fine use of spice and fresh herb flavours in his cooking. Rather than riding on the wave of current trends, he prefers to create inventive versions of the French classics he knows like the back of his hand.

A LA CARTE

FIRST COURSE	MAIN COURSE	DESSERT
• Macaroni farcis, truffe, artichaut et foie gras, gratinés au parmesan.	• Anguille des Sargasses sautée meunière.	• Sablé craquant au praliné et chocolat grand cru.
• Baba truffé au vin jaune, ailerons farcis, bouillon de poule infusé aux branches de sapin fumé.	• Poularde de Bresse cuite en vessie aux écrevisses.	• Diffusion de menthe fraîche glacée, framboises et chocolat lacté.

Champs-Élysées, Concorde, Madeleine

177

Champs-Élysées, Concorde, Madeleine

Ledoyen  ✿✿✿

Innovative XXXXX

A/C — carré Champs-Élysées ● Champs-Elysées Clémenceau

✉ 75008 **C3**

✆ 0153051001 – **Fax** 0147425501

P — **e-mail** pavillon.ledoyen@ledoyen.com **Web** www.ledoyen.com

VISA — closed 28 July-26 August, Monday lunch, Saturday and Sunday

MC — Menu €85 (lunch)/€284 wine included – Carte €148/244

AE

Ledoyen

This neo-Classical establishment has preserved the same environment of flowers and greenery since 1791, when Pierre Michel Doyen had his catering business here. It is only a stone's throw from the Champs-Élysées, yet seems so far from the madding crowd. Joséphine de Beauharnais is even said to have met Napoleon here. The friendly 18th century tavern was eventually transformed into a restaurant with luxurious decor. Its Lalique glass awning and monochrome façade conceal a superb ensemble of sculpted pale wood panelling, old paintings, Napoleon III armchairs, and furnishings. The inventive cuisine is by Christian Le Squer, who has taken this establishment to the top. "Meals are a time for sharing happiness", asserts this chef who fearlessly blends the classic and modern through his seasonal variations. The service and reception are well orchestrated. The cellar is well stocked. What else could you hope for?

A LA CARTE

FIRST COURSE

• Grosses langoustines bretonnes, émulsion d'agrumes.

• Araignée de mer rafraîchie d'une émulsion crémeuse liée de corail.

MAIN COURSE

• Blanc de turbot de ligne braisé, pommes rattes truffées.

• Ris de veau en brochette de bois de citronnelle, jus d'herbes.

DESSERT

• Le "Grand Dessert Ledoyen" en cinq compositions.

• Chocolat noir en fines feuilles croustillantes, lait de pistache glacé.

Taillevent ❀ ❀

Classic 🍴🍴🍴🍴

[A/C] 15 r. Lamennais   Ⓜ Charles de Gaulle-Etoile

✉ 75008   **B2**

📞 01 44 95 15 01 – **Fax** 01 42 25 95 18

e-mail mail@taillevent.com **Web** www.taillevent.com

Closed 28 July-27 August, Saturday, Sunday and public holidays – number of covers limited, pre-book

Menu €70 (lunch)/€190 – Carte €124/198

Taillevent

This is a family affair! Jean-Claude Vrinat and his father André, who preceded him here beginning in 1950, have made the former townhouse of the Duc de Morny a historic place for French gastronomy. The restaurant owes its name to the author of the *Viandier*, the first cookbook published in France, in 1486. The hushed and slightly austere decor give the place that air of refinement which attracts both politicians and businessmen. The ambiance features warm tones of brown, beige and red. A few contemporary works of art and the subdued lighting add a touch of conviviality. The cuisine remains a happy blend of tradition and novelty, with some Mediterranean influences from the chef. On the ground floor or upstairs, the service is crisp and precise, as it should be in such an establishment. With its variety of vintages – and prices – the Taillevent cellar is among the finest in the city.

A LA CARTE

FIRST COURSE	MAIN COURSE	DESSERT
• Rémoulade de tourteau à l'aneth.	• Selle d'agneau princier en rognonnade.	• Tarte inversée au chocolat et au café.
• Epeautre du pays de Sault en risotto, cuisses de grenouille dorées.	• Chausson feuilleté de ris de veau, tétragone et gremolata.	• Baba au rhum et aux raisins macérés.

Champs-Élysées, Concorde, Madeleine

Apicius ✿✿

Innovative XXXXX

20 rue d'Artois
✉ 75008
✆ 0143801966 – **Fax** 0144400957
e-mail restaurant-apicius@wanadoo.fr
closed August, Saturday and Sunday

Ⓜ St-Philippe du Roule
B2

Menu €140/€150 – **Carte** €79/156

Apicius

This has to be one of the most uncharacteristic Parisian venues, with its dining rooms furnished with art works and objects, its theatre chandeliers, still lifes bought for a bargain at auction houses and its fake fireplace. Since 6 December 2004, the monumental townhouse surrounded by a park is the new creative outlet for Jean-Pierre Vigato, a golf enthusiast and self-taught cook who got into the business by accident. Although the restaurant moved – it now has an impressive three dining rooms featuring amiable, smiling angels – Vigato preserved its name. Apicius was an Epicurian who lived during the time of the Roman Empire and left the first known cookbook to posterity. He is said to have invented blood sausage, duck with turnips, sole au gratin and bouillabaisse! You might even find it featured on a menu created by a chef who favours "authentic cuisine" without unnecessary complications and allows the produce to speak for itself.

A LA CARTE

FIRST COURSE

• Compote de cèpes frais et grillés, sabayon à la truffe blanche d'Alba (October to December).

• Terrine de concombre au raifort, caviar gros grains.

MAIN COURSE

• Milieu de gros turbot rôti, jus tranché aux épices.

• Tête de veau sauce ravigote.

DESSERT

• Soufflé au chocolat noir et chantilly sans sucre.

• Blanc manger au lait d'amande.

Lasserre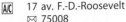

Classic XXXXX

17 av. F.-D.-Roosevelt	**Ⓜ** Franklin D. Roosevelt
✉ 75008	**B3**

☎ 0143595343 – **Fax** 0145637223

e-mail lasserre@lasserre.fr **Web** www.restaurant-lasserre.com

closed August, Saturday lunchtime, Monday lunchtime, Tuesday lunchtime, Wednesday lunchtime and Sunday

Menu €75 (lunch)/€185 – Carte €122/206

Lasserre

In this magical place, you reach the restaurant via a small velvet-upholstered lift. The impeccable decor features a roof that opens up to the Paris sky, with paintings by Touchagues. Diners relish their privacy among the window boxes full of flowers and little nooks and crannies. The traditional French service still in evidence here is hard to find elsewhere nowadays. The cuisine blends tradition and modernity, combining "essentials" with new dishes.

René Lasserre, who died in 2006 only a few years after selling his restaurant, was both the name and signature behind this establishment. As an adolescent, Lasserre left his native Basque country to find work in Paris, and opened the restaurant in 1942. With its consistent classical cuisine, unparalleled reception and service, this establishment became one of the most prestigious in the world.

A LA CARTE

FIRST COURSE
• Macaroni aux truffes noires et foie gras.

• Caviar osciètre aux poireaux et pomme de terre.

MAIN COURSE
• Selle d'agneau de lait au serpolet et artichauts poivrades.

• Homard breton à la coriandre, carottes et amandes fraîches.

DESSERT
• Tarte soufflée au chocolat.

• Timbale Elysée Lasserre.

8th ARRONDISSEMENT

Laurent ✿

Contemporary ✗✗✗✗

41 av. Gabriel 　　　　Ⓜ Champs-Elysées Clémenceau
✉ 75008 　　　　　　　　　　　　　　**C3**
✆ 0142250039 – **Fax** 0145624521
e-mail info@le-laurent.com **Web** www.le-laurent.com

closed Saturday lunchtime, Sunday and public holidays

Menu €75/€160 – Carte €132/213

Laurent

Was he a chef, a maître d'hôtel or simply an enlightened food-lover? Nothing much is known about Laurent, owner of the restaurant of the same name in 1860, except that he handed down his name to posterity! We do know that this former hunting lodge belonging to Louis XIV, subsequently an open-air café during the Revolution, was completely restored by the architect Hittorff who was commissioned by Louis-Philippe to develop the Champs-Elysées. The style was very innovative for the times and its main and private dining rooms are full of charm. Regulars can attest to the "Laurent spirit", characterised by attentive service and attention to detail. This is also true for the cuisine and its substantial classical menu, as well as the cellar stocked with fine wines. In fine weather, Paris society is fond of dining in its garden restaurant where guests can enjoy a moment of peace and quiet without a care for the passing of time.

A LA CARTE

FIRST COURSE
• Araignée de mer dans ses sucs en gelée, crème de fenouil.

• Opéra de foie gras, ris de veau et champignons de couche croquants.

MAIN COURSE
• Grosses langoustines "tandoori" poêlées, copeaux d'avocat à l'huile d'amande.

• Flanchet de veau braisé, blettes à la moelle et au jus.

DESSERT
• Fleurette fouettée à l'arabica en arlettes croustillantes, petit mystère aux noix de pécan.

• Gourmandise au chocolat noir marié aux framboises.

Pierre Gagnaire ❁ ❁ ❁

Innovative XXXX

A/C
VISA
MC
AE
Y

6 r. Balzac
✉ 75008
✆ 0158361250 – **Fax** 0158361251
e-mail p.gagnaire@wanadoo.fr

🚇 George V
A2

closed 21 July-20 August, 22 December-6 January, Sunday lunch and Saturday

Menu €95 (weekday lunch)/€245 – Carte €231/332

Pierre Gagnaire

Pierre Gagnaire started out in Saint-Étienne, but has been in Paris for ten years, a stone's throw from the Champs-Élysées. He spends most of his time here despite his other establishments in Paris (Gaya Rive Gauche), London and Tokyo. A few months before the French football team won the World Cup, Gagnaire won back the third star he had lost in Saint-Étienne two years earlier. The style of this iconoclastic chef – a jazz buff and lover of contemporary art – has been distilled over the years and is reaching towards something purer without relinquishing its originality. As a master of flavours, he likes to play around with clashing tastes and is expertly seconded by Michel Nave, a faithful companion in the kitchen and Meilleur Ouvrier de France. The intimate and contemporary atmosphere in the dining room is in perfect osmosis with the dishes, which are sometimes unorthodox, and often surprising.

A LA CARTE

FIRST COURSE	MAIN COURSE	DESSERT
• Langoustines de quatre façons.	• Pièce d'agneau de Lozère.	• Grand dessert Pierre Gagnaire.
• L'insolite.	• Tronçon de gros turbot rôti à l'arête.	• Soufflé caramel et angélique.

Champs-Élysées, Concorde, Madeleine

Champs-Élysées, Concorde, Madeleine

Le Jardin ⁜

Contemporary 🍴🍴🍴🍴

Hôtel Royal Monceau,
37 av. Hoche ⊠ 75008
☎ 01 42 99 98 70 – **Fax** 01 42 99 89 94
e-mail lejardin@royalmonceau.com **Web** www.royalmonceau.com

Ⓜ Charles de Gaulle-Etoile
A2

closed August, Monday lunch, Saturday and Sunday

Menu €59 (lunch)/€125 – Carte €86/126

G.Corbic/MICHELIN

This superb circular domed veranda is decorated in Second Empire style, with elegant glass walls and ceiling and large silk drapes for shade. The windows overlook the hotel gardens and the charming terrace, very popular in fine weather. The silk curtains, comfortable velvet chairs and soft music at dinnertime are all part of the delightfully luxurious decor and atmosphere created by Jacques Garcia.

In the kitchen, Christophe Pelé has upheld the highest standards. "True passion produces pleasure", maintains this chef who has worked in some excellent establishments. Using fine market ingredients, he creates subtle and inventive dishes with generous flavours. He likes to give his creations a touch of the Mediterranean, where he started out in the culinary world. High marks for the sommelier, who enjoys introducing diners to a new generation of winemakers and has put together a wine list that is full of great finds.

A LA CARTE

FIRST COURSE

• Langoustines rôties, confit d'oignons doux, râpée de truffe noire.

• Fleurs de courgette farcies de chair de tourteau.

MAIN COURSE

• Bar de ligne étuvé aux palourdes.

• Suprêmes de palombe dorés, foie gras.

DESSERT

• Fondant chocolat au curry et piments d'Espelette, croquant sablé à la cannelle, glace vanille.

• Mirabelles flambées à l'eau de vie, crème glacée vanille.

Les Élysées ✿ ✿

Innovative ✕✕✕

Hôtel Vernet, ◍ Charles de Gaulle-Etoile
25 r. Vernet ✉ 75008 **A2**
✆ 0144319898 – **Fax** 0144318569
e-mail reservations@hotelvernet.com **Web** www.hotelvernet.com
closed 28 July-27 August, Monday lunch, Saturday and Sunday

Menu €59 (lunch)/€130 – Carte €89/142

Les Élysées

Once past the threshold of the hotel, you walk up a few steps
and cross a small lounge with antique furniture and orchid floral
displays. Down a few more steps and you reach the rotunda
dining room bathed in soft light. The metallic structure of the
eye-catching glass roof was designed by Gustave Eiffel, and the
paintings by Charles Champigneulle. The decor features round
tables with damask tablecloths, raspberry-coloured velvet chairs
and modern canvasses on the walls. On the kitchen side, the
menu is the work of a "disciple" of Joël Robuchon. Refinement,
creativity and generosity are the name of the game here. Showing his technical mastery, Eric Briffard, who won the Meilleur
Ouvrier de France award, uses subtle flavours to shake up and
reinvent traditions without falling for passing trends. Diners on
a tight schedule will be delighted to know that, upon request,
everything on the menu can be served in exactly one hour.

A LA CARTE

FIRST COURSE	MAIN COURSE	DESSERT
• Tranche d'aubergine potagère, copeaux de foie gras, sorbet tomate.	• Homard bleu cuit sur sel aux aromates, jus au naturel, fenouil, artichaut, gnocchi.	• Citron de Menton confit, biscuit moelleux au thym-citron, sauce mélisse, crème glacée au mascarpone.
• Tourteau breton, pétales de daïkon marinés au miel-épices.	• Epaule d'agneau de Lozère fondante à l'orientale.	• Fruits rouges gelée d'hibiscus.

Champs-Élysées, Concorde, Madeleine

La Table du Lancaster ❀

Contemporary 𝕏𝕏𝕏

Hôtel Lancaster,
7 r. Berri ✉ 75008
✆ 0140764018 – **Fax** 0140764000
e-mail restaurant@hotel-lancaster.fr **Web** www.hotel-lancaster.fr

closed August

Ⓜ George V
B2

Menu €60 (weekday lunch)/€120 – Carte €75/135

La Table du Lancaster

The owner had an excellent idea in bringing in Michel Troisgros, since the restaurant won its first star in March 2005. This chef has never shied away from shaking up the most well-established culinary habits, benefiting from his travels to Tokyo and Moscow in particular. He has taken the same approach at this hotel, housed in an 18C building, by turning the kitchen over to Fabrice Salvador, who has added a contemporary approach. He has developed various themes for the dishes, and readily admits that "a new reading of the menu enables each diner to create the meal that he wants". From the age of twenty, this young chef had already discovered the Troisgros kitchens in Roanne. After training with Michel Guérard in Eugénie-les-Bains, he headed for New Orleans and Santa Barbara, then England and finally Paris, in March 2004. And the rest is history.

A LA CARTE

FIRST COURSE
· Cuisses de grenouilles au satay.
· Foie gras en escalope dorée, à la rhubarbe.

MAIN COURSE
· Langouste grillée indonésienne (spring-summer).
· Grillon de ris de veau, pissalat d'anchois.

DESSERT
· Feuille à feuille croustillantes au chocolat, granité à la bergamote.
· Doigts de meringue, petites griottes et glace pistache.

Maison Blanche

Contemporary XXX

15 av. Montaigne   **Ⓜ** Alma Marceau
✉ 75008   **B3**
✆ 0147235599 – **Fax** 0147200956
e-mail info@maison-blanche.fr **Web** www.maison-blanche.fr
closed Saturday lunch and Sunday lunch

Carte € 74/133

The Pourcel Brothers' Parisian establishment enjoys a grandiose setting. Like a cube placed on the roof of the Théâtre des Champs-Élysées, the restaurant seems to be observing the dome of Les Invalides and out to the west of the city through its huge glass window. And what a stunning view of the Eiffel Tower from the terrace. You hardly know which way to look in this ultra-contemporary duplex loft! Whether in one of the alcove-banquettes or up on the mezzanine, one never tires of the view. The chic brasserie food reflects the twins' native Languedoc. Fine choice of wines.

Fouquet's

Traditional XXX

99 av. Champs Élysées   **Ⓜ** George V
✉ 75008   **A2**
✆ 0147235000 – **Fax** 0147236002
e-mail fouquets@lucienbarriere.com **Web** www.lucienbarriere.com

Menu € 78/€ 110 – Carte € 72/128

From the beginning it has hosted the winners of the Molières and César awards; and every year the Jean Gabin, Romy Schneider, Louis Delluc and Marcel Pagnol prizes are presented here. As early as 1914, young aviators came to celebrate their exploits at the Bar de l'Escadrille. The famous sidewalk terrace on the "most beautiful avenue in the world" has been a meeting point for the Parisian smart set since time immemorial. Fouquet's is a legendary place, a luxury brasserie which people visit as they would the Eiffel Tower when in Paris. Renovated by Jacques Garcia in 1999, its beautiful interior, on the list of Historic Monuments, attracts prestigious and unknown patrons from around the world. An emblematic venue in the capital.

8th ARRONDISSEMENT

Senderens ✿ ✿

Innovative 🍴🍴🍴

A/C
VISA
MC
AE
◑
🍸

9 pl. Madeleine
✉ 75008
☎ 0142652290 – **Fax** 0142650623
e-mail restaurant@senderens.fr **Web** www.senderens.fr
closed Saturday and Sunday in July-August

Ⓜ Madeleine
D3

Carte € 73/91

Roberto Frankenberg

For many years number 9 Place de la Madeleine was occupied by Lucas-Carton, named after Richard Lucas, an English chef in the 18th century, and Francis Carton who bought the business in 1925. Eighty years later it is still there, but with a new name. Alain Senderens, who learned his culinary craft here and who held three stars since 1985, replaced the famous sign and launched Senderens.

The newly named restaurant has been doubly transformed. The white tablecloths were removed from the tables, and the Majorelle wood panelling now rubs shoulders with decidedly contemporary furniture. As for the chef, he has created a restaurant that is "in sync with the times", opting for less ceremonious service and simpler, less expensive produce in the kitchen. The result is a tapas and sushi bar upstairs and an unusual brasserie on the ground floor, producing a successful marriage of dishes and wine, and a considerably lower bill.

A LA CARTE

FIRST COURSE	MAIN COURSE	DESSERT
• Homard bleu et mangue en salade au basilic.	• Canard "Apicius" rôti au miel et aux épices.	• Coulant de samana, cerises amarena.
• Foie gras de canard rôti, tubes de navets caramélisés au poivre maniguette et noisettes torréfiées.	• Croustillant de merlan de ligne, émulsion à l'huile de sésame, cèpes marinés et roquette.	• Mille-feuille à la vanille de Tahiti.

Copenhague ✿

Scandinavian 🍴🍴🍴

142 av. Champs-Élysées
✉ 75008
☎ 0144138626 – **Fax** 0144138944
e-mail floradanica@wanadoo.fr
Web www.restaurantfloradanica.com

Closed 28 July-20 August, Saturday, Sunday and public holidays

Menu €55 (lunch)/€115 – Carte €79/114

🅜 George V
A2

Copenhague

Since 1955, this has been the prestigious showcase for the most southern kingdom among the Scandinavian countries. Gourmets have several selections to choose from. For a taste of Danish cuisine, opt for Flora Danica, which is both convivial and intimate with its subdued lighting and cosy atmosphere. For a more gastronomic meal, head for the upper floor where a portrait of Queen Margaret welcomes diners. Behind the large windows overlooking the Champs-Élysées, you will find the same peaceful and hushed atmosphere, but in an elegantly understated modern decor with red leather chairs and hanging garden.
Fish is naturally featured on the menu, with salmon in the forefront. The chef, who knows his classics, has created a lovely Franco-Danish blend inspired by Baltic flavours enriched with highly personal touches. Drinks include Danish beer and aquavit in addition to wines.

A LA CARTE

FIRST COURSE
• Foie gras poché à la bière.

• Blinis servis selon la tradition scandinave au saumon fumé sauvage de la mer Baltique.

MAIN COURSE
• Dos de cabillaud demi-sel au bouillon mousseux de palourdes.

• Noisettes de renne légèrement fumées et rôties, sauce venaison.

DESSERT
• Riz gonflé au lait cannelle-vanille, lait d'amande glacé.

• Le chocolat avec un peu de menthe.

Champs-Élysées, Concorde, Madeleine

189

Champs-Élysées, Concorde, Madeleine

Le Chiberta ⚜

Innovative 𝄖𝄖𝄖

A/C
📶
VISA
MC
AE
◐

3 r. Arsène-Houssaye — Ⓜ Charles de Gaulle-Etoile
✉ 75008 — **A2**
✆ 0153534200 – **Fax** 0145628508
e-mail chiberta@guysavoy.com **Web** www.lechiberta.com

closed 1st-21 August, Saturday lunchtime and Sunday

Menu €60/€100 – Carte €77/98

Stevens Fremont

A stone's throw from the Champs-Élysées and the place de l'Étoile, a corridor leads to the kitchen and adjoining bar and dining counter, where one can have a snack. With its dark, mainly slate tones, amazing walls covered with shelves of wine, and Traquandi paintings, the Chiberta is going for a relaxed look, with a *vinothèque* and little private rooms for business lunches and meetings in a peaceful environment. Guy Savoy himself was looking for just such an uncluttered ambiance, which he conceived with Jean-Michel Wilmotte, who designed the decor. Although he is still at his rue Troyon establishment, the "boss" has been closely following the development of this restaurant, which he rejuvenated. The inspired cuisine is the work of two chefs who trained at the "main restaurant". It features reinvented traditional dishes, at their best in the daily specials. By changing the market-based menu daily, they have begun to develop a clientele of regulars. The service is irreproachable and the cellar well-stocked.

A LA CARTE

FIRST COURSE	MAIN COURSE	DESSERT
• Crème de carottes citronnelle-gingembre, langoustines éclatées.	• Tronçon de turbot cuit sur l'arête, ratte du Touquet.	• Saveur praliné-citron vert.
• Suprême de colvert, foie gras et céleri, marmelade de coing aux poivres.	• Côte de veau de lait au four, petits navets et pommes Anna, jus à l'échalote confite.	• Poire et chocolat comme un millefeuille, sorbet poire.

Le Carpaccio

Italian XXX

Hôtel Royal Monceau,
37 av. Hoche ⊠ 75008
✆ 0142999890 – **Fax** 0142998994
e-mail ilcarpaccio@royalmonceau.com

closed Aug.

Carte €68/122

Ⓜ Charles de Gaulle-Etoile
A2

Le Carpaccio

The second gastronomic restaurant at the Hôtel Royal Monceau, near place de l'Étoile, is a true Italian enclave in Paris. The main dining room and two private rooms recall a Renaissance palace with their Florentine murals, Venetian chandeliers, Roman statues and mirrors in which a fresco of a Tuscan garden is reflected. As a final touch, mandolin music is played during dinner.

The atmosphere is highly romantic (and rather picturesque), for a guaranteed change of scenery. Likewise for the cuisine. Orazio Ganzi, a native of Sicily, has worked in the best Italian restaurants. His menu has two sections, one classic and one contemporary. The former is dedicated to the traditional cuisine from his country, whose original recipes he has adhered to. The latter features more personal dishes created with his generous touch. Don't miss the "white truffle" menu in the autumn – a must!

A LA CARTE

FIRST COURSE
• Carpaccio de filet de boeuf.
• Tagliatelles vertes au ragoût d'ossobuco.

MAIN COURSE
• Foie de veau à la vénitienne.
• Risotto au safran et poêlée de champignons de saison.

DESSERT
• Fraises des bois, chantilly et liqueur de fraise.
• Glace à la confiture d'orange amère.

El Mansour

Moroccan ♈♈♈

A/C
VISA
M©
AE
①
♈

7 r. Trémoille
✉ 75008
✆ 0147238818 – **Fax** 0140701353
closed Monday lunch and Sunday

Carte €45/68

Ⓜ Alma Marceau
B3

An elegant establishment in the Golden Triangle which cultivates the art of North African hospitality, with a decor worthy
of the finest restaurants in Casablanca – oak wood panelling,
sofas, large tables, lovely tableware, velvet armchairs – and
discreet and efficient service. Chef Mohamed Ezzyat knows Moroccan gastronomy like the back of his hand (he trained at La
Mamounia in Marrakech). The dishes include traditional *pastillas,
tajines* and couscous, all well-prepared and generously served.
And the extra touch? They serve the couscous from a little
serving trolley, an original and much appreciated gesture. The
short wine list has a few sunny North African vintages.

Le Marcande

 Classic ♈♈♈

VISA
M©
AE
♈

52 r. Miromesnil
✉ 75008
✆ 0142651914 – **Fax** 0142657685
e-mail info@marcande.com **Web** www.marcande.com
Closed 6-20 August, 24 December-1st January, Friday dinner from October to April, Saturday
except dinner from May to September and Sunday

Menu €40/€91 wine included – Carte €44/86

Ⓜ Miromesnil
C2

The delicious patio-terrace nestled in this restaurant is a rarity
in Paris. A few seconds are all it takes to forget the hustle and
bustle of the city in this oasis of calm where flowers, ivy and
bamboo blend in with the sound of a murmuring fountain. If
the sun is conspicuous by its absence, not to worry – it forms a
well of light, bathing the two part-traditional, part-contemporary
dining rooms in an amazing clarity. Stéphane Ruel, who has run
the kitchen since 2003, masterfully prepares traditional recipes
such as pike-perch *en meurette, entrecôte marchand de vin,* and
five-pepper duck breast. Follow the excellent advice of sommelier and proprietor Emmanuel Cazaux in choosing your wine.

Champs-Élysées, Concorde, Madeleine

Indra

Indian 🍴🍴🍴

A/C	10 r. Cdt-Rivière
VISA	✉ 75008
	✆ 0143594640 – **Fax** 0142250032
MC	**e-mail** toutounat@wanadoo.fr **Web** www.restaurant-indra.com
AE	closed Saturday lunchtime and Sunday
DC	

○ St-Philippe du Roule
B2

Menu €40 (lunch)/€65 – Carte €40/59

In 1976, talented and visionary businessman Yogen Gupta opened one of the first Indian restaurants in the land of foie gras and baguettes. Today it is as magical as ever. The secret? A refined decor with just the right touch of the exotic – patchwork quilts on the walls, finely sculpted wood panelling, well-laid-out tables and large mirrors. The kitchen adapts to Western palates while respecting Hindu gastronomic traditions. Northern India is particularly well-represented, as flavours from the south are considered more powerful. For the full experience, try the *thali* – a meal in itself served on a silver platter – to satisfy your food-lover's curiosity!

Spoon

Fusion 🍴🍴

A/C	12 r. Marignan
VISA	✉ 75008
	✆ 0140763444 – **Fax** 0140763437
MC	**e-mail** spoonfood@hotelmarignan.fr **Web** www.spoon.tm.fr
AE	closed 28 July-27 August, 22 December-2 January, Saturday and Sunday
DC	

○ Franklin D. Roosevelt
B3

Menu €45 (lunch)/€85 – Carte €49/79

The menu consists of one dish + a condiment or sauce + one side dish of your choice. Diners mix and match their own meals according to what they want. This playful concept, designed by Alain Ducasse, has quite a following, and the "zapping" gourmets love it! If that description fits you, chef Stéphane Colé has a variety of ingredients and recipes for you to choose from, which he has brought back from five different continents. The cellar nurtures dreams of distant getaways with its fine selection of national and international wines. The view of the kitchen in the chic, contemporary "zen" setting (modern furniture, leather banquettes and exotic wood) is another part of the journey. Don't forget to book your seat!

Champs-Élysées, Concorde, Madeleine

Champs-Élysées, Concorde, Madeleine

La Luna

Grilled fish 🍴🍴

A/C
VISA
MC
AE
♀

69 r. Rocher ✉ 75008
☏ 0142937761 – **Fax** 0140080244
e-mail laluna75008@yahoo.fr
closed 1st-22 August and Sunday

🅜 Villiers
C1

Carte €67/100

Its sea blue façade tips you off. People come to La Luna to enjoy the fish and shellfish specialities. The regularly renewed menu proposes recipes which sometimes have a touch of the exotic, such as large roasted gambas with vanilla oil and sea bream with ginger cooked in a banana leaf. This is a rather chic place, with an Art Deco interior (including an ancient fresco and a Lalique piece) which has recently been remodelled in a more discreet and up-to-date style (in light grey and red tones). The business clientele is very fond of the place and meets here on a regular basis, in particular for lunch. The restaurant is known for its famous *Baba de Zanzibar*, so the most ardent gourmets can't wait to get to the dessert course.

Le Relais Plaza

Contemporary 🍴🍴

A/C
VISA
MC
AE
🅞
♀

Hôtel Plaza Athénée,
25 av. Montaigne ✉ 75008
☏ 0153676400 – **Fax** 0153676666
e-mail reservation@plaza-athenee-paris.com
Web www.plaza-athenee-paris.com
closed 25 July-25 August

🅜 Alma Marceau
B3

Menu €50 – Carte €63/143

This brasserie frequented by the Parisian smart set is the chic and intimate "local" for the nearby couture houses. The Relais Plaza has certainly seen its share of celebrities, including Grace Kelly, Charles Aznavour, Liza Minelli, Yves Saint Laurent, John Travolta, Albert of Monaco and Junko Koshino. The well-preserved setting where this institution was born has an elegant, delicately renovated Art Deco interior inspired by the ocean liner, Le Normandie. Alain Ducasse has put Philippe Marc in charge of the cuisine, featuring classic dishes with a certain twist and an original menu where club sandwiches rub shoulders with tournedos Rossini (sautéed tournedos garnished with foie gras and truffles).

Tante Louise

Traditional ⅩⅩ

[A/C]
[VISA]

41 r. Boissy-d'Anglas   Ⓜ Madeleine
⊠ 75008   **D2**
℘ 0142650685 – **Fax** 0142652819
e-mail tantelouise@bernard-loiseau.com
Web www.bernard-loiseau.com
closed August, Saturday, Sunday and public holidays

Menu €34 (lunch)/€65 – Carte €47/66

Tante Louise – part of the Bernard Loiseau group – owes its name to Louise Blanche Lefeuvre, the Parisian "Mama" who founded this restaurant in 1929. The pretty Art Deco façade is a fitting invitation to take a seat in the 1930s dining room with its carefully preserved, rather plush decor. Or you might prefer to sit in the comfortable mezzanine with its warm pale wood panelling and large clock. In either case, the food is traditional and faithful to the principles of the master of Saulieu – simple, good and of course influenced by his native Burgundy, like the wine list elaborated by a sommelier who works at the famous Relais.

Les Saveurs de Flora

Contemporary ⅩⅩ

[A/C]
[VISA]

36 av. George V   Ⓜ George V
⊠ 75008   **A3**
℘ 0140701049 – **Fax** 0147205287
Web www.lessaveursdeflora.com
Closed August, February half-term holidays, Saturday lunch and Sunday

Menu €36 – Carte €56/88

Flora's flavours? They are brimming with originality and come from all over the world. Inspired by her travels, the proprietress reinvents traditional French and foreign recipes, making them more modern and "exotic". A dash of spice here and some herbs there, a sweet-and-savoury mixture or a blend of unexpected textures – and there's your new dish! This artist-chef's creative style is also evident in the decor of the three chic dining rooms (and a small lounge) designed with Dorothée Boissier, a disciple of Starck. With its naive wallpaper, Venetian mirror wall lamps, *fauteuils à médaillon* reupholstered in leather, climbing flowers, and paste butterflies, this is a charming place with a very personal touch.

Champs-Élysées, Concorde, Madeleine

Chez Catherine

Traditional 🍴🍴

A/C	3 r. Berryer
VISA	✉ 75008
MC	✆ 0140760140 – **Fax** 0140760396
AE	Closed 28 July-21 August, Saturday, Sunday and public holidays
①	
🍷	

Ⓜ George V
B2

Menu €48 (lunch)/€74

Two olive trees and a pretty white façade tell you that you have arrived Chez Catherine. But don't bother looking for her when you walk in. She's in the kitchen, busy cooking up one of her specialities (*petits farcis niçois, pressé de foie gras* with crab, duck breast with spices) or creating her "surprise menu". To try it out, have a seat in one of the two dining rooms (the smoking area has a glass partition and view of the kitchen). The pleasant, chic and modern setting has pearl grey walls, contemporary paintings and velvet armchairs. Lastly, allow yourself to be guided by the sommelier, who will recommend a bottle from among the fine selection of French wines in the cellar.

1728

Contemporary 🍴🍴

A/C	8 r. d'Anjou
VISA	✉ 75008
MC	✆ 0140170477 – **Fax** 0142655387
AE	**e-mail** restaurant1728@wanadoo.fr **Web** www.restaurant-1728.com
🍷	Closed 1st-15 August, Saturday lunch, Sunday and public holidays

Ⓜ Madeleine
D2

Carte €50/129

This townhouse is well worth a visit for the decor full of history. Built in 1728 by Antoine Mazin, it was the home of La Fayette from 1827 until his death. The sumptuous salons still have their period wood panelling and furniture, as well as the original wall hangings and paintings. Nothing seems to have changed, and the scrupulous restoration work has put all the charm and sparkle back into this unique and superb place. The food has zoomed into the 21C with a creative chef updating recipes from five continents, using aromatic plants and spices. You'll find some very fine bottles in the carefully composed wine list.

La Table d'Hédiard

Traditional ХХ

A/C

VISA

МС

AE

D

Y

21 pl. Madeleine   **Ⓜ** Madeleine
✉ 75008   **D2**
✆ 0143128899 – **Fax** 0143128898
e-mail latablehediard@hediard.fr **Web** www.hediard.fr
closed August and Sunday

Carte €47/69

Feeling a bit peckish after roaming the appetizing aisles of this famous luxury food store? Try the restaurant upstairs, formerly the *Comptoir des Épices et des Colonies*. Its colonial decor (design furniture and leather armchairs) lends itself perfectly to the culinary "safari" offered on the menu. A talented blend of local flavours and faraway fragrances, it is based on the daily market and, naturally, on the exotic ingredients selected by Hédiard. The friendly and professional staff makes sure that your journey is perfect in every way. This is a really enjoyable way to explore the establishment's "stars".

Le Sarladais

South-West of France ХХ

A/C

VISA

МС

AE

D

Y

2 r. Vienne   **Ⓜ** St-Augustin
✉ 75008   **D2**
✆ 0145222362 – **Fax** 0145222362
Web www.lesarladais.com
Closed 28 April-8 May, August, 24-31 December, Saturday except dinner from 22 September to 31 April, Sunday and public holidays

Menu €29 (dinner)/€54 – Carte €47/117

The robust and nourishing food here will satisfy any appetite and all cravings for foie gras and preserved *gésiers* (gizzards). Fans of Périgord specialities are fully aware that southwestern cooking is featured at this restaurant located between Saint-Augustin Church and Saint-Lazare Station. Seafood dishes are also on the menu, including sole (grilled or *meunière*), pike-perch steak grilled with thyme flowers, and market favourites depending on the catch of the day. The fine ingredients arrive straight from Carantec (Brittany). The decor is simple, with warm tones, wood panelling, floral compositions and paintings (for sale).

Champs-Élysées, Concorde, Madeleine

Fermette Marbeuf 1900

Traditional

A/C
VISA
MC
AE
DC
Y

5 r. Marbeuf
✉ 75008
☎ 0153230800 – **Fax** 0153230809
e-mail fermettemarbeuf@blanc.net
Web www.fermettemarbeuf.com

Ⓜ Alma Marceau
B3

Menu €25 (weekday lunch)/€30 – Carte €31/65

And to think that this exceptional establishment – an extraordinary Art Nouveau dining room (1898) evoking a winter garden with its cast-iron armature, superb stained glass and ceramics – might have sunk into oblivion! Discovered by accident during renovations, this work by architect Emile Hurté and painter Wielhorski has been admired by people from all over the world. Don't forget to ask for a table in the main room, even if the other rooms are also lovely. The excellent dishes prove that the decor is not the only reason to come here, and the classic, seasonal cuisine gets it just right. The faithful staff – the chef has been here since 1979! – and the discreet and friendly service are two more serious assets.

Marius et Janette

Seafood

4 av. George V
✉ 75008
☎ 0147234188 – **Fax** 0147230719

Ⓜ Alma Marceau
A-B3

Menu €46 (lunch)/€48 – Carte €60/140

Could the name refer to l'Estaque and Robert Guédiguian's films? It looks more like Saint-Tropez, to judge from the decor in the dining room evoking a yacht, and by the select clientele seated amongst the fishing poles, nets, plastic swordfish on the walls and brass portholes. As soon as the sun comes out, the decor changes altogether, and it's time to show off trendy sunglasses and suntans on the terrace on the Avenue Georges V. The cuisine also has a maritime bent, with a short menu featuring fish and shellfish dishes.

Stella Maris

Contemporary ✗✗

4 r. Arsène Houssaye
✉ 75008
☏ 0142891622 – **Fax** 0142891601
e-mail stella.maris.paris@wanadoo.fr **Web** www.stellamaris.com

Closed 10-20 August, Saturday lunch, Sunday and lunch on public holidays

Menu €43 (lunch)/€130 – Carte €100/140

Ⓜ Charles de Gaulle-Etoile
A2

Stella Maris

He is named Tateru Yoshino. But don't come here looking for food typical of the "land of the rising sun". As a chef who came to France in 1979 to train at Benoît, l'Archestrate and Robuchon, his orientation is clear: to make pure French cuisine. He did just that in the nineties in Tokyo, and customers at his three restaurants in his native country are still enjoying fine meals there today.

When Tateru Yoshino took over here, renovating the establishment in 2004 while preserving its Art Deco spirit, he gave it the same name as his restaurant in Odawara, in Japan. "I'll open a different restaurant if I decide to make Japanese food one day", he states quite clearly.

A LA CARTE

FIRST COURSE	MAIN COURSE	DESSERT
• Fondant de foie gras de canard et carotte (March to September). • Cervelas de homard breton, cuisses de grenouille, persil en émulsion.	• Saumon mi-cuit à l'émulsion de citron confit. • Tourte de pigeon (autumn).	• Kouign Amann façon Penthièvre, sorbet à l'ananas, sauce pomme verte. • Brochette de mini baba au rhum, crème vanille de Madagascar, fruits exotiques.

199

Sens par la Compagnie des Comptoirs

Contemporary ⅩⅩ

A/C
VISA
MC
AE

23 r. de Ponthieu ⓂFranklin D. Roosevelt
✉ 75008 **B2**
✆ 01 42 25 95 00 – **Fax** 01 42 25 95 02
e-mail resacdcparis@wanadoo.fr
Web www.lacompagniedescomptoirs.com
closed 1st-21 August, Saturday lunch and Sunday

Menu €45 (weekday lunch)/€90 wine included – Carte €44/74

Shades of grey set the tone in this second Parisian restaurant belonging to the Pourcel Brothers, with its "lounge" atmosphere clearly designed by their favourite architect, Imaad Rahmouni. It is contemporary, discreet and refined, with comfortable banquettes, Louis XVI chairs, little red lamps and a giant screen where films are projected. It is truly a delight to feel the spring sun flooding into the dining room through the glass roof, and to enjoy the sunny southern flavours permeating all the recipes prepared by the famous twins year round. The cheerful and professional waiters are an additional bonus!

Ginger

Thai ⅩⅩ

VISA
MC
AE

11 r. de la Trémoille Ⓜ Alma Marceau
✉ 75008 **B3**
✆ 01 47 23 37 32 – **Fax** 01 47 23 00 26

Carte €31/52

Here is an Asian restaurant whose name alone adds a dash of spice to the world of 8th arrondissement establishments! This is a fashionable place which doesn't take the easy route. The chef prepares fine Southeast Asian food (from Laos, Cambodia, Vietnam, etc.), making clever use of spices and exotic flavours. The enthic-inspired dining room has a zen atmosphere which is restful and unpretentious. And the little extra touch? The extremely kind and attentive waiters – a quality highly appreciated here in the heart of the ultra-chic Golden Triangle!

Ratn

Indian ✗✗

VISA

MC

AE

9 r. de la Trémoille
⊠ 75008
✆ 0140700109 – **Fax** 0140700122

Ⓜ Alma Marceau
B3

Menu € 39 – Carte € 39/48

Ratn has all the ingredients of a good Indian restaurant, starting with a "real" name – it means "jewel" – from the land of the Maharajas. The finely worked wood façade is like an invitation to embark on a journey. The interior is pleasantly understated and chic with its golden fabrics on the walls, velvet banquettes, sculpted wood panelling, statue of Shiva and hanging lamps. Another sign of authenticity is the Indian chef-proprietor's inexhaustible knowledge of the country and its gastronomy. His tasty dishes have just the right dose of spices. The service is very friendly.

Le Stresa

Italian ✗✗

A/C

VISA

MC

AE

①

⊉

7 r. Chambiges
⊠ 75008
✆ 0147235162

Ⓜ Alma Marceau
B3

closed 1st-8 May, August, 20 December-3 January, Saturday and Sunday – pre-book

Carte € 56/105

This tiny, chic trattoria is a favourite hangout of French and international "beautiful people", and both Alain Delon and Jean-Paul Belmondo are said to be regulars at Le Stresa; so the average mortal will have to book way in advance to get a table at this place run by the Faiola Brothers. Antonio is the one who welcomes diners into this timeless decor with paintings by Buffet and sculptures by César. The kitchen is Marco's domain, where he pampers demanding gourmet diners with his no-fuss Italian dishes prepared "just like at home" with generous portions and only the best ingredients. The prices are typically Parisian.

Champs-Élysées, Concorde, Madeleine

Bistrot du Sommelier

Contemporary ✕✕

A/C
🚻
VISA
💳

97 bd Haussmann
✉ 75008
☎ 01 42 65 24 85 – **Fax** 01 53 75 23 23
e-mail bistrot-du-sommelier@noos.fr
Web www.bistrotdusommelier.com

closed 28 July-26 August, 22 December-1st January, Saturday and Sunday

Ⓜ St-Augustin
C2

Menu € 39 (lunch)/€ 100 wine included – Carte € 46/68

It could also be called the Bistrot with the World's Best Sommelier, 1992 vintage, the title awarded at this prestigious contest's seventh ceremony to Philippe Faure-Brac, who has run this restaurant for the past 20 years. It is a true pleasure to taste the wine and food pairings invented by the sommelier and his chef partner, Jean-André Lallican, in the comfortable dining room and decor entirely devoted to Bacchus, with a convivial atmosphere and superb cellar with a host of labels. Winemakers' Fridays (*vendredis du vigneron*) are the latest concept, where proprietors present their estates and wines at thematic wine tasting-meals, an approach which is both gastronomic and educational.

Rue Balzac

Contemporary ✕✕

A/C
🚻
VISA
💳

8 r. Lord Byron
✉ 75008
☎ 01 53 89 90 91 – **Fax** 01 53 89 90 94
e-mail ruebalzac@wanadoo.fr

closed 1st-20 August, Saturday lunch and Sunday lunch

Ⓜ George V
A2

Carte € 32/88

Rue Balzac was created by a line-up of stars including Johnny and Laëticia Hallyday, Claude Bouillon and chef Michel Rostang. The six-bistro chef hired one of his students, Yann Roncier, to run the kitchen, and he does it with originality. Presented by theme and size of ingredients (small or large), the menu features their favourite recipes – thin pasta with green olives and Parmesan for Johnny, langoustines for Laëticia – and their associate's creations such as beef tartare. These "star acts" are often embellished with new, carefully prepared and up-to-date inventions. The huge dining room looks like a stylish contemporary apartment with a touch of the Baroque.

L'Angle du Faubourg ✿

Classic ✕✕

A/C	195 r. Fg St-Honoré
VISA	✉ 75008
ⓂⓄ	✆ 01 40 74 20 20 – **Fax** 01 40 74 20 21
AE	**e-mail** angledufaubourg@cavestaillevent.com
Ⓓ	**Web** www.angledufaubourg.com

Ⓜ **Ternes**
B2

Closed 28 July-27 August, Saturday, Sunday and public holidays

Menu €35/€70 (dinner) – Carte €45/71

L'Angle du Faubourg

According to owner Jean-Claude Vrinat, the idea of opening a new restaurant on the corner of rue du faubourg St-Honoré and rue Balzac was obvious to him. That might be because this food-lover's restaurant is located near the mythical Taillevent, for which it is a sort of annexe. But it is also – and perhaps especially – because it is next to the famous Caves Taillevent, an invitation to an interesting visit and possibly to tasting of some of the fine wines.

The setting is discreet and elegant, and the service is friendly and attentive. The cuisine is refined, classic but in keeping with the times, with no unnecessary complications. It features irreproachable produce and a fine selection of wines (by the bottle or glass). That about sums up this contemporary bistro with reasonable prices – a considerable asset when trying to bring in regular customers in this area.

A LA CARTE

FIRST COURSE	MAIN COURSE	DESSERT
• Etrilles farcies en gelée.	• Foie de canard poêlé au banyuls.	• Macaron aux fruits de saison.
• Langoustines rôties, barigoule d'artichauts à l'orange.	• Côte de veau en cocotte, jus à l'échalote confite.	• Coulant au chocolat, crème glacée au thym-citron.

Champs-Élysées, Concorde, Madeleine

Market

Fusion ☒☒

A/C **15 av. Matignon**   Ⓜ Franklin D. Roosevelt
VISA ✉ **75008**   **C2**
   ✆ 0156434090 – **Fax** 0143591087
ⓂⒸ **e-mail** prmarketsa@aol.com **Web** www.jeangeorges.com
AE **Menu** €43 (lunch)/€85 – **Carte** €48/82
♈

In 2002, Jean-Georges Vongerichten - that "most Alsatian of New Yorkers" - returned to his native country to open a restaurant in Paris. With his associates Luc Besson and François Pinault, he adapted his winning formula to French tastes. The result is this chic bistro with a discreetly contemporary decor designed by Christian Liaigre (raw materials, grey, beige and white tones, African masks). A friendly young staff presides over the two dining rooms, including one that is non-smoking and gives onto a courtyard. The menu, cooked up by the young Wim Van Gorp, blends French, Italian and Asian influences: pizza with black truffles, crab salad with mango, etc.

Maxan

Contemporary ☒☒

A/C **37 r. Miromesnil**   Ⓜ Miromesnil
   ✆ 0142657860 – **Fax** 0149249617   **C2**
VISA **Web** www.rest-maxan.com
   closed 6-21 August, Monday dinner, Saturday lunch and Sunday
ⓂⒸ **Menu** €38/€45 (dinner) – **Carte** €39/68
AE
♈

Where did the name of this discreet establishment on the rue de Miromesnil come from? It is simply a contraction of Maxime and Andrea, the children of Laurent Zajac, who is the chef – and "Daddy" – at this restaurant. The understated and original decor designed by Pierre Pozzi features white and striped technicolor walls, wood panelling and sensible bistro furniture. The same creative simplicity characterises the food. The menu features up-to-date flavours and carefully chosen seasonal ingredients with a classical base. The tasting menu is a good choice if you are feeling indecisive.

Village d'Ung et Li Lam

Thai ✗✗

A/C

VISA

10 r. J. Mermoz
✉ 75008
☎ 0142259979 – **Fax** 0142251206
closed Saturday lunchtime and Sunday lunchtime

🄼 Franklin D. Roosevelt
C2

Menu €35 – Carte €25/40

Ung and Li Lam will give you a warm welcome at their Asian
"Village" a stone's throw from the Champs-Élysées. As you walk
in, have a look at what you're treading on – a molten glass floor
inlaid with grains of sand and pottery shards. Then lift your gaze
to see the aquariums – hanging from the ceiling! You can also
see the live action in the kitchen, through a picture window. So
much for the decor. Now you can focus on the menu, featuring
the great classics of Chinese and Thai cuisine prepared exactly
as they should be, including an assortment of ravioli, caramel
spare ribs, beef sautéed in basil, and a host of other indispensable and flavoursome recipes! It is simple, good and entertaining, and the place is often booked up.

Al Ajami

Lebanese ✗✗

58 r. François 1st
✉ 75008
☎ 0142253844 – **Fax** 0142253839
e-mail ajami@free.fr **Web** www.ajami.com

🄼 George V
B2

Menu €24 (weekdays)/€41 – Carte €29/52

Tourists from the Middle East, Parisians of Lebanese origin and
businessmen from the city make up the clientele of this restaurant on the corner of rue François 1er and rue Lincoln. This
ambassador of traditional Lebanese cuisine is a Parisian offshoot
of an establishment created in Beirut in the 1920s, with branches
around the world. The decor is also inspired by the Land of
Cedars, with its Middle Eastern objects, vases, watercolours,
wood panelling, purple-and-gold striped wallpaper, comfortable
sofas, soft cushions and background music. Professional service
and family hospitality. Try the tasting menu with its assortment
of fragrant and flavoursome dishes.

Champs-Élysées, Concorde, Madeleine

Dominique Bouchet ✿

Traditional ✗

A/C **11 r. Treilhard**
✉ **75008**
📞 0145610946 – **Fax** 0142891114
MC **e-mail** dominiquebouchet@yahoo.fr
Web www.dominique-bouchet.com
AE closed August, February school holidays, Saturday, Sunday and public holidays

Ⓜ **Miromesnil**
C1

🍷 **Menu €90 – Carte €55/87**

Dominique Bouchet

After spending time in Japan, Dominique Bouchet made his comeback in the capital (on 6 December 2004) between Parc Monceau and Saint-Augustin. The prestigious Parisian restaurants in his star-studded CV include Jamin, La Tour d'Argent, and the Crillon. He is back in his own place now, in a small, lengthwise restaurant where you can watch the chef cooking in the kitchen. The peaceful, light and elegant space is simple and intimate, with pale stone walls highlighted by contemporary paintings. The small but well-designed menu changes according to the market and the chef's fancy. But don't expect unbridled fantasy or fusion; the repertoire is classical and perfectly mastered. The result is lively and titillating cuisine full of flavour. The fine selection of wines available by the glass is another plus.

A LA CARTE

FIRST COURSE
• Escargots petits gris, tarte aux olives.
• Foie gras de canard mariné au saké.

MAIN COURSE
• Gigot d'agneau de sept heures à la cuillère.
• Encornets poêlés, picadillos et chorizo.

DESSERT
• Sablé aux pommes, crème brûlée à la vanille bourbon, glace au lait d'amande douce.
• Eclair au chocolat, ganache sao-tomé, cerises noires et glace.

Bistro de l'Olivier

Mediterranean X

A|C
VISA
MC
AE
O
♀

13 r. Quentin Bauchart — **M** George V

✉ 75008 — **A3**

✆ 0147207863 – **Fax** 0147207458

closed August, Saturday lunch and Sunday – number of covers limited, pre-book

Menu €34 – Carte €65/75

Time flies at this warm bistro near the Champs-Élysées; and the bill is remarkably merciful given its location and quality. Naturally, the clientele from the neighbourhood know a good thing when they see it, so they have become regulars. What is the secret of this "eldorado"? Sun, sun, and more sun - in the colourful decor (walls in yellow tones, red banquettes, and regionalist paintings) and in the cuisine carefully prepared by chef Aurélien Marion. The menu changes frequently, featuring meticulously selected fresh ingredients in precise and tasty dishes with a Provençal flavour. This is the place to go when you need an antidote to grey Parisian skies!

Chez Cécile
la Ferme des Mathurins

Traditional X

VISA
MC
AE
♀

17 r. Vignon — **M** Madeleine

✉ 75008 — **D2**

✆ 0142664639

e-mail cecile@chezcecile.com **Web** www.chezcecile.com

closed August and Sunday

Menu €33 (lunch)/€36

It always feels great to be at this Madeleine area institution - but why exactly? Is it the friendly ambiance that reigns within these venerable walls? Or is it the good humour of the faithful clientele? Probably a bit of both. And this old-fashioned bistro – where Georges Simenon was a regular – hasn't lost any of its charm, with its traditional banquettes, snug tables and counter top with table settings for smokers. The new management has gone all out in the kitchen, with copious and well-prepared dishes (traditional seasonal and market-based cuisine) delivered to the table by the expert hands of the friendly and enthusiastic waiters. Jazz evenings on Thursdays. In short, don't forget to book!

207

Champs-Élysées, Concorde, Madeleine

Le Cou de la Girafe

Contemporary X

A/C

VISA

MC

AE

DC

☂

7 r. Paul Baudry
✉ 75008
☎ 0156882955 – **Fax** 0142252882
e-mail contact@coudelagirafe.com

closed 1st-20 August and Sunday

Ⓜ St-Philippe du Roule
B2

Menu €30 (lunch) – Carte €35/57

A trendy bistro? It does have all the necessary ingredients - a privileged location near the Champs-Élysées, contemporary decor designed by the highly sought-after Pierre-Yves Rochon (wood and shades of yellow and chocolate), hushed atmosphere and a clientele of regulars and businessmen at lunchtime. The cuisine is riding on the wave of current tastes, of course. But it pulls it off well - due to the talented chef who is a master of his art. The menu also features some fine fish recipes and *canaille* dishes. As a result, this establishment stands out from a good many other fashionable places. The little pavement terrace is enjoyable in summer.

Café Lenôtre-Pavillon Elysée

Brasserie X

🛜

A/C

⟐

P

VISA

MC

AE

DC

☂

10 av. Champs-Elysées
✉ 75008
☎ 0142658510 – **Fax** 0142657623
Web www.lenotre.fr

closed 1st-20 August, 1st-7 February, Monday dinner from November to February and Sunday dinner

Ⓜ Champs-Elysées Clémenceau
C3

Carte €42/65

The Pavillon Élysées is a kind of showcase for the famous Parisian caterer, with a shop, cooking school and restaurant. This mecca for food-lovers found the perfect setting – a magnificent and superbly restored Napoleon III pavilion, originally built for the 1900 World's Fair. The decidedly contemporary Café Lenôtre looks onto a very popular terrace, from which you can see the busiest avenue in the city. The appetizing menu features dishes with an international theme (Paris Oslo, Paris Cannes, Paris Bangkok), "Pasta Inventions", and updated traditional dishes. A most enjoyable place!

Cap Vernet

Seafood 🍴

[A/C]
[VISA]
[MC]
[AE]
[DC]
🍷

82 av. Marceau
✉ 75008
📞 0147202040 – **Fax** 0147209536
closed Saturday lunch and Sunday

🚇 Charles de Gaulle-Etoile
A2

Carte €45/61

If you feel like taking in the air of the seaside, head for Cap Vernet, an elegant and well-designed "ship" facing the Arc de Triomphe. Gangways, ship's rails and little tables in exotic wood give it an ocean liner look, while the taupe and plum colours, velvet armchairs and soft lighting create a hushed and intimate ambiance. So much for the decor; now the gastronomic cruise can begin. The menu features fish and shellfish. All the flavours and freshness of these meticulously chosen ingredients come out in the simple and refined recipes such as the tasty sole *petit bateau* cooked *à la plancha*.

L'Appart'

Traditional 🍴

[A/C]
[VISA]
[MC]
[AE]
🍷

9 r. Colisée
✉ 75008
📞 0153754200 – **Fax** 0153754209
e-mail de.appart@blanc.net **Web** www.lappart.com
closed Saturday lunch and Sunday in August

🚇 Franklin D. Roosevelt
B2

Menu €23 (lunch)/€30 (dinner) – Carte €29/57

With its sitting room, dining room, library and open kitchen, this restaurant has reproduced the rooms of a large and comfortable apartment on several floors. The cosy and original concept has developed a following – among businessmen at lunch, and hip young jet setters for dinner – thanks to its up-to-date cuisine inspired by the *terroir* and flavours of the South. The Sunday brunch menu is very popular. While parents enjoy their coffee, Mariage Frères tea, *viennoiseries* (pastries) and pancakes with maple syrup, younger gastronomes get a taste at the "Atelier des enfants" (Children's Corner), where they make cakes, cookies and lots of sweets to take home to their real apartment!

Champs-Élysées, Concorde, Madeleine

209

Toi

Contemporary ✗

A/C   27 r. Colisée   🖂 Franklin D. Roosevelt
VISA   ✉ 75008   **B2**

27 r. Colisée
✉ 75008
☎ 0142565658 – **Fax** 0142560960
e-mail restaurant.toi@wanadoo.fr **Web** www.restaurant-toi.com

Carte € 28/74

The 70s decor, contemporary lines and pop colours (red and orange) blend together well in this very "in" restaurant conceived by the designer Cherif. The hip, chic and original setting (with three levels: a ground floor, lounge bar, and mezzanine) is in tune with the truly inventive cuisine. The chef, who trained at several top establishments (Ritz, Crillon) comes up with some daring – and successful – combinations such as Cupid tomatoes and mozzarella brochettes, pan-fried gambas flambéed in pastis with quinoa, and fresh pistachio and raspberry macaroons with apricot sorbet. Diners in search of trendy spots will enjoy it here, and the fixed-price dinner menu is very reasonable. Buffet brunch on Sundays.

Devez

Terroir ✗

5 pl. de l'Alma   🖂 Alma Marceau
✉ 75008   **A3**
☎ 0153679753 – **Fax** 0147230948
e-mail contact@devezparis.com **Web** www.devezparis.com

Carte € 34/65

Devèses are large pastures found over the basaltic terrain of the Aubrac region – the pride and joy of stockbreeders in the Aveyron, like Christian Valette, who loves his native region and came to Paris to "sing its praises". This is his second establishment celebrating the famous breed of Aubrac beef. To give it the greatest chance of pleasing his diners, the chef cooks it different ways – simmered, roasted, *à la plancha* – and even serves as an appetizer ("gourmet tapas"). The decor is warm and up-to-date (wood everywhere and clean lines), and there is a heated terrace. Entirely non-smoking.

L'Atelier des Compères

Terroir ✗

VISA
⓿©
AE
♀

56 r. Galilée
☒ 75008
✆ 0147207556
e-mail contact@atelierdescomperes.com
Web www.atelierdescomperes.com

Ⓜ George V
A2

Closed August, 24 December-2 January, Saturday, Sunday and public holidays – number of covers limited, pre-book

Menu €33 (lunch)/€55

These talented fellows have set up their establishment in a cobblestone courtyard! With its up-to-date furniture and nicely set tables, barely covered by a large tarpaulin, it feels like walking into a chic *guinguette*! It is well-heated in winter, thus unaffected by inclement weather; and at the first sign of sunshine, the top comes off. Jacques Boudin and Eric Sertour were especially intent on making this little corner of paradise in the heart of Paris a generous and convivial place. To whet your appetite, the market-based dishes on the blackboard – changed daily – include roasted guinea fowl with cabbage, medallion of veal with morel mushrooms, and pineapple and pear crumble. This place has been packed ever since it opened.

La Maison de L'Aubrac

Terroir ✗

VISA
⓿©
AE
♀

37 r. Marbeuf
☒ 75008
✆ 0143590514 – **Fax** 0142252987

Ⓜ Franklin D. Roosevelt
B3

Menu €40/€55 – Carte €35/56

The name, La Maison de l'Aubrac, is very fitting. Christian Valette – a restaurateur who breeds cattle in Laguiole and loves his *terroir* – has made it a showcase for the Aubrac region. The rustic interior emulates that of a farm in the Aveyron, while the highly convivial atmosphere is sometimes a bit over-excited (understandable given the proximity of the Champs-Élysées). Beef – from Aubrac, naturally! – is featured in recipes from Aveyron, Lozère and Cantal. The straightforward and well-prepared dishes are accompanied by a very fine choice of wines (in particular the old vintages). And it is open 24 hours a day, 7 days a week. Fancy a rib of beef after an evening of clubbing?

Champs-Élysées, Concorde, Madeleine

Bocconi

Italian 🍴

10bis r. Artois
✉ 75008
☎ 01 53 76 44 44 – **Fax** 01 45 61 10 08
e-mail bocconi@wanadoo.fr

closed Saturday lunchtime and Sunday

Ⓜ St-Philippe du Roule
B2

Carte € 37/73

This is one of a group of chic and trendy trattorias in Paris. Bonuses include its unique location just behind the shopping galleries on the "most beautiful avenue in the world" and its really pleasant pavement terrace in summer. The decor is discreetly contemporary (yellow and reds tones, banquettes and cushions) and the typically Italian cuisine features fresh home-made pasta and other classics from across the Alps. Shared starters, which you can sample if there are several people in your party, are an original touch. A fun Italian jaunt!

Le Boucoléon

Traditional 🍴

10 r. Constantinople
✉ 75008
☎ 01 42 93 73 33 – **Fax** 01 42 93 95 44

Closed 12-26 August, Saturday lunch, Sunday and public holidays – number of covers limited, pre-book

Ⓜ Europe
C-D1

Carte € 34/43

All the charm of the Southwest seems to have been "contained" within this friendly neighbourhood establishment. Bright colours such as ocean blue - on the façade and in the paintings - light up the dark up-to-date setting (exposed stonework, immaculate walls, bistro floors and furniture) into which Richard Castellan welcomes you. A few souvenirs and posters are devoted to the sacrosanct rugby ball – the owner is an ardent fan! The warm ambiance is perfectly paired with the generous and delicious food made with ingredients from the Basque country; the menu changes every two months. *Dagizula* (bon appétit)!

Le Bistrot de Marius

Seafood

6 av. George V
✉ 75008
☎ 0140701176 – **Fax** 0140701708

Ⓜ Alma Marceau
B3

Carte € 35/65

If, when in Paris, you can't have a game of *pétanque* (bowls), a glass of *pastis* under the southern sun or a bouillabaisse on a lively quayside, then head for this bistro – just like the ones on the old port of Marseille! Sitting at your snug table in the dining room decorated in Provençal colours, the "Bonne Mère" (basilica of Notre Dame de la Garde) won't seem so far away as you sample the excellent market cuisine featuring seafood dishes. Particularly since the prices seem to have remained closer to Marseille than to Paris. This is an authentic and convivial place with no frills. Booking advised!

Daru

Russian ✗

19 r. Daru
✉ 75008
☎ 0142272360 – **Fax** 0147540814
e-mail restaurant.daru@orange.fr **Web** www.daru.fr

Ⓜ Courcelles
B1

closed August and Sunday

Menu € 34 (lunch) – Carte € 45/70

This is the first Russian grocer's – created by one of Nicolas II's officers in 1918 – and oldest Russian restaurant in the city. The red-and-black decor bursting with warmth and conviviality will take you right back you to old Russia, with its casks, bottles of rare vodka, portraits of the Czars, precious paintings and materials, dark wood panelling, and dolls. Traditions are still strong here, where they treat guests to *zakouskis* (*tarama* for two, sea urchins, smoked salmon, marinated herring, etc.), caviar and the quintessential beef Stroganoff with paprika and potato blinis. Enjoy the balalaika music in the background while sipping your vodka.

Cô Ba Saigon

Vietnamese ♈

A/C   181 r. Fg St-Honoré   **Ⓜ** Charles de Gaulle-Etoile
✉ 75008   **B2**
VISA   ☎ 0145637037 – **Fax** 0145637037
Ⓜ©   **e-mail** khanguyen@cobasaigon.fr **Web** www.cobasaigon.com
AE   closed 1st-19 August and Sunday
♈   **Menu** €29 (dinner) – **Carte** €27/39

This is the kind of place you keep coming back to for the refined and carefully prepared Vietnamese cuisine (prices are very reasonable too). Come for dinner, when the menu and dishes are more elaborate, to enjoy the fragrant soups, salads, grilled food and other specialities. The table settings are smarter in the evening too. At lunchtime they serve simpler, more traditional dishes. There are knick-knacks and paintings from back home to add that exotic touch, an extremely welcoming proprietress, and a fine range of teas. The beautiful Cô Ba – whose face graced a stamp in colonial Indochina – would have no reason to blush at this restaurant named after her.

Shin Jung

Korean ♈

A/C   7 r. Clapeyron   **Ⓜ** Rome
✉ 75008   **D1**
VISA   ☎ 0145222106 – **Fax** 0142941096
Ⓜ©   closed Sunday lunchtime and lunchtime public holidays
♈   **Menu** €28 (dinner)/€36 (dinner) – **Carte** €20/38

Regulars at this friendly family establishment come here for the really fine and authentic Korean cooking. The dishes are often less well-known than those from neighbouring Asian countries, although equally appetizing. Raw fish and barbecue dishes are often the specialities, somewhere in-between traditional Chinese and Japanese recipes. The *bibimbap*, another Korean speciality, is delicious here. The calligraphy drawings on the walls, highly discreet decor with a "zen" ambiance, fast and unfussy service guarantee an authentic experience.

Opéra, Grands Boulevards

Richer X/MICHELIN

Opéra, the Grands Boulevards, Saint-Lazare form a triangle. The 9th is central, busy, commercial and larger than the tiny riverside arrondissements, but it is also denser, more dynamic and smaller than the arrondissements closer to the ring road. It is a concentrate of Paris and symbolises the movement and variety that endow the capital with its distinctive character. Wedged between place Pigalle, boulevard des Italiens and the rue d'Amsterdam and rue du Faubourg Poissonnière, it has a little of everything and lacks nothing: one of the largest railway stations in France (Saint-Lazare), an international calibre opera house, several outstanding churches and more department stores than one could ever hope to raid in an entire lifetime... .

A BIT OF HISTORY...

The Opéra district was born out of Napoleon III's desire to leave his imprint on Paris: the new avenues that were to be built and would soon be qualified as "Haussmannian" needed a focal point, an architectural and aesthetic construction that would draw the eye. Designed by Garnier, the Opéra de Paris is now the "Palace of Dance" but has retained all its original splendour and decor including an abundance of marble and stucco work and a profusion of grandiose frescoes and gilt-trimmed facades that create a somewhat extravagant picture. Yet despite its luxury and massive outline, the edifice continues to inspire a certain lightness. The immediate vicinity was built in the same style despite an impressive number

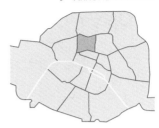

of banks, whose headquarters are fully capable of holding their own next to the imperial constructions. At lunchtimes, the district is awash with employees and businessmen in a hurry, mingling with the crowds of tourists in a joyful pandemonium, which is also probably the reason for the high density of restaurants and pubs, particularly around Havre-Caumartin, serving lunchtime specials and offering happy hours to appeal to this wide ranging clientele.

From
THE GOLDEN ERA TO THE GOUTTE D'OR

The Grands Boulevards – Italiens, Haussmann and Poissonnière – were initially designed to decongest Paris but soon

Sauvignier S./MICHELIN

became well-known districts devoted to entertainment and pleasure. Popular with walkers right from the start, they were quickly engulfed with cafés, theatres, shops and restaurants. Today the area is home to all the leading high-street chain stores, temples of fashion and consumerism, in addition to a number of cinemas beloved by Parisians such as the Grand Rex

and the Max Linder which continue to uphold French cinema loving traditions. All around the brasseries and cafés overflow with customers to such a point that the area sometimes resembles an anthill. It is however not difficult to find a little peace and quiet by heading north along one of the streets that lead to Pigalle. The steeple of the church of La Trinité, characteristic of the second Empire, dominates the surrounding, quieter and more residential streets.

Further east, rue des Martyrs will thrust you into the joyful and effusive atmosphere near Montmartre whose sun-drenched markets, food shops of every possible type and unlikely bars are already a foretaste of the north of Paris and the nearby Goutte d'Or district – so very different from the sumptuous luxury of the Emperor's court.

Sauvignier S./MICHELIN

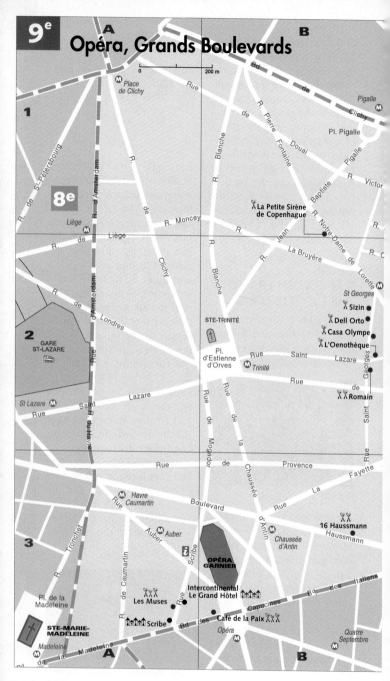

9e Opéra, Grands Boulevards

0 — 200 m

M Place de Clichy

Rue

Bd de

Pigalle **M** Clichy

8e

Pl. Pigalle

R. Pierre Fontaine

R. de Douai

R. Blanche

R. de St-Pétersbourg

R. d'Amsterdam

Liège **M**

de

R. Moncey

R. de Liège

R. Victor

Baptiste

R. Notre-Dame de

X **La Petite Sirène de Copenhague**

La Bruyère

R. Jean

Clichy

R. Blanche

de

Lorette

St Georges **M**

X **Sizin**

● **Dell Orto**

X **Casa Olympe** ●

X **L'Oenothèque**

STE-TRINITÉ

GARE ST-LAZARE

R. de Londres

Rue de Stuttgart

Rue Saint

Pl. d'Estienne d'Orves

M Trinité

Lazare

St Lazare **M**

Rue Saint Lazare

Rue

de

X X **Romain**

Rue Saint Georges

Rue de Mogador

Rue de la Chaussée

Rue de Provence

La Fayette

Rue de

Boulevard

Havre Caumartin **M**

Rue

de

X X **16 Haussmann** ●

Haussmann

d'Antin

Auber **M** Auber

Chaussée d'Antin

Rue de Caumartin

Scribe

OPÉRA GARNIER

Rue Tronchet

Pl. de la Madeleine

X X **Les Muses**

🏨 **Scribe**

Intercontinental Le Grand Hôtel 🏨

Bd des Capucines

Café de la Paix X X X

Opéra

Bd des Italiens

Quatre Septembre

STE-MARIE-MADELEINE

Madeleine

R. de la Madeleine

de

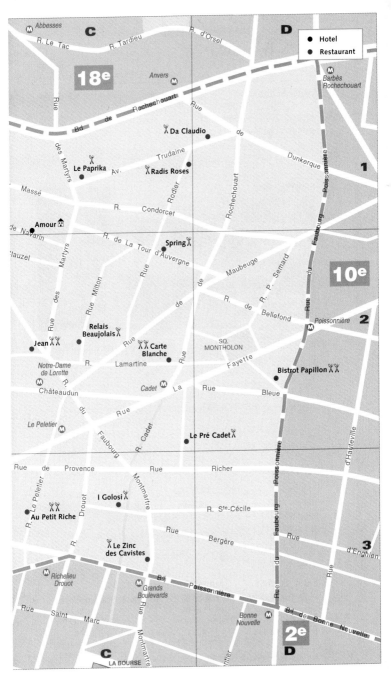

18e

C — Abbesses
R. Le Tac
R. Tardieu
R. d'Orsel
D

● Hotel
● Restaurant

Barbès
Rochechouart

Anvers

Bd de Rochechouart Rue de Dunkerque

1

✗ Da Claudio

de

Trudaine

✗ Le Paprika

Av. ✗ Radis Roses

des Martyrs

Massé

Rodier

Rochechouart

R. Condorcet

de Navarin

🏠 Amour

R. de La Tour d'Auvergne

Clauzel

✗ Spring

10e

Maubeuge

R. P. Semard

des

Rue Milton

Rue

de

R. de Bellefond

Rue du Faubourg Poissonnière

Poissonnière

2

Rue

✗✗ Jean

Relais Beaujolais ✗

✗✗ Carte Blanche

SQ. MONTHOLON

Bistrot Papillon ✗✗

Notre-Dame de Lorette

Rue

Lamartine

Fayette

Châteaudun

Cadet

La

Rue

Bleue

Le Peletier

du

Faubourg

Rue

R. Cadet

● Le Pré Cadet ✗

d'Hauteville

Rue de Provence

Rue

Richer

R. Le Peletier

Drouot

✗✗ I Golosi ✗

Montmartre

R. Ste-Cécile

● Au Petit Riche

Rue

Bergère

3

d'Enghien

R.

✗ Le Zinc des Cavistes

Bd Poissonnière

Rue du Faubourg Poissonnière

Rue

Richelieu Drouot

Grands Boulevards

Rue Saint Marc

Montmartre

Poissonnière

Bonne Nouvelle

Bd de Bonne Nouvelle

2e

C

D

LA BOURSE

9th ARRONDISSEMENT

Les Muses ❀

Contemporary ✗✗✗

   Hôtel Scribe,
   1 r. Scribe ✉ 75009
   ✆ 01 44 71 24 26 – **Fax** 01 44 71 24 64
   e-mail h0663-re@accor.com
   Closed August, Saturday, Sunday and public holidays

Ⓜ Opéra
A3

Menu €45 (lunch)/€95 – Carte €70/85

Les Muses

Don't be afraid of going down into the hotel basement, where the dining room tables are located. Calliope, the muse of eloquence, would undoubtedly recognise a kindred quality in the culinary art of Franck Charpentier. As the master chef at the "most Parisian of hotels" since early 2006, he has opted for a highly contemporary style of cooking, asserting his love of the land and unadulterated tastes. The chef readily explains that his "grandmother's leg of lamb" and Paul Bocuse's appearances on television are what triggered his desire to become a chef. Fond of very graphic displays of food, he focuses on creating refined dishes in a modern cooking style that happily blends elegance and technical virtuosity.

The restaurant menu states the origins of the produce (lamb from Lozère, veal from Corrèze, farm-raised pork from Brittany) and changes themes during different seasons (asparagus, morel mushrooms, etc.).

A LA CARTE

FIRST COURSE
· Foie gras de canard rôti.
· Homard breton et ravioli aux girolles.

MAIN COURSE
· Filet de bar de ligne poêlé au beurre demi-sel.
· Agneau de Lozère tout simplement rôti.

DESSERT
· Tomates confites au vin de Modena parfumé au thym frais, crème glacée minute.
· Croustillant de cerises, crème brûlée glacée pistache.

Café de la Paix

Traditional 🍴🍴🍴

Intercontinental Le Grand Hôtel,
12 bd Capucines ✉ 75009

🚇 **Opéra**
B3

☎ 0140073636 – **Fax** 0140073613

e-mail legrand.reservations@ichotelsgroup.com
Web www.paris.intercontinental.com

Menu €45 (lunch)/€85 – Carte €50/106

Surely it needs no introduction. The legendary brasserie of the Grand Hôtel Intercontinental (1862) is without a doubt where the Parisian smart set, and well-to-do tourists, love to meet. And well they should, for the setting is sublime, with a magnificent painted ceiling, beautiful frescoes (by Garnier), gilded wood panelling, and Second Empire-style furniture. It is luxurious and unique. So, you may have to wait a bit between courses, and the bill is not what you'd call skimpy; but this is the Café de la Paix, where Maupassant, Oscar Wilde, Gide and Zola were once regulars. The service plays out in three acts (from 7am to midnight), featuring a smooth, updated classical repertoire.

16 Haussmann

Contemporary 🍴🍴

Hôtel Ambassador,
16 bd Haussmann ✉ 75009

🚇 **Richelieu Drouot**
B3

☎ 0148000638 – **Fax** 0144834057

e-mail 16haussmann@concorde-hotels.com
Web www.hotelambassador-paris.com

closed 4-25 August, Saturday lunch and Sunday

Menu €32 (dinner)/€41 (lunch) – Carte €52/60

Sybille de Margerie has created a talented blend of elegance, understated taste and contemporary design here. The royal blue, ochre and mahogany Bayadères stripes, red chairs designed by Starck, reddish pale wood, drapes and trompe-l'œil materials are all part of the style at this establishment at the Ambassador, a cut above the usual hotel restaurant. Chef Michel Hache and his team create up-to-date recipes with a classical base, including langoustine ravioli with a creamy basil mousse, wild mushroom risotto with truffle oil and Parmesan *tuiles*. The service is good and the environment is lively (with a picture window that looks out onto the boulevard); the terrace is a favourite in the summer.

Opéra, Grands Boulevards

Opéra, Grands Boulevards

Au Petit Riche

Traditional 𝕏𝕏

A/C

25 r. Le Peletier   **Ⓜ** Richelieu Drouot
✉ 75009   **C3**
☎ 0147706868 – **Fax** 0148241079
e-mail aupetitriche@wanadoo.fr **Web** www.aupetitriche.com
closed Sun

VISA
ⓂⓒⒺ
AE
Ⓓ
♈

Menu €27/€35 wine included – Carte €30/56

This is truly an institution, mentioned by Maupassant in *Bel Ami*, and frequented by Mistinguett and Maurice Chevalier. Its 19C dining rooms haven't changed a bit since it opened in 1854, with its red velvet banquettes, finely chiselled mirrors, hat racks, elegant snug tables, etc. The only change of note is the clientele. Bankers and stockbrokers have made it their "local", while stars and theatre-goers flock here until the midnight hours. Its charm remains intact. Enjoy the recipes inspired by Touraine cuisine at this historic venue, along with a bottle chosen from the superb list featuring wines from the Loire Valley.

Bistrot Papillon

Traditional 𝕏𝕏

A/C

6 r. Papillon   **Ⓜ** Cadet
✉ 75009   **D2**
☎ 0147709003 – **Fax** 0148240559

VISA
Ⓜⓒ
AE
Ⓓ
♈

Closed 1st-9 May, 5-31 August, 23 December-2 January, Saturday except dinner from October to April and Sunday

Menu €27 – Carte €36/48

The Papillon in a nutshell? Classic, without a doubt. And that's what people like here – its "textbook", "exemplary" and almost "endangered species" side. It feels like one of those country inns where everything seems to have been carefully preserved for decades. The authentic Belle Epoque decor features wood panelling and bouquets of flowers everywhere, fabrics creating more privacy between tables, and pretty bistro chairs. The ideal setting for enjoying the great culinary classics "reverently" re-created by Jean-Yves Guion. Since 1983 he has been regaling regulars, businessmen and tourists in the family atmosphere expertly maintained by his wife Evelyne.

Jean ✿

Innovative ✗✗

VISA
MC
AE
DC

8 r. St-Lazare
✉ 75009
✆ 0148786273 – **Fax** 0148786604
e-mail chezjean@wanadoo.fr **Web** www.restaurantjean.fr

closed 7-15 April, 28 July-28 August, Saturday and Sunday

Ⓜ Notre Dame de Lorette

C2

Menu €39/€78 (dinner) – Carte €50/66

The name refers to the proprietor, Jean-Frédéric Guidoni, long with the "Taillevent school" where he was the maître d'hôtel before striking out on his own. This Baroque establishment with a neighbourhood bistro look - counter, pale wood panelling, floor mosaics, banquettes and brass - is a place you shouldn't miss. Kindness and conviviality are the watchwords. Benoît Bordier, in the kitchen, has great technical mastery. His captivating and inspired food is precise, contemporary and playful – in its expression, pairings and presentation. The wine list has a selection of "young guard" winemakers whose wines are of particular interest. Have a look upstairs at the Mezyana, a bar-smoking lounge where the chef once tried out some culinary experiments, and which can be booked as a private room. The service is friendly and efficient.

Opéra, Grands Boulevards

A LA CARTE

FIRST COURSE
• Rouget saisi, potiron, poivron rouge, yaourt au raifort.

• Lapin et tétragone, café-badiane, artichaut.

MAIN COURSE
• Poitrine de cochon fermier cuite huit heures.

• Epaule d'agneau, maïs, aubergine et condiments au genièvre (winter).

DESSERT
• Figues rôties, verveine et radis, sorbet framboise.

• Biscuit chocolat, craquant, sorbet menthe crépue.

Carte Blanche 🍴

Traditional 🍴🍴

A/C

VISA

MC

AE

🍷

6 r. Lamartine
✉ 75009
📞 0148781220 – **Fax** 0148781221
e-mail rest.carteblanche@free.fr

closed 1st-20 August, Saturday lunch and Sunday

Ⓜ Cadet
C2

Menu €25/€38

Who says that all the new bistros have to be trendy? Behind its simple façade, this one has its own particular charm with its stone walls, exposed beams and clean lines. Some photographs – and tableware – from a trip add a personal touch to the decor. The two globe-trotting proprietors have also drawn their culinary inspiration from around the world, with a knack for how to choose just the right ingredients and give them an original twist. The resulting dishes are quite a success – blending French tradition and exotic flavours. This is a gustative adventure that will delight your taste buds!

Romain

Italian 🍴🍴

VISA

MC

AE

DC

🍷

40 r. St-Georges
✉ 75009
📞 0148245894
e-mail restaurant_romain@yahoo.fr

Ⓜ St-Georges
B2

Menu €33 – Carte €35/66

This establishment tells its very own love story, between the Bürkli family and Italy. Mr. Bürkli is in the kitchen, concocting a short but inspired menu – renewed each month – dedicated to Italian gastronomy and featuring fresh homemade pasta and excellent cold meats, as well as tasty dishes all prepared here with the freshest ingredients. In the dining room, Mme. Bürkli extends a warm welcome to the diners, already won over by the simple but very pleasant setting. Their son Romain, after whom the restaurant was named, knows the Italian wine list like the back of his hand. A really charming restaurant just behind Notre-Dame-de-Lorette – when you're in the mood for a Roman adventure.

La Petite Sirène de Copenhague

Danish

47 r. N.-D. de Lorette   **Ⓜ** St-Georges
⊠ 75009   **B1**
✆ 0145266666

closed 29 July-27 August, 24 December-2 January, Saturday lunch, Sunday, Monday – pre-book

Menu € 28 (lunch)/€ 32 – Carte € 48/64

You'll be under its spell the minute you walk into this genuine ambassador of Danish cuisine. But rather than charming you with her singing, this siren catches gourmets in her net with delicious sweet-and-sour herring and incomparable smoked salmon, two undisputed stars on this sweet and savoury menu from the land of Hans Christian Andersen. The rest is naturally in the same spirit. Peter and his friendly staff take your order with their delightful Nordic accents, while proposing an excellent øl (Danish beer) or obligatory aquavit – to be enjoyed in moderation of course. The warm decor completes the local colour with its polished floor tiles, whitewashed walls, soft lighting, candles and paintings by Scandinavian artists. A real treat!

Casa Olympe

Traditional

48 r. St Georges   **Ⓜ** St-Georges
⊠ 75009   **B2**
✆ 0142852601 – **Fax** 0145264933

closed 1st-12 May, 1st-25 August, 22 December-3 January, Saturday and Sunday – number of covers limited, pre-book

Menu € 38/€ 55

Dominique Versini – alias Olympe (also her mother's first name) – was the culinary mastermind of the 1980s, one of the first women chefs and instigator of what was known as "nouvelle cuisine". Out of the limelight these days, she now holds sway in two small ochre dining rooms on the rue Saint-Georges, and nothing seems to have changed. She still has the same strong character and the same faculty for reinventing traditional cuisine inspired by dishes with a Mediterranean touch. So the financiers and insurance men fight over tables at their "local" at noon, while the artists fill it up in the evening. Who cares if your ten neighbours can hear what you're saying? The food is well worth the close quarters!

9TH ARRONDISSEMENT

L'Oenothèque

Traditional 🍴

AC

VISA

MC

AE

D

🍷

20 r. St-Lazare
✉ 75009
✆ 0148780876 – **Fax** 0140161027

Ⓜ Notre Dame de Lorette
B2

closed 1st-8 May, 13 August-2 September, 25 December -1st January, Saturday and Sunday

Carte € 29/50

Feeling a bit peckish after your walk through the Nouvelle Athènes neighbourhood? Try this wine bar that willingly worships at the altar of Dionysus. Daniel Hallée, a former sommelier with the prestigious Jamin establishment, is in charge of this pocket bistro which doubles as a boutique selling wines and spirits. The place is popular with a regular crowd, won over by the chef's imagination in the kitchen. New recipes grace the blackboard every day, depending on the ingredients he brings back from the market. Needless to say, there is an interesting selection of wines to accompany his tasty dishes.

I Golosi

Italian 🍴

AC

VISA

MC

🍷

6 r. Grange Batelière
✉ 75009
✆ 0148241863 – **Fax** 0145231896
e-mail i.golosi@wanadoo.fr

Ⓜ Richelieu Drouot
C3

closed 5-20 August, Saturday dinner and Sunday

Carte € 25/48

Murano glass lamps and "Venetian terrace" floors are just part of the magic at this trattoria in the Passage Verdeau. The contemporary decor upstairs, combined with the waiters' accents, has given this establishment an incomparably chic air – and a solid reputation to go with it. And it's no wonder, with its extensive list of Italian wines (over 500 vintages, many of them served by the glass), huge variety of antipasti, seasonal soups and pasta dishes which change by the week. Can't resist? You can find all these flavours from Italy at the adjoining shop to take home with you – your own secret weapon. Booking advised!

Le Pré Cadet 😊

Traditional ⚒

AC

VISA

MC

AE

D

10 r. Saulnier
✉ 75009
☎ 0148249964 – **Fax** 0147705596

Ⓜ **Cadet**
C2

closed 1st-8 May, 1st-21 August, 22 December-1st January, Saturday lunch and Sunday
– number of covers limited, pre-book

Menu €30 – Carte €34/47

This establishment starts out as a "local" for the banking and insurance company crowd in the daytime, then turns into a meeting place for night owls later on. The grass is always green at the Pré Cadet, and the place is always packed. One look at the blackboard will tell you the reason for its success – the copious traditional food at friendly prices. Offal – including calf's head with *sauce gribiche* (vinaigrette sauce with chopped boiled eggs, gherkins, capers and herbs), *andouillette* sausage and calf's liver – is featured among the house specialities. The long list of coffees available is inspiring, promising subtle flavours of fruit and caramel.

Dell Orto

Italian ⚒

VISA

MC

AE

🍷

45 r. St-Georges
✉ 75009
☎ 0148784030

Ⓜ **St-Georges**
B2

closed August, 24 December-2 January, Sunday and Monday – dinner only

Carte €32/62

Honouring Italian cuisine while adding his own creative touch is the leitmotiv of the chef-proprietor of this friendly restaurant which is only open for dinner. Why not at lunchtime? Because Patrizio Dell'Orto needs time to put together the daily market-based dishes which complete his short menu, to make his fresh pasta and think up appetising names for his creations. It is well worth the wait; the recipes from his native land, subtly seasoned with spices from afar, have already earned him a wide following. The same Mediterranean influence is present in the decor of the two dining rooms, with a warm and charming interior blending Italian and North African designs.

Opéra, Grands Boulevards

Da Claudio

Italian ✕

10 av. Trudaine
✉ 75009
✆ 0148785581 – **Fax** 0148780601

closed August, Saturday lunch and Sunday

Carte € 27/42

Ⓜ **Anvers**
D1

This Italian restaurant is characterised by its tasteful bistro decor. There is a discreet southern touch in the large dining room with its central bar, simple table settings, paintings on display, dark parquet floors, and cream-coloured walls. Some of the tables on the veranda look out over the street, while the terrace is full as soon as the good weather sets in. In the evening there is a different atmosphere, with soft lighting creating an intimate ambiance to the delight of romantic diners. In the kitchen, Claudio the chef-proprietor prepares dishes with fresh ingredients from southern Italy featuring generous, sun-drenched Mediterranean flavours.

Le Paprika

Hungarian ✕

28 av. Trudaine
✉ 75009
✆ 0144630291 – **Fax** 0144630962
e-mail domi@le-paprika.com **Web** www.le-paprika.com

Ⓜ **Anvers**
C1

Menu € 14 (weekday lunch)/€ 30

Hungarian gastronomy is not very well known when you think about it, apart from the inevitable goulash. So what about Hortodagy pancakes, stuffed cabbage, *körösöt*, strudel and *beigli* (a poppy-and-walnut roll)? There is only one place to get a taste of real Magyar flavours, and that is Le Paprika, which has held the top spot for about ten years. The Czekö family generously shares all the riches of its country in the simple and authentic food, washed down with Tokay and other wines from the Eger region. A gypsy orchestra fills the elegant retro dining room with the sounds of folklore melodies from November to May. In summer, the lovely terrace is always a favourite. And you can bring back a gourmet souvenir from the small boutique.

Relais Beaujolais

Lyonnais cuisine

3 r. Milton ⓂNotre Dame de Lorette
✉ 75009 **C2**
✆ 01 48 78 77 91

closed August, Saturday, Sunday and public holidays

Carte € 29/47

There is something reassuring about this establishment. Perhaps it's that when you walk in here – and browse the menu – you realise that the *terroir* is still a force to be reckoned with. Or could it be that its sweet country atmosphere tells you there are still some "rust-proof" representatives of tradition amongst all the trendy restaurants? One thing is certain – this place is high up on the list of diners who enjoy specialities from Lyon and wines from Beaujolais, a region where the chef finds most of his ingredients and from which he draws his considerable inspiration! The dishes are always consistent, and as for the friendly ambiance created by Marie-Christine and Alain Marzeau, it has won over a steady stream of new diners.

Radis Roses

Traditional

68 r. Rodier Ⓜ Anvers
✉ 75009 **C1**
✆ 01 48 78 03 20

e-mail radisroses@tele2.fr **Web** www.radis-roses.com

Closed 1st-15 August, Sunday except dinners in winter and Monday – pre-book

Menu € 33

Welcome to one of the rare Parisian establishments that features specialities from the Drôme. The recipes have been slightly updated, but they are indeed authentic, skilfully blending regional ingredients and contemporary culinary practices. The ambiance is unaffected in the somewhat "trendy" dining room, which is simple and tasteful. The warm welcome from the proprietors is an added bonus in this altogether charming restaurant which has already won over the hearts of vegetarians and carnivores alike. Non smoking.

Opéra, Grands Boulevards

Spring 🐌

Traditional 🍴

A/C
VISA
💳
🍷

28 r. Tour d'Auvergne
✉ 75009
☎ 01 45 96 05 72

e-mail freshsnail@free.fr **Web** www.springparis.blogspot.com

dinner only – number of covers limited, pre-book

Ⓜ Cadet
C2

Menu €32/€36 (No-choice menu)

All the ingredients for a successful *table d'hôte* have been combined right here – in the heart of Paris! That is the challenge brilliantly met by Daniel Rose, who came here from Chicago to study philosophy and fell in love with the idea of becoming a restaurateur. And he shares that passion with his diners, as they watch him prepare his delicious set menu, developed daily in the kitchen-dining area based on the market and his fancy. As for the wines, a group of handpicked wine-growers have selected their best bottles for you. Generosity by the score, a liberal dose of conviviality and just the right equation of talent. Please, sir, can we have some more?!

Sizin

Turkish 🍴

VISA
💳
🍷

47 r. St-Georges
✉ 75009
☎ 01 44 63 02 28

e-mail ekilic@free.fr **Web** www.sizin-restaurant.com

closed August

Ⓜ St-Georges
B2

Carte €20/30

One look at the thorough, bilingual menu and you will know this is the best Turkish restaurant in the 9th arrondissement. It is like taking a one-way trip to Istanbul and discovering new dishes at each meal, such as hummus, stuffed vine leaves (*yaprak sarma*), appetizing hot starters and a wide variety of grilled meats – with or without sauce – including leg of lamb kebabs (*sis*), veal cutlets stuffed with kasar cheese, mushrooms and pistachios (*dana sarma*). Last call for the attractive dining rooms with their old engravings, Iznic faience, Oriental lamps and background music! On board, you will have a very pleasant journey thanks to the friendly Kilics and their excellent suggestions.

Le Zinc des Cavistes

Bistro 🍴

A|C
VISA
💳

5 r. fg Montmartre
✉ 75009
☎ 01 47 70 88 64 – **Fax** 01 44 79 01 83

Closed Saturday lunch, Sunday and public holidays

🍷 Carte € 24/38

Ⓜ Grands Boulevards
C3

The name is explicit, and it keeps its promise, for behind this very discreet façade lies a genial wine bar. The decor has an understated modern look with silvery-grey tones around the zinc bar, bottle racks, shades of orange in the dining room area and a very pleasant hushed ambiance throughout. Bistro classics are featured, with some snack menus at lunch which regulars are very fond of. And naturally an interesting selection of wines – by the glass in particular – to try out amongst friends and family (with 70 place settings, the upstairs room has plenty of room for groups).

Opéra, Grands Boulevards

Gare de l'Est, Gare du Nord, Canal St-Martin

Richer X./MICHELIN

The 10th arrondissement, an ethnically diverse district caught up in the world of fashion, has a multitude of facets. On one side, it remains working-class and off the main tourist tracks, while on the other, it has been snatched up by the bourgeois-bohemian wave that has awakened the sleepy banks of Canal St-Martin.

CANAL ST-MARTIN, A FALSE PICTURE POSTCARD

Little remains today of the mythical almost brash "atmosphere" of the canal St-Martin immortalised by Carné, Simenon, Doisneau and many others. The warehouses have been demolished and only the façade of the famous Hôtel du Nord, converted into a restaurant, remains. However, the "old-fashioned" charm of the canal's bridges, locks and barges continues to operate to the delight of the lovers of romantic Paris.

While it has no inclination to disown its picture postcard cinematographic past, the canal is also keen to keep up with fashion. A meeting-place for Parisian bourgeois-bohemians, the trendy cafés that line **quai de Valmy and quai de Jemmapes** are never empty. The terraces are inevitably so crowded, that people take their drinks across the street to the cobbled embankments. This is particularly true at the weekends when they become pedestrian and are very popular with families. Rue Beaurepaire is home to some of the capital's most avant-garde fashion stylists and also to highly specialised bookshop-galleries devoted

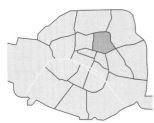

to graphic arts and fashion. The capital's trendiest urbanites and up-and-coming artists are regulars to the district, if they aren't lucky enough to live in one of the workshop-lofts, rare in this district devoid of major museums. However the surrounding little streets can offer simple less crowded bistros.

DOORSTEP TO THE EAST

The ambience around the noisy, populous **gare de l'Est and gare du Nord** is in total contrast and resounds to the rhythm of the shops' cash registers and the hurried steps of travellers. However there is no need to take the Thalys to Amsterdam or the Eurostar to London to discover distant horizons. A world tour of savours from the most classical to the most exotic is just a stone's throw away. While the traditional flavour of Alsace continues to animate the hundred-year-old Art Deco brasseries, **porte de St-Martin and porte de St-Denis** are now an open door to the East and Africa. From authentic tandoori chicken and kebabs sold in tiny booths or colourful fragrant

Legac H./MICHELIN

spices hawked from roadside stalls to the cheap hairdressing and barbers' salons, **rue du Faubourg St-Denis** offers a cosmopolitan setting for the Turkish and Pakistani communities, while **boulevard de Strasbourg** for its part is the headquarters of the African population and the dilapidated **passage Brady and passage du Prado** have become a genuine Little India.

BUT THAT'S NOT ALL

The 10th arrondissement also offers a host of unique sites that are worth exploring. For example, the **couvent des Récollets**, a haven of peace and quiet and now the Maison de l'Architecture and a popular meeting-place, the delightful village ambience of **place Ste-Marthe** or the pleasant garden of **St-Louis Hospital.** In terms of entertainment, the choice is vast from the mythical **New Morning** jazz club, the more eclectic **Point Ephémère** to countless theatres. If in search of a tempting treat, you could not do better than try the confectioner Furet's "Bonheur supreme" or the "Verre volé" bistro-wine cellar.

233

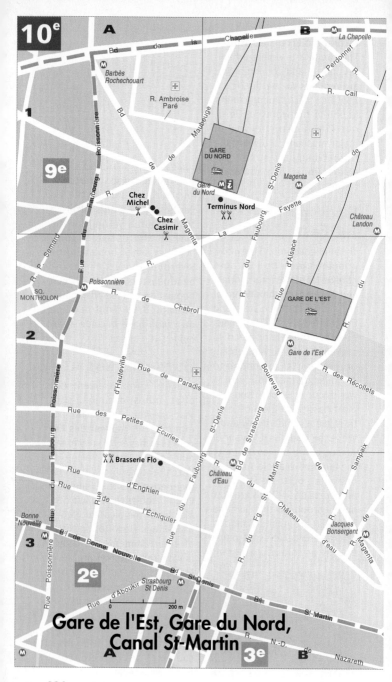

Gare de l'Est, Gare du Nord,
Canal St-Martin

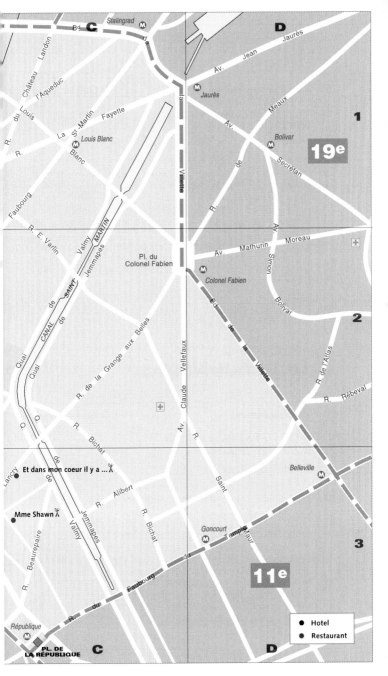

Brasserie Flo

Brasserie 🍴🍴

7 cour Petites-Écuries
⊠ 75010
☎ 0147701359 – **Fax** 0142470080
Web www.floparis.com

Ⓜ Château d'Eau
A3

Menu €21/€31 – Carte €28/80

The picturesque cobblestone Cour des Petites-Écuries, located behind the rue du Faubourg Saint-Denis, is the enchanting setting for this Alsatian institution. The interior decor exemplifies this historic place, with its painted wood walls and ceiling, multi-coloured stained glass evoking a Germanic abbey and its venerable banquettes topped by shiny brass hat-and-coat racks. Classics are featured in the kitchen, where tasty brasserie specialities – sole meunière with steamed potatoes, grilled chateaubriand, Baba au rhum – are prepared with high-quality ingredients. The oysters and other shellfish are as fresh as they come.

Terminus Nord

Traditional 🍴🍴

23 r. Dunkerque
⊠ 75010
☎ 0142850515 – **Fax** 0140161398
Web www.terminusnord.com

Ⓜ Gare du Nord
B1

Menu €31 – Carte €29/69

Last stop! Time to get off – and eat! This authentic Parisian brasserie across from the Gare du Nord station must have seen its share of Picards, Lillois, Wallons, Flemish – and with the Chunnel, British – passengers coming through! Art Deco and Art Nouveau blend together beautifully here in the atmospheric ceiling, period frescoes and high mirrors, posters and sculptures everywhere, magnificent mosaic tiles and chocolate leather furniture. The highly cosmopolitan clientele comes to enjoy the menu's classics such as *choucroute, andouillettes*, oysters and rib of beef, and greatly appreciate the quality of the service and the variety on the menu.

Chez Casimir

Bistro 🍴

6 r. Belzunce
✉ 75010
☏ 01 48 78 28 80

Ⓜ Gare du Nord
A1

closed Saturday and Sunday

♟ Menu €29

This restaurant in the shadow of the neighbouring church is none other than the annexe of Chez Michel. Its rather ageing façade conceals a bistro-style dining room with a small bar by the entrance, walls painted in yellow with a plywood dado and decorated with copperware and retro paintings. The convivial, minimal design consists of snug and narrow tables surrounded by brown imitation leather banquettes. The cuisine features straightforward and tasty dishes without a lot of fuss but always prepared lovingly by the chef. The seasonal game is excellent, the desserts often inventive and the wine list equal to the task. Efficient service.

Chez Michel

Traditional 🍴

10 r. Belzunce
✉ 75010
☏ 01 44 53 06 20

Ⓜ Gare du Nord
A1

♟ closed 29 July-20 August, Monday lunch, Saturday and Sunday

Menu €30 – Carte €45/65

Again, the somewhat worn façade of this establishment has clearly been around a long time. Never mind, you are not here for the decor anyway. You came to taste Thierry Breton's cooking, and right you are. Given excellent marks in the international press, the chef welcomes both regulars from the neighbourhood and tourists from all over, all of whom enjoy his flavoursome and skilfully prepared traditional menu from Brittany (his native region). The blackboard varies according to the seasons and market, but don't miss the succulent game dishes such as roasted wild pigeon with *cèpes* (mushrooms) and chestnuts – truly a delight.

Sidebar: Gare de l'Est, Gare du Nord, Canal St-Martin

Mme Shawn

Thai ✗

A/C
VISA
MC
AE
Y

34 r. Y. Toudic   Ⓜ Jacques Bonsergent
✉ 75010   **C3**
✆ 0142080507 – **Fax** 0142022560
e-mail reservation@mmeshawn.com **Web** www.mmeshawn.com

Menu €17 (lunch)/€35 (dinner) – Carte €25/35

Good Thai cuisine is rare in Paris, making Mme. Shawn all the more of a delicious exception. The welcoming glass façade of this restaurant, on a rather quiet street near the canal Saint-Martin, houses a charming dining room decorated in the Thai spirit with bamboo stalks between the relatively snug tables, attractive place settings with little enamel cups and wooden chopsticks. The tasty and aromatic dishes owe much to the quality of the preparation and the spices, blending together flavours such as galanga, coriander, lemon grass and ginger.

Et dans mon coeur il y a...

Bistro ✗

A/C
VISA
MC
AE
Ⓓ
Y

56 r. Lancry   Ⓜ Jacques Bonsergent
✉ 75010   **C3**
✆ 0142380737 – **Fax** 0142025260
e-mail reservation@etdansmoncoeur.com
Web www.etdansmoncoeur.com
closed Saturday lunch and Sunday dinner

Menu €20 (lunch) – Carte €31/45

The dishes have catchy names – "*filet très mignon*", "*véritable entrecôte pour connaisseurs*" – which reflect the straightforward, authentic and up-to-date cuisine at this brand new bistro. A stone's throw from the canal, it blends old and modern with the vestiges of a Belle Epoque decor (superb spiral staircase and zinc bar), cosy purple velvet banquettes, neo-Baroque chandeliers and a bookcase. The snug tables, warm wood panelling and soft lighting give it a charming, convivial air, and the service is most congenial. The perfect place for the neighbourhood Bobos (Bohemian bourgeois) and everyone else too!

Nation, Voltaire, République

Sauvignier S./MICHELIN

Encircled by place de la République, boulevard de Ménilmontant, boulevard de Charonne and rue du **faubourg Saint-Antoine,** the essentially residential 11th arrondissement is no less rich in history. It hosts two of the three squares that are still hotbeds of political unrest in the east of Paris, place de la République and place de la Nation. Synonymous with protest marches, rallies and demonstrations, these two squares alone symbolise two of the components held most sacred by the French people: democracy (République) and a community of fate (Nation). It may be the overpowering memory of some of France's most troubled moments that has contributed to the incessant, almost frenetic, activity of the 11th, visible in the jumble of markets, bars, nightclubs and restaurants that leave the walker in no doubt as to the district's amazing diversity.

NATION – RÉPUBLIQUE - THE ROAD TO ENLIGHTENMENT?

Both squares are linked by **boulevard Voltaire,** named after the satirist philosopher who is probably the figure that best represents the era of Enlightenment. In an amusing coincidence, the urban fabric along the boulevard reveals an immense variety of small booths and stalls, Haussmannian and dilapidated buildings and bars and restaurants of all sorts in a splendid illustration of what could be deemed to be the diverse nature of open-minded societies. The height of animation along the boulevard can be found at the crossroads

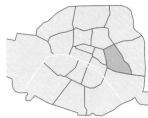

with rue de Charonne. Here excutives pressed for time rub shoulders with the fruit and vegetable vendors of **place de la Nation** and hard-up students, hence the range of restaurants for all budgets that cater to this vast socio-professional melting pot. The vicinity around place de la République is equally rich in **brasseries** and **large bistros,** which can be highly useful when an army of strikers require feeding during demos!

The atmosphere around Nation is both quieter and more marginal, with wide avenues almost entirely residential. **Rue de Charonne** runs from Bastille to Père-Lachaise cemetery, parallel with **rue de la Roquette** with which it shares more than one similarity. Both these long, narrow and sometimes winding streets are also increasingly popular with yuppies who are attracted by the district's lively character, range of leisure pursuits and social diversity.

Blackwell K./MICHELIN

TRENDSETTING BOHEMIA

The scenery changes as you reach the corner of **rue Saint-Maur** and **rue Oberkampf** to reveal a breeding ground of bourgeois-bohemian style festive effervescence. Formerly deeply working-class, the district has been fundamentally transformed under the impetus of a generation of young trendsetters in search of a certain authenticity that can still be felt in the countless **café-theatres and concert halls,** small gastronomic (or otherwise) cafés and picturesque unpretentious eating houses frequented by an ill-assorted clientele. The locals sometimes mutter and curse about being invaded in this way, but those exploring the district are overjoyed. Going down rue Oberkampf towards boulevard **Richard Lenoir,** look out for the handsome **winter circus** (formerly the "cirque Napoleon") built by Hittorff on the model of an antique coliseum. The surrounding streets are extremely well equipped in bars and restaurants of all types, although not renowned for haute cuisine.

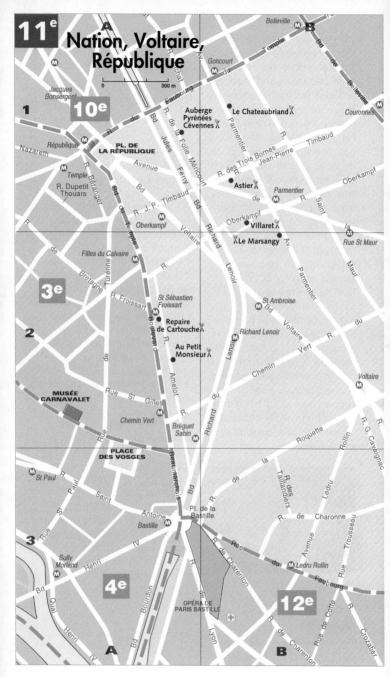

Belleville

Jacques Bonsergent

10e

République

PL. DE LA RÉPUBLIQUE

Nazareth

Temple

R. Dupetit Thouars

Filles du Calvaire

3e

Bretagne

Turenne

R. Froissart

St Sébastien Froissart

Repaire de Cartouche

Au Petit Monsieur

MUSÉE CARNAVALET

Rue St Gilles

Chemin Vert

PLACE DES VOSGES

St Paul

Sully Morland

Henri

4e

Bourdon

Antoine

Bastille

Pl. de la Bastille

OPÉRA DE PARIS BASTILLE

Lyon

Goncourt

du

Temple

Belleville

Le Chateaubriand

Auberge Pyrénées Cévennes

Couronnes

Timbaud

Parmentier

Jean-Pierre

R. des Trois Bornes

Astier

Oberkampf

Parmentier

Oberkampf

Villaret

Le Marsangy

Rue St Maur

Maur

St Ambroise

Richard Lenoir

Voltaire

Chemin

Vert

Roquette

Rollin

R. G. Cavaignac

Charonne

Ledru Rollin

Faubourg

Trousseau

Crozatier

Rue de Corte

de Charenton

12e

B

A

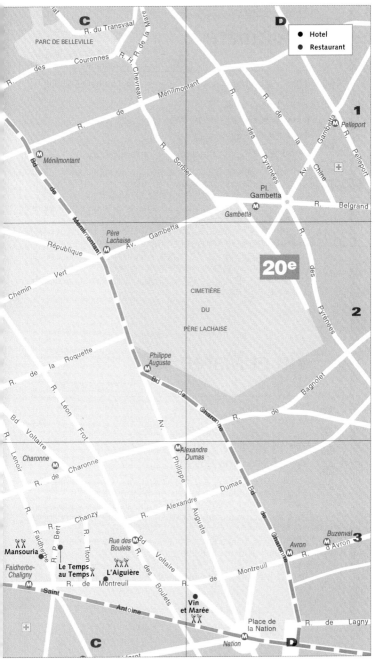

L'Aiguière

Contemporary XXX

A/C 37bis r. Montreuil Ⓜ Faidherbe Chaligny
⊡ ✉ 75011 **C3**
VISA ✆ 01 43 72 42 32 – **Fax** 01 43 72 96 36
e-mail contact@laiguiere.com **Web** www.l-aiguiere.com
Ⓜ© closed Saturday lunchtime, Sunday and public holidays
AE Menu €33/65 wine included – Carte €64/96
Ⓓ
⅋ This establishment is recommended by all wine-lovers – and
♀ with good reason. The owner, a passionate sommelier, has
continued to enrich his superb cellar. It's no surprise that nearly
all the wine-making regions (in France and around the world)
are represented on the amazingly plentiful list. In short, you will
delight in the remarkable combinations of wine and food here.
Dining is a pleasure in this elegant setting with its fine Gustavian-
inspired mezzanine dining room – French ceiling, shades of
yellow, shimmering fabrics and lovely collection of ewers – and
private rooms. The up-to-date seasonal recipes are served with
politeness and discretion.

Vin et Marée

Seafood XX

A/C 276 bd Voltaire Ⓜ Nation
VISA ✉ 75011 **D3**
✆ 01 43 72 31 23
Ⓜ© **Web** www.vin-et-maree.com
AE Menu €24 – Carte €33/51
♀
Simply cooked seafood is on offer at Vin et Marée – like the
other three Parisian restaurants of the same name. The blackboard exclusively features fresh fish and shellfish in season. The
sea is also honoured on the dessert menu, with roasted papaya
à la tahitienne and Zanzibar baba au rhum. Enjoy a little seaside
adventure in a discreet brasserie-style decor (large mirrors, mosaic murals and comfortable banquettes), with a view of the
kitchen and an efficient wait staff. There is no shortage of takers
among the crowds on the Boulevard Voltaire – and well beyond.

Mansouria

 Moroccan ✗✗

A/C   11 r. Faidherbe   Ⓜ Faidherbe Chaligny
       ✉ 75011   **C3**
VISA   ☎ 0143710016 – **Fax** 0140242197

MC   closed 13-19 August, Monday lunch, Tuesday lunch and Sunday

Menu €30/46 wine included – Carte €31/50

Fatema Hal is a well-known figure in the Parisian world of Moroccan gastronomy, and her restaurant is quite an institution. Trained as an ethnologist, she has written about recipes from her country and has imparted the best of her roots to this authentic spot. That's why the Parisian smart set never tires of dining in this Moorish decor and tasting the true North African specialities – *tajines*, couscous, *pastillas*, custard scented with orange blossom water, etc. – prepared by the skilful cooks. The incomparable service is friendly, courteous and efficient. It goes without saying that booking is advised, especially for dinner during the weekend.

Le Chateaubriand

 Contemporary ✗

VISA   129 av. Parmentier   Ⓜ Goncourt
       ✉ 75011   **B1**
MC   ☎ 0143574595

AE   closed 15 August-9 September, 17 December-3 January, Saturday lunch, Sunday and Monday

♀   Menu €19 (lunch)/€39 (dinner)

It looks like a 1930s bistro transplanted into the present. From the past it has preserved its slightly retro decor, while the food is up-to-date and the waiting staff right off a fashion runway. This bevy of dazzlingly "gorgeous guys" do a terrific waiting job. It's the least they can do to present the dishes created by Inaki Aizpitarte, the famous young Basque chef who is now in charge here. At lunchtime, businessmen and office workers on a tight schedule enjoy the thousand and one flavours of his straightforward and ultra-fresh creations. In the evening he caters to food-lovers who prefer to take their time, with more elaborate and simply delicious dishes – to the delight of his clientele, already won over.

Nation, Voltaire, République

Au Petit Monsieur

Bistro 🍴

VISA	50 r. Amelot	Ⓜ Chemin Vert
	✉ 75011	**A2**
MC	✆ 0143555404 – **Fax** 0143147703
AE	**e-mail** aupetitmonsieur@wanadoo.fr **Web** www.aupetitmonsieur.fr
♈	closed August, Saturday lunch, Sunday and Monday

Carte € 29/50

The Petit Monsieur – formerly the C'Amelot – embodies the best of Parisian bistros. It has it all, from the snug tables and moleskin banquettes to the elegant table settings and very friendly service. That includes the pleasure of seeing and hearing what's being cooked up in the kitchen. Perhaps it will help you choose from among the daily suggestions and the very appetising dishes on the menu, including the fine cold meats (from Auvergne, Spain, Corsica and Italy) and a selection of delicious *bouchées fines* (tapas), available individually, as a tasting platter (a blend of all the items) or in your own combination.

Le Temps au Temps

Bistro 🍴

VISA	13 r. Paul Bert	Ⓜ Faidherbe Chaligny
	✉ 75011	**C3**
MC	✆ 0143796340 – **Fax** 0143796340
🎗	closed August, 24 December-1st January, Sunday and Monday
♈	**Menu € 30**

In the wings of this little neighbourhood bistro is a congenial and enthusiastic couple. The lady of the house is in charge of the service and sustaining the convivial atmosphere (she also did the portraits of "chefs with stars" on the walls). The man of the house handles the cooking operation with a magic touch. His secret lies in selecting only the freshest ingredients and using them in streamlined dishes where he distils their essence. The result is delicious and well-prepared food that is slightly alternative without being convoluted. This is an establishment with a future. Non-smoking.

Nation, Voltaire, République

Repaire de Cartouche

Traditional ✗

VISA

99 r. Amelot
⊠ 75011

🚇 St-Sébastien Froissart
A2

MC

☎ 0147002586 – **Fax** 0143388591

closed August, February school holidays, 1 week in May, Sunday and Monday

♀ Menu € 16 (weekday lunch)/€ 25 (lunch) – Carte € 33/52

This restaurant seems to be cultivating its country inn look with its exposed beams, wood panelling, solid wood furniture, small-paned windows and frescoes to the glory of the impetuous Cartouche (who is said to have taken refuge here after he deserted the army in 1713). Could it be a nod to chef-owner Rodolphe Paquin's native Normandy? His traditional cuisine ignores trends which come in and out of fashion, sometimes borrowing from the bistro repertoire, and is fond of game in autumn. Needless to say, the well-stocked cellar – featuring numerous small producers and natural wines – has the perfect beverage for each of these dishes. The lunch formula and menu are offered at very reasonable prices.

Auberge Pyrénées Cévennes

Terroir ✗

A/C

106 r. Folie-Méricourt
⊠ 75011

🚇 République
A1

VISA

☎ 0143573378

MC

closed 30 July-20 August, Saturday lunch and Sunday

AE

♀ Menu € 29 – Carte € 27/60

The good humour in this establishment strikes you the minute you walk in the door. Jokes start flying and the proprietress gives you the warmest of welcomes. In the dining room where hams and sausages hang from the ceiling, the tables are snug. There's no doubt about it – diners here have a good time. The cuisine features dishes from the Pyrénées and the Cévennes, but doesn't neglect the other regions either. The recipes are authentic and generous, "plats canailles" and "lyonnaiseries", washed down with a very drinkable jug of Beaujolais, for example. This place has the charm of a regional inn at reasonable prices, and without any fuss. Wet blankets should stay at home!

Le Marsangy

Traditional ✕

A/C **VISA** **MC**

73 av. Parmentier
✉ 75011
☎ 0147009425 – **Fax** 0147009425

Ⓜ Parmentier
B2

closed 1st-8 May, 1st-15 August, 24 December-4 January, Saturday lunch and Sunday

♈ Menu €28 – Carte €29/35

The façade is as discreet as they come and the environment quite lively. You won't regret walking into the Marsangy, a warm bistro whose name refers to the little Burgundy village where the chef-proprietor was born. At the stove, he lets his inspiration guide him in composing market-based recipes that are generous and epicurean – like the chef himself. This cheerful man knows how to share his love of the good things in life; and, next to his specialities of the day on the slate menu, he always writes the names of choice wines he would like you to try. Quite simply a delicious moment to enjoy.

Astier

Bistro ✕

VISA **MC** **Ⓓ**

44 r. J.-P. Timbaud
✉ 75011
☎ 0143571635
e-mail restaurant.astier@wanadoo.fr

Ⓜ Parmentier
B1

pre-book

♈ Menu €30

The exceptionally well-stocked wine list is the main asset at this true institution. Little bottles and great vintages "lie dormant" in the cellar, patiently waiting to fill the glass of one of the many regulars, and all at very reasonable prices – proof that it hasn't fallen prey to its own success. The food keeps things on the simple side, as if keeping a low profile before such a tribute to Bacchus. Diners eat at snug, simply laid formica tables, under slightly kitsch lamps, in a rather lively atmosphere. Just the kind of bistro that is the soul of Paris.

Nation, Voltaire, République

Villaret

Bistro

  13 r. Ternaux
☒ 75011
☏ 0143577556

closed August, Saturday lunch and Sunday

Menu € 27 (lunch)/€ 50 (dinner) – Carte € 35/53

Behind this discreet façade on the rue Ternaux is a really nice little establishment. Its motto is "do things well, in all simplicity". The pretty but unassuming bistro decor features a fine zinc bar of the kind one rarely sees anymore, exposed beams and wood everywhere. Looking over the menu, the *plats canailles* which the chef cooks his own way, are what stand out, although the market-inspired recipes look tempting too. As for the cellar, you dream of going down for a look at all those vintage bottles and other prestigious wines. Fans of Burgundy and Côtes-du-rhône will have lots of great ones to choose from!

◎ Parmentier
B1

Nation, Voltaire, République

Bastille, Bercy, Gare de Lyon

Sauvignier S./MICHELIN

A substantial slice of the city between Bastille, the Seine and the town of Vincennes, the 12th is one of those arrondissements where versatility is second nature. It would be fruitless to try and limit the area to its legendary square, the historic **Bastille,** now witness to the extravagant behaviour of the city's night-birds. It is of course a high spot of Parisian nightlife and the location of an international symphonic stage in harmony with the capital, but other districts a little further afield are also worth exploring. Along the Seine, pause and admire the titanic efforts deployed along the embankment, in particular on the former site of **Bercy's wine warehouses.** Near the ring road, the 12th reveals yet another facet, a quieter, greener and friendlier face as you approach Vincennes and its parks and woods.

TO WAR!

The rifles and grenades of the great revolutionary struggles gave way to more festive and peaceful events. The Bastille is home to national celebrations (July 14) and also demonstrations. The district has changed immensely over the last 20 years, particularly with the construction of the Opera House and shops, cafés and restaurants have sprung up in a joyful and some-what chaotic mixture of styles and ambiences. Time-worn and freshly renovated buildings stand alongside modern edifices in what has become one of the capital's most attractive districts. The dock of the nearby **Arsenal** marina, shaded by plane trees and dotted with little harbour-side cafés, is

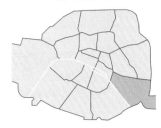
extremely pleasant to stroll round.

A VILLAGE IN THE CITY

Apart from the imposing outline of the **Ministry of Finance,** Bercy used to be above all known for the grassy pyramid of its **Palais Omnisport,** whose immense hall, one of the largest in Paris, has given rise to a host of cafés, bars and grocery shops in the immediate vicinity that refuel the hungry music lovers on concert nights. Now however the rest of the embankment, which stretches as far as the ring road, has been treated to a major redevelopment plan including a landscaped flo-

Sauvignier S./MICHELIN

ral park "à la française", the conversion of the old wine storehouses into restaurants, cafés and shopping malls, a new **cinema complex** and a long façade of neo-Haussmannian buildings, all of which has radically changed the appearance of this district. The area is alive and animated from morning until late into the night and **"Bercy-Village"** should not be missed.

LITTLE-KNOWN POINTS OF INTEREST

Two other areas are worth a detour, at least in gastronomic terms. First, **Gare de Lyon** and its surroundings, whose **traditional brasseries** that specialise in quick service make it a point of honour to cater to everyone at all times. Next, the district around the covered market of **place d'Alligre,** less well-known, even to Parisians, is now home to a friendly micro-district of "ordinary" folk, where old-fashioned bistros welcome regulars and a few rare visitors with equal cordiality. Every weekend a flea market and African fruit and vegetables stalls add colour to the traditional market fare.

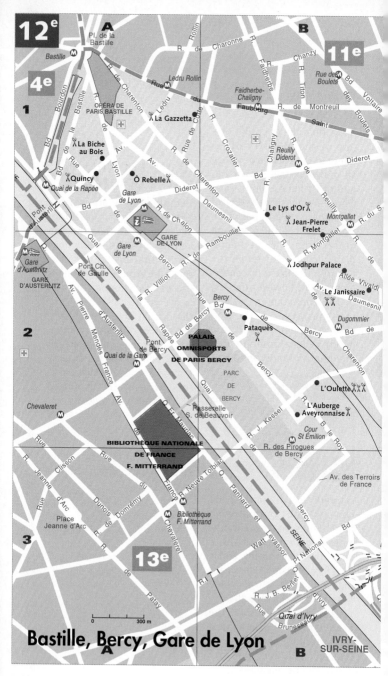

Bastille, Bercy, Gare de Lyon

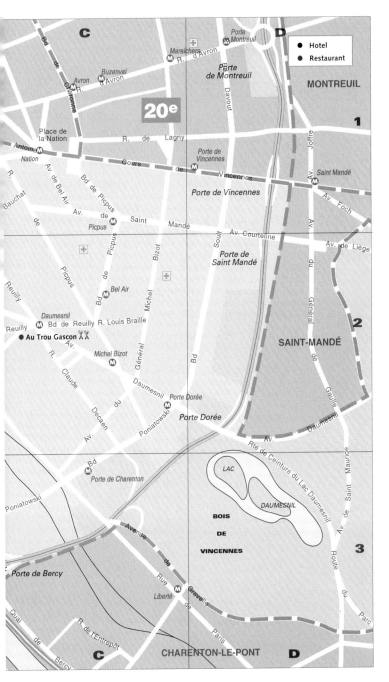

C

Bd de Charonne

Avron
d'Avron

Buzenval
Avron

Maraichers
R. d'Avron

Porte
Montreuil

Porte
de Montreuil

MONTREUIL

Davout

Joffre

20e

1

Place de
la Nation

Antoine
Nation

R.   de   Lagny

R.
Bauchat

Av. de Bel Air

Bd de Picpus

Cours   de   Vincennes

Porte de
Vincennes

Porte de Vincennes

Saint Mandé

Av.

Av.   de   Liège

Av. Foch

Av. de   de   Picpus

Saint   Mandé

Av. Courteline

Porte de
Saint Mandé

Soult

du

Picpus

Bd   de

Bel Air

Michel

Bizot

Général

Reuilly

Daumesnil
Bd de Reuilly R. Louis Braille

● **Au Trou Gascon** ✕✕

Av.

Michel Bizot

Général

Bd

SAINT-MANDÉ

de

Gaulle

2

R.

Reuilly

Claude

du

Daumesnil

Porte Dorée

Daumesnil

Poniatowski

Porte Dorée

Av.

Rte de Ceinture du Lac Daumesnil

Av. de Saint Maurice

Decaen

Av.

Bd

Porte de Charenton

LAC

DAUMESNIL

BOIS

DE

VINCENNES

Route

du

Parc

3

Poniatowski

Avenue

de

Rue

Porte de Bercy

Liberté

Gravelle

de

Paris

Quai

de

Bercy

R. de l'Entrepôt

C

CHARENTON-LE-PONT

D

● Hotel
● Restaurant

L'Oulette

South-West of France

15 pl. Lachambeaudie   Cour St-Emilion
✉ 75012   **B2**
✆ 0140020212 – **Fax** 0140020477
e-mail info@l-oulette.com **Web** www.l-oulette.com
closed Saturday and Sunday

Menu €43/70 – Carte €48/73

What is Marcel Baudis cooking up in his "Oulette", the Occitan name for a small pot? Specialities from the Southwest, his native land, which he reinvents with talent. Among these flavourful dishes are his cream of artichoke soup with truffle cream, roasted codfish with a spice crust, braised oxtail, and the original *pain d'épice perdu à la coque* (gingerbread French toast). His ideas are drawn from areas such as Quercy, Corbières, Gascogne and the Cévennes. The ingredients and wines are expertly chosen (the cellar has about a hundred labels). As for the warm atmosphere in the discreetly contemporary, hushed dining room, it cheers up the "suit-and-tie" crowd at lunchtime. Special feature: the charming terrace shaded by thuja trees.

Au Trou Gascon

A/C VISA MC AE ① ✿

40 r. Taine

✉ 75012

📞 01 43 44 34 26 – **Fax** 01 43 07 80 55

Web www.autrougascon.fr

closed August, Saturday and Sunday

Menu €38 (lunch)/€50 – Carte €52/60

Ⓜ Daumesnil

C2

Au Trou Gascon

The revealing name is quite indicative of the menu! Alain Dutournier took over this former 1900s bistro next to the Palais Omnisports de Paris-Bercy when he first came to Paris, before establishing himself in the smart area between Opéra and Concorde.

As soon as you enter, the tremendous collection of Armagnacs sets the tone of authenticity. The cuisine here has retained its Adour-Océan trademark, with dishes favouring Gascony in general and the southwest in particular. Tradition and creativity are blended with a light hand, in the most subtle and interesting ways, and the well-stocked wine list features wines from the terroir so dear to the owner's heart. The decor makes elegant and moderate use of soft beiges and greys, creating a warm setting and highlighting the mouldings and contemporary paintings. To top it off, the service is friendly and attentive.

A LA CARTE

FIRST COURSE

• Gambas poêlées, royale de foie gras, cappuccino de châtaignes (autumn-winter).

• Pâté en croûte de foie gras de canard pistaché.

MAIN COURSE

• Filet de pigeonneau cuit rosé, cuisse compotée, légumes façon tajine (summer).

• Cassoulet "Trou Gascon" aux haricots de maïs.

DESSERT

• Soufflé glacé litchi.

• Russe, pistache glacée, marbré d'abricots secs.

Le Janissaire

Turkish 🍴🍴

22 allée Vivaldi
✉ 75012
☎ 0143403737 – **Fax** 0143403839
e-mail karamanmus@hotmail.com **Web** www.lejanissaire.com
closed Saturday lunchtime and Sunday

Ⓜ Daumesnil
B2

Menu €13 (weekday lunch)/€42 – Carte €21/40

Le Janissaire offers an excellent overview of Turkey, authenticated by the staff whose origins lie in the country. The terrace invites you to take a seat here before even seeing the dining room, which is equally attractive with its Ottoman rugs, paintings and stained glass. In short, this is a fine environment in which to explore the gastronomic specialities from this land, such as *ezme* (spicy tomato purée), *borek* (cheese puff pastries), and *tavuk* (chicken brochettes). For dessert, try the rare and surprising *kabak tatlisi* and *yeniceri tatlisi* (pumpkin and aubergine preserves). While the regional wine is perfectly fine, if you want to try something really different, have the *ayran*, a drink made from salty yoghurt and lemon.

Ô Rebelle

Innovative 🍴

24 r. Traversière
✉ 75012
☎ 0143408898 – **Fax** 0143408899
e-mail info@o-rebelle.fr **Web** www.o-rebelle.fr
closed 13 August-2 September, 24 December-2 January, Saturday lunch and Sunday

Ⓜ Gare de Lyon
A1

Menu €30/38 – Carte €46/57

The name promises something revolutionary, but does the food really live up to it? The answer is yes, judging from the creative international cuisine cooked up by the Japanese chef. The dishes are a subtle blend of flavours: fricassee of squid in cuttlefish ink, tuna carpaccio with miso vinaigrette, snail pancakes on leek *croustillants* with vanilla, marshmallows with red berries. The cellar is equally exotic, featuring wines from the New World (Chile, Australia, California). The decor is less exuberant, preferring the current refined and tasteful look with beige banquettes, chairs covered in red canvas, leafy green walls and modern paintings. The perfect place for globe-trotting aesthetes!

Jean-Pierre Frelet

Traditional 🍴

A/C	25 r. Montgallet	Ⓜ Montgallet
VISA	✉ 75012	**B1-2**
⑩©	✆ 0143437665	
♀	**e-mail** marie_rene. frelet@club-internet.fr	

closed 7-22 April, 1st-18 August, Saturday lunch and Sunday

Menu €27 (dinner) – Carte €38/46

The Frelets welcome you into their restaurant like longstanding friends. Passionate about their profession, they work with the precision of true artisans. They form the perfect couple – she in the dining room and he in the kitchen – combining her warm reception with his know-how in cooking straightforward market-based cuisine with no false notes. The focus is on the ingredients here, freshly prepared in dishes that change by the day. That is the reason for the success of this little neighbourhood restaurant with a minimalist decor. Informed gourmets are inevitably drawn to the well-designed lunch menu, and consider themselves lucky to get in, as there are only twenty places per sitting. Book without delay.

Pataquès

Bistro 🍴

A/C	40 bd Bercy	Ⓜ Bercy
VISA	✉ 75012	**B2**
⑩©	✆ 0143073775 – **Fax** 0143073664	
Ⓐ🄴	**e-mail** pataquesbercy@aol.com **Web** www.pataques.fr	
♀	closed Sun	

Menu €30 – Carte €30/42

This bistro-brasserie has become with time the "local" for the Ministry of Finance, just across the street. Its sunny decor suits the Mediterranean – and more specifically, Provençal – cuisine to a tee. The simply prepared dishes speak for themselves: tuna and eggplant *millefeuille*, codfish lasagna, *sauté de veau aux olives et citron* (veal with olives and lemon), and *patience d'Aix* served with nougat ice cream and a raspberry coulis. The flavours will transport you straight to the land of Cézanne. Furthermore, the contagious good cheer in the dining room, the attentive service and very attractive menu make Pataquès a very likable place.

Quincy

Traditional ✗

A/C	28 av. Ledru-Rollin	**Ⓜ** Gare de Lyon
	✉ 75012	**A1**

☎ 01 46 28 46 76 – **Fax** 01 46 28 46 76
Web www.lequincy.fr

closed 12 August-12 September, Saturday, Sunday and Monday

Menu € 50/70 – Carte € 46/71

Although Paris is becoming more and more upscale, there are still some establishments outside the trends and fashions. The Quincy is one of them, and so much the better! Unchanged for the past thirty years, this rustic bistro "like they don't make them anymore" (watch out – they don't even take credit cards!) resembles its owner, Michel Bosshard, known as Bobosse. This generous, talkative bon vivant proposes dishes which are like him - 100% homemade and with influences from the Ardèche and Berry regions. Meat and cold meats are featured, as well as foie gras, *terrine fermière*, stuffed cabbage, *cassoulet*, and chocolate mousse. Better than a nostalgic *madeleine,* these recipes with their good old-fashioned flavours will bring you sheer delight.

La Biche au Bois

Classical ✗

VISA	45 av. Ledru-Rollin	**Ⓜ** Gare de Lyon
MC	✉ 75012	**A1**
AE	☎ 01 43 43 34 38	

closed 22 July-22 August, 24 December-2 January, Monday lunch, Saturday and Sunday

Menu € 24

Fans of La Biche au Bois like this establishment for its quality and reasonable prices. The conscientious, dynamic owner takes pride in preserving tradition here, in the simple setting of a classic, convivial bistro with snug tables sporting tablecloths, fine silverware and old-style cooking. *Foie gras au torchon, terrine de campagne au poivre vert* (country terrine with green pepper sauce), *pavé de saumon sauce forestière* (salmon steak with mushroom and bacon sauce) are featured. Other dishes include game in season. For dessert, try the house *Opéra Biche* (a creamy cake with custard cream) or the fruit tart. In short, a menu with a strong flavour of the *terroir*, the reason for this establishment's success.

Le Lys d'Or

Chinese 🍴

5 pl. Col-Bourgoin
✉ 75012
☎ 0144689888 – **Fax** 0144689880
Web www.lysdorming.com

Ⓜ Reuilly Diderot
B1

Menu € 22/26 – Carte € 20/39

Here you can enjoy all the gastronomic flavours of China in Paris, and in the setting of a luxurious palace where the colour red and greenery are the dominant notes (including an indoor garden with bamboo, streams and fountains). The award-winning Lys d'Or, which has been open for over 10 years, is an invitation to explore the underappreciated culinary art of the Middle Kingdom. The four regional cooking styles – Sechuan, Shanghai, Canton and Beijing – are surprisingly diverse and extremely refined. Although you will find the usual *dim sum* on the menu, try something different like the *gui fei* (grilled meat), tofu tartare with coriander, crab with crispy vegetables, or *gou fen* (Asian paella). The wine list has both Chinese and French wines.

La Gazzetta

Fusion 🍴

29 r. de Cotte
✉ 75012
☎ 0143474705 – **Fax** 0143474717
e-mail team@lagazzetta.fr **Web** www.lagazzetta.fr
closed 5-27 August, Sunday dinner and Monday

Ⓜ Ledru Rollin
A1

Menu € 29 (dinner) – Carte € 36/40

The team from the China Club and the Fumoir has opened a third establishment, La Gazetta, half cosy bistro and half modern brasserie. The all-in-one concept – restaurant, wine bar and cultural café (French and foreign-language press available) – has made this a trendy spot with fine food and a menu featuring Mediterranean ingredients. After a hesitant start, La Gazzetta has hit its stride thanks to Petter Nilsson (ex-chef at Les Trois Salons in Uzès). A Swede, he is perfectly at home with Corsican, Italian and Spanish specialities, favouring simple flavours. The shoulder of lamb with honey and the *cassata* (chilled sweet Sicilian ricotta with candied fruit) are delicious, and the regional wines bursting with sun.

12th ARRONDISSEMENT

L'Auberge Aveyronnaise

Terroir 💥

 40 r. Lamé
⌧ 75012
☎ 0143401224 – **Fax** 0143401215
e-mail lesaubergistes@hotmail.fr

closed 1st-15 August

Ⓜ Cour St-Emilion
B2

Menu € 24/30 – **Carte** € 28/41

The name says it all: welcome to the Aveyron! More a brasserie than an inn, this establishment in the modern Bercy area is solidly rooted in the Rouergue terroir. The menu is filled with mouth-watering specialities: *tripoux, boudin* (blood sausage), *jarret aux lentilles, chou farci*, cold meats, *aligot, millefeuille à l'ancienne, flan à la louche*. The generous portions are made with the best of ingredients (Ségala veal, Aubrac beef, fresh Laguiole tome), and watered down with jugs of local wine. In addition to the neo-rustic rooms – with fireplace and checkered table-cloths naturally – you can enjoy the two terraces, on the street or in the private courtyard (only open at lunchtime in the summer).

Jodhpur Palace

Indian 💥

 42 allée Vivaldi
⌧ 75012
☎ 0143407246 – **Fax** 0143401702
e-mail jodhpur-palace@yahoo.fr **Web** www.jodhpurpalace.com

Ⓜ Daumesnil
B2

Menu € 24/35 – **Carte** € 20/42

Indian cuisine, once scarce in the 12th arrondissement, has found a home in this spacious Oriental "palace" with its enticing red façade. Baldev Singh has chosen a quiet street near the Coulée Verte walkway for his second Parisian establishment. In this wonderful haven of peace (especially on the shady terrace) you will be transported to the land of saris and spices. The surprising decor blends traditional frescoes and mahogany wood panelling with the very modern-looking spotless white walls. This is a far cry from the usual atmosphere with subdued lighting (although it has that too, in a small alcove at the back). The menu features classic recipes from around the country, from Jodphur in the North all the way to the South of India.

Place d'Italie, Austerlitz, Bibliothèque Nationale de France

Richer X./MICHELIN

As populous as it is vast, the 13th is one of the rare Parisian arrondissements to still show signs of demographic growth. In full boom since the rehabilitation of its embankments, this area of Paris is both a new rental bonanza and an attractive economic, commercial and cultural centre. Impressively enterprising, its multiple facets provide a surprising juxtaposition of scenery. From **Gare d'Austerlitz** and nearby Jardin des Plantes to **Place d'Italie** opening onto a more working-class and cosmopolitan district of the "left bank", the 13th is proud of its contrasts.

ASIA-ON-SEINE

The largest Asian community in Paris lives south of Place d'Italie, down the avenue of the same name, around the Olympiades, a vast complex of high-rise dwellings that watches over Chinatown. This pocket handkerchief of Asia is however a far cry from the suburbs of Peking and its population of Chinese, Vietnamese, Cambodians and Laotians has woven a tight net of combined linguistic, artistic and culinary influences. Visitors are invariably surprised by the ideograms of the illuminated shop signs that light up these tightly packed streets. Once the first surprise over, you cannot fail but be caught up in the spicy scents and the steam from the rice wafting out of the countless restaurants and which fill the air with the perfume of the East. Let yourself be tempted, or

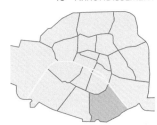

even better, venture into **Tang Frères,** a supermarket on avenue d'Ivry, whose shelves are piled high with unknown fruit and exotic spices, and see the produce first hand. If in the area at the beginning of the year, don't miss the **Chinese New Year** celebrations when red and gold dragons burst out of shops and tower blocks to wind their way through the traffic to the sound of beating drums.

PARIS YESTERDAY AND TODAY

The scenery and decor change radically in the new **"Paris Rive Gauche"** district that is being developed around the four "open books" of the **Bibliothèque Nationale de France** (referred to as the "BNF" by its regulars). Formerly the site of the mills of Paris, the sector is somewhat reminiscent of an architectural exhibition by its sundry assortment of

Sauvignier S./MICHELIN

buildings of all shapes, colours and materials. A testing ground for the most daring projects in smoked or printed glass, metal, brick, wood and most of all concrete.

PARIS VILLAGE

The neighbourhood around the **Butte aux Cailles** is no doubt more human and the townscape is comprised essentially of low-rise buildings and early 20C working-class houses. Its original village identity continues to prevail, despite its current appeal to the bourgeois-bohemians of Paris and the **bistros** continue to play a role in local life while negligently conjuring up the district's communard past. A similar if more floral picture can be seen around **Hénocque** between Tolbiac and Maison Blanche whose colourful little ivy-clad houses definitely have a picture postcard appeal.

The district is not however home to the capital's top restaurants, but rather to authentic Parisian bistros with a warm family atmosphere. The final touch to this working-class heritage lies in the small triangle of the **cité florale** between **Montsouris Park** and the **Cité Universitaire,** a tiny world where time seems to have stood still

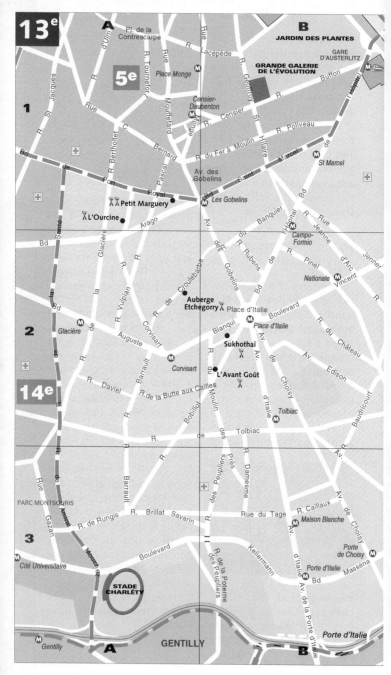

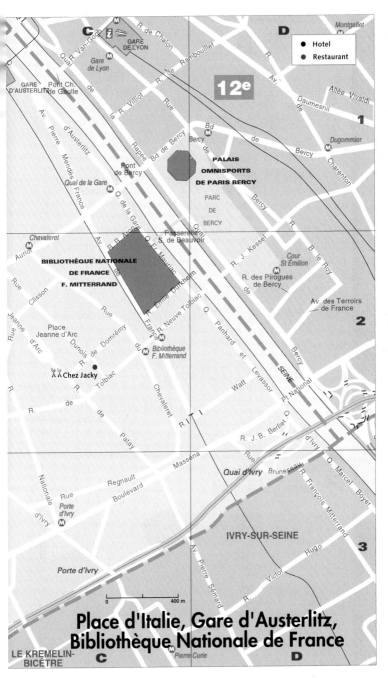

Place d'Italie, Gare d'Austerlitz,
Bibliothèque Nationale de France

Chez Jacky

Traditional ✗✗

A/C
VISA
MC
Y

109 r. du Dessous-des-Berges
✉ 75013
☏ 0145837155 – **Fax** 0145865773
Web www.chezjacky.fr

Ⓜ Bibliothèque F. Mitterrand

C2

Closed 30 July-26 August, 24-30 December, Saturday, Sunday and public holidays

Menu €43 wine included – Carte €45/86

Venture into the quiet streets around the Bibliothèque F. Mitterrand to find this unusual inn, where time seems to have stopped its course. Cheerfully run by three brothers, it stands out in the urban landscape with its provincial and pleasantly old-fashioned look. The setting is rustic, the atmosphere warm and the cuisine features fine recipes straight from the French tradition such as *foie gras de canard*, *tête de veau* and *cuisse de poularde*. The service is equally flawless and well-executed, both in form (starters and desserts placed on a side table) and content, with a staff that is attentive without being overly sollicitous. Diners, take note: they take tradition seriously here, and Escoffier remains the main reference!

Petit Marguery

Bistro ✗✗

A/C
VISA
MC
AE
Y

9 bd Port-Royal
✉ 75013
☏ 0143315859 – **Fax** 0143367334
e-mail marguery@wanadoo.fr **Web** www.petitmarguery.fr

Ⓜ Les Gobelins

A1

closed August, Sunday and Monday

Menu €24 (lunch)/€35

The reputation of the Petit Marguery is already well established. Apart from the arrival of chef Christophe Bisch – who has done a brilliant job taking over from the Cousin Brothers – nothing has changed within these august pink and burgundy walls, including the cooks at their posts, the waiters who wouldn't remove their classical black-and-white outfits for anything, and the spirit of the place, just as warm as ever. Regulars come back to taste the copious bistro dishes and game specialities, including the *lièvre à la royale*. Others are cordially invited to try it. There's no doubt they will be won over by the food and Belle Epoque decor, fine enough to be a national monument.

L'Avant Goût

Bistro ✕

[A/C]

26 r. Bobillot
✉ 75013
[VISA]
☎ 0153802400 – **Fax** 0153800077

[MC]

closed Sunday and Monday – number of covers limited, pre-book

⦿ Place d'Italie
B2

Menu €31/42 – Carte €35/43

The craze over this contemporary bistro on the Butte aux Cailles has not abated; on the contrary, it seems to be increasing by the year. As a result, it is always full – noon and night. So reservations are a must. Its success is due to Christophe Beaufront, who trained with Guérard and Savoy and is constantly inventing new associations of flavours, with a penchant for spices. In addition to the emblematic *pot-au-feu de cochon*, try the *terrine de foie gras à la vanille*, the *dos de cabillaud* or the tiramisu strawberries. The menus change once a month – gourmets take note! Displayed on the blackboard, they are part of the pleasant and simple decor (with red banquettes and snug tables) which goes with the relaxed atmosphere.

Auberge Etchegorry

Basque ✕

41 r. Croulebarbe
✉ 75013
[VISA]
☎ 0144088351 – **Fax** 0144088369
[MC]
Web www.etchegorry.com

closed 2-22 August, Sunday and Monday

[AE]

⦿ Les Gobelins
A2

Menu €26/55 wine included – Carte €32/43

It feels like Bayonne or St-Jean-Pied-de-Port, but this attractive red inn with a deeply Basque spirit is right in the 13th arrondissement. It's all there in the rustic dining room, from the sausages and hams to the *piments d'Espelette* (hot peppers) and *chisteras* hanging from the ceiling. The dishes, full of southwest tradition, are simple and generous. Connoisseurs will be delighted, and novices won over. Fine frescoes provide an unusual touch to admire between mouthfuls. Famous figures shown include Victor Hugo, Chateaubriand and Béranger, all regulars in the days when Madame Grégoire held her illustrious cabaret here. The façade still reflects those days.

Place d'Italie, Gare d'Austerlitz, BNF

13th ARRONDISSEMENT

L'Ourcine

Bistro 🍴

♀ 92 r. Broca
✉ 75013
📞 0147071365 – **Fax** 0147071848

Ⓜ Les Gobelins
A1

closed Sunday and Monday

Menu €30

Quality and modesty are a fitting description of the spirit at l'Ourcine, a tasteful bistro which is always packed. It could be due to the eye-catching dark red façade that instantly tells you this is a place where they take food and wine seriously! Chef Sylvain Danière (who trained with Camdeborde) is passionate about authentic food. His pure market cuisine, changing daily and seasonally, uses only the freshest ingredients and flavours. The wines come from carefully chosen small winemaking estates. Booking is advised, as the number of place settings is deliberately limited.

Sukhothaï

Thai 🍴

VISA
ⓂⒸ

12 r. Père Guérin
✉ 75013
📞 0145815588

Ⓜ Place d'Italie
B2

closed 6-26 August, Monday lunch and Sunday

Menu €20/24 – Carte €19/32

This authentic Thai local is a stone's throw from the Place d'Italie. It's less expensive than a direct flight to Bangkok, and is well worth the trip. The decor affords a change of scenery without going overboard, thus avoiding the pitfalls of affected folklore. A few sculpted buddhas, some engravings and flowers here and there suffice to create a pleasant hushed atmosphere. The service also exemplifies refinement and discretion. As for the cooking, prepared by the owner's wife, it is an explosion of flavours and spices. Beef, duck, pork and shellfish coincide with lemon grass, basil, peppers and coconut milk. It's no wonder so many Thais come to Sukhothaï when they're in Paris. Booking is strongly advised.

美 麗

PLATS À EMPORTER
欢迎外卖

VILLE DE PARIS · DÉBIT DE BOISSONS · LICENCE IV N°3242

Daroulau F./PHOTONONSTOP

Montparnasse, Denfert-Rochereau

Richer X/MICHELIN

The relatively extensive 14th arrondissement is quite representative of the large residential neighbourhoods of southern Paris. It too, like its neighbours the 13th and the 15th, has a village past that can still be felt in the structure of the streets and the variety of buildings and architectural trends, and a pleasantly provincial air continues to float around the 14th, annexed to Paris somewhat later than other arrondissements.

BOHEMIAN NIGHTS

There is however nothing "provincial" about **Montparnasse**. The district may well be named after the pleasure-loving gods of Olympus, but is now more well known as a high spot of Parisian night-life. Easy to find, the 200-metre high Montparnasse **Tower** can be seen from everywhere in Paris and its summit commands a grandiose panorama of the city (and the Eiffel Tower to boot). The surrounding streets literally swarm with typical Parisian **cafés, Irish pubs** and restaurants of every culinary tradition. **Rue de la Gaîté** is well known for its theatres and charms, while practically every high street chain and department store has a foothold on **rue de Rennes** that runs from the tower as far as Saint-Germain-des-Prés. The 300-metre long **rue du Montparnasse** itself, that runs from Edgar Quinet to Notre-Dame-des-Champs, is the location of nearly twenty Breton pancake houses.

The atmosphere gradually changes as you leave the centre

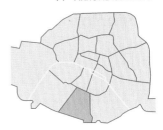

and head towards Montrouge. First stop, **Denfert-Rochereau** and its immense statue of the **Lion of Belfort,** built in memory of the soldiers of 1870-1871. Here the mood is both less audacious and more Bohemian and its network of narrow streets is packed with traditional bistros and small relaxed restaurants. The pedestrian **rue Daguerre,** two minutes from the metro station, provides a wide choice of food shops and delicatessens that pay homage to French produce. The locals do their daily shopping here, amidst holiday-makers and busy executives from avenue du Général Leclerc. On the other side of the square, between rue Froidevaux and rue Campagne Première, **Montparnasse cemetery** (the second largest in Paris) is an enclave and a world unto itself. It is here that Baudelaire, Camille Saint-Saëns, Jean-Paul Sartre and Serge Gainsbourg, among others, are buried. The paths, lined in splendid lime, cedar and sophora trees, are a perfect invitation to meditation.

Hills and Dales

The last portion of the 14th around **Montsouris Park,** before the ring road, is well worth the visit. The garden itself is beautifully landscaped with artificial grottoes, waterfalls and a splendid ornamental lake. Practically uninhabited prior to 1860, the area was entirely reorganised by Napoleon III around the park created in his honour and which is the highest point of the left bank (at an altitude of 75 metres no less!). Highly popular on Sunday afternoons, the neighbourhood is the perfect expression of the "village" character of the south of the arrondissement. George Braque, Salvador Dali and Henri Rousseau could be seen walking down the little streets to the west and their delightful houses and small apartment blocks continue to perpetuate the memory of those legendary years.

Garet H./MICHELIN

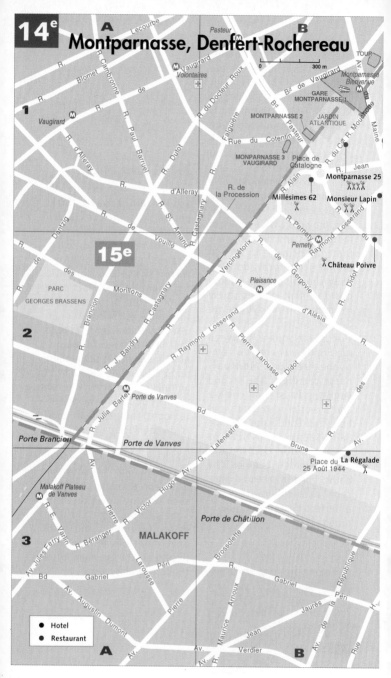

14ᵉ Montparnasse, Denfert-Rochereau

A   B

Lecourbe

Pasteur

M Vaugirard
Volontaires

Bd de Vaugirard

TOUR
Montparnasse
Bienvenue
M

GARE
MONTPARNASSE 1

R. Blomet

R. Camronne

R. du Docteur Roux

R. Lalgulère

Bd Pasteur

Vaugirard

R. de

MONTPARNASSE 2
JARDIN
ATLANTIQUE

R. du Cdt R. Mouchotte

Maine

1

Vaugirard M

Rue du Cotentin

R. Paul Barruel

R. Dutot

MONTPARNASSE 3
VAUGIRARD

Place de
Catalogne

Jean

Montparnasse 25

R. d'Alleray

d'Alleray

R. de
la Procession

R. Alain

Millésimes 62

Monsieur Lapin

R. St. Amand

R. Castagnary

R. Pernety

R. Raymond Losserand

15ᵉ

R. de Vouillé

Pernety M

du

R. de Dantzig

R. des

PARC
GEORGES BRASSENS

Morillons

R. Brancion

R. Castagnary

Vercingétorix

Plaisance
M

R. de Gergovie

Château Poivre

Didot

2

R. J. Baudry

R. Raymond Losserand

R. Pierre Larousse

Didot

d'Alésia

R. des

Porte de Vanves
M

R. Julia Bartet

Porte de Vanves

Bd

R. G. Lafenestre

Brune

Av.

Porte Brancion

Porte de Vanves

Place du
25 Août 1944

La Régalade

Malakoff Plateau
de Vanves
M

Av. Hugo

Victor

Porte de Châtillon

3

Av. Jules Ferry

R. H. E. Varlin

Pierre

R. Béranger

Péri

Larousse

MALAKOFF

Brossolette

R.

Gabriel

Bd

Gabriel

Av. Augustin Dumont

Péri

Pierre

Maurice

Arnoux

Jean

Verdier

Av. de la République

Jaurès

● Hotel
● Restaurant

A   B

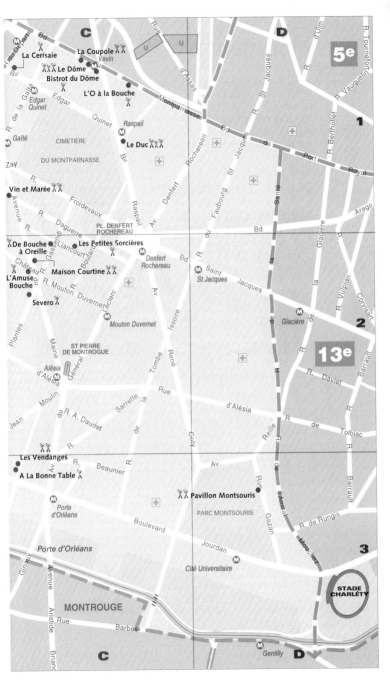

C

D

5e

R. d'Ulm

R. Tournefort

R. Vauquelin

Bd
Raspail

La Cerisaie

La Coupole
Vavin

Le Dôme
Bistrot du Dôme

L'O à la Bouche

Montparnasse

Rue

U   U

d'Assas

St Jacques

R. St Jacques

R. Berthollet

1

R. de la Gaité

Edgar
Quinet

Edgar

Quinet

Raspail

Bd
de
Port
Royal

Galté

CIMETIÈRE

Le Duc

Rochereau

St Jacques

de
la Santé

Zay

DU MONTPARNASSE

Denfert

du Faubourg

Arago

Vin et Marée

Froidevaux

Raspail

Av.

Bd

Glacière

R. Vulpian

Corvisart

Avenue

R.

R.
Daguerre

PL. DENFERT
ROCHEREAU

R. du Faubourg

St Jacques

Bd

De Bouche
à Oreille

Liancourt

Les Petites Sorcières

Château

Maison Courtine

L'Amuse
Bouche

R. Mouton Duvernet

Boulevard

Leclerc

Denfert
Rochereau

Saint
St Jacques

Jacques

de

Glacière

la

R.

R. Daviel

2

13e

Severo

Mouton Duvernet

Issoire

Plantes

Maine

ST PIERRE
DE MONTROGUE

Alésia
d'Alésia

Général

Tombe

René

d'Alésia

Reille

de

Tolbiac

Barrault

Jean

Moulin

du R. A. Daudet

Sarrette

de

la

Rue

Goty

de

R. de Rungis

Barrault

Les Vendanges

A La Bonne Table

R.

R.

Beaunier

Av.

Pavillon Montsouris

PARC MONTSOURIS

Rue

Amiral

Mouchez

3

Porte
d'Orléans

Boulevard

Jourdan

Gazan

STADE
CHARLÉTY

Porte d'Orléans

Cité Universitaire

Ginoux

Avenue

Aristide

MONTROUGE

Rue

Barbès

Gentilly

Briand

C

D

Montparnasse, Denfert-Rochereau

Montparnasse'25 ❀

Contemporary 🍴🍴🍴🍴

A/C
P
VISA
MO
AE
D
❀
♈

Hôtel Méridien Mont-
parnasse,
19 r. Cdt Mouchotte ✉ 75014
✆ 01 44 36 44 25 – **Fax** 01 44 36 49 03
e-mail meridien.montparnasse@lemeridien.com
Web www.montparnasse.lemeridien.com
Closed 7-15 April, 7 July-2 September, Saturday, Sunday and public holidays

Ⓜ Montparnasse Bienvenüe

B1

Menu €49 (weekday lunch)/€110 – Carte €91/109

Montparnasse'25

This hotel with its stone-and-mirror façade is ideally located near the train station, numerous shops, brasseries and pedestrian streets. The lobby is flanked by silhouettes of Sartre, Modigliani and Foujita, whose presence can still be felt in the neighbourhood they immortalized. The Art Deco setting in the gastronomic restaurant upstairs, inspired by the 1930s, is both attractive and surprising with its black-and-grey-toned walls and huge picture window, which overlooks a garden courtyard and diffuses a soft and soothing light. Reproductions of Modigliani paintings are a reminder that this artist had his studio nearby and was a regular at neighbourhood bars. In his masterful cuisine, which is classic yet up-to-date, the chef brings out the best of his fine ingredients – without resorting to unnecessary fads. The service is as good as ever.

A LA CARTE

FIRST COURSE
• Langoustines à l'huile de vanille (spring).

• Lapin braisé, foie gras poché au vin rouge, huile de truffe.

MAIN COURSE
• Sole, filets en bourride au vin du Jura et cèpes (autumn).

• Ris de veau rôti au comté.

DESSERT
• Allumette aux fruits d'été, fleurette battue, jus de ratafia, crème glacée au nougat.

• Tartelette citron basilic, barbe à papa, sorbet gin fizz.

Le Duc ✿

Seafood ✗✗✗

A/C
VISA
MC
AE
DC
Y

243 bd Raspail
✉ 75014
☎ 0143209630 – **Fax** 0143204673
closed 31 July-22 August, 24 December-2 January, Saturday lunch, Sunday and monday

Ⓜ Raspail
C1

Menu €46 (lunch) – Carte €48/138

Le Duc

The riveted sheet metal façade with handrails is the first sign of the establishment's maritime ambiance. Regulars enjoy the informal lunch menu at the bar lined with high leather stools. The plush and intimate dining room faithfully reproduces the atmosphere of a yacht with its mahogany ceiling, polished wood panelling, cabin lamps and shiny brass. Giant stuffed tortoises and colourful illustrations on the walls provide a lesson in the anatomy of marine fauna, evoking a natural history museum. As you may have guessed, the sea is the main theme here. The choice fish is delivered directly from France's fishing ports. The fresh seafood ingredients ensure the quality of the straightforward cuisine, enjoyed by a large business clientele which has made this their "local", filling the place up at lunchtime. The raw fish and shellfish platter is Pascal Hélard's signature dish.

A LA CARTE

FIRST COURSE	MAIN COURSE	DESSERT
• Poissons crus.	• Homard à l'orange.	• Pâtisseries maison.
• Encornets poêlés à l'ail.	• Langoustines rôties au gingembre.	• Entremets.

Le Dôme

Seafood ✗✗✗

A/C
VISA
MC
AE
D

108 bd Montparnasse
✉ 75014
✆ 0143352581 – **Fax** 0142790119

closed Sunday and Monday in August

Carte €51/119

Ⓜ Vavin
C1

Welcome to what was once a temple of the Bohemian literary and artistic crowd in the Roaring Twenties. Le Dôme is a famous Montparnasse seafood brasserie with a unique lively and chic atmosphere which has been carefully preserved over the years. The fine Art Deco interior full of photographs from that era and a fresco by the painter Carzou – once a regular here – is a testimony to those glorious days. Every detail contributes to the spirit of this establishment, with wood panelling everywhere, green and tawny-coloured banquettes, stained glass and soft lighting. The cuisine and service are of the same quality. The freshly delivered seafood is nicely presented in generous dishes, and served with well-chosen wines.

Maison Courtine ✿

Terroir ✗✗

A/C
VISA
MC
♀

157 av. Maine
✉ 75014
✆ 0145430804 – **Fax** 0145459135
e-mail yves.charles@wanadoo.fr
closed 3-27 August, 24 December-3 January, Monday lunch, Saturday lunch and Sunday

Ⓜ Mouton Duvernet
C2

Menu €38/43

Maison Courtine

"My main task is to find exceptional wines and produce," says Yves Charles, who has been the owner here for nearly ten years, in an attempt to explain why he is in the business. He handles the service in the dining room, advises diners on their choice of wines and provides the impetus for the cooking developed together with his chef.

When he arrived in Montparnasse to take over Lou Landès, Yves Charles knew that the establishment, run by Georgette Descat at the time, was considered to be a true ambassador of South-western French cooking. Nowadays the cassoulet is still served, and the emblematic cook would be proud of her successor's decision to keep that same tradition on the menu. The decor is airier, with a "bar area" – which has its regulars – in orange, green and yellow.

A LA CARTE

FIRST COURSE
• Escalopes de foie gras de canard poêlées aux raisins.

• Fine tête de veau tiède en vinaigrette de basilic.

MAIN COURSE
• Canard sauvage rôti entier au poivre long (October to February).

• Médaillon de veau de lait et lentilles blondes de la Planèze.

DESSERT
• Croustillant de pruneaux à l'Armagnac et glace caramel.

• Moelleux de chocolat, coulis d'orange.

277

Montparnasse, Denfert-Rochereau

Pavillon Montsouris

Traditional XX

20 r. Gazan
⊠ 75014
☏ 01 43 13 29 00 – **Fax** 01 43 13 29 02

Ⓜ Cité Universitaire
D3

Closed February half-term holidays and Sunday dinner from mid September to Easter

Menu €49/75

This establishment's charm lies in its exceptional location in the Parc Montsouris. The superb Belle Epoque pavilion offers diners the rare and enviable luxury of the countryside right in Paris. The smart colonial-style decor (russet wood, plants, bronze lamps) under the large glass roof – bathing the place in light – makes you instantly forget the nearby hustle and bustle. The feeling of escaping it all is even greater on the lovely terrace surrounded by vegetation, which opens as soon as the weather permits. Both are charming settings where you can peacefully enjoy the up-to-date market cuisine proposed on the menu. Private dining rooms are available upon request.

La Coupole

Brasserie XX

102 bd Montparnasse
⊠ 75014
☏ 01 43 20 14 20 – **Fax** 01 43 35 46 14
e-mail jtosi@groupeflo.fr **Web** www.flobrasseries.com

Ⓜ Vavin
C1

Menu €24/31 – Carte €30/75

The legendary Coupole has lost none of its original splendour, thanks to its fine renovations. Built in 1927 by the architects Barillet and Le Bouc, it was a hot spot for Parisian nightlife during the Roaring Twenties. Famous figures from the Montparnasse artistic and literary crowd who dined here include Kessel, Picasso, Man Ray, Sartre, Giacometti and Hemingway. From that illustrious past it has preserved its flamboyant Art Deco interior, renowned for its 32 pillars decorated with artwork from the era (paintings by Fernand Léger among others). Add to that the remarkably courteous and efficient waiters, and brasserie food such as copious seafood platters and *choucroute au riesling* . Now, sit back and enjoy it!

Vin et Marée

Seafood ✕✕

A/C
VISA
MC
AE
♀

108 av. Maine
✉ 75014
☎ 0143202950
e-mail vin.maree@wanadoo.fr

Ⓜ Gaîté
C1

Menu €25 – Carte €39/53

You are hardly back in Montparnasse and already feeling nostalgic for Brittany? Head for Vin et Marée Maine! The lobsters in the tank give a hint to the seafood specials on the blackboard, featuring seasonal fish and shellfish. Starters and desserts are in line with this Parisian chain's classics, including *huîtres spéciales perle blanche* (oysters) and *baba de Zanzibar*. The smart marine decor has a personal touch (mahogany wood panelling, blue and white tones, and faience with aquatic themes). The dining room on the veranda enjoys full daylight; the upstairs room is reserved for non-smokers.

Monsieur Lapin

Traditional ✕✕

A/C
VISA
MC
AE
♀

11 r. R. Losserand
✉ 75014
☎ 0143202139 – **Fax** 0143218486
Web www.monsieur-lapin.fr

Ⓜ Gaîté
B1

closed August, Saturday lunch and Monday – number of covers limited, pre-book

Menu €34/45 – Carte €43/66

There is only one celebrity here - in the decor and in the dishes - and that is Monsieur Lapin (Mr. Rabbit). Like the Mad Hatter in Alice in Wonderland, he is all over the place: on the shelves, in a framed photograph, on the fine pewter bar and in little niches. In the kitchen he turns into *salade de Monsieur Lapin* according to the chef's inspiration, rabbit terrine in aspic with herbs from the *garrigue* or *croustillant de lapin* with dried fruit and wild mushrooms. To satisfy all tastes, the menu also features fish and other meats in rather modern dishes. Impatient diners can rest easy: if it involves a delicious meal, Lewis Carroll's famous hero is never late for such an important date!

Les Vendanges

Classic ✗✗

VISA
MC
AE
DC
æ

40 r. Friant
✉ 75014
✆ 0145395998 – **Fax** 0145397413
e-mail guy.tardif@wanadoo.fr **Web** www.lesvendanges-paris.com

Closed 28 July-26 August, 23 December-1st January, Saturday except dinner from November to January and Sunday

Menu €35

The name and bunches of grapes shown on the façade tip you off: the "treasure" at this congenial restaurant is in the cellar. And it is well-stocked and adventurous. In addition to the multitude of fine labels from all of France's wine-growing regions, it also has some good vintages from little known estates, and offers them at moderate prices. That is a godsend for anyone hoping to learn about new wines from experienced professionals. The same serious approach is evident in the menu, prepared with fresh ingredients and renewed seasonally. It features a wide range of classic recipes and a few dishes from the Southwest. The friendly staff gives the place an added charm.

Ⓜ Porte d'Orléans
C3

Les Petites Sorcières

Traditional ✗

VISA
MC

12 r. Liancourt
✉ 75014
✆ 0143219568 – **Fax** 0143219568

closed 13 July-16 August, Monday lunch, Saturday lunch and Sunday

Menu €33 – Carte €30/39

Ⓜ Denfert Rochereau
C2

Rest assured – these *sorcières* are very good little witches! Whether they are hanging from the ceiling, hiding in a corner or about to fly off on a broom, they are here to make your meal go smoothly. There is no magic formula here, simply a very nice little establishment with a personalized decor in shades of red, snug and nicely set little tables, an up-to-date menu carefully prepared with fine ingredients (such as the green bean and haddock salad with sweet onions, fillet of cod with a broad bean ragout, or the pineapple and raisin crumble with coconut sorbet), and prices which haven't skyrocketed!

La Régalade

Traditional ✗

A/C
VISA
MC
⚇

49 av. J. Moulin
✉ 75014
☏ 0145456858 – **Fax** 0145409674
e-mail la_regalade@yahoo.fr

Ⓜ Porte d'Orléans
B3

closed 26 July-20 August, Monday lunch, Saturday and Sunday – pre-book

Menu €32

Beware of overindulging on the delicious welcome terrine – you may regret not having enough room when the other courses arrive! Bruno Doucet is not the kind to serve skimpy portions. His part-*terroir*, part-market-based cuisine (*cochonailles, pomme Macaire au boudin noir*, preserved tomatoes stuffed with herbs) is generous and full of flavour, to the delight of gourmets and food-lovers of all persuasions. The fine wines and the extremely kind service are added bonuses. It is easy to see why so many people have made this their "local" and have only one regret - that they can only taste La Régalade's delights during the week! (Be sure to book, or you may be sorely disappointed.)

L'O à la Bouche

Terroir ✗

A/C
VISA
MC
AE
♀

124 bd Montparnasse
✉ 75014
☏ 0156540155 – **Fax** 0143210787
e-mail loalabouche2@wanadoo.fr

Ⓜ Vavin
C1

closed 5-27 August, Monday from May to October and Sunday

Menu €22 (lunch)/€33 – Carte €36/44

It could be the title of a Surrealist manifesto by André Breton and his gang from the period between the two world wars. In fact, it is the name of a restaurant run by Franck Paquier. With the solid experience of working for Troisgros and Guy Savoy under his belt, he finally settled on the boulevard Montparnasse and looked south for his inspiration. You can see that love of sunny climes in the decor – ochre and burnt sienna walls – and in the updated cuisine from the *terroir* which features genuine southern flavours. With its warm bistro spirit and congenial ambiance, this place gives you a true taste of the Mediterranean art of living.

Montparnasse, Denfert-Rochereau

Montparnasse, Denfert-Rochereau

La Cerisaie ☺

VISA 70 bd E. Quinet   Ⓜ Edgar Quinet
☒ 75014   **C1**
Ⓜ© ✆ 0143209898 – **Fax** 0143209898

closed 14 July-20 August, 23 December-6 January, Saturday and Sunday – pre-book

Ⓨ Menu €31 – Carte €31/37

If you try to get in without a reservation, Maryse Lalanne will tell you with that disappointed – but charming – look on her face: "It's already full!". And the size (20 place settings) has very little to do with it. The answer would probably be the same even if there was room for 30, 40 or 50 people. People love coming to this (non-smoking) pocket restaurant just to see what's on the blackboard - specialities slowly cooked and re-created based on the market, reflecting the talent of a chef who worked in the finest establishments in Toulouse. The cellar has a fine selection of regional wines, well-paired with these delicious dishes. La Cerisaie stands out as a fine representative of the Southwest in the heart of this "Breton" neighbourhood!

L'Amuse Bouche

VISA 186 r. Château   Ⓜ Mouton Duvernet
☒ 75014   **C2**
Ⓜ© ✆ 0143353161

Ⓨ closed August, Sunday and Monday

Menu €32

Philippe Dubois recently took over this friendly neighbourhood restaurant, where soufflés are the speciality. Well-represented on the rather traditional menu, they come in a wide variety to satisfy all tastes, whether sweet or savoury, as a starter, main course or dessert (with Grand Marnier, for instance). As for the decor, virtually nothing has changed since the arrival of the new chef-proprietor. It still has the same snug little tables and bright orange walls with just a few copper pots and personal touches added. The clientele of regulars can rest assured that all is well, and continue to enjoy the fare at this pleasant establishment.

Bistrot du Dôme

Seafood ☓

A/C | 1 r. Delambre | ⓜ Vavin
VISA | ✉ 75014 | **C1**
| ☎ 0143353200
ⓂⓒⒶ | closed Sunday and Monday in August
AE | Carte € 35/46
ⓨ

This is the annexe of the Dôme, its prestigious neighbour and "older brother". With its decidedly bistro look (old counter, wood and pewter bar, waiters in black-and-white outfits), the family resemblance doesn't jump right out at you - unless you're looking at the menu with its wide choice of seafood dishes. The large blackboard features such mouth-watering specials as haddock carpaccio, langoustine risotto, and skate with capers. As the "baby", the Bistrot du Dôme has a more "well-behaved" side than its older sibling. Here, the chic brasserie with its brisk and lively service is replaced by a convivial and rather relaxed ambiance. The large dining room, with its grape-leaf decorations on the ceiling, is all the more pleasant for it.

A La Bonne Table

Traditional ☓

A/C | 42 r. Friant | ⓜ Porte d'Orléans
VISA | ✉ 75014 | **C3**
| ☎ 0145397491 – **Fax** 0145436692
ⓂⓒⒶ | closed 8-29 July, 23 December-6 January, 27 February-4 March, Saturday lunch and Sunday
AE | Menu € 25 (lunch)/€ 29 – Carte € 31/46
ⓄⒹ
ⓨ

At his Bonne Table, Yoshitaka Kawamoto – who trained in the French style – features traditional French food. But connoisseurs of Japanese gastronomy will detect that special Nipponese touch which makes all the difference in his recipes. The influences from the Land of the Rising Sun are definitely there - in the choice of ingredients, in the specific preparation and in the seasoning, giving each dish a unique character. That originality easily makes up for the rather retro decor (banquettes, ceiling mouldings and rustic furniture), particularly when the prices are so reasonable.

Montparnasse, Denfert-Rochereau

Severo ⬡

Meat ✕

VISA
MC

8 r. Plantes
✉ 75014
✆ 0145404091

Ⓜ Mouton Duvernet
C2

closed 7-15 April, 21 July-20 August, 22 December-2 January, Saturday and Sunday

Carte €28/46

This excellent and unpretentious bistro has developed a fine reputation. And rightly so, since owner William Bernet puts a great deal into it, as he whirls around the tables and shares his love of wine with diners. That passion is expressed on the large blackboards placed all along the walls. There are wines from all the different *terroirs* and for all budgets. This treasure house is paired with a deliberately short, traditional menu honouring the Auvergne and Limousin regions. The dishes are cooked up with great care; the owner, a former butcher, prepares the meat himself, and the chef still makes homemade French fries!

De Bouche à Oreille

Traditional ✕

VISA
MC

34 r. Gassendi
✉ 75014
✆ 0143277314 – **Fax** 0143251423
e-mail baobenoit@hotmail.com

Ⓜ Denfert Rochereau
C2

closed 1st-15 August, Monday lunch, Saturday lunch and Sunday

Carte €30/49

The chef-owner at this congenial bistro is Benoît Chagny, who trained – and opened the A & M restaurant – with Jean-Pierre Vigato. For his own first establishment he chose a simple setting (exposed stonework and walls in yellow tones for a restrained look) as if to underline the essential element – his cuisine. He has clearly succeeded. In the kitchen, he cleverly reinvents the great classics of the culinary tradition (veal chops, duck terrine, etc.). Sampled in the convivial atmosphere here, his special blackboard dishes have a flavour that is both authentic and novel. My compliments to the chef!

Château Poivre

Terroir 🍴

VISA

MC

AE

DC

145 r. Château   **Ⓜ** Pernety
⊠ 75014   **B2**
✆ 01 43 22 03 68 – **Fax** 01 43 22 82 13
e-mail chateaupoivre@noos.fr

Closed 10-23 August, 23 December-3 January, Sunday, Monday and public holidays

Ⓨ   Menu €19 – Carte €22/53

With the Impasse Florimont nearby, the Languedoc wine cellar on the Place de Moro-Giafferi, and the proprietors' fine moustache, it was impossible not to be reminded of Georges Brassens, especially here in his own neighbourhood! The Dalbera Brothers have been here for twenty years and have been very successful. In the kitchen, Alain prepares straightforward, copious recipes with influences from the Southeast (tripe *à la niçoise*, fish *à l'antiboise*) and Southwest (preserved duck with Sarlat potatoes). In the dining room, Michel extends a friendly welcome in a rather retro setting, brightened up by the contemporary lighting and warm yellow and orange tones. And the prices are inversely proportionate to the size of the dishes!

Millésimes 62

Traditional 🍴

VISA

MC

AE

13 pl. Catalogne   **Ⓜ** Gaîté
⊠ 75014   **B1**
✆ 01 43 35 34 35 – **Fax** 01 43 20 26 21
e-mail millesime62@wanadoo.fr   **Web** www.millesimes62.com

closed 5-26 August and 24 December-2 January

Ⓨ   Menu €26

Millésime 62 has all the elements of a fine little establishment, starting with its enviable location on a square designed by Ricardo Bofill, a stone's throw from the TGV (high-speed train) station, and major hotels and theatres in Montparnasse. The setting is that of a charming contemporary bistro in muted yellow and chocolate tones, with a terrace facing the fountain. It is very pleasant, with nothing extravagant about it. There is a fine selection of wines – in particular by the glass – chosen by oenologist Jacques Boudin, and tasty market cuisine. As you may well imagine, the restaurant is very popular. Not to worry – prices have not gone up as a result.

Montparnasse, Denfert-Rochereau

Vaugirard, Porte de Versailles, Beaugrenelle

Blackwell K./MICHELIN

The most densely populated arrondissement of Paris is also one of its least well known. Its impressive dimensions conceal a dual heritage that is typical of both western and southern Paris; bourgeois and opulent in areas, but also deeply marked by its former "village" past, prior to being annexed to the rest of Paris. The variety of the streets, architecture and populations make it difficult to define its identity and the locals claim that it takes a whole lifetime to discover its secret nooks and crannies.

INTERNATIONAL PARIS

A genuine town within a town, the Porte de Versailles **exhibition centre** attracts millions of visitors from all over the world every year. It is the site of the most awaited (and the most visited) shows such as the **automobile show, agricultural show** and the famous **Paris Fair** and its Lépine invention competition. The area can become frankly overpopulated during some of these international events, rendering the road network almost impracticable and pushing the bus and metro system to its limits. There are however bonuses to this inconvenience and the area is chock-full of brasseries, small bistros and even restaurants with gastronomic claims, all at reasonable prices to attract the crowds of visitors.

VILLAGERS AT HEART

The real heart of the arrondissement, where the genuine locals live, lies between the **Vaugirard** and Grenelle districts.

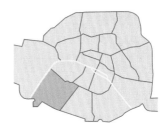

These former suburbs were annexed to Paris at a relatively late date and today represent a tightly woven mesh of typically Parisian mini-districts. Convention and George Brassens to the south, **La Motte Piquet** and Commerce to the north, they are made up of tiny squares and crossroads that are frequently adorned with gardens, music stands, unassuming little churches or the statue of some long forgotten war hero. Extremely well endowed in terms of neighbourhood shops, these havens of village life in the heart of Paris continue to nurture a genteel way of life, made up of discreet sociability and long-standing customs.

MANHATTAN-PARIS

The contrast afforded by **Beaugrenelle,** a shopping and financial centre built on the embankment of the former Javel district, couldn't be more marked. The sheer height of these tower blocks, built out of smoked glass, steel and concrete, is such that the skyline seems more akin to that of a North American city than to Paris, an impression that is even more pronounced from the hill on the other side of the river in the 16th. If you can manage to ignore the cruelly out-of-date architectural style, you will enjoy the district's several lounge bars and trendy restaurants, some of which command stunning views of the Seine.

Blackwell K/MICHELIN

Far from the frantic pace of the rest of Paris or the denser, and if the truth be known, less intimate, living conditions of the central arrondissements, these islands of quiet tranquillity reveal a little-known and relatively affluent side of Paris. Book lovers should not miss the **book market** every Sunday on rue Brancion, two minutes from the lawns and gardens of **Georges Brassens Park**.

Vaugirard, Porte de Versailles, Beaugrenelle

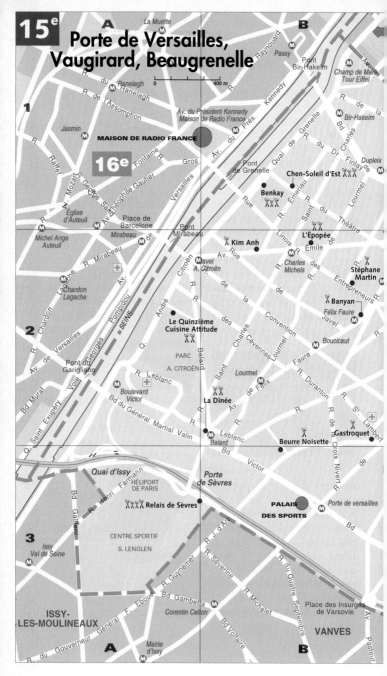

15e

A

B

Porte de Versailles, Vaugirard, Beaugrenelle

La Muette

R. du Ranelagh
R. de l'Assomption

Raynouad

Passy

Pont
Bir-Hakeim

Av. du Président Kennedy
Maison de Radio France

Kennedy

M Bir-Hakeim

Champ de Mars
Tour Eiffel

Jasmin

Quai de Grenelle

R. de

Bd

Charles

R. du Dr Finlay

Dupleix

MAISON DE RADIO FRANCE

16e

Fontaine

Gros

Versailles

Pont
de Grenelle

Rue

Chen-Soleil d'Est 🍴🍴🍴

George Sand
Av. Théophile Gautier

Église
d'Auteuil

Place de
Barcelone

Pont
Mirabeau

St Émeriau

Lourmel

R. du Théâtre

R. Mozart

Benkay 🍴🍴🍴

Michel Ange
Auteuil

Mirabeau

R. de Mirabeau

🍴 **Kim Anh**

Linois

Émile

L'Épopée 🍴

M de

Av. Rue

Citroën

Mavel
A. Citroën

Charles
Michels

R. des

**Stéphane
Martin** 🍴

Le Chardon
Lagache

R. Chardon

AV.

Pompidou

SEINE

R. André

R. de

de la

Convention

Entrepreneurs

🍴 **Banyan**
Félix Faure
Xavier

M Boucicaut

**Le Quinzième
Cuisine Attitude**

PARC
A. CITROËN

Balard

R. des

St Charles Cévennes

Lourmel

Faure

R. Duranton

R. St Lambert

🍴 **Gastroquet**

Pont du
Garigliano

Av. de Versailles

Voie Georges

R. Leblanc

**Boulevard
Victor**

Bd du Général Martial Valin

Av. de Félix

Lourmel

🍴🍴 **La Dînée**

R. de Croix Nivert R.

Bd Murat

Q. Saint Exupéry

R. Leblanc
Balard

Bd

Victor

Beurre Noisette

Quai d'Issy

HÉLIPORT
DE PARIS

Porte
de Sèvres

🍴🍴🍴🍴 **Relais de Sèvres**

Bd Gallieni

Bd Henri Farmann

CENTRE SPORTIF
S. LENGLEN

**PALAIS
DES SPORTS**

Porte de versailles

Bd

Issy
Val de Seine

ISSY-
LES-MOULINEAUX

R. du Gouverneur Général F. Eboué

R. Guynemer

Bd Gambetta

Corentin Celton

Bd Voltaire

R. J. d'Arc

R. Séverine

R. Michelet

R. du Quatre Septembre

Place des Insurgés
de Varsovie

Av. Pasteur

VANVES

Mairie
d'Issy

A

B

0   400 m

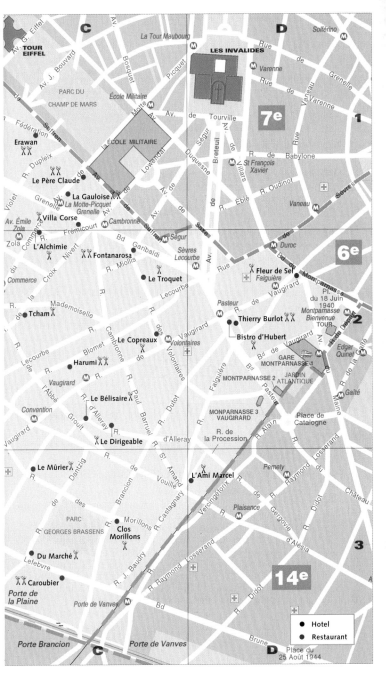

Benkay

Japanese ✗✗✗

Novotel Paris Tour Eiffel,
61 quai de Grenelle ⊠ 75015
✆ 01 40 58 21 26 – **Fax** 01 40 58 21 30
e-mail h3546@accor.com **Web** www.novotel.com

Ⓜ Bir-Hakeim
B1

Menu €30 (lunch)/€125 – Carte €42/131

Located on the top (fourth) floor of a small building next to the Novotel (ex-hotel Nikko), this comfortable Japanese restaurant is in a choice setting with a pretty view of the Seine and the Maison de la Radio. The sobre, zen-like decor features clean lines, light-coloured marble, dark wood, and spacious, traditional Japanese tables. The food focuses on quality ingredients and delicious eye-catching dishes such as fillet of beef seared on a hotplate at the tableside, sautéed calamari and crêpes flambées, tasty and spectacular. A fine culinary experience for those in search of something a bit exotic.

Chen-Soleil d'Est

Chinese ✗✗✗

15 r. Théâtre
⊠ 75015
✆ 01 45 79 34 34 – **Fax** 01 45 79 07 53
closed Aug. and Sun.

Ⓜ Charles Michels
B1

Menu €40 (weekday lunch)/€160 – Carte €55/225

Chen probably doesn't get much sun in this underground tunnel under Beaugrenelle, where it is almost invisible. Luckily there is plenty of light in the plates here, with its tasty and authentic Asian cuisine featuring wok and steamed food, sweet-and-savoury flavours and scents of ginger and lemon grass. The typical, elegant setting doesn't hurt either. The Asian decor in the plush dining room features Venetian blinds, a plush red carpet and imported furniture. The kitchen can be seen from the entrance, decorated with Chinese-style wood. A true gastronomic journey into the land of the Han.

Le Quinzième Cuisine Attitude

Fashionable ✗✗

 14 r. Cauchy
✉ 75015
VISA ℰ 0145544343 – **Fax** 0145572296
e-mail resa@lequinzieme.com
Web www.restaurantlequinzieme.com

🅐🅔 closed 11-20 August, Saturday lunch and Sunday

Ⓜ Javel
A2

Ⓨ Menu €35 (weekday lunch)/€95 – Carte €45/90

The talented Cyril Lignac, already famous due to his show, "Oui Chef !", is behind this elegant restaurant a short distance from the Parc André Citroën. The place rather resembles him, as he is the first to admit. The chic contemporary setting features pure wood, glass and ceramics, and the furniture in discreet tones confirms the impression of an open, light and comfortable space. Quality and innovation are also present in the kitchen, where the inventive dishes combine choice ingredients and tried-and-tested recipes. Sweet-and-savoury tastes and crispy-creamy textures create contrasts and surprises. A view of the kitchen through a wide picture window allows diners to admire the chef at work.

Harumi

Japanese ✗✗

🅐🅒 99 r. Blomet
✉ 75015
VISA ℰ 0142502227 – **Fax** 0142502227
e-mail contactharumi@wanadoo.fr **Web** www.harumi.fr

🅐🅔 closed 15 July-15 August, Sunday dinner and Monday

Ⓜ Vaugirard
C2

Ⓨ Menu €38 – Carte €48/52

Franco-Japanese fusion is the name of the game at this small, pleasantly refined neighbourhood establishment. The female chef – a rarity in Paris – is Japanese and has a masterful command of both culinary traditions. The decor, like the chef, is charming and tactful, a comfortable and colourful setting with pastel furniture and many Japanese touches. The cuisine features quality ingredients, reinventing traditional recipes from the Land of the Rising Sun, such as belly of Mediterranean tuna *mi-cuit* in a spice crust, *rognons de veau et jus de shitaké* (veal kidneys in shitake juice), or the delicious *côte de cochon de lait aux 5 épices asiatiques* (suckling pig with 5 Asian spices). Fine wine list.

Porte de Versailles, Vaugirard, Beaugrenelle

La Dînée

Contemporary ✗✗

VISA
MC
AE
DC

85 r. Leblanc
✉ 75015
📞 0145542049 – **Fax** 0140607376
e-mail postmaster@ladinee.com **Web** www.restaurant-ladinee.com
closed Saturday and Sunday

Ⓜ Balard
B2

Ⓨ

Menu € 36

This little seafood restaurant with a discreet façade is located on a street near Balard. It has developed a blue-chip reputation in the neighbourhood by using fresh, high-quality ingredients and making simple, well-balanced dishes. The long dining room has a pleasant contemporary decor with pastel walls and banquettes, abstract paintings and soft lighting. Well-prepared dishes from the sea include pan-fried squid with lemon, scallop and sea snail tartare, and braised Cajun-style salmon. There are also plenty of treats for those who are fond of game and poultry.

La Gauloise

Traditional ✗✗

📶
🚌
VISA
MC
AE
Ⓨ

59 av. La Motte-Picquet
✉ 75015
📞 0147341164 – **Fax** 0140610970

Ⓜ La Motte Picquet Grenelle
C1

Carte € 32/50

Judging from the number of signed photographs proudly displayed on the walls, La Gauloise must have hosted a fair amount of political and media figures over the course of its long history. With its Spartan banquettes, venerable mirrors and cascading chandeliers, the 1900s-style decor evokes the sturdy bistros of the good old days and the Golden Age of Parisian brasseries. The standard traditional dishes are simple and well-prepared, including onion soup, duck *confit* and rib steak. Enjoy the pleasant terrace in summer, or the small dining room for a meal in private.

Thierry Burlot 🏠

Contemporary ✗✗

A/C 8 r. Nicolas Charlet   ⓜ Pasteur
VISA ✉ 75015   **D2**
⓪⓪ ☎ 0142190859 – **Fax** 0145670913
A/E closed Saturday lunchtime and Sunday
♈ **Menu** €35/59 – **Carte** €41/51

The atmosphere is hushed and peaceful in this Pasteur neighbourhood institution a few hundred metres from the Montparnasse TGV station. The decor is discreet and cosy, with lacquered wood panelling, soft lighting and smoked glass partitions, suffused with a relaxing jazzy ambiance. Thierry Burlot has earned a solid reputation in this arrondissement and beyond with his well-prepared up-to-date cuisine. The dishes are elegant and often inventive. Try the gambas dimsum with *cumbava* and *rougail*, or the preserved suckling pig with *lardons* and onion compote, always delicious. Fine selection of wines.

Caroubier 🏠

Moroccan ✗✗

A/C 82 bd Lefebvre   ⓜ Porte de Vanves
VISA ✉ 75015   **C3**
⓪⓪ ☎ 0140431612 – **Fax** 0140431612
A/E closed 21 July-20 August and Monday
♈ **Menu** €15 (weekday lunch)/€28 – **Carte** €27/45

A real North African oasis, a short distance from the Parc des Expositions, the Caroubier has embodied the best of Moroccan cuisine for 30 years. In its rather contemporary setting adorned with rugs, photographs and objects from North Africa, this family restaurant proposes tasty traditional food prepared in just the right way. All the great classics are made flawlessly and served in copious portions, including generous couscous dishes, tajines with subtle and candid flavours, and *pastillas* full of the Atlas sun. The reception is thoughtful, the service quick and efficient and the prices reasonable. This is a place which you leave feeling very satisfied.

Fontanarosa

Italian 🍴🍴

28 bd Garibaldi
✉ 75015
📞 0145669784 – **Fax** 0147839630
e-mail contact@fontanarosa-ristorante.eu
Web www.fontanarosa-ristorante.eu

Ⓜ Cambronne
C2

Menu €21 (weekday lunch)/€30 – Carte €31/69

This friendly trattoria is ideally located on the boulevard Garibaldi, named after the father of Italian unity. This ambassador of Sardinian culinary traditions found a place for itself straight away here in the heart of the Grenelle district. The pretty pink façade, sheltered green terrace and interior in pastel tones highlighted by paintings of vegetation evoke Sardinia. In this characteristic setting you can enjoy the well-prepared, flavourful and copiously served Italian specialities. Various seasonal antipasti, gnocchi with the frank flavours of the Italian sun or the Milanese-style risotto will give you a delicious taste of this great culinary tradition. The well-stocked wine list covers all the different regions in the country.

L'Épopée

Traditional 🍴🍴

89 av. É. Zola
✉ 75015
📞 0145777137 – **Fax** 0145777137
closed 22 July-22 August, Saturday lunch and Sunday

Ⓜ Charles Michels
B2

Menu €34/€40

A meal at l'Epopée (Epic) can easily turn into an adventure, especially if you allow the proprietor to share his passion for wine with you. The lyricism and hyperbole are present in the dishes too. This restaurant, located next to the Charles Michel metro station, has a plush interior with light parquet floors, watercolours on the walls and comfortably spaced tables, creating a relaxed, low-key atmosphere. In addition to the well-stocked cellar, regulars come back for the traditional food that is well-made and rather copious. The fresh ingredients are carefully prepared, and the excellent service can make it a truly epic experience!

Porte de Versailles, Vaugirard, Beaugrenelle

Erawan

Thai ✗✗

[A/C]
[VISA]
[MC]
[AE]

76 r. Fédération
⊠ 75015
℘ 0147835567 – **Fax** 0147348598
closed 5-20 August and Sunday

Ⓜ La Motte Picquet Grenelle
C1

Menu € 23/38 – Carte € 20/52

In Thai mythology, Erawan was a three-headed elephant with an uncommon appetite. There is no doubt that it would have felt quite at home in this pleasant Thai restaurant hidden behind a rather all-purpose Asian façade. The dining room is decorated with traditional art work and highlighted by wood panelling and tantric bas-reliefs, a hushed ambiance and soft lighting – a decor that evokes the minimalist mystique of Southeast Asian culture. A father-and-son team takes care of the service and prepares the characteristic light and fragrant cuisine. The dishes with flavours of coconut, lemon grass and curcuma are mouthwatering.

Le Père Claude

Traditional ✗✗

[A/C]
[VISA]
[MC]
[AE]
[♀]

51 av. de la Motte Picquet
⊠ 75015
℘ 0147340305 – **Fax** 0140569784
e-mail lepereclaude@free.fr

Ⓜ La Motte Picquet Grenelle
C1

Carte € 34/69

This establishment, a real institution in the neighbourhood, is located on a broad avenue near the Champ de Mars and is protected from the noise of the street by a pleasant terrace. The tone is set the minute you enter, with a superb rotisserie where poultry, sausages, bacon and *andouillettes* are roasted. Claude Perraudin has left his lively and colourful mark on the place, where local figures and servicemen from the nearby École Militaire mix in the low-key yet convivial atmosphere. In addition to the meat dishes, there are tapas specialities and a fine – and much appreciated – selection of wines by the glass.

Porte de Versailles, Vaugirard, Beaugrenelle

Stéphane Martin

Contemporary ✗

A/C	67 r. Entrepreneurs
VISA	⊠ 75015
	✆ 01 45 79 03 31 – **Fax** 01 45 79 44 69
MC	**e-mail** resto.stephanemartin@free.fr
🍷	closed 30 July-21 August, 23 December-2 January, Sunday and Monday

M Charles Michels
B2

Menu €22 (weekday lunch)/€35 – Carte €36/49

Stéphane Martin is a very popular place, and not just with locals; this friendly establishment has earned an enviable reputation with most of the food-lovers on the Left Bank. The setting is cosy and tasteful, with a wine and caramel colour scheme, dark wood furniture and a fresco of an ancient library. The food features appetizing up-to-date recipes which are well-prepared with carefully selected ingredients. Try the éminced of duck foie gras or the ham hocks braised in honey, ideal blends of inventiveness and quality.

Kim Anh

Vietnamese ✗

A/C	51 av. Emile Zola
VISA	⊠ 75015
	✆ 01 45 79 40 96 – **Fax** 01 40 59 49 78
MC	Closed Easter holidays, 6-20 August and Monday – dinner only
AE	
🍷	

M Charles Michels
B2

Menu €34 – Carte €40/69

Sheltered from the very busy Avenue Émile Zola by a line of shrubs, this establishment proposes authentic and enticing Vietnamese specialities. Forget the plain façade and unassuming interior decor with a few floral bouquets. You are here for the food. The menu features the whole gamut of spicy and sweet Tonkin flavours, including delicious caramelized langoustines and grilled tripe seasoned with garlic, hot peppers, sugar and lemon. You are about to embark on a memorable cruise on the Mekong to explore the culinary marvels of faraway Cochin China, with a nice French wine to accompany the trip.

Porte de Versailles, Vaugirard, Beaugrenelle

Le Copreaux

Traditional ✗

A|C

VISA

MC

Ⓨ

15 r. Copreaux
✉ 75015
✆ 0143068335

closed 1st-20 August, Sunday and Monday

Ⓜ Volontaires
C2

Menu €27 wine included – Carte €27/40

The eponymous street, only a stone's throw from the Volontaires metro station, is tiny and nearly invisible. The restaurant is equally discreet behind its glass façade hidden from the pavement by velvet curtains. But once inside you will appreciate the qualities of this charming family establishment. Wood panelling and paintings on the walls, small, discreetly laid tables form the rustic and warm ambiance with a country feel. The chef, who is the husband of the proprietress, prepares subtle and flavourful traditional cuisine. Non smoking.

Bistro d'Hubert

Bistro ✗

VISA

MC

AE

Ⓓ

Ⓨ

41 bd Pasteur
✉ 75015
✆ 0147341550 – **Fax** 0145670309
e-mail message@bistrodhubert.com **Web** www.bistrodhubert.com

closed Saturday lunchtime, Monday lunchtime and Sunday

Ⓜ Pasteur
D2

Menu €34 – Carte €40/72

The setting at this restaurant on the boulevard Pasteur, a stone's throw from Montparnasse station, is very attractive. The dining room looks like an inn from the Landes region with its light wood walls and ceiling, its rustic tables and shelves filled with bottles and jars from the *terroir*. The legendary Hubert is no longer in the kitchen, but his daughter has inherited his passion for the good things in life. Updated traditional recipes are proposed in the bistrot, using fine and carefully selected ingredients. If you are tempted by a choice after-dinner liqueur or a good cigar, the proprietress will be glad to share her excellent recommendations.

Porte de Versailles, Vaugirard, Beaugrenelle

Beurre Noisette

Contemporary ✗

VISA
MC
AE
♀

68 r. Vasco de Gama
✉ 75015
☎ 0148568249
closed 30 July-19 August, 31 December-6 January, Sunday and Monday

Ⓜ **Lourmel**
B2-3

Menu €22 (weekday lunch)/€42

While the name of this restaurant in a quiet street between Balard and Lourmel is already quite enticing, the dishes served here are truly mouth-watering. The two dining rooms with warm colours and soft lighting make you feel right at home, the staff is welcoming, and the ambiance pleasantly convivial. The chef, who has worked at some of the finest establishments in Paris and is all alone here, lovingly cooks up delicious up-to-date food, with dishes featured on the blackboard which change according to the market. At lunchtime the menu is simple and less ambitious. Nice selection of wines by the glass.

L'Ami Marcel

Traditional ✗

A/C
VISA
MC
AE
♀

33 r. Georges Pitard
✉ 75015
☎ 0148566206 – **Fax** 0148566206
e-mail lamimarcel@lamimarcel.com **Web** www.lamimarcel.com
closed 30 July-20 August, Sunday and Monday

Ⓜ **Plaisance**
D3

Menu €32 – Carte €26/37

It's hard not to take a fancy to l'Ami Marcel, as the dishes here are appealing and the ambiance deliciously lively. This little restaurant hidden in a lost corner of the 15th arrondissement rather far from the Plaisance metro station, is indeed full of charm. Its typical Parisian bistro decor with banquettes, snug tables and a zinc bar covered in zebrano – a tropical wood from Africa – highlights the paintings by neighbourhood artists on the walls. The well-prepared and reasonably-priced traditional cuisine, served in an ultra-convivial ambiance, includes talented renditions of dishes from the *terroir* such as homemade foie gras terrine and ox cheeks braised in red wine. It's no wonder Marcel has so many friends!

Clos Morillons

Contemporary ☓

 50 r. Morillons   Ⓜ Convention

✉ 75015   **C3**

℘ 0148280437 – **Fax** 0148287077

☗ closed 6-19 August, Sunday dinner and Monday

Menu €26

This friendly neighbourhood restaurant is hidden in a quiet street near the Parc Georges Brassens and its Sunday book fair. The pleasant decor, with its bistro-style façade, discreet interior in pastel yellow tones, rattan and bamboo furniture and simply laid tables, stays tactfully in the background, allowing the flavoursome up-to-date cuisine carefully prepared with well-chosen ingredients to speak for itself. The dishes feature original associations and various subtly used spices: tiny scallops and shrimp with ginger, swordfish fillet with chorizo and vegetables, etc. Friendly service, and the wine list is rather well-stocked.

Le Troquet ⍟

Terroir ☓

 21 r. F. Bonvin   Ⓜ Cambronne

✉ 75015   **C2**

℘ 0145668900 – **Fax** 0145668983

☗ closed 2-10 May, 5-27 August, 24 December-1st January, Sunday and Monday

Menu €28 (weekday lunch)/€40

Who would have thought that an anonymous little street between Cambronne and Lecourbe would have such a fine restaurant? This little establishment with a discreet façade is the quintessential *troquet* with its colourful bistro decor of tiled floors, moleskin banquettes and convivial ambiance around the rather snug tables. The food is why people come here, with its enticing set menu which changes according to the market and includes a few Basque specialities. Superb ingredients, flavourful dishes and very reasonable prices – what more could you ask for?

Porte de Versailles, Vaugirard, Beaugrenelle

Gastroquet

Traditional

VISA
MC
AE

10 r. Desnouettes
✉ 75015
✆ 01 48 28 60 91 – **Fax** 01 45 33 23 70
closed August, Saturday dinner from March to July and Sunday

Ⓜ Convention
B2

Ⴅ Menu €22 (lunch)/€29 (dinner) – Carte €49/58

This authentic gastronomic *troquet* (small wine cafe), a short distance from the Parc des Expositions, is quite charming. A wide, curtained picture window in the discreetly comfortable dining room gives onto narrow rue Desnouettes. The place is masterfully run by an energetic couple with an enduring passion for fine ingredients which has drawn in neighbourhood gourmets as well as occasional diners. The traditional, market-based cuisine on the menu is simple and often copious, while the friendly family atmosphere delights customers. Good choice of wines by the glass.

Villa Corse

Corsican

A/C
VISA
MC
AE

164 bd Grenelle
✉ 75015
✆ 01 53 86 70 81 – **Fax** 01 53 86 90 73
e-mail lavillacorse@wanadoo.fr
closed Sunday

Ⓜ La Motte Picquet Grenelle
C1

Carte €49/56

Dreaming of Corsica in Paris? This elegant restaurant in the Cambronne neighbourhood takes the island's gastronomic delights to new heights, proposing food with the powerful flavours of the *maquis* (scrubland). The place amazingly evokes a Corsican villa, with vaulted arcades, wrought-iron balustrades and lithographs illustrating the Isle of Beauty. The three dining rooms, decorated in different styles, have something to please everyone: library, bar-lounge or terrace. The dishes are proud to show off their origins, featuring cold meats with character, local herbs with strong aromas, and robust local wines – a vigorous and noble cuisine.

Porte de Versailles, Vaugirard, Beaugrenelle

Du Marché

Bistro

VISA

59 r. Dantzig
✉ 75015
✆ 0148283155 – **Fax** 0148281831
closed August, Sunday and Monday

Ⓜ Porte de Versailles
C3

Menu €29/€32

This establishment, a stone's throw from the Parc Georges Brassens, has an unpretentious look evoking the old-fashioned charm of a 1950s bistro with mosaic tiles, *boule* lamps, an imitation leather banquette and zinc counter. But don't be fooled – they are very serious about the food here. The chef proposes specialities from the Southwest, enhanced by a touch of the Mediterranean terroir, with tasty and generous dishes. The classic ingredients are excellent: duck breast and preserved duck from the Lot-et-Garonne, *foie gras et blonde d'Aquitaine* are carefully cooked and served up perfectly. Fish aficionados will enjoy the swordfish in aioli sauce.

Fleur de Sel

South-West of France

VISA

32 bd Montparnasse
✉ 75015
✆ 0145485203 – **Fax** 0145485217
e-mail restaurant.fleurdesel@wanadoo.fr **Web** www.fleur-de-sel.fr
Closed Saturday lunch, Sunday and lunch on public holidays

Ⓜ Falguière
D2

Menu €20/25 – Carte €38/44

This restaurant with a warm atmosphere, located right on the Boulevard du Montparnasse, has been a smash hit ever since it opened. Wine comes first here – white or red – served by the glass, carafe or bottle, and sold at cost price! The three dining rooms are decorated in the 1950s bistro style with posters of films and showbiz stars from the era on the walls. The fine market-based food features carefully prepared, updated versions of classics such as chef's terrine with preserved onions, Salers beef in *maître d'hôtel* sauce (butter, parsley and lemon), and braised lamb shanks. A few daily specials are also posted on the blackboard.

Porte de Versailles, Vaugirard, Beaugrenelle

L 'Alchimie

Traditional ⚔

VISA   34 r. Letellier   Ⓜ La Motte Picquet Grenelle
MC   ✉ 75015   **C2**
DC   ✆ 01 45 75 55 95
     Web http://alchimie.lesrestos.com
♀   closed 29 July-20 August, 24 December-1st January, Sunday and Monday

Menu €28

What is the secret chemistry at work in this friendly little establishment with a discreet façade in the Grenelle area? Quite
simply, a blend of talent and know-how. The chef knows his
classics well after years of working for some of the all-time greats,
including Senderens, Faugeron and Raymond Blanc. His tasty
and carefully prepared traditional recipes feature seasonal ingredients enhanced by his magical touch. Livened up with
exotic spices and sweet-and-savoury touches, they take on a
whole new dimension; dishes such as venison chops with *grand
veneur* sauce and swordfish steak with sweet potato and ginger
aioli are absolutely wonderful.

Le Mûrier

Traditional ⚔

VISA   42 r. Olivier de Serres   Ⓜ Convention
MC   ✉ 75015   **C3**
♀   ✆ 01 45 32 81 88
     e-mail lepimpecmartin@yahoo.fr
     closed 13-19 August, Saturday and Sunday

Menu €19 (lunch)/€25

The ambiance is peaceful and convivial, and the prices reasonable at this unpretentious establishment in a rather quiet street
near the Convention metro station. Behind the unassuming
façade is a long dining room in shades of yellow, which is simply
laid out and decorated with turn-of-the-century posters that
give it an "old café" look. The place is brightened up with little
touches of blue and some greenery here and there. Like the
setting, the simple and carefully prepared cuisine has great
respect for tradition. Classics include the fine grilled beef, veal
kidneys with mustard and house terrines. The service is efficient
and unpretentious.

Le Bélisaire

Bistro ✗

VISA
MC
AE
♀

2 r. Marmontel
✉ 75015
✆ 0148286224 – **Fax** 0148286224
closed 8-15 April, 29 July-21 August, 23-30 December, Saturday dinner and Sunday

🄼 Vaugirard
C2

Menu €20 (weekday lunch)/€30

This restaurant, named after the eponymous novel by Marmontel, has little in common with the Byzantine general. The atmosphere is calm, and the up-to-date cuisine tasty – a far cry from the rigours of military life at any rate. While it may look like an unassuming café, the establishment has built up a solid reputation among local gourmets thanks to its young chef, Mathieu Garrel. The carefully prepared, market-based dishes vary according to the seasons. Try the game in autumn – the excellent venison stew for example – or the vegetable starters in the spring. Efficient service in the two pleasant dining rooms with a country bistro feel.

Le Dirigeable

Traditional ✗

VISA
MC
AE
♀

37 r. d' Alleray
✉ 75015
✆ 0145320154
closed 1st-20 August, 23 December-2 January, Sunday and Monday

🄼 Vaugirard
C2

Menu €19 (weekday lunch) – Carte €28/45

Embark on a true culinary cruise in this discreetly charming aerostat just a few minutes from the Vaugirard metro station. This friendly neighbourhood restaurant has a simple, laid-back decor with chocolate banquettes, wooden furniture and light-coloured walls with wide mirrors. Well-prepared traditional food is made with the most carefully selected ingredients. The menu is attractive at lunchtime, with daily blackboard suggestions, and bolder in the evening. A large clientele of regulars has been built up over the years due to the high-quality dishes, convivial ambiance and kind staff.

Porte de Versailles, Vaugirard, Beaugrenelle

Tcham

Korean ✗

A/C
VISA
MC
Y

89 r. Croix-Nivert
✉ 75015
☎ 01 45 30 38 14 – Fax 01 45 30 38 14
e-mail kobiz128@hotmail.com
closed 23 December-2 January and Sunday

Ⓜ Commerce
C2

Menu €20/€26 wine included – Carte €23/35

This peaceful residential area of the 15th arrondissement is the perfect spot for this discreet restaurant specializing in cuisine from the land of morning calm. The food is the main focus here, so don't expect anything fancy from the understated design and deliberately minimalist decor with just a few simple paintings on the walls. But the excellent and tasty Korean food, more elaborate in the evening, features talented versions of the major local specialities. Try the famous *Bibimbap*, or beef with fresh and raw vegetables served with an egg yolk on a base of rice, warmed in a stone pot. Delicious!

Banyan

Thai ✗

A/C
VISA
MC
AE
Y

24 pl. E. Pernet
✉ 75015
☎ 01 40 60 09 31 – Fax 01 40 60 09 20
e-mail lebanyan@noos.fr Web www.lebanyan.com
closed 6-20 August and Sunday

Ⓜ Félix Faure
B2

Menu €35/55 – Carte €33/53

Don't be put off by the ordinary-looking façade. The Banyan is a genuine piece of Thailand right in Paris. Oth Sombath, the talented young chef who started out at the Blue Elephant, creates his own tasty and inventive version of Thai food. His flavourful recipes featuring curcuma and galangal, and scented with basil and the powerful aromas of lemongrass and curry, have the sweet smell of Thailand's gardens. Meals are served on simple wooden tables in the comfortably designed, low-key dining room decorated with traditional etchings. Takeaway dishes are also available.

Porte de Versailles, Vaugirard, Beaugrenelle

Étoile, Trocadéro, Bois de Boulogne, Passy, Auteuil

Blackwell K./MICHELIN

The 16th is so vast that it has two postal codes, an exception in Paris, and indeed the differences between the north and south sectors of the arrondissement extend far beyond a mere digit. From the luxury and opulence around **place de l'Étoile** to the peaceful lawns of the **bois de Boulogne,** without forgetting the splendid vista from the **palais de Chaillot,** this arrondissement, in which it is said that nothing ever happens, in fact has much to offer visitors. Bordered by the Seine, avenue Marceau and the Bois de Boulogne, it has far more to recommend it than well-heeled streets and luxury boutiques.

TRIUMPHAL

On the main road into the west of Paris, the Étoile has conquered more than one visitor in its time. Is it because of the grandiose symbolism of the **triumphal arch** built by Napoleon to celebrate his victories? Or is it because of the memory of the unknown soldier, whose tomb is the culminating point of an annual military parade? More prosaically though, it is most probably the nightlife and shops that explain its constant popularity with tourists. By day its tightly-packed shopping malls and luxury boutiques, and come sunset, its nightclubs, among the most exclusive of the capital, never empty. It is also

home to some of the capital's finest restaurants, providing of course that you are prepared to foot the bill.

A PARISIAN OASIS

To the southwest of the Étoile, the climate progressively mellows as the presence of shops grows rarer and we can only urge visitors to take advantage of this break from the urban bustle to explore the Bois de Boulogne and its neighbourhood. A survivor of the forest of Rouvray that bordered Paris in the Middle Ages, this gigantic wood is two and a half times larger than Central Park. Lakes and waterfalls add interest to the dozens of kilometres of roads and paths through the

Blackwell K./MICHELIN

wood, as do several of the capital's most beautifully located gastronomic restaurants. Several portions of the wood are in fact parks in their own right, such as the **Jardin d'Acclimatation,** an immense playground with a zoo and theme park, the **Jardins de Bagatelle,** laid out in an "Anglo-Chinese" style and the **Pré-Catelan,** landscaped gardens inspired by the

works of Shakespeare. Even though the "bois", as the Parisians affectionately refer to it, can hardly be called unspoilt countryside, it is sufficiently varied to appeal to everyone!

BOURGEOIS AND VILLAGERS

Few areas of Paris have retained their village-like features in the same way as **Passy and Auteuil;** formerly towns on the outskirts of Paris, they were annexed to the capital under Napoleon III but continue to display their original charm. Bourgeois, even select, they are the epitome of carefree, unchanging Paris. Rue de Passy for example is lined with all sorts of shops, in particular clothing, while around Auteuil are some of the capital's best gourmet establishments where each café, delicatessen and restaurant has its own speciality. East of Passy don't forget to pause on **place du Trocadéro** and savour the splendid view of the Tour Eiffel before branching out into the surrounding streets to sample the fare of the smart bistros and trendy restaurants.

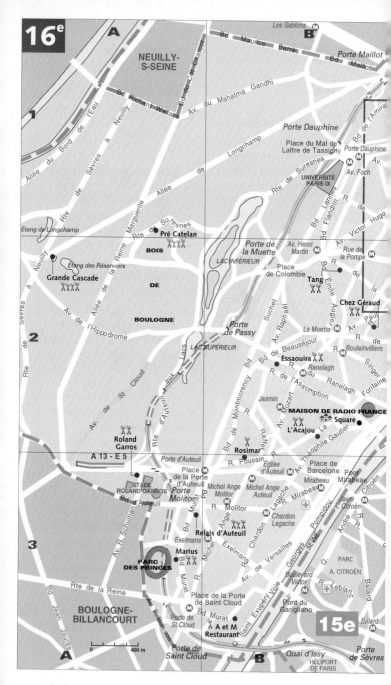

16e

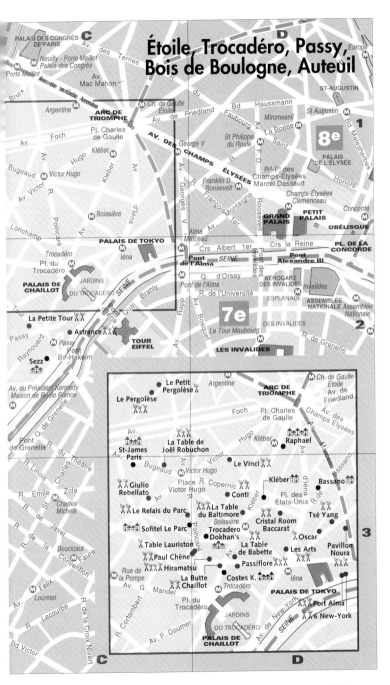

Étoile, Trocadéro, Passy, Bois de Boulogne, Auteuil

Pré Catelan ✿✿✿

Innovative 𝕏𝕏𝕏𝕏

rte Suresnes
✉ 75016 **A1**
✆ 01 44 14 41 14 – **Fax** 01 45 24 43 25
e-mail leprecatelan-restaurant@lenotre.fr **Web** www.lenotre.fr
Closed 28 October-6 November, 17 February-11 March, Sunday except lunch from May to October and Monday

Menu €75 (weekday lunch)/€180 – Carte €151/200

Pré Catelan

This sumptuous Napoleon III building is hidden deep inside the Bois de Boulogne, only a few minutes from the Arc de Triomphe. In fine weather one can dine in the gardens and on the shady terrace, while the classically designed luxury dining room features a ceiling decorated with friezes by Caran d'Ache. For several years now, the inventive cuisine here has been prepared by Frédéric Anton, awarded the Meilleur Ouvrier de France prize. This fashioner of tastes – who wanted to be a cabinetmaker – has created a menu combining balance, harmony and generosity. He cares about the graphic effect of his dishes – without neglecting their flavour – and is fond of inventing unusual combinations and variations on the same ingredients. This playful side only adds to his appeal. Not to mention the impeccable reception and service, and the impressive wine list. These are just a few of the arguments in favour of this noble house, which has made it all the way to the top.

A LA CARTE		
FIRST COURSE	**MAIN COURSE**	**DESSERT**
• TOUS CES PRODUITS ACCOMMODÉS SELON L'HUMEUR OU LA SAISON :		
• La tomate.	• Le pigeonneau.	• Le café "expresso".
• La langoustine.	• L'agneau.	• Le chocolat.

Grande Cascade ✿

Contemporary ✕✕✕✕

---

 allée de Longchamp (In the Bois de Boulogne)
✉ 75016 **A2**
✆ 0145273351 – **Fax** 0142889906
 e-mail contact@lagrandecascade.fr **Web** www.lagrandecascade.fr
Closed February half-term holidays

Menu €70/€165 – Carte €130/170

The well-to-do clientele that frequents this place is well aware of the appeal of this former hunting lodge, which belonged to Napoleon III and is tastefully furnished in the Belle Époque style. With its elegant rotunda dining room lit up by a huge glass roof and its beautiful terrace – booked up at the first sign of good weather – they flock to the Bois de Boulogne for a bit of charm and "country air" and a taste of the slightly old-fashioned but ever-so-sweet and stylish Paris of yesteryear. While reassuringly classical – although not without a touch of modernity – the food has kept up with the times, like its young owners. Georges and André Menut took over from their father André, once in charge of awakening this "sleeping beauty" himself. They gave carte blanche to Frédéric Robert, a chef who worked at the Grand Véfour, the Vivarois and Lucas Carton, including ten years with Alain Senderens. All of which enables this establishment, whose short menu is quite mouth-watering, to climb up the gastronomic ladder of Paris.

A LA CARTE

FIRST COURSE
• Fleurs de courgette ivres de girolles, coques et couteaux.
• Canelloni farci de truffes noires, foie gras et céleri.

MAIN COURSE
• Homard de Nouvelle-Ecosse façon newburg.
• Pomme de ris de veau cuite lentement, olives, câpres et croûtons frits.

DESSERT
• Grande assiette de chocolat.
• Annanas rôti aux écorces de gingembre, baba au vieux rhum, crème fouettée au citron vert.

Étoile, Trocadéro, Passy, Bois de Boulogne

Étoile, Trocadéro, Passy, Bois de Boulogne

Hiramatsu ❀

Innovative 🗙🗙🗙🗙

A/C

VISA

MC

AE

D

🎐

🍷

52 r. Longchamp
✉ 75116
✆ 0156810880 – **Fax** 0156810881
e-mail paris@hiramatsu.co.jp **Web** www.hiratamatsu.co.jp
closed 28 July-26 August, 29 December-6 January, Saturday and Sunday – number of covers limited, pre-book

◉ Trocadéro
D3

Menu € 48 (lunch)/€ 130 – **Carte** € 103/140

Don't be fooled by the Japanese-sounding name (the owner's real name); Hiramatsu is an ambassador of French cuisine, blending contemporary classicism with a touch of sophistication with perfect harmony. Formerly on the île Saint-Louis, Hiroyuki Hiramatsu left his small space with twenty tables for what had long been the domain of Henri Faugeron, an ardent defender of a certain classicism in cooking. The choice is not really an accident, and the story is worth telling. Hiramatsu came to learn his craft in France when he was a mere chef's assistant in the late 1970s. He knocked on the door of 52 rue de Longchamp and was turned away. In short, he has come full circle in his Parisian journey by becoming the owner of that very same place. The restaurant is elegant with a discreet zen décor; and the service, like the food, is extremely refined.

A LA CARTE

FIRST COURSE
· Foie gras de canard aux choux frisés, jus de truffe.

· Filet de bar de ligne en fine croûte d'herbes, mousseline de vermouth, purée de chou-fleur.

MAIN COURSE
· Feuilleté de homard au parfum de truffe, jus d'estragon.

· Fines lamelles d'agneau, compotée d'oignons blancs, jus de truffe.

DESSERT
· Risotto de riz noir au vin rouge, crème glacée à la noix de coco.

· Croûte "Tahiti" et tuiles de banane, crème glacée à la pistache.

Relais d'Auteuil ✿

Classic ✗✗✗

A/C
VISA
MC
AE
D
✿
♉

31 bd. Murat
✉ 75016
☎ 0146510954 – **Fax** 0140710503
e-mail pignol.p@wanadoo.fr
closed August, Christmas holidays, Monday lunchtime, Saturday lunchtime and Sunday

Menu €55 (lunch)/€148 – Carte €110/164

Ⓜ Michel Ange Molitor
A3

Christophe Biche

After working at some fine establishments, Patrick Pignol chose to have his own little place rather than work in a large restaurant that belonged to someone else. In 1984, at the age of 23, this native of Lozère, who grew up in the Paris area, set up shop on the Boulevard Murat near Roland Garros Stadium. Although he started his career in the dining room, he now leaves that side to his wife, Laurence. The service is discreet with a personal touch; the atmosphere in the flower-decked dining room is elegant and refined. The generous home cooking features the major classics while keeping up with the times. The faithful clientele knows that the game season is the chef's favourite, when he transforms his establishment into a kind of hunting lodge. He confesses in all simplicity that "cooking is either good or it isn't". You could get dizzy just from reading the wine list, which has some particularly fine vintages.

A LA CARTE

FIRST COURSE
• Amandine de foie gras.
• Langoustines croustillantes infusées au citron et parfum de coriandre.

MAIN COURSE
• Grosse sole de ligne.
• Côte de veau de lait.

DESSERT
• Beignets de chocolat bitter.
• Madeleines tièdes, glace au miel et noix.

Étoile, Trocadéro, Passy, Bois de Boulogne

La Table de Joël Robuchon ✿✿

Classic ✗✗✗

A/C
VISA
MC

16 av. Bugeaud
✉ 75116
☏ 01 56 28 16 16 – **Fax** 01 56 28 16 78
e-mail latabledejoelrobuchon@wanadoo.fr

Ⓜ Victor Hugo
C3

Menu €55 (lunch)/€150 – Carte €55/152

La Table de Joël Robuchon

Joël Robuchon is now established... all over the world. From Las Vegas to Tokyo and Monte-Carlo, his name is known on several continents. All his restaurants attract a clientele that is fond of the classicism of this exceptional chef who is not afraid of being a visionary. Thankfully, he is also present in Paris, where he has been collecting stars again. L'Atelier features straightforwardly 21st century cuisine; La Table is a pleasure for its quality as well as the well-designed prices on the daily set menu. The tasteful and refined decor is quite restrained.

The appealing menu, featuring ingredients prepared in a traditional way, has some original choices of "small portions" for an interesting gourmet experience. The balanced and moderate cuisine is well worth the trip.

A LA CARTE

FIRST COURSE
- Oeuf mollet et friand au caviar osciètre.
- Chair de tourteau en gelée.

MAIN COURSE
- Pavé de bar, macaroni de ricotta et herbes.
- Caille farcie de foie gras et caramélisée avec pomme purée truffée.

DESSERT
- Chocolat sensation.
- Baba au rhum.

Étoile, Trocadéro, Passy, Bois de Boulogne

La Table du Baltimore ✿

Contemporary XXX

A/C
VISA
MC
AE
D
Y

Hôtel Sofitel Baltimore,
1 r. Léo Delibes ✉ 75016
✆ 01 44 34 54 34 – **Fax** 01 44 34 54 44
e-mail h2789-fb@accor.com **Web** www.sofitel.com

M Boissière
D3

closed 28 July-27 August, Saturday and Sunday

Menu €48 (lunch)/€95 – Carte €46/64

G.Corbic/MICHELIN

Jean-Philippe Pérol, who has been in charge here since 2001, is well aware of the difficulty in attracting an outside clientele to a hotel restaurant. But it is easy to get over that apprehension by going to La Table at the Sofitel Baltimore, where you are sure to have "very good cooking in its category".

The restaurant, where the old wood panelling contrasts nicely with the contemporary furniture, features warm colours and old photographs of the city of Baltimore – thus the name given to this 19th century building.

The chef, a classicist who has worked in several fine establishments (the Pré Catelan and the Meurice, in particular), believes in "enjoyable cuisine" on his menus, which change with the seasons and their ingredients. With the intent of creating good value for money, he has done his utmost to win over any food-lovers who may still feel hesitant to dine at a hotel, inviting them to simply come and enjoy it.

A LA CARTE

FIRST COURSE

• Tourteau effiloché au parfum d'aneth.

• Saint-Jacques cuites au plat, bouillon à la citronnelle (season).

MAIN COURSE

• Mulet poêlé, confit de pommes de terre au parfum d'ail.

• Osso-bucco en cocotte, fondue de tomate et fricassée de légumes à l'huile d'olive.

DESSERT

• Chocolat en ganache moelleuse.

• Tarte fine au cacao amer, quartiers d'orange confite.

Étoile, Trocadéro, Passy, Bois de Boulogne

Le Pergolèse ✿

Classic XXX

A/C
VISA
MC
AE
Y

40 r. Pergolèse
✉ 75116
✆ 01 45 00 21 40 – **Fax** 01 45 00 81 31
e-mail le-pergolese@wanadoo.fr **Web** www.lepergolese.com
closed 4-26 August, Saturday and Sunday

M Porte Maillot
C2

Menu €30 (lunch)/€80 – Carte €68/124

Le Pergolèse

"I wanted to create a beautiful place to receive diners, as if it were my own home," acknowledges Stéphane Gaborieau, who moved to Paris in the summer of 2005 after a long stay in Lyon. Having succumbed to the charms of the capital, this winner of the Meilleur Ouvrier de France award took over from high-profile Albert Corre. It was a risky bet when you think how faithful his customers were. But with his kindness and good nature, the chef, helped out in the dining room by his wife Chantal, succeeded in his idea of transporting the "spirit of the countryside" to the 16th arrondissement. His cooking is appealing and has great respect for the produce he uses. Although his Lyon touch is quite pronounced and the basis of his cooking quite traditional, there is a Mediterranean verve in there as well. That comes as no surprise, in fact, since this chef trained in southern France. The plush dining room has a timeless air of "good taste" with its bronze statuettes and paintings that liven up the walls. The wine list has some interesting items to explore.

A LA CARTE

FIRST COURSE

• Ravioli de langoustines en duxelles, émulsion de crustacés au foie gras.

• Croustillant de cuisses de grenouilles à l'ail des ours.

MAIN COURSE

• Aiguillette de Saint-Pierre meunière, cannelloni aux multi-saveurs (winter).

• Double côte de veau rôtie en cocotte.

DESSERT

• Croustillant de mangue et de pomme au miel de romarin, jus passion, glace au nougat.

• Moelleux de chocolat chaud, sorbet cacao.

Astrance ✿✿✿

Innovative 🍴🍴🍴

4 r. Beethoven
✉ 75016
☎ 0140508440

Ⓜ Passy
C2

Closed 1st-6 March, August, autumn half-term holidays, Saturday, Sunday and Monday
– number of covers limited, pre-book

Menu €70 (lunch)/€270

Astrance

Improvisation is the name of the game here! Pascal Barbot and Christophe Rohat have created a place which is timeless and far from the madding crowd. Like them, it disregards fashion, embodying their idea of the perfect restaurant. Located near Trocadéro, it has only one small room with a discreet contemporary decor and twenty place settings. The chef creates a new menu every day based on the market – and the customers. Only the ingredients are decided upon beforehand; the rest is developed according to his inspiration. Yes – it is a form of improvisation, but one that is measured and well thought out. The chef, who is eager for his cuisine to remain open to the world, combines the exotic with the *terroir* in a seamless blend of flavours and textures. The harmony between the dining room and the kitchen is perfect, adding to the charm of this unconventional restaurant. The wine list is ample enough to satisfy the most demanding palates and also to highlight the food.

A LA CARTE

FIRST COURSE	MAIN COURSE	DESSERT
• Galette de champignons de Paris, foie gras mariné au verjus, citron confit.	• Selle d'agneau grillée, aubergine laquée au miso.	• Sorbet au lait d'amande et piment.
• Endive caramélisée, beurre de spéculoos, condiment banane.	• Foie gras poêlé, huître tiède, ormeau et bouillon de crevettes grises.	• Ile flottante au fruit de la passion et noix grillée.

Étoile, Trocadéro, Passy, Bois de Boulogne

317

16th ARRONDISSEMENT

Pavillon Noura

Lebanese XXX

A/C

VISA

MC

AE

DC

21 av. Marceau
✉ 75116
✆ 0147203333 – **Fax** 0147206031
e-mail noura@noura.fr

Ⓜ Alma Marceau
D3

Menu €36 (lunch)/€64 – **Carte** €37/54

This temple of Lebanese cuisine, on one of the smartest avenues in the city, has a sumptuous Middle Eastern decor - walls decorated with Levantine frescoes, chairs upholstered in ultramarine velvet and beautiful table settings. Dining at Noura's is a true gastronomic voyage to the land of Cedars and a systematic exploration of Phoenician flavours. The meat and vegetarian *mezzés* are tasty, and the variety on the pastry trolley is spectacular, with semolina, honey and almonds combined in a thousand different ways. Fine selection of local wines – often with spicy aromas – and traditional Arak liqueur.

Les Arts

Traditional XXX

9 bis av. d'Iéna
✉ 75116
✆ 0140692753 – **Fax** 0140692708
e-mail maison.des.am@sodexho.prestige.fr
Web www.sodexho-prestige.fr

Ⓜ Iéna
D3

Closed 28 July-28 August, 23 December-1st January, Saturday, Sunday and public holidays

Menu €38 – **Carte** €61/79

The magnificent Hôtel d'Iéna is the prestigious setting for this elegant classical restaurant. Since 1925 this building has been the headquarters of the Société des Ingénieurs des Arts et Métiers, for which this establishment was named. The splendid ornamental opulence of the main dining room features a high ceiling decorated with mouldings, Doric columns and copies of masterpieces. A classic cuisine mainly strives to please the clientele of engineers and businessmen. In summer, book a table on the terrace with its superb garden.

Passiflore ❀

Classic 🗴🗴🗴

[A/C]	33 r. Longchamp
✉	75016
[VISA]	☎ 0147049681 – **Fax** 0147043227
	e-mail passiflore@club-internet.fr
[MC]	**Web** www.restaurantpassiflore.com
[AE]	closed 14 July-20 August, Saturday lunch and Sunday

Ⓜ Trocadéro
D3

🍷 Menu €35 (lunch)/€54 (dinner) – Carte €63/95

Passiflore

Things often come in threes. After Le Camélia and Le Restaurant du Quai in Bougival, with an interlude at Lenôtre, in February 2001 Roland Durand began working at Passiflore, which had been a Chinese restaurant before. Thus, the scent of Asia was already in the air. It was somewhat of a symbol to this chef from Auvergne – Meilleur Ouvrier de France and an avid traveller – who readily admits that his cooking is "permeated with his trips to Asia, and especially Southeast Asia". To compose a menu that seems to be in perpetual motion, this explorer of flavours also steeps himself in old recipe books, which he admits being very fond of. In fact, the culinary approach taken by this man, who is not afraid of shaking up gastronomic habits, can be summed up in a few words: noble rusticity and exotic flavours. The decor is a perfect reflection of that philosophy, with its low-key, zen ambiance enhanced by a baroque blend of African and Asian objets d'art, evoking a journey to some far-away place.

A LA CARTE

FIRST COURSE	MAIN COURSE	DESSERT
· Ravioles de homard.	· Tête de veau aux huîtres (October to April).	· Viennoise en pain perdu, fruits rôtis au miel de châtaignier.
· Petite crème de mousserons à la chair de langoustines.	· Tournedos de pied de cochon.	· Riz au lait à la cardamome, fruits du dragon au sirop d'érable.

Étoile, Trocadéro, Passy, Bois de Boulogne

Port Alma

Seafood XXX

A/C
VISA
MC
AE
D
Y

10 av. New York
✉ 75116
☎ 0147237511 – **Fax** 0147204292
e-mail restaurantportalma@wanadoo.fr
closed 24 December-2 January and Sunday

Ⓜ Alma Marceau
D3

Menu €29 (lunch)/€39 (dinner) – **Carte** €28/105

The Port Alma, a mecca for Parisian seafood-lovers, is located on the quayside of the Left Bank a short distance from the Pont de l'Alma. The marine decor has a decidedly classical look – dining room with exposed beams and a veranda, velvet arm-chairs in ultramarine shades, and many other elements evoking the deep blue sea. The same breath of fresh air permeates the menu, featuring impeccable ingredients in seaside dishes that will delight your taste buds such as sole and scallop fricassée, roasted langoustines with preserved tomatoes, and the more traditional grilled, line-caught sea bass.

Cristal Room Baccarat

Innovative XX

A/C
VISA
MC
AE
D
Y

11 pl. des Etats-Unis
✉ 75116
☎ 0140221110 – **Fax** 0140221199
e-mail cristalroom@baccarat.fr
closed Sun – pre-book

Ⓜ Boissière
D3

Menu €120 – **Carte** €55/117

In addition to the restaurant, this splendid townhouse also houses the headquarters of the Baccarat crystalworks, as well as a shop and museum. Like the brand, the setting is exceptional with its Empire decor completely redesigned by Philippe Starck, preserving the original marble, parquet floors and exposed beams, offset by the boldly modern look. The decor only serves to enhance the high-quality menu with tasty, up-to-date food including marinades, meat and fish à la plancha, spit-roasted poultry and simmered casserole dishes. An extraordinary black crystal chandelier – one of a kind – hangs from the dining room ceiling.

Le Relais du Parc

Traditional ✗✗

Hôtel Sofitel Le Parc,
55 av. R. Poincaré ✉ 75116
☎ 01 44 05 66 10 – **Fax** 01 44 05 66 39
e-mail le.relaisduparc@accor.com **Web** www.sofitel.com

Ⓜ Victor Hugo
C3

Closed 7-25 August, 22 December-5 January, Saturday lunch from 15 September to 6 May, Sunday and Monday

Carte €65/83

Le Relais du Parc

Joël Robuchon and Alain Ducasse were highly successful at this same address. Since then, the vocation of this fine townhouse has changed. Le Parc remains, with its terrace and summer garden. The decor, by Gilles Le Gall, transforms the establishment according to the seasons. Warm tones dominate in autumn and winter, in a harmonious blend of caramel, raspberry and chocolate, with a large fireplace adding extra warmth and charm. Beige and green are the prevailing colours in spring and summer, creating a fresh and cheerful ambiance. The contemporary paintings also change, trading browns for shades of red berry. But the memory of Robuchon and Ducasse lives on, in the library which contains some of their works, and through their enduring influence on the food. The young chef has even included several dishes on the menu that are "classics" from one or the other. In keeping with the times, the food here focuses on quality market ingredients.

A LA CARTE

FIRST COURSE
- Coquillettes aux truffes, jambon, jus d'un rôti.
- Cocotte de légumes en aigre-doux.

MAIN COURSE
- Baudroie piquée de chorizo, légumes de couscous, condiments, pois chiches, harissa.
- Jarret de veau fondant, os à moelle, gnocchi de pomme de terre (winter).

DESSERT
- Petits pots vanille et chocolat.
- Pommes cuites en cocotte, parfait glacé caramel.

Tsé Yang

Chinese ✗✗

[A/C]
[⟷]
[VISA]
[MC]
[AE]
[♀]

25 av. Pierre 1er de Serbie
✉ 75016
✆ 0147207022 – **Fax** 0147207534
Web www.tseyang.fr

Ⓜ Iéna
D3

Menu €49/€59 – **Carte** €37/66

This elegant Chinese restaurant located just behind Trocadéro will transport you to the halls of the Forbidden City the minute you walk through the door. The decor redesigned by James Tinel and Emmanuel Benet taps into the hidden sources of the Middle Kingdom, with monumental jade lions at the entrance, a rich interior with dark fabrics and a gilded ceiling, and black wood furniture with sculpted motifs. The classic Chinese cuisine features traditional spicy soups, dim sum, Peking duck and beef sautéed with soy sprouts, prepared with a talented twist by the inventive young chef. This establishment should appeal to even the most unaccustomed Western palates!

La Table de Babette

French West-Indies ✗✗

[A/C]
[⟷]
[VISA]
[MC]
[AE]
[Ⓓ]
[♀]

32 r. Longchamp
✉ 75016
✆ 0145530007 – **Fax** 0145530015
e-mail tabledebabette@wanadoo.fr **Web** www.tabledebabette.com
closed 15-31 August, Saturday lunch and Sunday

Ⓜ Trocadéro
D3

Menu €38 (lunch)/€45 – **Carte** €47/77

La Table de Babette – a delicious journey to the sunny isles in the heart of the 16th arrondissement – has earned a solid reputation with neighbourhood gourmets and Caribbean food-lovers from all over Paris. You have to admit the proprietress of this haven of colourful flavours and spicy aromas knows what she's doing. The traditional Caribbean dishes served here are subtly reinterpreted with a playful touch. The warm and cosy decor evokes a tropical bijou flat with its exotic wood furniture, luxuriant plants and flowery carpet. The music appropriately draws on beguine classics, creating an atmosphere that is both hushed and joyful.

Giulio Rebellato

Italian XX

A/C

VISA

MC

AE

136 r. Pompe
⊠ 75116
𝒸 0147275026

closed August

Carte €48/60

Ⓜ Victor Hugo
C3

Sumptuous fabrics, old engravings and sparkling, finely worked mirrors are part of the upscale decor at this comfortable restaurant – designed by Garcia and inspired by the golden age of Venice – where you can enjoy Italian specialities. The establishment has drawn in a demanding clientele from the rue de la Pompe for ages, and has built up a solid reputation for its quality ingredients and generous cuisine. The ample menu is a superb tribute to Italian gastronomy, featuring delicate dishes such as the lovingly baked lasagna, copious ravioli, delicious risottos and traditional Italian desserts.

Tang

Chinese XX

A/C

VISA

MC

AE

125 r. de la Tour
⊠ 75116
𝒸 0145043535 – **Fax** 0145045819
e-mail charlytang16@yahoo.fr

closed 29 July-21 August, 23 December-3 January, Sunday and Monday

Menu €39 (weekday lunch)/€98 – Carte €56/152

Ⓜ Rue de la Pompe
B2

Paris now has three different Chinatowns! This tiny restaurant on a discreet and rather forlorn street in the chic 16th arrondissement is indeed a true institution in the city. The Chinese food here is straightforward and authentic – a nice change from the usual spring rolls. Creation is ever present at Tang, where excellent ingredients are used to prepare the reinvented traditional dishes, including spring salad with langoustine tails and fresh pasta, spicy Peking duck *croustillant* with green pepper sauce, thin crepes and chive julienne – bold and delicious! The setting does credit to both tips of Eurasia with its subtle fusion of French elegance and traditional elements.

Étoile, Trocadéro, Passy, Bois de Boulogne

La Petite Tour

Classic ✗✗

A/C
VISA
MC
AE
◑
▯

11 r. de la Tour
✉ 75116
☎ 0145200997 – **Fax** 0145200931
closed 25 July-20 August, Saturday lunch and Sunday

Menu €28 – **Carte** €43/77

Ⓜ Passy
C2

With its discreet and somewhat dated façade, this little restaurant on a modest street corner in the smart 16th arrondissement is proud of its classic, old-fashioned inn look. The long dining room has a 1960s decor, red velvet banquettes and armchairs, attractive and well-spaced tables, and floral compositions. But classic doesn't necessarily mean basic, and the young chef who has taken over the kitchen at this not-to-miss establishment in the Trocadéro area, knows how to combine flavours while respecting tradition. His tasty dishes vary with the market and seasons, and daily specials are featured on the blackboard. Attentive service.

Paul Chêne

Traditional ✗✗

A/C
VISA
MC
AE
◑
▯

123 r. Lauriston
✉ 75116
☎ 0147276317 – **Fax** 0147275318
Closed Easter holidays, August, 24-31 December, Saturday and Sunday

Menu €38/€48 – **Carte** €42/75

Ⓜ Trocadéro
C-D3

More than an institution, this is a true piece of history with its venerable zinc bar polished by the years, opulent fifties-style red banquettes, and snug, lively tables. Time seems suspended here, where the years go by, but nothing disturbs the well-oiled operation at this fine establishment. That experience has clearly paid off, judging from the traditional recipes served up in generous portions in dishes such as veal kidneys, rack of lamb and the house terrine, and especially in the famous *merlan en colère* ("angry" whiting), a huge fish served with its tail in its mouth. It's pleasant and entertaining. What more could you ask for?

Roland Garros

Contemporary ✗✗

VISA
MC
AE
D
Y

2 bis av. Gordon Bennett
✉ 75016
☎ 0147434956 – **Fax** 0140718324
e-mail contact@laffiche.fr **Web** www.laffiche.fr

Closed 1st-27 August, 23 December-3 January, Saturday and Sunday from October to April
and Sunday dinner from May to September

🅜 Porte d'Auteuil
A3

Menu €50/€65 – Carte €45/86

The ambiance is airy and pleasantly country-like at this terrace restaurant – one of the finest in the city – located inside the Porte d'Auteuil complex, with its contemporary furniture, comfortable velvet banquettes, lovely wood veranda and sunny terrace planted with grass. Marc Veyrat assists in composing the up-to-date menu, which evolves with the market and the seasons. The ingredients are fresh, and the poultry roasted in the impressive rôtisserie is mouth-watering. The beautiful setting nearly puts the high-quality food in the background. Tennis fans will enjoy it here.

Conti

Italian ✗✗

A/C
VISA
MC
AE
D
❀
Y

72 r. Lauriston
✉ 75116
☎ 0147277467 – **Fax** 0147273766

Closed 4-26 August, 24 December-1st January, Saturday, Sunday and public holidays

🅜 Boissière
D3

Menu €32 (lunch) – Carte €39/64

Stendhal's emblematic colours are the theme at this Italian restaurant run by two Frenchmen in love with food from across the Alps. The dark wood panelling and red velvet in the dining room celebrate Italy at its most refined and luxurious, under the soft lighting from crystal chandeliers. As for the dishes, they are more Franco-Italian fusion than traditional, featuring the best ingredients from both countries, including top-quality seafood, numerous fresh pasta dishes and a sumptuous tiramisu full of flavour. The wine list, with the best of French and Italian vintages, is well worth perusing.

Étoile, Trocadéro, Passy, Bois de Boulogne

Marius

Seafood ✗✗

82 bd Murat
✉ 75016
✆ 0146516780 – **Fax** 0140718375
closed August, Saturday lunch and Sunday

Ⓜ Porte de St-Cloud
A3

Carte €45/67

A real institution in the Porte de Saint-Cloud neighbourhood, Marius creates talented blends of the finest seafood ingredients with a very Provençal personal touch. The decor of the restaurant, which has a shady summer terrace, is understated and comfortable, with light-coloured walls adorned with mirrors, chairs upholstered in yellow velvet, pleasantly spaced tables and discreet marine touches. Seafood is naturally featured on the menu, including some wonderfully fresh fish and shellfish specialities, including bouillabaisse, which is particularly delicious. The chef's specialities change daily, and the fine selection of wines are well paired with the dishes.

L'Acajou

Contemporary ✗✗

35bis r. La Fontaine
✉ 75016
✆ 0142880447 – **Fax** 0142889512
Web www.l-acajou.com
closed August, Saturday lunch and Sunday

Ⓜ Jasmin
B2

Menu €35/€40 – Carte €50/68

Dynamic young chef Jean Imbert has made his mark in the neighbourhood with this recently renovated, elegant restaurant located between the Maison de la Radio and the Eglise d'Auteuil. Everything at l'Acajou is lovely, including the decor with dark wood panelling, caramel banquettes, cream-coloured walls and contemporary art work. The hushed, tasteful atmosphere is further enhanced by the ample space with roomy tables. The chef-proprietor's imaginative cuisine features well-prepared, up-to-date recipes with a creative twist.

Le Vinci

Italian ✗✗

A/C
VISA
MC
AE
Ⴘ

23 r. P. Valéry
✉ 75116
☎ 0145016818 – **Fax** 0145016037
e-mail levinci@wanadoo.fr

closed 28 July-26 August, Saturday and Sunday

Ⓜ Victor Hugo
D2-3

Carte € 47/63

Behind the discreet façade of this *ristorante*, on a quiet street near the Avenue Victor Hugo, is a little gem of Italian gastronomy. The tone is set the minute you walk into the restaurant, with its bright and happy colours characteristic of the *mezzogiorno*, and comfortable, elegantly set tables that create an airy and convivial atmosphere. The kitchen features all the great classics of Italian cuisine, often reinvented with panache, such as various kinds of gnocchi, polenta and dry-cured ham gratin, risottos and osso buccos, and naturally the unbeatable tiramisu. Good selection of French and Italian wines.

Essaouira

Moroccan ✗✗

VISA
MC
Ⴘ

135 r. Ranelagh
✉ 75016
☎ 0145279993 – **Fax** 0145275636

closed August, Monday lunch and Sunday

Ⓜ Ranelagh
B2

Menu € 15 (lunch) – Carte € 35/47

This typically Moroccan restaurant derives its name from Essaouira, the colourful fishing port on the Atlantic Ocean once known as Mogador. The traditional rugs and North African crafts set the mood straight off; the fine mosaic fountain in the centre of the room and soft music complete the attractive ambiance. The cuisine features all the great Moroccan classics, including tasty and copious couscous, tajines filled with flavours from the Atlas, and other skilfully prepared specialities. Friendly service and fine selection of local wines.

Étoile, Trocadéro, Passy, Bois de Boulogne

327

Chez Géraud 😳

Bistro ✗✗

VISA
MC
🍷

31 r. Vital
✉ 75016
☎ 0145203300 – **Fax** 0145204660
closed 28 July-28 August, 25 December-2 January, Saturday and Sunday

Ⓜ La Muette
B2

Menu €30 – Carte €50/72

This restaurant – with a reputation that extends far beyond its quiet neighbourhood – has a welcoming, traditional bistro decor. The painted façade enhanced by Longwy faience evokes the fine old establishments of yesteryear, hinting at the equally delightful interior with its large ceramic fresco and matching plates on rather rustic, nicely laid-out tables. A rather chic place, highly appreciated by a clientele of businessmen from the 16th arrondissement. In the kitchen, the chef proves that tradition can be a good thing, with classic dishes such as *pot-au-feu* (stew), rib steak and homemade terrines, along with tasty game specialities in season. You will undoubtedly leave this smart and reasonably priced place with a smile on your face!

La Butte Chaillot

Bistro ✗✗

A/C
VISA
MC
AE
DC
🍷

110 bis av. Kléber
✉ 75116
☎ 0147278888 – **Fax** 0147274146
e-mail buttechaillot@guysavoy.com **Web** www.buttechaillot.com
Closed 6-26 August and Saturday lunch from April to September

Ⓜ Trocadéro
D3

Menu €33/€50 – Carte €37/57

This further star in the Guy Savoy galaxy is nestled on the famous Avenue Kléber, a few minutes from the place du Trocadéro. The look of the establishment is decidedly 21C bistro. The copper-coloured modern decor designed by Jean-Michel Wilmotte has contemporary furniture in shades of chocolate and contemporary artwork highlighted by clever indirect lighting. This comfortable and rather trendy interior gives a free hand to the very up-to-date and flavourful cuisine featuring well-prepared, high-quality ingredients. The free-range spit-roasted poultry with its potato purée and jus is one of the outstanding dishes featured on the enticing menu.

6 New-York

Innovative ✗✗

A/C
VISA
MC
AE
D
Y

6 av. New-York
✉ 75016
☎ 0140700330 – **Fax** 0140700477
e-mail 6newyork@wanadoo.fr

closed August, Saturday lunch and Sunday

Ⓜ Alma Marceau
D3

Menu €30 – Carte €48/58

The cuisine is not American at this trendy restaurant giving onto the Avenue de New York and the lively quais de Seine; but the interior is chic and contemporary, with a minimalist decor in chocolate and mustard tones and a few floral compositions. The matching clientele includes the elegant "happy few" and well-informed tourists. The food is flawless – fresh and tasty up-to-date dishes with an inventive touch, including crab charlotte with avocado and curry, *pièces de cochon en éventail*, and tuna in three styles with ginger sauce. Attentive and efficient service.

A et M Restaurant

A la mode ✗

hTi
VISA
MC
AE
Y

136 bd Murat
✉ 75016
☎ 0145273960 – **Fax** 0145276971
e-mail am-bistrot-16@wanadoo.fr

closed August, Saturday lunch and Sunday

Ⓜ Porte de St-Cloud
B3

Menu €30 – Carte €29/49

Chic and relaxed are the words for this "hip" restaurant a stone's throw from the Seine. The A and M refer to the founders of Apicius and Marius, two historic pillars of Parisian gastronomy who partnered up here to create a resonably priced bistro. The resolutely modern decor has a comfortable contemporary look with cream and tobacco shades and soft lighting. The same creative restraint is evident in the kitchen, where the chef cooks up precise and well-prepared up-to-date dishes such as cream of mushroom soup with foie gras shavings, or the amazing pan-fried pig's ear *croustillant* with shallots and parsley. Daily specialities and wines of the month are featured on the blackboard.

Étoile, Trocadéro, Passy, Bois de Boulogne

Étoile, Trocadéro, Passy, Bois de Boulogne

Le Petit Pergolèse

Bistro 🍴

[A/C]
[VISA]
[MC]
[🍷]

38 r. Pergolèse
⊠ 75016
✆ 0145002366 – **Fax** 0145004403

closed August, Saturday and Sunday

Carte €31/61

🚇 Porte Maillot
C2

As its name indicates, this restaurant is an annexe of the famous Pergolèse located a short distance away on the same street. In short, this is a chef's bistro which strives for quality through simplicity. The contemporary decor of the dining room, the unpretentious layout with snug tables and spirited atmosphere create a lively and functional setting which attracts a wide clientele of hurried and demanding businessmen. Judiciously updated and flavoursome cuisine features simple and well-prepared dishes. The blackboard changes according to the market, like the chef's daily specialities, announced out loud.

Table Lauriston

Traditional 🍴

[A/C]
[VISA]
[MC]
[AE]
[🍷]

129 r. Lauriston
⊠ 75016
✆ 0147270007 – **Fax** 0147270007

closed 4-28 August, Saturday lunch and Sunday

Carte €39/63

🚇 Trocadéro
C-D3

It was inevitable that someone would eventually open a traditional Parisian bistro in a neighbourhood better known for hushed gourmet restaurants than for authentic *troquets*. The Table Lauriston, a stone's throw from the rue de Longchamp and Avenue Poincaré, offers what all Parisian gourmets dream of – traditional, invigorating bistro cuisine using the freshest of ingredients. Dive in without delay and sample the menu full of classics such as herring cured in oil with warm potatoes, choice rib steak, and calf's liver tournedos in vinegar. The wide selection of wines by the glass is an added bonus.

Rosimar

Spanish X

AC | 26 r. Poussin | **M** Michel Ange Auteuil
VISA | ✉ 75016 | **B2-3**
MC | ☎ 0145277491 – **Fax** 0145207505
AE | Closed August, 24-31 December, Saturday, Sunday and public holidays

Menu €32/€34

This restaurant on rue Poussin seems quite unassuming behind its small glass façade, but the long dining room is decorated with numerous mirrors which give it a feeling of ample space. Two words suffice to define the spirit here – family-run and Spanish. The menu is loaded with Catalan and Andalusian specialities which are carefully prepared with excellent ingredients. The generous and sun-filled homemade paella, powerfully flavoured cold meats and garlic-and-parsley *chipirons* are full of the rich tastes of the Iberian *terroir*. Try one of the bottles on the wine list, with selections from both sides of the Pyrenees. *Salud*!

Oscar 😊

Traditional X

VISA | 6 r. Chaillot | **M** léna
MC | ✉ 75016 | **D3**
AE | ☎ 0147202692 – **Fax** 0147202793
 | closed 6-19 August, Saturday lunch and Sunday

Menu €21 – Carte €30/46

Behind its discreet glass façade on a quiet street in the most well-to-do part of the 16th arrondissement, this authentic neighbourhood bistro is a rare species in Paris – a bastion of gourmet tradition with reasonable prices. Run by two experienced associates, it has become a big success with a reputation far beyond the area. The simple and unassuming setting is anything but eye-catching, with its snug tables, stainless steel cutlery and paper tablecloths. But the food is truly a delight, with straightforward and generous dishes such as the homemade terrine, classic rib steak cooked to perfection and the daily blackboard suggestions. Copious and delightful!

Palais des Congrès, Wagram, Ternes, Batignolles

Legac H./MICHELIN

Appreciated for its tranquillity, the 17th is nonetheless an arrondissement unlike others. Wedged in between avenue de Saint-Ouen and avenue de la Grande Armée, this formerly very rural sector was annexed to Paris in 1860. Most of the buildings date from the 1860-1920 period, making it an homogenous monument of Haussmannian architecture, and its graceful facades of dressed stone bourgeois buildings and flawlessly straight wide avenues create a picture of ordered, if unsurprising, urban planning. Practically devoid of parks or gardens, such was the need for housing at the time it was annexed. With the exception of the very exclusive Monceau Park and a few railway lines running out of Saint-Lazare station, almost all the arrondissement has been developed. Three distinct districts are nonetheless worth taking the time to explore. Near Étoile, the **Ternes-Wagram** sector with its **cabarets** and shows is in fact more characteristic of the 8th than the quiet 17th. Next, towards the ring road and **porte Maillot** stands the **Palais des Congrès,** a major shopping and tourist attraction. Lastly, towards the 18th, just before **place de Clichy,** the walker will enjoy the typically Parisian "village" spirit of the Batignolles area, a rarity in the arrondissement.

IMPERIAL SHOW TIMES

A stone's throw from place de l'Étoile, the area between avenue des Ternes and avenue de Wagram combines the bourgeois appeal of its Haussmannian architecture with intense commercial and leisure activity. The famous salle Wagram, built

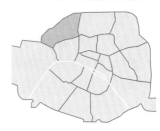

in 1865 on the site of a former dance hall and two minutes from the former Empire Theatre, has been a high spot of entertainment for almost 150 years. Ever at the forefront of modernity, it was the first to host new cultural forms that emerged in the 20C. The scene of the first Paris automobile show, it also staged boxing fights at the time of Al Brown and Marcel Cerdan and some of the greatest post-War jazz musicians from Bud Powell to Duke Ellington played here. No doubt this glorious past is partly the reason for the abundance of relatively upmarket restaurants and brasseries. Heading down towards place des Ternes, the district becomes livelier and also more commercial: the **Ternes Fnac** music and bookshop is still the largest in Paris and the flower market (everyday except Mondays) on place des Ternes is a genuine institution in the neighbourhood. A few more or less exclusive nightclubs provide a pleasant setting for a late night drink.

CULTURAL EXCEPTION

Heading eastwards along boulevard de Courcelles, make sure you stop at Parc Monceau, the only garden worthy of the name in the arrondissement, and admire the splendid landscaping à la française and elegant perspectives as you stroll past manicured lawns in a relaxing break from the frantic pace of the city. The surrounding buildings overlooking the park are among the most sought after of the capital because of their calm location and elegant Haussmannian architecture.

The real soul of the 17th lies just a short distance away further east. Batignolles village, a genuine exception in the arrondissement, rises like a refreshing island from the mists of a monotonous ocean of dressed stone. Cosy restaurants serving fine cuisine at reasonable prices, friendly bistros and gourmet grocery stores line the narrow streets up towards square des Batignolles and its adjoining church, endowing the village with a delightfully provincial feel. To such an extent, that it has caught the fancy of a population of stylish yuppies and bourgeois-bohemians, who could hardly be qualified as needy, attracted by the charm and authenticity of a small suburban town, without the inconvenience.

Legac H./MICHELIN

Palais des Congrès, Wagram, Ternes, Batignolles

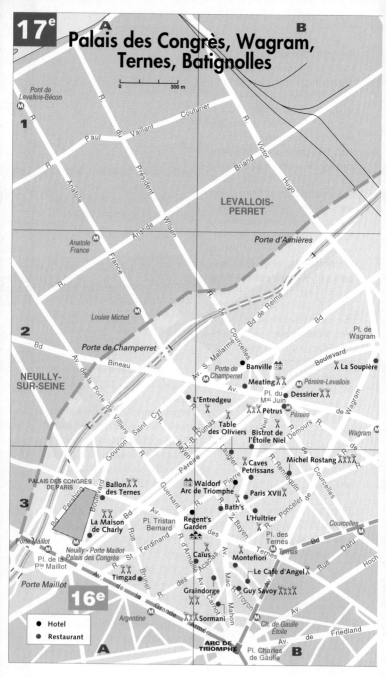

17ᵉ

Palais des Congrès, Wagram, Ternes, Batignolles

0   300 m

Pont de Levallois-Bécon

R. Paul

R. du Vaillant

Couturier

R. Anatole

Président

Wilson

Victor

Briand

Hugo

LEVALLOIS-PERRET

Anatole France

Aristide

Porte d'Asnières

Louise Michel

Bd de Reims

Bd

R.

Pl. de Wagram

Bd

Porte de Champerret

Bineau

Av. de la Porte de Champerret

Courcelles

Av. S. Mallarmé

Banville

Boulevard

La Soupière

NEUILLY-SUR-SEINE

Meating

Péreire-Levallois

Av.

Pl. du Mᵃˡ Juin

Dessirier

L'Entredgeu

R. Saint CYR

Pétrus

Niel

Péreire

de Wagram

R. J.-B. Dumas

Table des Oliviers

Bistrot de l'Étoile Niel

Péreire

de Demours

Wagram

Gouvion

R.

R. de Villiers

Guersant

R. Bayen

Lauger

R. Pierre

Caves Petrissans

Michel Rostang

R. Renéquin

R. de Courcelles

PALAIS DES CONGRÈS DE PARIS

Boulevard Pershing

Ballon des Ternes

Waldorf Arc de Triomphe

Paris XVII

Bath's

L'Huîtrier

Courcelles

Porte Maillot

La Maison de Charly

Pl. Tristan Bernard

Av. R. Ferdinand

Regent's Garden

des

Pl. des Ternes

Bd

Daru

R.

Hoch

Neuilly - Porte Maillot Palais des Congrès

Pl. de la Pᵗᵉ Maillot

R. St.

R. d'Armaillé

Caïus

Av. des Acacias

Av. Bayen

Montefiori

Le Café d'Angel

Rue Ternes

M

Porte Maillot

Brunel

R.

Timgad

des

Graindorge

Mac

R. Troyon

Guy Savoy

Grande

Mahon

Ch. de Gaulle Étoile

Friedland

16ᵉ

Argentine

Av. de la

Armée

Sormani

Carnot

Av.

de

A

● Hotel
● Restaurant

ARC DE TRIOMPHE

Pl. Charles de Gaulle

B

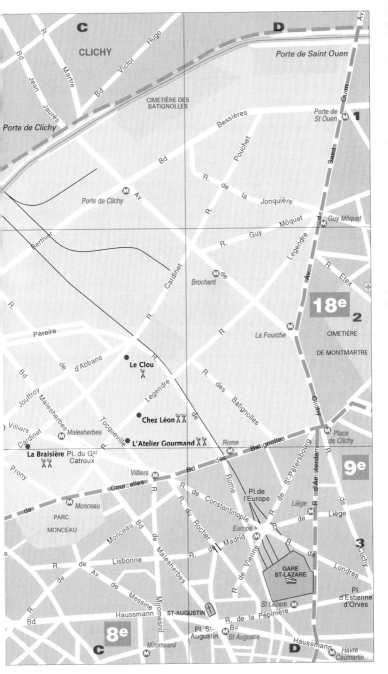

Guy Savoy ✿ ✿ ✿

Innovative 🍴🍴🍴🍴

Palais des Congrès, Wagram, Ternes, Batignolles

A/C	18 r. Troyon
	⊠ 75017
	✆ 01 43 80 40 61 – **Fax** 01 46 22 43 09
VISA	**e-mail** reserv@guysavoy.com **Web** www.guysavoy.com
MC	closed August, 24 December-2 January, Saturday lunchtime, Sunday and Monday
AE	

Ⓜ Charles de Gaulle-Etoile
B3

Menu € 230/285 – **Carte** € 112/223

Guy Savoy

In 1987 Guy Savoy moved from the rue Duret – his first Parisian address – to this spot near Étoile. But the move hasn't changed anything; he calls himself an innkeeper – in all simplicity. The label may seem a bit paradoxical for this kind of establishment, but he has stuck to it. In 2000, Jean-Michel Wilmotte undertook the "reconstruction" of the restaurant, where large canvasses by contemporary artists mingle with African sculptures. It is muted and refined, uncluttered and warm all at once. Rather than one large dining room, there are several small nooks creating an intimate atmosphere for diners. The cuisine is streamlined, generous and authentic, inventive without excess, drawing from its roots in the terroir and highlighting its most emblematic products. Seamless service by the restaurant manager and the staff eager to satisfy the clientele. There is no danger of being bored by the wine list.

A LA CARTE

FIRST COURSE
· Soupe d'artichaut à la truffe noire, brioche feuilletée aux champignons et truffes.
· Crème légère de lentilles et langoustines.

MAIN COURSE
· Côte de gros turbot à l'oeuf en salade et soupe.
· Ris de veau rissolés, "petits chaussons" de pommes de terre et truffes.

DESSERT
· Terrine de pamplemousse, sauce au thé.
· Millefeuille "minute" à la gousse de vanille.

Live in Italian

At finer restaurants in Paris, London, New York and of course, Milan.

the **MICHELIN** guide

a collection to savour !

Belgique & Luxembourg
Deutschland
España & Portugal
France
Great Britain & Ireland
Italia
Nederland
Österreich
Portugal
Suisse

Also :

Paris
London
New York City
San Francisco
Main Cities of Europe

Michel Rostang ⭐⭐

Classic 🍴🍴🍴🍴

20 r. Rennequin · **Ⓜ** Ternes
✉ 75017 · **B3**
✆ 0147634077 – **Fax** 0147638275
e-mail rostang@relaischateaux.com **Web** www.michelrostang.com

closed 1st-21 August, Monday lunchtime, Saturday lunchtime and Sunday

Menu €70 (lunch)/€175 – Carte €124/202

Michel Rostang

In 2007, Michel Rostang will celebrate his thirtieth anniversary in Paris, where he started out as a kitchen boy, notably at Lasserre. Coming from a long line of chefs from the Isère – his father Joseph won three stars at La Bonne Auberge in Antibes in 1980 – he was destined to enter the profession, which has proven to be the right choice. A collector of fine objects (Lalique, Robj porcelain statuettes, etc.) elegantly highlighted in showcases, the chef welcomes diners into a refined setting with wood panelling and dark lacquerware. Meals are served in various dining rooms, each named after its particular style of decoration; the excellent classical cuisine has some contemporary touches. In short, it is reassuring and welcome, like the wine list that pays tribute to Côtes du Rhône.

A LA CARTE

FIRST COURSE
· Tarte tiède et croustillante de cuisses de grenouilles.

· Gratin de queues d'écrevisses en cassolette.

MAIN COURSE
· Foie gras chaud de canard rôti d'une fine croûte de sésame dorée.

· Canette au sang servie saignante en deux services.

DESSERT
· Le cigare croustillant de tabac de Havane, mousseline au cognac, marsala et arlettes glacées.

· Barre de chocolat crousti-fondante au praliné noisette.

Palais des Congrès, Wagram, Ternes, Batignolles

Sormani

Italian ✗✗✗

[AC]
[VISA]
[MC]
[AE]
[symbols]

4 r. Gén. Lanrezac ⓜ Charles de Gaulle-Etoile
⊠ 75017 **B3**
℡ 01 43 80 13 91 – **Fax** 01 40 55 07 37
e-mail sasormani@wanadoo.fr

Closed 4-20 August, Saturday, Sunday and public holidays

Menu €44 (lunch)/€150 – Carte €53/176

All the charms of baroque Italy are evoked – with restraint – in the plush dining rooms of this comfortable restaurant with its red colours, majestic Murano glass chandeliers, elegant place settings, mirrors and mouldings. Pascal Fayet's cuisine naturally follows this *dolce vita* theme in his resolutely Italian menu, half of which is devoted (in season) to the rare truffle. The wine cellar goes by the same refrain with its superb labels from the finest winemaking areas in Italy. Regulars at this chic establishment include a large clientele of businessmen, who enjoy the privacy of the lounge on the ground floor.

Pétrus

Traditional ✗✗✗

[symbols]
[AC]
[VISA]
[MC]
[AE]

12 pl. Mar. Juin ⓜ Pereire
⊠ 75017 **B2**
℡ 01 43 80 15 95 – **Fax** 01 47 66 49 86

closed 5-21 August

Carte €34/65

Pétrus has recently taken a different tack. The marine ambiance and fish specialities are out, and the new co-owners and chef have given the place a new lease of life. It is still a deluxe brasserie with the same elegance and attention to detail, but the style has been updated with rattan armchairs, light colours, a refined decor, pretty place settings and attentive service. The same modern trend is evident in the kitchen, where classical recipes are carefully reinvented with select up-to-date ingredients, skilfully complemented with market-based specialities. In summer, enjoy the pleasant terrace across from the Place du Maréchal Juin.

Palais des Congrès, Wagram, Ternes, Batignolles

La Braisière ಜ

South-West of France ✗✗

AC
VISA
MC
AE
D
%
Y

54 r. Cardinet
✉ 75017
☎ 01 47 63 40 37 – **Fax** 01 47 63 04 76
e-mail labraisiere@free.fr
closed August, 1st-8 January, Saturday lunch and Sunday
Menu € 33 (lunch) – Carte € 50/58

Ⓜ Malesherbes
C2

La Braisière

Humorist Alphonse Allais once suggested "transporting cities to the countryside" for the fresh air. The idea could also apply to restaurants, to give them an appealing "country" feeling. That is exactly what has been done with great success in the Ternes neighbourhood of Paris by Jacques Faussat, in (voluntary) exile from his native Gascony. With its contemporary paintings by Alain Jacquier (another Gascon), the restaurant is a true South-western enclave in the capital. It is a charming and friendly place, with a modern decor featuring clean lines and taupe hues. You feel almost as if you were in a private home, with the host working in the kitchen while his wife Elizabeth (a Beaux Arts graduate who designed the illustrations on the menu) takes care of the dining room. That impression is confirmed by the warm welcome and unaffected service. The market-based cuisine, with a Southwest flavour of course, offers top-quality products with a simple, gentle and delicate touch.

A LA CARTE

FIRST COURSE
• Gâteau de pommes de terre au foie gras.

• Salade de homard bleu et oeuf lucullus, crème d'oursin en homardine.

MAIN COURSE
• Gibier (October to January).

• Jarret de veau braisé longuement, cocotte de céleri au vieux jambon.

DESSERT
• Tarte mirliton aux fruits de saison.

• Fondant au chocolat noir, glace verveine et citron vert.

Palais des Congrès, Wagram, Ternes, Batignolles

Palais des Congrès, Wagram, Ternes, Batignolles

Dessirier

Seafood ✕✕

A/C
VISA
MC
AE
D
🕸
🍷

9 pl. Mar. Juin
✉ 75017
✆ 0142278214 – **Fax** 0147668207
e-mail dessirier@michelrostang.com **Web** www.michelrostang.com
closed 13-19 August

Ⓜ Pereire
B2

Carte €51/90

An appetising oyster bar tips you off immediately – people come here to enjoy the fine seafood specialities. The delicious roasted line-caught sea bass for two is one of the best dishes of the house. But the kitchen produces a multitude of other enticing seafood dishes prepared with ingredients selected with great care by Michel Rostang, proprietor of five other bistros. The elegant and unfussy decor is worthy of the great Parisian brasseries with its banquettes and upholstered armchairs, wood panelling, engravings and pretty painted plates. This lively place is mainly frequented by a business clientele at lunchtime.

Timgad

Moroccan ✕✕

A/C
VISA
MC
AE
D

21 r. Brunel
✉ 75017
✆ 0145742370 – **Fax** 0140687646
e-mail contact@timgad.fr **Web** www.timgad.fr

Ⓜ Argentine
A3

Menu €45/60 wine included– Carte €38/71

Welcome to the days when Timgad reigned supreme! This little corner of North Africa, with a name that refers to an ancient city, is well worth it just for the decor: gilded chandeliers, Moorish furniture and – to top it off – the superb, finely worked stucco sculpted by Moroccan craftsmen, which took over a year to finish! The menu is equally impressive with its rich selection of couscous (the semolina is extremely delicate), *tajines* and *pastillas* enjoyed for their generosity and thousand and one flavours. After that, what could be finer than prolonging your meal in the lovely hushed salon with a murmuring fountain? A guaranteed change of scenery!

Graindorge 🎈

VISA
MC
AE
Y

15 r. Arc de Triomphe ⓜ Charles de Gaulle-Etoile
✉ 75017 **B3**
✆ 01 47 54 00 28 – **Fax** 01 47 54 00 28
e-mail le.graindorge@wanadoo.fr
closed 1st-15 August, Saturday lunch and Sunday

Menu €28 (weekday lunch)/€32 – Carte €43/56

Bernard Broux has "sown his *Graindorge* (barley seed)" (read: opened his Flemish restaurant) in the capital. The climate around l'Étoile has worked well for him – undoubtedly because he has succeeded in adapting the charm of an inn from his native Flanders to Parisian tastes. It is a pleasure to sit down in his amusing (1930s bistro-style) Art Deco dining room to enjoy a *bintje en brandade de morue* or a seafood *waterzoï* with grey Ostende shrimp, generous recipes taken from the chef's *terroir* and complemented with market specialities. There is a very fine selection of artisanal beers from across the Quiévrain (Angélus, Moinette Blonde) to wash them down with, and plenty of treats for wine-drinkers too.

Meating

VISA
MC
AE
Y

122 av.de Villiers ⓜ Pereire
✉ 75017 **B2**
✆ 01 43 80 10 10 – **Fax** 01 43 80 31 42
e-mail chezmichelpereire@wanadoo.fr

Carte €33/84

Yes, the pun in the name is intended. In other words, this restaurant is a kind of steak house designed for a chic neighbourhood – the latest trendy concept. The place is unique and carries it off well. Its talented American chef selects the finest meats, carefully checks their origins, and cooks them "to within a degree" (likewise for the fish). The key to its success is the fashionable decor in dark shades, catering to a hip clientele of carnivores who have become regulars. Simple as pie? Well, someone had to think of it first, and he was the one bold enough to open this establishment where l'Apicius once stood. Could I have one rare rib steak over here, please?!

L'Atelier Gourmand

Classic ✗✗

A/C
20 r. de Tocqueville ⓜ Villiers
⊠ 75017 **C2**
☎ 01 42 27 03 71 – **Fax** 01 42 27 03 71

VISA Closed 14-20 May, 1st-21 August, Saturday except dinner from 15 September to 15 June and Sunday

MC
Menu €36

AE
⚏

Guy-Antoine Fontana is a very likable man who specialises in the great classics, and does it very well. From conception to the finished recipe, he eliminates everything superfluous and highlights the essential – fine and meticulously selected ingredients. And since he likes to please people, he makes sure "classic" doesn't mean "routine" by changing the menu every month. As for the decor in this former painter's studio – some would call it busy, while others might call it highly colourful – it won't leave you indifferent with its modern paintings, antique objects, collection of 19C table tidies, and "flashy" orange and green tones. In short, this is an eclectic mix with an Italian touch – worth having a look at from the mezzanine above.

Ballon des Ternes

Brasserie ✗✗

103 av. Ternes ⓜ Porte Maillot
⊠ 75017 **A3**

VISA
☎ 01 45 74 17 98 – **Fax** 01 45 72 18 84

MC
e-mail leballondesternes@fr.oleane.com

AE
closed 1st-21 August

⚏
Carte €36/63

If you want to show your colleagues from across the Atlantic an authentic 1900s brasserie, then look no further. Take them to the Ballon des Ternes between conventions at the Palais des Congrès. It has it all, from the red velvet banquettes and bistro chairs to the little lamps, ceiling *fixé sous verre*, furniture from the Champagne region and mirrors on all the walls; not to mention the smiling waiters zooming around the tables and the impressive menu featuring seafood and traditional dishes. For the "French Touch", don't forget to point out the upside down table on the ceiling!

Chez Léon

Traditional ✗✗

32 r. Legendre ⊕ Villiers
⊠ 75017 **C2**
☎ 0142270682 – **Fax** 0146226367
e-mail chezleon32@wanadoo.fr

closed 30 July-24 August, 24-31 December, Saturday and Sunday

Menu €26 – Carte €28/52

Chez Léon, they don't toy with tradition. This 1950s bistro is proud of its strong identity, with a simple setting that is appealing precisely because of its retro Parisian quality. Most of the "ambasssadors" of timeless French gastronomy are present on the menu – from chicken liver terrine and Burgundy snails for starters, to turbot in a *beurre blanc*, andouillette sausages, *jambon persillé*, veal kidneys, *sole meunière*, and *saumon à l'oseille*, before ending with the homemade profiteroles or lukewarm pear soup with blackcurrants. The tasty recipes are well-prepared and served with speed and a smile. Guaranteed conviviality at this excellent little establishment – a place to remember.

La Maison de Charly

Moroccan ✗✗

97 bd Gouvion-St-Cyr ⊕ Porte Maillot
⊠ 75017 **A3**
☎ 0145743462 – **Fax** 0145743536
Web www.lamaisondecharly.com

closed August and Monday

Menu €42

The two olive trees are like a landmark in front of the dark ochre façade. When you walk into La Maison de Charly, you can tell right away that this is not one of those Moroccan restaurants loaded with flashy stucco and gold decorations. There's nothing kitsch about the Moorish decor here, which has discreet and elegant contemporary touches. But the lovely ambiance has a definite North African flavour, with flowers and trees all over, fine materials, sculpted doors and even a palm tree under the large glass roof. The traditional couscous-tajines-pastillas trio is doubly delicious; and specialities such as *tanjia* (baby lamb preserved with spices) will have you hurrying back for more.

Bath's ✿

Contemporary ✗

A/C
VISA
MC
AE
♀

25 r. Bayen
✉ 75017
☎ 01 45 74 74 74 – **Fax** 01 45 74 71 15
e-mail contact@baths.fr **Web** www.baths.fr
Closed August, Sunday and public holidays

Ⓜ Ternes
B3

Menu € 25 (lunch) – Carte € 40/60

Bath's

An electric blue sign and a reception area with soft lighting are the prelude to the new world of Jean-Yves Bath and his son Stéphane, who have gone from the 8th to the 17th arrondissement, and from sophistication to a simplicity that is closer to today's tastes. That is the spirit in which they created this very personal place, dotted with sculptures by the owner and paintings by Jean-Pierre Rives (yes, the one who played in the French rugby team in the 1980s!). Curiously, the dining room evokes Asia with its ceiling and wall lamps creating soft lighting, and its black lacquer tables offsetting the orange walls. But the ham hanging from the ceiling, bistro table settings and subtly presented products from the *terroir* situate this establishment in a very French location, with a rather Southwestern orientation. The Bath method consists of two or three discreetly and simply presented ingredients of irreproachable freshness and quality.

A LA CARTE

FIRST COURSE	MAIN COURSE	DESSERT
• Cassolette d'oeufs brouillés.	• Escalope de saumon poêlée aux lentilles.	• Riz au lait.
• Salade tiède de homard.	• Tatin de pieds de porc.	• Confiture de "vieux garçon".

Caïus

Innovative ✗

AC
VISA
MC
AE
Ⓨ

6 r. d'Armaillé Ⓜ Charles de Gaulle-Etoile
✉ 75017 **B3**
✆ 0142271920 – **Fax** 0140550093

Menu €38

Hidden behind the unassuming façade and traditional neighbourhood bistro look is a rather chic establishment. And what inventive food! Jean-Marc Notelet's cuisine is full of originality. His secret? Spices and rare ingredients. He has a knack for transforming ordinary recipes into trendy dishes with a pinch of vanilla and a dash of argan oil. Bursting with new ideas, he changes the listings on the huge blackboard every day. As a result, one never tires of the food, nor of the atmosphere in the little modern dining room with clean lines, light wood panelling and photographs of precious condiments. This is a place where all the senses are celebrated.

Montefiori

Italian ✗

AC
VISA
MC
AE

19 r. de l'Etoile Ⓜ Charles de Gaulle-Etoile
✉ 75017 **B3**
✆ 0155379000
e-mail montesiori@wanadoo.fr

closed 1st-20 August, 24 December-1st January, Sunday and Monday

Menu €22 (weekday lunch) – Carte €31/66

If you like Italian cuisine, preferably in a trendy restaurant, this establishment with a beautiful façade is the place for you (a former bakery, it is now a historic monument). The Montefiori has a clientele of regulars from the neighbourhood and a rather "fashion-conscious" red-and-green decor (Italy's colours) with clean lines and a few objects with a Baroque touch (chandeliers, statues) which give it a well-designed personal style. Tradition is also the main theme in the kitchen, where they don't fool around with the great Italian classics such as veal Milanese, tiramisu – although the chef sometimes adds his own twist here – linguine with clams, peach and champagne sorbet.

Palais des Congrès, Wagram, Ternes, Batignolles

La Soupière ☺

A/C
VISA
MC
AE
Ŷ

154 av. de Wagram
✉ 75017
℘ 0142270073 – **Fax** 0146222709

closed 1st-19 August, Saturday lunch and Sunday

Ⓜ Wagram
B2

Menu €32/60 – Carte €36/57

You feel like lifting the lid of the *Soupière* (soup tureen) just to taste Christian Thuillart's one-of-a-kind Wild or Spring Mushroom Menus. In season, this passionate chef concocts meals celebrating the delicate flavours of these precious mycelia. The menu also features traditional dishes with tasty, carefully selected and skilfully prepared ingredients. The setting includes a fine trompe-l'œil garden and colonnade, giving the hushed little dining room (with 30 place settings) a mock-Tuscan look. Warm reception.

Table des Oliviers

A/C
VISA
MC
Ⓘ
Ŷ

38 r. Laugier
✉ 75017
℘ 0147638551 – **Fax** 0147638581
e-mail latabledesoliviers@wanadoo.fr
Web www.latabledesoliviers.fr

closed 26 February-3 March, 30 July-20 August, Monday lunch, Saturday lunch and Sunday

Ⓜ Pereire
B3

Menu €30 – Carte €48/53

Mr. and Mrs. Olivier have a restaurant. What should they call it? La Table des Oliviers, naturally. And what is on the menu? Specialities from Provence, of course! Apart from that, everything depends on when you dine here. The Niçois like to sample their *socca* (crepes) on Thursday, while the Marseillais prefer to have their *bouillabaisse* on Friday or Saturday. Every day has its particular dish, but Sunday – as the chef explains on the blackboard – is a day for relaxation! During the rest of the week, you can enjoy the homemade olive oil bread, the dishes seasoned with thyme and basil, and the very pleasant southern French decor. You can almost hear the cicadas chirping.

Bistrot de l'Étoile Niel

Bistro ✕

75 av. Niel
✉ 75017
✆ 0142278844 – **Fax** 0142273212
e-mail gensdarmesb@aol.com
closed Saturday lunch and Sunday

Ⓜ Pereire
B2

Menu €29 (weekday lunch) – Carte €31/48

A chic but relaxed bistro, rather like Bruno Gensdarmes himself, now alone at the helm of this fine ship after fifteen years with Guy Savoy. This experienced chef cooks up typical bistro dishes in his own special way, with flavours from here, ingredients from there – Argentine rib steak in mustard butter, warm leeks and "Arrosagarai" salt-cured ham –, well-dosed condiments and spices; then his creativity takes care of the rest. The short and original menu has no chance of falling into a routine since it changes every two months. In summer, the deliciously shady terrace is a real favourite.

Le Café d'Angel

Traditional ✕

16 r. Brey
✉ 75017
✆ 0147540333 – **Fax** 0147540333
Closed 30 July-20 August, 24 December-6 January, Saturday, Sunday and public holidays

Ⓜ Charles de Gaulle-Etoile
B3

Menu €20/24 – Carte €40/48

This is a really pretty café with plenty of appeal – imitation leather banquettes, faïence on the walls and little square tables with paper placemats. Not to mention the highly friendly and communicative ambiance, which you can already see through the glass façade before even stepping in. This is a place for people who feel nostalgic for the Parisian bistros of yesteryear. The food is exactly what you would expect in a restaurant like this, with good, 100% homemade traditional recipes. They change every day, so just have a look at the blackboard while strolling by. There's a good chance that, without even realizing it, the Café d'Angel will become your favourite local establishment! This place was surely born under a lucky star.

Palais des Congrès, Wagram, Ternes, Batignolles

Palais des Congrès, Wagram, Ternes, Batignolles

Caves Petrissans

Traditional ✗

30 bis av. Niel
✉ 75017
✆ 0142275203 – **Fax** 0140548756
e-mail cavespetrissans@noos.fr

Ⓜ Pereire
B3

Closed 28 July-27 August, Saturday, Sunday and public holidays – pre-book

Menu €34 – Carte €38/55

The regulars at this hundred-year-old cellar are legion. And delightful Marie-Christine Allemoz – the fourth generation! – greets newcomers with the same warm welcome, seating you in a flash at one of the tables where Céline, Abel Gance or Roland Dorgelès may have eaten in their day. Follow the proprietors' excellent advice on which wine to choose. They will find the best bottle for you from their amazing adjoining shop, taking the homemade terrine, *tête de veau sauce ravigote* or one of the numerous bistro classics – all delicious! – to a whole new level. There is a more private room in the back and a terrace covered with Virgina creeper.

Le Clou

Terroir ✗

132 r. Cardinet
✉ 75017
✆ 0142273678 – **Fax** 0142278996
e-mail le.clou@wanadoo.fr **Web** www.restaurant-leclou.fr

Ⓜ Malesherbes
C2

closed 13-26 August and Sunday

Menu €21 (weekday lunch)/€32

The pretty painted wood façade, old posters, blackboard, wood panelling, snug and simply laid tables tell you that you are in a typical neighbourhood bistro. And yet, there is valet parking at lunch and dinner, and great vintages (Petrus, Château Margaux) to accompany your meal. Who said conviviality and refinement couldn't go together? Certainly not Christian Leclou, the chef-proprietor of this restaurant, as evidenced by his dishes. Going by traditional names, they clearly demonstrate his skill as he follows the seasons and highlights fine ingredients from the *terroir*, in particular from Poitou, the chef's native region.

Paris XVII 🐾

Bistro ※

VISA

MC

🍷

41 r. Guersant
✉ 75017
☏ 01 45 74 75 27

Ⓜ Porte Maillot
B3

closed 17-23 April, 31 July-20 August, 25 December-1st January, Sunday and Monday

Menu €20/30 – Carte €20/31

The trendiness of the neighbouring arrondissements will never spill over into this pocket bistro, where Madame André and her son are doing everything to prevent it. In both the dining area and kitchen, they have preserved the charm of this smart and simple establishment. And no one is going to complain about it. Have a look at the blackboard to find out the market specialities of the day – fresh and well-executed bistro dishes that match the place to a tee. You can enjoy them amidst the jolly close quarters and convivial atmosphere; and you could easily forget that you are only a short drive from the ring road that encircles Paris.

L'Huîtrier

Seafood ※

A/C

VISA

MC

AE

🍷

16 r. Saussier-Leroy
✉ 75017
☏ 01 40 54 83 44 – **Fax** 01 40 54 83 86

Ⓜ Ternes
B3

closed Sunday from June to August, Sunday dinner in September and Monday

Carte €29/69

It's no mystery that people come here for the oysters, which is clear from the name and the attractive oyster bar at the entrance. But there are other fish and seafood on the generous blackboard besides these famous shellfish. Watch it carefully, to catch the appetizing seasonal and tide-based novelties. The dishes are simply prepared to highlight the extremely fresh ingredients delivered constantly throughout the year. Enjoy them in the warm and discreetly contemporary setting.

Palais des Congrès, Wagram, Ternes, Batignolles

L'Entredgeu

VISA · 83 r. Laugier   Ⓜ Porte de Champerret
MC · ✉ 75017   **A2**
🍷 · ✆ 01 40 54 97 24 – **Fax** 01 40 54 96 62

closed 1st-22 August, 24 December-1st January, and Monday

Menu €22 (weekday lunch)/€30

The ambiance in this place is amazing! You'd think the entire 17th arrondissement had made it their "local" – and with reason. Philippe Tredgeu (the chef-proprietor) and his wife Pénélope know how to please gourmet diners. With fine market ingredients, perfectly mastered traditional recipes and restrained prices, their formula is a hit and has already developed a large clientele of regulars. Furthermore, the warm welcome extended by the proprietress makes it even more enjoyable! Due to this great success, it is often booked and the service is sometimes a bit rushed. But the friendly atmosphere makes you forgive and forget. After all, what would this place with a touch of the southwest be without all the banter and clinking glasses?

Palais des Congrès, Wagram, Ternes, Batignolles

Montmartre, Pigalle

Blackwell K./MICHELIN

Montmartre is famous for its artists, its tourists, its basilica unique in the world and its steep streets. The portrait is clearly that of Paris, but how can we describe Pigalle with its frilly cabarets, Can-can girls and neon lights that never sleep? At times it seems as if the 18th embodies all on its own the entire fantastical dimension of Paris. This is however unsurprising when one thinks of the sheer size of this arrondissement, bordered by boulevard de Rochechouart, avenue de Saint-Ouen and the ring road. The range of ambiences and panoramas is as broad as it is unexpected, from festive, almost brazen in Pigalle, picturesque and more bohemian around Montmartre to distinctly cosmopolitan at the Goutte d'Or.

PARIS BY NIGHT

Considered broadly, **Pigalle** is made up of several distinct sectors: first of all, place Pigalle itself, at the meeting point of avenue de Clichy and boulevard de Rochechouart, then rue Pigalle that goes down towards the 9th and finally the informal jumble of lanes at the foot of the hill of Montmartre. It would be pointless to try and pretend that Pigalle is not known first and foremost for its nightlife; it is home to some of the capital's most famous **cabarets,** such as the **Moulin Rouge,** a multitude of bars and discos and a growing number of pubs with dance floors in answer to the fun-loving demands of a new generation of party-goers. What the visitor should however also know is that the area is literally crammed with tiny restaurants, gourmet cafés and friendly eateries serving every imaginable type of cuisine from Indian and Chinese to Basque, Auvergne, African and even Balkan. Apart from Montmartre (see below), another area bran-

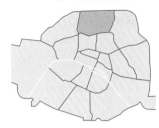

ching off from Pigalle is worth exploring. Head directly north towards the town of Saint-Ouen along the street of the same name and the famous **flea market of Clignancourt,** located on several hectares of land and paradise for lovers of bric-a-brac and antiques.

PICTURE POSTCARD MONTMARTRE

Clichés are often long-lived but that of **Montmartre** remains fully justified: picturesque narrow cobbled streets and long flights of steps with wrought-iron railings paint this picture postcard portrait of Paris, crowned by the basilica of the **Sacré-Cœur** and its stunning view of the city. Formerly the haunt of artists of all kinds, tourism is gradually overtaking the hillock, with its good and bad side effects. Bar a few notable exceptions, it is dotted with

Blackwell K./MICHELIN

authentic bistros that continue to survive. Nor should one forget that the **artistic tradition** of Montmartre has far from said its last word as is proven by the aptly named Montmartre-aux-artistes on rue Ordener that provides workshops and housing for painters, sculptors and creators of all kinds.

Finally, it would be unthinkable to leave without mentioning the **Goutte d'Or** area around Barbès. The district vibrates in permanence to the rhythm of its international communities speaking languages from around the world, offering a unique picture in Paris. Lovers of exotic food, from fruit to spices, are sure to find what they're looking for in the district's countless specialised shops or, even better, on market days (Wednesday and Saturday).

restaurants that the Parisians somewhat sneeringly refer to as "tourist traps", meaning that they are expensive and uninteresting. However the district still has a few genuine locals and aficionados who meet up for a drink in one of the many

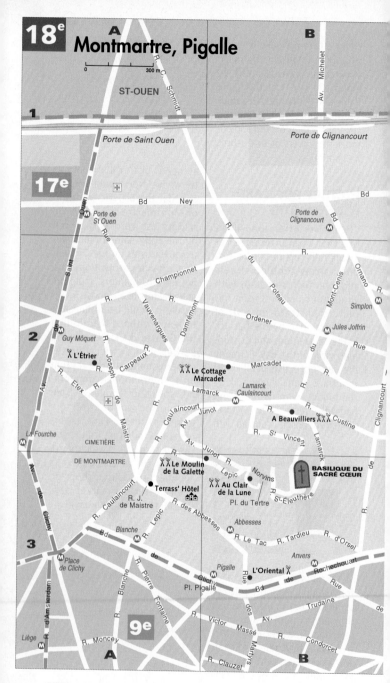

Montmartre, Pigalle

ST-OUEN

Porte de Saint Ouen

Porte de Clignancourt

17ᵉ

Bd   Ney   Bd

Porte de
St Ouen

Porte de
Clignancourt

Championnet

Poteau

Ordener

Simplon

Jules Joffrin

Guy Môquet

L'Étrier

Marcadet

Le Cottage
Marcadet

Lamarck
Caulaincourt

Lamarck

A Beauvilliers   Custine

CIMETIÈRE

La Fourche

DE MONTMARTRE

Le Moulin
de la Galette

Au Clair
de la Lune

BASILIQUE DU
SACRÉ CŒUR

Terrass' Hôtel

Pl. du Tertre

St-Eleuthère

R. J.
de Maistre

Blanche

Abbesses

R. Le Tac   R. Tardieu   R. d'Orsel

Place
de Clichy

Anvers

Pigalle

L'Oriental

Pl. Pigalle

9ᵉ

Liège

Trudaine

R. Moncey

Condorcet

R. Clauzet

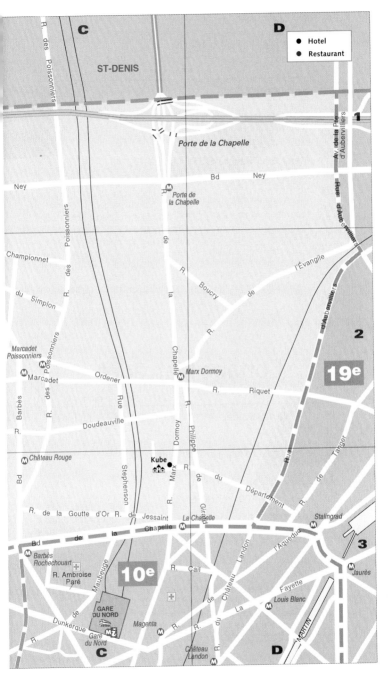

A Beauvilliers

Contemporary ✗✗✗

52 r. Lamarck
✉ 75018
☎ 0142550542
Web www.abeauvilliers.com

closed Sunday and Monday

Ⓜ Lamarck Caulaincourt
B2

Menu €35 (lunch)/€63 – Carte €61/74

Yohan Paran, now fully in control here, has given this Montmartre institution a new lease of life. His talent lies in revitalizing this establishment while preserving what earned it such a fine reputation in the first place – its name, to begin with, which comes from Antoine de Beauvilliers, chef for the Comte de Provence. Then there is the elegant decor, remodelled in a more up-to-date and equally refined style. As for the pleasant shady terrace full of flowers, it is still a favourite in summer. In the kitchen, the talented Yohan has opted for a contemporary style blending different flavours. Don't miss his truffle dishes in season.

Le Cottage Marcadet

Contemporary ✗✗

151 bis r. Marcadet
✉ 75018
☎ 0142577122
e-mail contact@cottagemarcadet.com
Web www.cottagemarcadet.com

closed August, Sunday and Sunday

Ⓜ Lamarck Caulaincourt
B2

Menu €35/100 – Carte €57/89

The decor at this elegant restaurant at the foot of the Butte is comprised of yellow and salmon tones, Louis XVI-style furniture, paintings by local artists and smart table settings. The soft lighting creates a hushed ambiance which offsets the up-to-date seasonal cuisine on the attractively priced set menus. The à la carte menu features various dishes including sardine fillets with onion compote, caramelized sea bream with sweet spices, and a caramel bavarois with salted butter. Drawn by the setting, the chef's touch and the professional service, the local business clientele has made it one of their preferred restaurants. Remember to book, as there are less than thirty place settings.

Le Moulin de la Galette

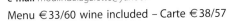

Contemporary XX

83 r. Lepic
☒ 75018
✆ 01 46 06 84 77 – **Fax** 01 46 06 84 78
e-mail moulindelagalette@yahoo.fr

Ⓜ Abbesses
A-B3

Menu €33/60 wine included – Carte €38/57

You have to climb up the famous rue Lepic – praised in song by Yves Montand and walked by Amélie Poulain – to reach this charming mill with a historic background. Built in 1622, it was the last of the 30 mills in Montmartre to resist the industrial age. Transformed into a *guinguette* (open-air café), immortalized in paintings by Renoir and Toulouse-Lautrec, it sent many a Parisian heart reeling. Today it houses a pleasant and up-to-date restaurant serving traditional bistro dishes. As for the *guinguette*, it was turned into a terrace where people no longer dance, but they certainly enjoy sitting there in fine weather. A fabulous destiny indeed.

Au Clair de la Lune

Traditional XX

9 r. Poulbot
☒ 75018
✆ 01 42 58 97 03 – **Fax** 01 42 55 64 74
closed 19 August-16 September, Monday lunch and Sunday

Ⓜ Abbesses
B3

Menu €30 – Carte €37/67

The affable Jerfauts brothers, twins who have run this establishment for over fifteen years, will welcome you into their inn located just behind the Place du Tertre. One is in the dining room and the other in the kitchen, forming the perfect duo for pampering diners and serving up classic dishes celebrating traditional French cuisine. The pleasant atmosphere is quite charming with its murals of the Butte in earlier times, Louis-Philippe furniture and convivial ambiance. Welcome to the heart of Jean-Pierre Jeunet's Montmartre.

L'Oriental

VISA

76 r. Martyrs
✉ 75018
☎ 0142643980 – **Fax** 0142643980
Web www.loriental-restaurant.com

Ⓜ Pigalle
B3

Menu € 14,50 (weekday lunch/wine included)/€ 34
– Carte € 27/39

This North African restaurant benefits from the cosmopolitan hustle and bustle of Pigalle. What distinguishes it from other establishments in the neighbourhood? The pleasant eastern setting – tables decorated with *zelliges, moucharabiehs*, banquettes with cushions and a small fountain – has just the right touch of the exotic without overdoing it. The menu features tajines and couscous, as well as other great classics of Moroccan cuisine. The friendly welcome rounds out the picture and proves why this restaurant is what you could call a really nice little place.

L'Étrier

A/C
VISA

154 r. Lamarck
✉ 75018
☎ 0142291401 – **Fax** 0146271915

Ⓜ Guy Môquet
A2

closed 6-26 August, 1st-7 January, Sunday and Monday

♀ Menu € 20 (weekday lunch)/€ 48 – Carte € 25/50

Regulars at this pocket bistro know to book a table here before showing up. There are only twenty place settings in this place, and with its warm decor and loads of good cheer, it is no surprise that people fill it up for lunch and dinner. The two associates who run this charming restaurant are well-versed in the art of how to please diners – and treat them to simple and well-prepared traditional dishes. The blackboard is changed regularly to satisfy all tastes and take advantage of seasonal ingredients. It is well worth climbing up the steep streets of the Butte for this kind of treatment!

La Villette, Cité des Sciences – Buttes Chaumont

Typical of sprawling northeastern Paris, the 19th arrondissement covers a vast area between place de Stalingrad, rue de Belleville and the ring road. The result of the annexation of the former towns of Belleville, Villette and parts of Pantin and Aubervilliers, traces of its multiple and composite past can still be seen. It is impossible to reduce the 19th to a single definition due to the many changes and evolutions brought about by the massive urban development programmes implemented by the city of Paris and the French government. As a result, the distinctive futurist quality of the Villette district has little in common with the steep narrow lanes of the Buttes-Chaumont, all of which ensure that a stroll through the 19th will afford surprises that are both aesthetic and culinary.

OLD AND NEW

A 19C fruit and vegetable vendor would indeed be hard put to recognise his old district around the **Villette** today because the entire sector has been developed to make way for the **Cité des Sciences et de l'Industrie**, the **Cité de la Musique** and immense expanses of lawn. The old abattoirs, no longer in use, were pulled down, as were the fruit and vegetable stalls, and replaced with immense esplanades, manicured lawns and footbridges spanning the canals of the **Ourcq** and **Saint-Denis,** creating what is now an urban zone that is both modern and luminous and highly popular with walkers. The sector is home to several cinemas, including the famous **Géode** and its amazing 360° screen,

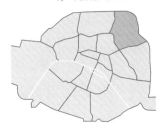

and to the **Zénith** concert hall, a genuine institution in Paris. The outlying areas, particularly towards Pantin, have retained their former charm, but it is not here that you will taste fine cuisine. The area is home to a tightly meshed network of little restaurants of every imaginable culture. Further west, you will encounter rue de Flandre that cuts across the entire north segment of the arrondissement as far as Stalingrad. Relatively opulent (and bourgeois-bohemian) towards the canal, it occasionally evokes a Haussmannian boulevard, but is more populous and working-class on the other bank, where it features some of the most daring, if not always the most attractive, examples of residential housing in Paris.

THE DISCREET CHARM OF THE BUTTES CHAUMONT

Buttes-Chaumont Park, another of Napoleon III's ambitious projects, is one of the capital's largest parks and the centre of tiny districts of sometimes unexpected charm. The park itself is worth a trip for its landscaped splendid mineral formations, several artificial grottoes and a temple of Greek inspiration that dominates the site. Around the park you will discover another surprisingly green facet of the 19th. Towards the ring road lies the **Mouzaïa district,** an unspoilt steep island of greenery; built on former gypsum quar-

ries, none of its comfortable little houses with gardens are over two storeys high giving the overall impression of a sleepy residential suburb of a small provincial town.

Southwest of the park, towards rue Simon Bolivar, a few minutes' walk suffices to climb up the Bergeyre mound to a district, also seemingly forgotten by time, of small 1920's working-class houses lining staircase streets interspersed with flower-decked gardens. The view over **Belleville** is outstanding, giving the impression of flying over the city, while to the west you will have no difficulty in picking out the details of the Sacré-Coeur. The district, devoid of fancy restaurants and gourmet halts, is rather home to lively neighbourhood bars steeped in history, where the locals will happily wax lyrical on the merits of their beloved district.

Blackwell K./MICHELIN

La Villette, Cité des Sciences – Buttes Chaumont

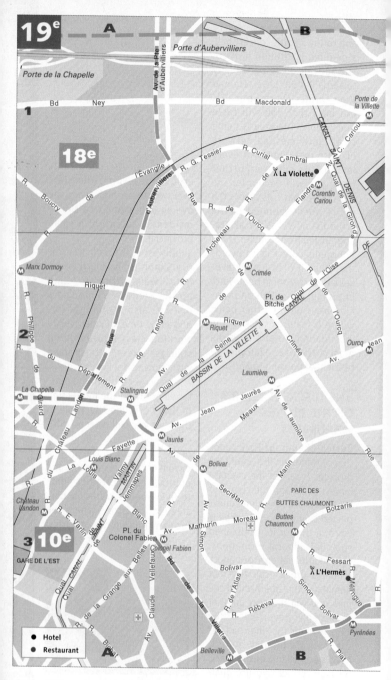

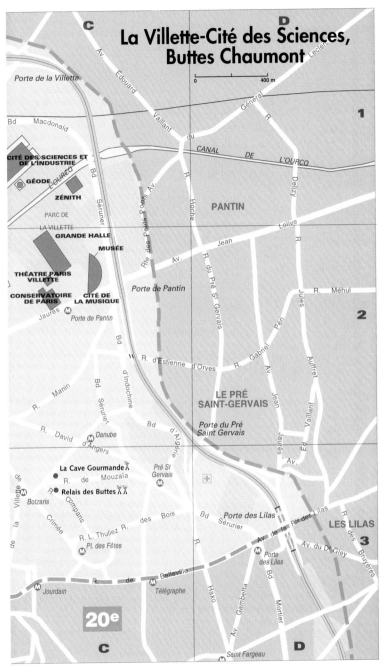

La Villette-Cité des Sciences, Buttes Chaumont

0   400 m

Porte de la Villette

Bd   Macdonald

CITÉ DES SCIENCES ET DE L'INDUSTRIE

GÉODE

ZÉNITH

PARC DE

LA VILLETTE

GRANDE HALLE

MUSÉE

THÉÂTRE PARIS VILLETTE

CONSERVATOIRE DE PARIS

CITÉ DE LA MUSIQUE

Jaurès Ⓜ

Porte de Pantin

Av. Édouard Vaillant

CANAL DE L'OURCQ

Bd Sérurier

Rte des Petits Ponts Av.

R. Hoche

PANTIN

Av. Jean

Av. Général Leclerc

R. Delizy

Lolive

Porte de Pantin

R. d'Estienne d'Orves

R. du Pré St Gervais

R. Méhul

R. Jules

R. Gabriel Péri

Av. Jean Jaurès

Auffret

R. Manin

Bd Sérurier

Bd d'Indochine

Bd d'Algérie

LE PRÉ SAINT-GERVAIS

Porte du Pré Saint Gervais

R. David

Danube d'Angers Ⓜ

La Cave Gourmande ⚔

R. de Mouzaïa

Relais des Buttes ⚔⚔

Pré St Gervais Ⓜ

Botzaris Ⓜ

Compans

Crimée

R. L. Thuliez R. des Bois

Pl. des Fêtes Ⓜ

Porte des Lilas

Bd Sérurier

Ⓜ Porte des Lilas

LES LILAS

Av. de la Pte des Lilas

Av. du Dr Gley

R. des Bruyères

Av. Ed. Vaillant Jaurès Av.

de la Villette

Jourdain Ⓜ

R. de Belleville

Télégraphe Ⓜ

Haxo

Av. Gambetta

Bd Mortier

20e

Saint Fargeau Ⓜ

C   D

Relais des Buttes

Classic ✗✗

86 r. Compans
✉ 75019
☎ 0142082470 – **Fax** 0142032044

Ⓜ Botzaris
C3

closed August, 24 December-3 January, Saturday lunch and Sunday

Menu €34 – Carte €43/57

Escape from the hustle and bustle of Paris and recharge your batteries in this peaceful restaurant which has the look of a country house. In winter you can sit by the fire in the dining room decorated with colourful paintings. In fine weather, trade in the warm fireplace for the warm sun on the delicious flowery patio. Throughout the year you will enjoy the classic cuisine prepared by chef Marc Gautron, including fine seafood specialities (oyster and scallop timbale with Bourbon, fillet of red mullet). You couldn't dream of a better place to enjoy a meal in a little country inn – on the hills of the Buttes-Chaumont.

La Cave Gourmande ☺

Bistro ✗

10 r. Gén. Brunet
✉ 75019
☎ 0140400330 – **Fax** 0140400330
e-mail lacavegourmande@wanadoo.fr

Ⓜ Botzaris
C3

Closed 5-26 August, February half-term holidays, Saturday lunch and Sunday

Menu €36

This pleasant establishment has everything going for it. The key to its success? Undoubtedly, the little touch of inventiveness which the chef sprinkles in all his dishes, carefully prepared with fresh seasonal and market-based ingredients. Or could it be the warm ambiance? The first room - with a view of the kitchen - has a bistro look (wooden tables, bottle racks, mirrors), while the second is simpler. One thing is for sure; the gracious hospitality of the proprietors has won them a clientele of regulars, who like to treat themselves to a well-deserved meal here - after walking up and down the paths of the largest and steepest public garden in Paris!

L' Hermès

Bistro

VISA
MC
♀

23 r. Mélingue
✉ 75019
☎ 0142399470
e-mail lhermes@wanadoo.fr

Ⓜ Pyrénées
B3

closed 8-16 April, 5 August-4 September, 25 February-3 March, Wednesday lunch, Sunday and Monday

Menu €16 (weekday lunch)/€30 – Carte €32/52

You have to go all the way to the end of the rue Mélingue to find this establishment, which is somewhat hidden but worth hunting for. It is easier to find at night with its string of fairy lights (on the painted wood façade) indicating the road to l'Hermès – better than a compass – and giving it the look of a *guinguette* (open-air café). Inside, the rustic dining room has a deliciously country charm with its old sideboard, ochre tones, wood furniture, lace curtains, colourful paintings and plaid table-cloths. This is the kind of place that just makes you feel good. The menu features bistro dishes presented on the blackboard, ingredients from the *terroir*, and a cellar with some pleasant surprises.

La Violette

Contemporary

🖨
VISA
MC
♀

11 av. Corentin Cariou
✉ 75019
☎ 0140352045
e-mail restolaviolette@free.fr **Web** www.restaurant-laviolette.com

Ⓜ Corentin Cariou
B1

closed 14-20 May, 6-12 August, 25 December-2 January, Saturday and Sunday – number of covers limited, pre-book

Carte €35/46

There is only one exception in the black-and-white decor at this restaurant - a purple banquette! It runs the length of this room exclusively in wood and marble (on the bar, tables, and walls), where the atmosphere evokes the 1930s. Photographs of the city and a wine-growing theme – wine crates, racks and brass plaques engraved with names of vintages – give the place a style that is both hip and cosy. It is smart, like the cuisine featuring tasty and up-to-date little dishes enjoyed by the clientele of businessmen, with whom it is very popular at lunchtime. Remember to book (there are less than thirty place settings), and request the smaller room for more privacy.

Sauvignier S./MICHELIN

Père Lachaise, Belleville

Composed of the former town of Belleville and the Père-La-chaise district, the 20th sports relatively ample dimensions within its immense tangle of lanes and passageways. It is no doubt due to the rural and working-class past of Belleville that this part of the capital has continued to exhibit such a propensity for diversity since its annexation. Formerly a zone of vineyards and slopes, it first became a working-class district of immigrants, before it evolved into a hunting ground for Parisians in search of more reasonably priced housing. Nowadays the district is a genuine melting pot of constantly changing influences and populations from all over the world, bohemian artists in search of authenticity or inspiration and occasional walkers who pass each other without always mixing, making the 20th a district of contrasts.

366

DIVERSITY

An enthusiastic enterprising spirit seems to characterise the Belleville district. You only have to take a walk round the market (every Tuesday and Friday) to discover the tastes and smells of five continents with produce from all over France in addition to West Indian, African and Asian spices and craftwork from nearly everywhere. The housing and shops of the district reflect this variety of cultures, as do the dozens of tiny restaurants that proudly represent every culinary tradition in the world.

The scenery changes radically as you head further south, around the Buzenval, Alexandre Dumas and porte de Montreuil metro stations. Here the bourgeois-bohemians are progressively settling areas

formerly abandoned. As a result **Buzenval** has become the favourite haunt of artists in search of space and also of more or less legal squats wedged in between waste ground and buildings to be demolished. Those in search of authenticity will however adore the area and will no doubt want to stop in one of the many nearby popular cafés for a well-earned pastis.

BETWEEN TWO WORLDS

A visit to **Père-Lachaise cemetery** also offers the chance to take a walk through the history of France (and the world) and the list of its famous residents is seemingly endless from Oscar Wilde to Jim Morrison and from Auguste Comte to Marcel Proust. The necropolis, set on 45 hectares of land and home to some 70 000 graves, is a real town within a town with avenues lined in neo-Byzantine mausoleums and imposing burial vaults.

The surrounding quiet residential streets make a welcome break from the effervescence of the nearby **Ménilmontant** district. Here, exotic restaurants, trendy cafés and old-fashioned bistros joyfully cohabit in a tangled web of steep streets and shaded squares. Then, heading down towards **place de la Nation,** the district becomes surreptitiously bourgeois: Asian influences are gradually supplanting the former North African and African communities, and many of the restaurants and delicatessens are well worth a pause.

In the opposite direction, towards **place de Bagnolet** and its high-rise council flats, don't miss the chance for a quick walk in the village referred to as "the countryside in Paris", a delightful 1910 estate perched on a hill and dotted with terraced gardens; almost Montmartre in the heart of the 20th!

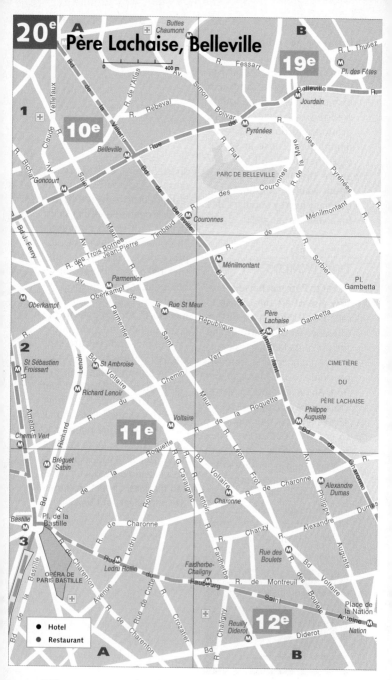

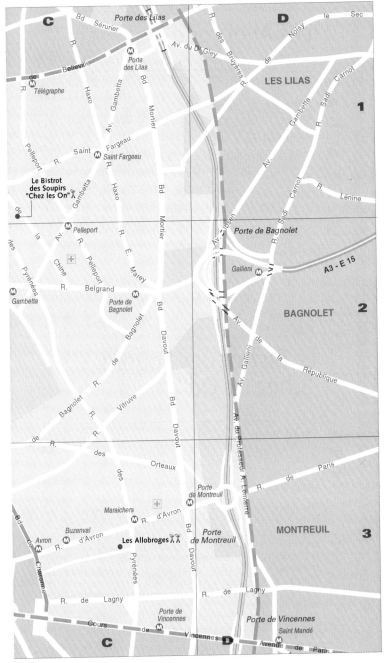

Les Allobroges 😊

Contemporary 🍴🍴

VISA
MC
AE

71 r. Grands-Champs
✉ 75020
✆ 01 43 73 40 00 – **Fax** 01 40 09 23 22

Closed 16-22 April, August, 24 December-2 January, Sunday, Monday and public holidays

Ⓜ Maraîchers
C3

Menu €21/€34

Olivier Pateyron (who trained with Dalloyau and Guérard) has been the chef here for over twenty years! Needless to say, he is a master at his work and never tires of it. The proof is in his delicious up-to-date cuisine which features herbs and vegetables and uses the finest ingredients. He has won over the entire 20th arrondissement and well beyond! Diners come from all over the city to enjoy a treat at this place a stone's throw from the Porte de Montreuil. With its simple interior, charming reception and well-prepared food, this is a real find in the neighbourhood.

Le Bistrot des Soupirs "Chez les On"

Terroir 🍴

VISA
MC
�images

49 r. Chine
✉ 75020
✆ 01 44 62 93 31 – **Fax** 01 44 62 77 83

closed 1st-6 May, 30 July-19 August, 24 December 1-st January, Sunday and Monday

Ⓜ Gambetta
C1

Menu €35 (lunch)/€41 – **Carte** €28/43

This fine establishment in the 20th arrondissement falls in the bistro category. Although small in size, it is larger-than-life in terms of its atmosphere, which is distinct and always fun. The decor has an authentic and unpretentious charm with its fine oak counter, wood everywhere and carefully preserved 1930s ambiance. Regulars never tire of its "country" appeal and blackboards with their delicious specials such as homemade terrines, generous *canaille* and bistro dishes (snails, homemade foie gras, *andouillettes*), and seasonal game. The generous and well-prepared food is paired with an interesting selection of proprietors' wines. Unbeatable value for money.

Where to stay

Alphabetical list of hotels

A

Le A (8ᵉ)		426
Amour (9ᵉ)		433
Aubusson (Hôtel d') (6ᵉ)		398

B

Banville (17ᵉ)		431
Bassano (16ᵉ)		430
Bourg Tibourg (4ᵉ)		419
Le Bristol (Hôtel) (8ᵉ)		380

C

Caron de Beaumarchais (4ᵉ)		421
Le 123 (8ᵉ)		427
Chambiges Élysées (8ᵉ)		425
Costes (1ᵉʳ)		385
Costes K. (16ᵉ)		397
Crillon (8ᵉ)		381

D - E

Daniel (8ᵉ)		409
Duc de Saint-Simon (7ᵉ)		404
Élysées Céramic (8ᵉ)		428
Esprit Saint-Germain (6ᵉ)		400

F

Fouquet's Barrière (8ᵉ)		391
Four Seasons George V (8ᵉ)		379
François 1er (8ᵉ)		408

G - H

Grands Hommes (5ᵉ)		422
L'Hôtel (6ᵉ)		399
Hyatt Regency (8ᵉ)		394

I - K

Intercontinental Le Grand Hôtel (9ᵉ)		382
K+K Hotel Cayré (7ᵉ)		406
Kléber (16ᵉ)		429
Kube (18ᵉ)		415

L

Lancaster (8ᵉ)		392
Little Palace (3ᵉ)		418
Lutetia (6ᵉ)		390

M - N

Le Meurice (Hôtel) (1ᵉʳ)		374
Montalembert (7ᵉ)		405
Murano (3ᵉ)		389
Napoléon (8ᵉ)		393
Noailles (2ᵉ)		416

P

Park Hyatt (2ᵉ)		377
Pavillon de la Reine (3ᵉ)		388
Pershing Hall (8ᵉ)		424
Petit Moulin (Hôtel du) (3ᵉ)		417
Plaza Athénée (8ᵉ)		378
Pont Royal (7ᵉ)		403

Le Meurice

íO 228 r. Rivoli
⊠ 75001
✆ 01 44 58 10 10 – **Fax** 01 44 58 10 15
e-mail reservations@lemeurice.com
Web www.lemeurice.com

Ⓜ Tuileries
A1

137 rm – ┇€520/610 ┇┇€620/725, ⌷€48 – 23 suites

íO **le Meurice** (see restaurant index)

Le Meurice

Just near Place de la Concorde, a stone's throw from the Tuileries Gardens, the Meurice seems to have been at 228 rue de Rivoli for an eternity. Since 1835, in fact, when Augustin Meurice, postmaster in Calais and owner of the hotel during the Restoration, decided to move it from 223 rue Saint-Honoré.

He was aiming for the clientele from across the Channel, to such an extent that an advertisement at the time asserted that "no other hotel in Paris offers so many advantages to English travellers." In 1935, when the hotel was enlarged through complete renovations (except for the historic façades), the poet Léon-Paul Fargue declared that there were three kinds of clients in Parisian hotels: "the bad ones, the good ones, and those who stay at the Meurice", including numerous celebrities and crowned heads.

Today, after the face-lift undertaken in 1998 (the renovations lasted two years and employed up to five hundred and sixty workers), the Meurice is dazzling them again and offering the kind of service one expects from a luxury hotel, including Yannick Alleno's sublime cuisine.

Ritz

🍴○ 15 pl. Vendôme   Ⓜ **Opéra**
📠 75001   **B1**
✆ 01 43 16 30 30 – **Fax** 01 43 16 36 68
e-mail resa@ritzparis.com
Web www.ritzparis.com

106 rm – ♦€710/810 ♦♦€710/810, ⌂ €44 – **56 suites**

🍴○ *L'Espadon* (see restaurant index)

Ritz

An apprentice wine waiter in his native Switzerland, he studied in the most luxurious establishments in Europe. Then César Ritz imagined creating an ideal residence that would offer "all the refinements a prince could want in his own home". He admitted "dreaming of a house that he would be proud to associate his name with". In Paris, a sumptuous home built in the 18th century was for sale at n° 15 Place Vendôme. Thus, on 1st June 1898, the former townhouse of the Duke de Lauzun became the Ritz. A temporary hospital for soldiers in the First World War, it regained its former magnificence in the Roaring Twenties. In 1944 a soldier named Ernest Hemingway, who later became a regular, helped remove the German occupants who had been there for four years. "Whenever I dream of paradise and beyond, I find myself transported to the Ritz in Paris," he wrote.

In 1979 the Ritz family sold the establishment to Mohamed Al Fayed, an Egyptian businessman based in the U.K. After nine years of restoration work, he gave the Ritz back its glamour, and the legend goes on.

The Westin Paris

3 r. Castiglione
✉ 75001
☎ 0144771111 – **Fax** 0144771460
e-mail reservation.01729@starwoodhotels.com
Web www.westin.com/paris

Ⓜ Tuileries
A1

409 rm – ♦€249/730 ♦♦€249/730,⚌€31 – 29 suites

The Westin Paris

The superb location of the Westin Paris, between the Place Vendôme and the Tuileries Gardens, is ideal for shopping on the elegant rue du faubourg Saint-Honoré or exploring the collections in the Louvre Museum. This Haussmannian building (from 1878) has preserved its sumptuous Napoleon III salons, and also features a more intimate and contemporary touch in its leather and red velvet bar. The rooms – some with a view over the Tuileries Gardens – are done in a variety of traditional styles including Directoire, Consulat and Empire. Le First, its new boudoir-style restaurant designed by Jacques Garcia, has a hushed atmosphere with subdued lighting where you can enjoy brasserie-style cuisine with a contemporary twist. La Terrasse Fleurie, the outdoor summer restaurant with the same menu, is located in the central courtyard. The refreshing decor is composed of foliage and a fountain. A haven of peace and quiet in the heart of Paris.

Park Hyatt

5 r. Paix
✉ 75002
✆ 0158711234 - **Fax** 0158711235
e-mail vendome@hyattintl.com
Web www.paris.vendome.hyatt.com

Ⓜ Opéra
A2

143 rm - €580/650 €690/760, €44 - 35 suites

VISA

Park Hyatt

Ed Tuttle is an art-lover and architect. He has been living in Paris since 1977. Hyatt chose him for its establishment on rue de la Paix. He had already designed several dream hotels around the world. At 5 rue de la Paix, where five Hausmann buildings were put together, he intended to create a place where artwork held a predominant place in the decor. He also wanted to highlight a certain French classicism by reworking traditional styles and materials in a contemporary way, with furniture he designed entirely, carefully blending various French styles from Louis XVI to the thirties.

When the "elegant, sophisticated and very Parisian" Park Hyatt Paris-Vendôme opened its doors on 20 August 2002, it was clear that this artist had succeeded. Jean-François Rouquette, who worked in several establishments with stars along the way and has accepted a wonderful challenge here, is in the kitchen in both restaurants: les Orchidées, with its glass conservatory and open-air courtyard, as well as the more low-key Pur'Grill.

Plaza Athénée

25 av. Montaigne
✉ 75008
☎ 0153676665 – **Fax** 0153676666
e-mail reservation@plaza-athenee-paris.com
Web www.plaza-athenee-paris.com

Ⓜ Alma Marceau
B3

145 rm – 🛉€575 🛉🛉€705/790, ☕ €35 – 43 suites

Alain Ducasse au Plaza Athénée and **_Le Relais Plaza_** (see restaurant index)

VISA MC AE

Plaza Athénée

This legendary Parisian hotel, where the watchwords are luxury, elegance and refinement, is the epitome of excellence. Since its inauguration in 1911, the Plaza has attracted a clientele that includes the most illustrious figures in business, entertainment and politics. After the majestic lobby, the eye is drawn to the colours of the Cour Jardin and Galerie des Gobelins. Flowers, marble, gilt work and famous paintings adorn each room, creating an impression of absolute comfort, enhanced by the extremely attentive service.
The first six floors of the hotel offer large rooms with traditional Louis XV, Louis XVI and Regency-style furnishings.
The hotel's two upper floors are entirely dedicated to the Art Deco movement; some suites are duplexes with sauna, fitness facilities and a view of the Eiffel Tower. At 500 square metres (5382 square feet), the Royal is the largest suite in Paris and affords a truly spectacular view of the city. In short, this is a dream come true.

Four Seasons George V

ⅢO 31 av. George V

⊠ 75008

✆ 0149527000 – **Fax** 0149527010

e-mail par.lecinq@fourseasons.com

Web www.fourseasons.com

184 rm – ♦€680 ♦♦€710,☲€35 – 61 suites

ⅢO **Le Cinq** (see restaurant index)

Ⓜ George V

A3

Four Seasons George V

The legendary George V has been "the" luxury hotel in Paris ever since it opened in 1928. Walking past the porch and awning, one is immediately struck by the majesty of the huge marble lobby, followed by the lobby-gallery and a succession of lounge areas where brunch is served. White marble and gilt work are everywhere, illuminated by magnificent floral arrangements. The light in the grand dining room, with its Louis XVI decor worthy of a palace, comes from an inner courtyard – an oasis of greenery designed as a hanging garden. The food is extremely refined, and the superb wine list makes it even more appealing. The two stylish private dining rooms can be booked in advance. The same 18C spirit pervades the guestrooms, decorated with old engravings. All the rooms have a terrace or balcony on the upper floors, where the same floral exuberance is on display. The hushed ambiance and absolute comfort make this the quintessential Parisian luxury hotel, and one of the most sought after by the international jet set.

Champs-Elysées, Concorde, Madeleine

Le Bristol

112 r. Fg St-Honoré
⊠ 75008
📞 0153434300 – **Fax** 0153434301
e-mail resa@lebristolparis.com
Web www.lebristolparis.com

Reopening scheduled for 22 March on completion of work

Ⓜ Miromesnil
C2

124 rm – †€590/610 ††€640/1130, ⊋€51 – 38 suites

¶○ *Le Bristol* (see restaurant index)

Le Bristol

For its clientele, this superb hotel, built in 1925 around a magnificent garden, remains the symbol of a certain kind of luxury with the accent on comfort and well-being. With its Louis XVI furniture and old masters, the decor in the rooms and suites, some of which have terrace gardens, plays on soft nuances highlighted by rare wood panelling and precious fabrics. The marble bathrooms are comfortably sized.

The reception and concierge area were restructured at the beginning of the year, and the fitness centre and beauty salon were also reorganised. The winter and summer restaurants are made for food-lovers, and the amazing pool like a barge on the top floor, surrounded by teak and glass, gives onto a solarium with a view over the whole of Paris. Although time seems to have stopped in this haven of calm and luxury, 2007 will see a big change. A new building on the corner of the rue du faubourg Saint-Honoré and avenue Matignon has been added, with thirty rooms and a restaurant grill that will open in the autumn.

Crillon

🛏️ 10 pl. Concorde Ⓜ️ **Concorde**
✉️ 75008 **D3**
✆ 01 44 71 15 00 – **Fax** 01 44 71 15 02
e-mail crillon@crillon.com
Web www.crillon.com

119 rm – ♦€615/1160 ♦♦€615/1160, ☕ €47 – 28 suites

🍽️ **Les Ambassadeurs** (see restaurant index)

Crillon

"Here, all is order and beauty, luxury, calm, and delight." Baudelaire's *L'invitation au voyage* is a fitting description of this luxury hotel à la française, ideally located a stone's throw from the rue du faubourg Saint-Honoré, the Champs-Élysées and the Louvre. Overlooking the Place de la Concorde, with which it shares a rich history, this majestic building is an 18th century masterpiece designed by Jacques-Ange Gabriel (architect of the Petit Trianon at Versailles).

Without rejecting this prestigious past, Sonia Rykiel and Sybille de Margerie have redesigned the rooms and suites, blending a personal touch with the sumptuous antique furniture. Luxurious apartments look out over the square, while the Bernstein and Louis XV suites on the top floor have terraces with a view of Paris.

Parisian chic is in evidence everywhere, from the reception rooms to the bar. At Les Ambassadeurs, the gastronomic restaurant, one of the best chefs of his generation has put together a classic yet innovative French menu. Sheer bliss.

Champs-Elysées, Concorde, Madeleine

Intercontinental Le Grand Hôtel

2 r. Scribe
75009
01 40 07 32 32 - **Fax** 01 42 66 12 51
e-mail legrand.reservations@ichotelsgroup.com
Web www.paris.intercontinental.com

Opéra
A3

450 rm - €335/650 €335/650, €35 - 28 suites

Café de la Paix (see restaurant index)

VISA

AE

G.Corbic/MICHELIN

1862 and 2003 are two historic dates for the Grand Hôtel. The first marks the inauguration of this establishment a stone's throw from the Opéra Garnier. The second is when this monumental Napoleon III style building was reopened after a complete renovation lasting many months. Rooms and suites are decorated in a Second Empire spirit with a range of blues, reds and gold. With its varnished mahogany furniture, refined prints and raised beds with elegant plaid covers, you will have all the luxury and comfort you need and, hidden behind this classical decor, the best state-of-the-art technology to keep the hotel up with the times.

The restaurant, which has had its moments of glory in the past, is quite up to the challenge. Since the spring of 2006, Laurent Delarbre (Meilleur Ouvrier de France 2004) has taken over the kitchen at the Café de la Paix. Meals are served continuously here, from breakfast to late-night dinner, under the period frescoes in this historic monument.

Scribe

1 r. Scribe
✉ 75009
☎ 01 44 71 24 24 – **Fax** 01 42 65 39 97
e-mail h0663@accor.com
Web www.sofitel.com

Ⓜ Opéra
A3

208 rm – 🛏€ 540/685 🛏🛏€ 540/685, ⌓ €28 – 5 suites

🍴 **Les Muses** (see restaurant index)

Scribe

Every floor in this hotel – renovated over the past year – is devoted to a particular figure, from Jules Verne, Auguste and Louis Lumière (who held their first public cinema screening here in 1895) to Diaghilev, Marcel Proust, Joséphine Baker, as well as the Jockey Club. Panels explaining the hotel's history line the corridors. The high ribbed columns of the façade are illuminated, while the lobby features a huge checkerboard of black and white stones. The rooms are in a similar style to the ground floor, with noble materials, rich textures and lighting effects. The elegant decor, designed in a classic style with a twist, is not averse to current trends. You can relax in the fitness room and spa on the first floor, while – in addition to Les Muses – food-lovers will appreciate the contemporary gastronomy in the conservatory with its glass roof and two fireplaces.

Raphael

17 av. Kléber
✉ 75116
☎ 0153643200 – **Fax** 0153643201
e-mail reservation@raphael-hotel.com
Web www.raphael-hotel.com

Ⓜ Kléber
D2

61 rm – ♦€335/475 ♦♦€335/570, ⌒€37 – 25 suites

Raphael

With its portrait of Raphaël in the grand lobby, a Turner painting, wood panelling, gilt and 15th century English furniture, the Hôtel Raphael, in the heart of the prestigious Golden Triangle Parisian business district, is a must. This valiant centenarian offers its guests the slightly old-fashioned but ever-so-reassuring charm of the luxury hotels of the Belle Époque. The lift takes you up to the Grand Siècle rooms and apartments, as well as to the Jardins Plein Ciel featuring seasonal-based dining with a 360º panoramic view of the capital. Traditional food is also served in the dining room and at the Bar Anglais.

As the owners of the Regina and Majestic hotels too, Léonard Tauber and Constant Baverez would be proud of the Raphaël, which they originally opened in the spring of 1925. Eighty years later, after a long period of renovation work and of integrating the latest technological innovations, it remains an independent, family-oriented, private place – unheard of in Paris.

A WATER THAT BELONGS ON THE WINE LIST.

MICHELIN MAPS
Let your imagination carry you away.

With Michelin maps, travelling is always a pleasure
- Quality road network coverage, updated annually
- A wealth of tourist information: picturesque routes and must-see sites
- Route-planning made easy: travel as you please

www.ViaMichelin.com

A better way forward

Costes

🍴 239 r. St-Honoré   Ⓜ Concorde
✉ 75001   **A1**
☎ 0142445000 – **Fax** 0142445001

79 rm – 🛏€350 🛏🛏€500, 🍽€30 – 3 suites

G.Corbic/MICHELIN

A discreet façade bearing the name of the establishment, a solid building in the Napoeon III style near the Place Vendôme, and a unique atmosphere after you cross the threshold of the hotel. That's the Costes, located a few blocks from what was once the Hotel Meurice in the 19th century.

The reception and lounges give onto a delightful Italian courtyard decorated with antique statues, where you will enjoy dining at the first sign of good weather. *Très* Costes. Little nooks for intimate conversations with love seats in pear wood and tub chairs. *Très* Costes.

The purple and gold bedrooms are decorated with refined details, harmonious colours, stylish furniture and monogrammed linens, giving it a Baroque touch. It has a swimming pool and fitness centre, as well as a bar designed by Jacques Garcia. *Très* Costes, as is the restaurant, a temple of the "contemporary lounge" trend.

De Vendôme

🍽 1 pl. Vendôme
✉ 75001
✆ 0155045500 – **Fax** 0149279789
e-mail reservations@hoteldevendome.com
Web www.hoteldevendome.com

🄼 Opéra
B1

19 rm – 🚻€430/660 🚻€510/780,⌣€30 – 10 suites

De Vendôme

This former 18th century townhouse is a unique gem, fitted out in the finest tradition of French decorative arts. The reception boasts pilasters with gilt capitals, inlaid polychrome marble floors and a desk made of fine wood. The spacious rooms come in sparkling or pastel colours, all with elegant draperies, as well as antique and period furniture.

The hushed atmosphere of the bar recalls that of an English club, and your imagination can easily fly across the Channel as you sip a glass of Scotch surrounded by the subdued lighting, mahogany furniture and Chesterfield armchairs. Meanwhile, in the kitchen, the chef makes good use of spices. The presidential suite, which can be used for private parties, is on the top floor of the hotel, with a vast lounge and terrace. Here is your chance for a breathtaking view over the rooftops of Paris. In short, this is a charming and magical place, located at number 1, Place Vendôme.

Renaissance Paris Vendôme

4 r. Mont-Thabor
75001
01 40 20 20 00 – **Fax** 01 40 20 20 01
e-mail francereservations@marriotthotels.com
Web www.renaissanceparisvendome.com

Tuileries
B1

85 rm – €330/610 €330/610, €29 – 12 suites

Pinxo (see restaurant index)

Renaissance Paris Vendôme

A very Parisian address, between the Opéra Garnier and the Jardin des Tuileries. Pierre-Yves Rochon has transformed this 19C building into a chic and elegant contemporary hotel, with an interior decor from the 30s and 50s remodelled according to current tastes. The noble materials and range of warm, soft colours envelop you in a bright yet intimate world the minute you cross the threshold. The rooms, in an array of light shades, have a pleasant and serene glow. The fireplace in the lobby is another spot to enjoy a moment of peace and quiet surrounded by the warm and elegant decor. More relaxation awaits you in the heated swimming pool, steam room and fitness centre, where you may also enjoy a massage. Or, have a change of scenery in the exotic Bar Chinois, the perfect place for a private talk. The modern black-and-white decor at the Pinxo restaurant is ideal for tasting the delicious new creations of Alain Dutournier, who has won two stars at the neighbouring Carré des Feuillants.

PLAN 3rd ARRONDISSEMENT

Pavillon de la Reine

28 pl. Vosges		**Ⓜ** Bastille
✉ 75003		**D3**

✆ 0140291919 – **Fax** 0140291920

e-mail contact@pavillon-de-la-reine.com

41 rm – †€360 ††€415, ⌑€25 – 15 suites

Pavillon de la Reine

The Place Royale was inaugurated in 1612, built at the initiative of "good king" Henri IV, assassinated two years earlier. The Place des Vosges soon turned the Marais district into a haven for high society, frequented by writers such as the Marquise de Sévigné, Racine, La Fontaine and Molière. Nowadays it is a delight to stroll and window shop under the arcades of the square, full of art galleries and antique shops. Wandering around this soulful neighbourhood, one must take the time to breathe in its special scent.

In the heart of historic Paris, the Pavillon de la Reine is in a unique location, close to the bubbling Place de la Bastille, the Marais' prestigious townhouses-turned-museums, and the picturesque Jewish quarter. Rooms are available on the courtyard or garden side. Its flowered courtyards and luxurious accommodation – part 17th century - are hidden from sight, giving it the look of a charming pied-à-terre.

Murano

┇○ 13 bd du Temple   Ⓜ Filles du Calvaire
✉ 75003   **C1**
✆ 01 42 71 20 00 – **Fax** 01 42 71 21 01
e-mail paris@muranoresort.com
Web www.muranoresort.com

 42 rm – ┇€350/650 ┇┇€400/650, ⌂ €38 – 9 suites

Murano

The eye-catching façade combines classicism and modernity. The upper floors of the building are true to their 19th century origins, while the ground floor is all steel and frosted glass. The Murano Urban Resort, in one of the oldest neighbourhoods in Paris, is a holiday destination of a completely new kind. The phenomenal renovations included two years of reflection, five hundred architectural plans and fifteen months of construction work, transforming this hotel into a unique setting where one can move freely between the various areas.

The Murano opens onto a gallery of white marble decorated by flowing organdie drapes, with glass sculptures lining the passageway. Luminous cubes, discrete precision lighting, modern paintings and contemporary furniture make for immaculate, airy decor without walls. Each of the rooms is equipped with a personal lighting system allowing you to select a colour to suit your mood, from sky blue, lilac and solar yellow to emerald green and turquoise. The hotel also features modular suites and a central lounge with fireplace. The height of modern refinement...

Lutetia

‖○ 45 bd Raspail   Ⓜ Sèvres Babylone
     ✉ 75006   **B2**
     ✆ 01 49 54 46 46 – **Fax** 01 49 54 46 00
     e-mail lutetia-paris@lutetia-paris.com
     Web www.lutetia-paris.com

220 rm – ♦€230/950 ♦♦€230/950, ⌓ €25 – 11 suites

‖○ *Paris* (see restaurant index)

This exceptional historic establishment was the first Art Deco hotel in Paris, built in 1910 by the owners of the Bon Marché department store. A stone's throw from the government ministries and Saint-Germain-des-Prés, it is easy to spot with its sumptuous façade celebrating the Bacchanalia and nature. Inside, the reception and lobby illustrate the Rykiel era, with works by Philippe Hiquily, Arman, César and Chemiakin – a reminder of the cultural effervescence here. Numerous paintings and lithographs decorate the rooms, all in the spirit of the Roaring Twenties. The well-equipped marble bathrooms are truly luxurious in the suites and junior suites. The pure Art Deco style is also on display at Le Paris, serving excellent food in a warm setting with wood panelling, elegant oval tables and colourful tableware, directly inspired by the ocean liner, Le Normandie. The Brasserie Lutetia has the same marine accent, with a menu devoted to seafood. There is live jazz music at the bar in the evenings from Wednesday to Saturday.

St-Germain-des-Prés, Quartier latin, Luxembourg

Fouquet's Barrière

🍴 46 av. Georges V
🏷 75008
📞 01 40 69 60 00 – **Fax** 01 40 69 60 05
e-mail hotelfouquets@lucienbarriere.com
Web www.fouquets-barriere.com

Ⓜ George V
A2

91 rm – 🛏€690 🛏🛏€690, ☕€30 – 15 suites, 1 duplex

🍴 **Fouquet's** (see restaurant index)

Véronique Mati

This establishment on the corner of Avenue des Champs-Élysées and Avenue George V is a true legend. It was here in 1899 that Louis Fouquet bought a former coachman's café. Since English was quite in fashion, he proudly posted the new name on the façade: Fouquet's American Drinks-Cocktails. The restaurant became famous, won three stars in the Michelin guide in the 1930s and was declared a Historic Monument in 1990.

Later, the Barrière group took over and decided to add a luxury hotel onto the restaurant built around an event garden designed by Édouard François. Since autumn 2006, the one hundred rooms and suites have been completed. Decorator Jacques Garcia has made wonderful use of mahogany, silk and velvet. On the ground floor, guests at the latest great hotel opened in the capital can have drinks at the bar, Le Lucien, and dine at the restaurant, Le Diane. On the top floor, the François André terrace affords a fantastic view of the Eiffel Tower.

Champs-Elysées, Concorde, Madeleine

Lancaster

🍴 7 r. Berri

✉ 75008

✆ 01 40 76 40 76 – **Fax** 01 40 76 40 00

e-mail reservations@hotel-lancaster.fr

Web www.hotel-lancaster.fr

46 rm – 🛏€310 🛏🛏€410/590, ☕ €32 – **11 suites**

🍴 *La Table du Lancaster* (see restaurant index)

Ⓜ George V

B2

Lancaster

In the late 19th century a Spanish businessman had his residence built on the rue de Berri, a quiet street that once bordered the Pépinières Royales. A quarter of a century later, Swiss hotelier Émile Wolf, who professed to have "no clients, only friends", turned the building into a hotel. Its privileged location away from the hustle and bustle of Paris and its courteous and discreet hospitality and service create the kind of warm and intimate atmosphere the owner was striving for. The rooms and suites, spread out over four floors, reflect a perfect balance between tradition and comfort. The decor features imaginative colours and a variety of precious fabrics including silk velvet, wool and large wall hangings. And don't be surprised to see so many paintings on the walls by Boris Pastoukhoff. He was a long-time resident at the Lancaster, and paid for his room with his art work!

Another major asset here is Michel Troisgros, who supervises the restaurant.

Napoléon

🍴 40 av. Friedland   Ⓜ Charles de Gaulle-Etoile
⬍ ✉ 75008   **A2**
✆ 0156684321 – **Fax** 0156684440
e-mail napoleon@hotelnapoleon.com
Web www.hotelnapoleonparis.com

101 rm – 🛏€440/590 🛏🛏€440/590, ⌿€26

Napoléon

You have just arrived from New York and the minute you walk into the Napoléon, it's as if you were plunged into the early 19C Paris of the emperor himself. Better than a museum, this establishment created in 1928 is the living embodiment of a part of French history that was full of splendour and magnificence. Here, you can experience life as it was in those times, with the addition of modern comforts. Consider the fine collection of paintings, autographs and figurines to the glory of Napoleon punctuating the plush Empire and Directoire decor, the wood panelling and warm tones, soft lighting and thick curtains creating a hushed atmosphere. Every inch of the hotel exudes refinement and elegance – a delight for tourists and Parisians fond of authenticity and style. For this place is truly exceptional, through its location at the foot of the Arc de Triomphe and clientele of legendary figures such as Joséphine Baker and Errol Flynn, who said this was quite simply "The Place to be"!

Champs-Elysées, Concorde, Madeleine

Hyatt Regency

24 bd Malhesherbes
🖂 **75008**
☎ 01 55 27 12 34 – **Fax** 01 55 27 12 35
e-mail madeleine@hyattintl.com
Web www.paris.madeleine.hyatt.com

86 rm – ∮€290/465 ∮∮€350/525, ⌕€28

Ⓜ Madeleine
D2

Hyatt Regency

An oasis of peace and quiet in the centre of Paris! Behind its elegant façade on the Boulevard Malesherbes, this hotel reopened eight years ago after undergoing an eleven-month total renovation, undertaken by Italian architect Aldo Riva. By choosing to preserve its residential style, he transformed this Haussmanian building into a Parisian hotel in keeping with the pace of the entertainment world on the grands boulevards. There is a huge choice of stylishly decorated rooms (a range of beige, chamois and ivory highlighted by pale wood) many with paintings by artist Nathalie Schmitt. A few rather privileged regular guests like to stay in the famous suite 706, located on the top floor of the building. Its panoramic terrace overlooks the whole of Paris!

The hotel started a trend with its literary brunches, held one Sunday per month at its Café M since October 2003, giving avid readers a chance to meet some great writers.

St-James Paris

🍴 43 av. Bugeaud   **Ⓜ** Porte Dauphine
✉ 75116   **C3**
☎ 0144058181 – **Fax** 0144058182
e-mail contact@saint-james-paris.com
Web www.saint-james-paris.com

38 rm – 🛏€370 🛏🛏€480, ☕€28 – 10 suites

St-James Paris

The Saint James is quite unique in that it is the only château-hotel in Paris and is also one of the few with a huge private garden. Its story is quite fascinating.

Born in Marseille in 1797, Adolphe Thiers, a former minister in the government of Louis-Philippe who opposed Napoleon III, was for two years the first president of the 3rd Republic. A large townhouse was built in his memory in 1892 on the site of the first Parisian aerodrome for hot-air balloons.

Long a special place reserved for France's best students, it was bought by the English in 1986 and became a typical London club; six years later, it changed hands again and was turned into a luxurious hotel residence. According to tradition in this vast home, access to the lovely oval dining room is reserved for residents and members of the club, who are the only ones permitted to dine there.

Étoile, Trocadéro, Passy, Bois de Boulogne

Sofitel Le Parc

55 av. R. Poincaré
⌷ **75116**
☎ 0144056666 – **Fax** 0144056600
e-mail h2797@accor.com

Ⓜ Victor Hugo
C3

116 rm – ♦€210/580 ♦♦€230/580, ⌷ €26 – 5 suites

Ⓣ **Le Relais du Parc** (see restaurant index)

This Sofitel is one of the jewels of the ACCOR group, embodying the "discreet charm of the bourgeoisie" in the 16th arrondissement of Paris. The reception, lounges and rooms have a decidedly British touch, with cosy print fabrics cleverly concealing the state-of-the-art facilities. Some of the suites even have canopy beds. To ensure optimal peace and quiet, most of the rooms are arranged around the terrace garden. The library-lounge in tartan colours and the bar in shades of chocolate and rust are ideal for cocktails. The sculptures by Arman – both here and at the reception desk – impart an elegant touch. Beware of the "hunting" ambiance at breakfast, served in a room with numerous trophies! You may prefer the terrace in the verdant cobblestone courtyard, the perfect place to enjoy your meal far from the noisy city. A short, up-to-date menu has been designed for your enjoyment by two great names in French cooking.

Costes K.

81 av. Kléber
⌧ 75116
☏ 01 44 05 75 75 – **Fax** 01 44 05 74 74
e-mail resak@hotelcostesk.com
83 rm – ♦€ 300 ♦♦€ 350/550, ⌑ € 20

Ⓜ Trocadéro
D3

Costes K.

This "little brother" of the older Costes establishment (on rue Saint-Honoré) has its own personality – a new concept and style for a different clientele. Conceived by Spanish architect Ricardo Bofill, it occupies a special place among the top ten most modern hotels in the city. The minimalist interior decor, with a deluxe "zen" ambiance and inimitable sense of detail, features clean lines and noble materials such as polished stucco, marble, colourful sycamore wood and immaculate glass. The feeling of absolute peace and quiet in the heart of Paris is reinforced by the delicious interior patio and Japanese garden, around which the rather spacious and generously equipped rooms and junior suites are arranged. The same care is evident in the extra facilities. Between the superb fitness room (in exotic wood) and the lovely little swimming pool, you can enjoy a wonderful moment of relaxation without even leaving the premises. In fact, you may never want to leave this haven of peace.

D'Aubusson

33 r. Dauphine
✉ 75006
✆ 01 43 29 43 43 – **Fax** 01 43 29 12 62
e-mail reservations@hoteldaubusson.com
Web www.hoteldaubusson.com

Ⓜ Odéon
D1

49 rm – ♦€295/465 ♦♦€295/465, ⌷€23

D'Aubusson

The hotel is named for its large antique Aubusson tapestries. This is old Paris - in the heart of Saint-Germain-des-Prés, and a stone's throw from the Seine and the Carrefour de l'Odéon. The Burgundy stone paving, age-old beams and majestic Louis XV salon – where, in winter, there is always a crackling fire going in the monumental fireplace – create a unique and intimate atmosphere enhanced by the attentive service. The bar is set up in the peaceful patio or in the Café Laurent where - on Thursday, Friday and Saturday evenings - jazz groups play late into the night in an international ambiance and British-style decor. The nightlife notwithstanding, you can still find all the peace and quiet you need in the rooms, which are rather spacious for this neighbourhood. Those in the 17C part of the building have preserved their exposed beams, and all of them have a personal touch. The smart Modern Style bathrooms are another excellent reason to stay here.

L'Hôtel

13 r. Beaux Arts   **Ⓜ** St-Germain des Prés
✉ 75006   **C1**
☎ 0144419900 – **Fax** 0143256481
e-mail stay@l-hotel.com
Web www.l-hotel.com

16 rm – **†**€255/640 **††**€255/640, ⌑ €18 – **4 suites**

L'Hôtel

The restrained façade is a striking contrast to the inside with its absolutely Baroque blend of genres! This hotel built in 1816 was given a facelift by Jacques Garcia, and it is one of his finest accomplishments. First, there is the Empire spirit faithfully reproduced in the dizzying central shaft and skylight overlooking the reception, and the row of little lounges with marbled red and green colonnades. The atmosphere is intimate and cosy despite this lofty elegance. The rooms range from scrupulously historical to freer reconstructions in different styles, including Pondichéry, Coti, Charles X, Roi de Naples and "Merteuil" - all with marble bathrooms. Not to mention the sumptuous suite that was the last dwelling place of Oscar Wilde, which inspired him to say: "I am dying beyond my means!". The cosy restaurant topped by a large glass roof resembles a winter garden with its heavy fabrics and plush armchairs and sofas. The earthly nourishment is in the classic genre, prepared by a young and ambitious team.

St-Germain-des-Prés, Quartier latin, Luxembourg

Esprit Saint-Germain

🔟 22 r. Saint-Sulpice
✉ 75006
✆ 0153105555 – **Fax** 0153105556
e-mail contact@espritsaintgermain.com
Web www.espritsaintgermain.com

Ⓜ Mabillon
C2

31 rm – 🛏€310/550 🛏🛏€310/550, ☕€26 – 1 suite

Esprit Saint-Germain

"Just like at home" is how the owners describe this establishment, a charming hotel open since late 2004 in the heart of the arrondissement, between Luco and Boulevard Saint-Germain.

Except for the discreetly highlighted name, nothing distinguishes the façade from the neighbouring buildings. But once inside, the elegance, conviviality, comfort and refinement give you a taste of the subtle differences at work here.

The owner, Laurence Taffanel, was involved in decorating her "house" and creating a warm atmosphere with its verdigris partitions in the lobby, neo-Romantic figurative paintings on the walls, and bookcases full of books. After thirty months of renovations, she transformed this typical 17th century building into "an historic hotel with a modern infrastructure". It has great 19th century charm and a lounge area with a view over the rooftops of Paris.

Sénat

10 r. Vaugirard
✉ 75006
☎ 0143545454 – **Fax** 0143545455
e-mail reservations@hotelsenat.com
Web www.hotelsenat.com

Ⓜ Luxembourg
D2

41 rm – ♊€ 185/385 ♊♊€ 185/385, ☕ €15

Sénat

From some of the windows on the street side – sometimes you have to lean out a bit – you can see the lofty façade of the Senate and the gates of the Luxembourg Gardens.
The hotel reception is hidden behind a traditional shop front. As you cross the threshold, you can feel the sense of harmony and well-being in the lobby, salon-library and patio. It took fifteen months of renovation work in 2003 and 2004 to provide clients with this warm and comfortable, large six-floor "family home" nestled in the heart of Saint-Germain des Près. It is just waiting to be explored, with its harmonious blend of classic and contemporary styles, its decor with clean lines, soft beige, brown and violet tones, and exotic wood furniture. It is chic and cosy, like the duplex suites on the top floor where the view of Paris from the little terrace is breathtaking.

St-Germain-des-Prés, Quartier latin, Luxembourg

Relais St-Germain

○|○ **9 carrefour de l'Odéon**
✉ **75006**
✆ 0143291205 – **Fax** 0146334530
e-mail hotelrsg@wanadoo.fr

22 rm ⌓ – ∤€210 ∤∤€275/420

○|○ *Le Comptoir* (see restaurant index)

Ⓜ Odéon
C2

Denis Clément

As a child in his native Béarn, he dreamt of rugby and never thought he would live in Paris. But this rugby fan is now established in the capital, near Odéon in the heart of Saint-Germain des Prés. The star-winning restaurants he once frequented and the famous Régalade are now long forgotten. With his wife Claudine, who was involved in decorating the place, Yves Camdeborde is now the owner of a fashionable restaurant that is always full for lunch and dinner, as well as a charming hotel with twenty rooms next door to the Comptoir.

Crossing the threshold of this 17th century house is an invitation to take a voyage back in time through art, history and culture. The rooms, huge and all different, are cosy and decorated with great attention to detail, from the original beams to the precious fabrics, furniture and antique objects. The suite with terrace has been designed with intimacy and comfort in mind. The copious and surprising breakfast is the perfect way to start out your day on the right foot!

Pont Royal

⍾○ 7 r. Montalembert
✉ 75007
✆ 01 42 84 70 00 – **Fax** 01 42 84 71 00
e-mail hpr@hroy.com
Web www.hotel-pont-royal.com

Ⓜ Rue du Bac
D2

& 65 rm – ♦€390/450 ♦♦€390/450, ⌇€26 – 10 suites

⍾○ *L'Atelier de Joël Robuchon* (see restaurant index)

Pont Royal

The Pont Royal is considered to be one of the very chic places on Paris' Left Bank, a refined literary hotel once frequented by Apollinaire and Gide, where writers still enjoy meeting at the elegant and cosy bar. The place still echoes with the voice of F. Scott Fitzgerald, who was fond of staying here with his wife Zelda. You can easily imagine them running into André Malraux, who is said to have enjoyed teaching his conquests about American cocktails.

This is a hotel that has kept up with the times – steeped in history, yet decidedly modern.

It is no accident that Joël Robuchon, whose team takes care of breakfasts and room service, chose this place to set up the first unit of his Atelier, now a worldwide venture.

PLAN 7th ARRONDISSEMENT

Duc de Saint-Simon

14 r. St-Simon
75007
0144392020 – **Fax** 0145486825
e-mail duc.de.saint.simon@wanadoo.fr
Web www.hotelducdesaintsimon.com

Rue du Bac
C-D2

VISA
AE

34 rm – †€220 ††€375, ☕ €15

Duc de Saint-Simon

Curiously, although the Duc de Saint-Simon had several residences in the area, he never lived on the street that bears his name. Consequently, this well-known 17th century French memoirist never lived in the eponymous hotel either. Never mind!

This fine establishment near Les Deux Magots and Le Flore, the two most famous cafés in the historic neighbourhood of Saint-Germain des Près, is a haven of comfort and tranquillity – just like being at home. Past the courtyard with its climbing wisteria, a cosy salon with a warm and elegant decor awaits you.

Each of the rooms is individually styled; but there is an overall unity in the furniture and matching colours. A lift takes you down to the bar in a nicely arranged 17th century cellar. The shady flower-decked courtyard is an added touch for guests to enjoy in fine weather.

Montalembert

 3 r. Montalembert
✉ 75007
 ☎ 0145496868 – **Fax** 0145496949
e-mail welcome@montalembert.com
Web www.montalembert.com

 56 rm – 🛏€199/350 🛏🛏€199/450, ☕€20 – 8 suites

🄼 Rue du Bac
D2

Montalembert

On the Left Bank, in the heart of Saint-Germain-des-Prés, close to the Louvre and Musée d'Orsay, this hotel was built in 1926 and recently renovated. The spirit is more that of an urban holiday residence where the guest should feel at home. How so? By focusing on the cosy comforts and intimate atmosphere. That is the clear intention of the Soldevila family who took over the establishment in 2005. Already the long-time owners of the Palace Hotel Majestic and the Hotel Inglaterra, in the heart of Barcelona, they decided to develop a more international business.

The rooms are either decidedly contemporary, or quite classical in the Louis-Philippe style. It's up to the guests to choose. In each room, marked with the stamp of architect Christian Liaigre, there are bedspreads in taupe, tobacco or cinnamon, bronze lamps designed by Eric Schmitt, photographs by Jean-Pierre Godeault, and prints by Guiseppe Castigioni. In the restaurant, the dishes come in two sizes and four themes: earth, sea, sun and vegetable.

Tour Eiffel, École Militaire, Invalides

K+K Hotel Cayré

4 bd Raspail
75007
0145443888 – **Fax** 0145449813
e-mail reservations@kkhotels.fr
Web www.kkhotels.com/cayre

Rue du Bac
D2

125 rm – €310/401 €338/650, €24

K+K Hotel Cayré

K + K, as in Josef and Helmut Koller, who created their hotel group in 1961, comprising 10 establishments in Europe. The same initials and the same identity can be found in London, Munich, Salzburg, Vienna, Budapest, Prague and Bucarest. In Paris too, of course, where the writer George Bernanos and the musician Pablo Casals were regulars at the Hôtel Cayré.
Set in an area known for its involvement in fashion and the arts, the hotel was completely renovated in a decidedly modern spirit. The contrast is striking between the Haussmanian façade overlooking the Boulevard Raspail and the contemporary design of the rooms with their soft, clean lines. Pastel and vivid colours blend in well together in the hall and reception, as well as in the bar and bistro. This is an ideal place for business people, and the Business Lounge is the perfect setting for confidential meetings. Not to mention the Wellness Centre, ideal for getting in shape and eliminating stress.

Tour Eiffel, École Militaire, Invalides

De Sers

41 av. Pierre 1er de Serbie
✉ 75008
☏ 0153237575 – **Fax** 0153237576
e-mail contact@hoteldesers.com
Web www.hoteldesers.com

🅜 George V
A3

45 rm – †€480/550 ††€480/650, ⚏ €29 – 6 suites

De Sers

Architect Thomas Vidalenc describes his approach in redesigning the Hôtel de Sers as trying to create "a home where the traveller experiences time in a new way, articulating a feeling of contemporary melancholy."To achieve that soothing effect, he opted for a design with clean lines, solid fabrics and airy spaces where nothing is out of place. Comfort, aestheticism and modernity are the key concepts in all the rooms, expressed with restraint and refinement in the parquet floors, cosy beds, bathrooms with light Italian marble and white faience, grey, beige and violet tones, and designer furniture.The building has preserved traces of its origins (the former home of the Marquis de Sers, a health care establishment, and as of 1935, a hotel) such as the monumental staircase visible from the reception. The garden has also been converted into a lovely patio-terrace where breakfast is served in summer. In addition to these fine facilities, there is also a gym, a sauna and hammam, massage and a "bath menu" with a variety of options available upon request. Now, take a deep breath|

François 1er

7 r. Magellan

✉ 75008

📞 0147234404 – **Fax** 0147239343

e-mail hotel@hotel-francois1er.fr

Web www.the-paris-hotel.com

Ⓜ George V

A2

40 rm – 🛉€300/780 🛉🛉€350/1000, ☕€22 – 2 suites

Blending old elegance and contemporary comforts appears to have been the leitmotiv for Pierre-Yves Rochon when he redesigned the François 1er at the dawn of the year 2000. And he certainly succeeded. The proof is in the luxurious and charming rooms cleverly combining canopies, thick curtains, *toile de Jouy*, plush carpeting, old lithographs, mouldings and antique furniture. In the bathrooms, Italian marble and modern designer facilities fit together in a smart retro style. The stylish details further enhance the charm of the place. The result is a soothing and rather comforting "stately homes" feeling, exemplified by the plush and muted dining room with a fireplace, and the winter garden with flowers in all seasons; as well as the antique knick-knacks, elegant armchairs and precious marble decorating every nook and cranny. In short, this is the height of refinement. It is also a model of hospitality with its discreet, pleasant and friendly staff.

Daniel

‖○
|⧩|
♿
A/C
☎
SAT
🚗
VISA
Ⓜ©
AE
Ⓓ

8 r. Frédéric Bastiat
✉ 75008
☏ 0142561700 – **Fax** 0142561701
e-mail danielparis@relaischateaux.com
Web www.hoteldanielparis.com

Ⓜ St-Philippe du Roule
B2

22 rm – ☖€320/450 ☖☖€380/450, ⧢ €30 – 4 suites

Daniel is intimate and elegant, with a townhouse sort of charm. Since it was redecorated by Tarfa Salam, and reopened in September 2004, it feels like being in the cavern of Ali Baba, and is ideally located between the Champs-Élysées and rue du Faubourg Saint-Honoré. Here, Eastern and Western aesthetics are happily combined in a well-conceived blend of styles – a cosmopolitan marriage of motifs and materials. The owners are said to be real antique buffs, and this is quite clear from the decoration mixing carpets from Kazakhstan, vases from Asia, Chinese wallpaper, *toile de Jouy fabrics,* English sofas with lots of cushions, ebony furniture from Lebanon, Moroccan ceramics (in the bathrooms), Syrian chairs and silver platters from Turkey. You can savour this soothing atmosphere, oscillating between a love of the East and Chinese curios, under the glass roof in a corner of the lounge. Comfortably settled in, you can forget all about time and dream of journeys to distant places.

Square

🍴○ 3 r. Boulainvilliers

✉ 75016

☎ 0144149190 – **Fax** 0144149199

e-mail hotel.square@wanadoo.fr

Ⓜ Mirabeau

B2

22 rm – 🛏€270/350 🛏🛏€270/350, ☕€20 – 2 suites

G.Corbic/MICHELIN

The Square grew out of a rather wild idea. With its sinuous and elliptical curves, and covered in marble, it looks like a trans-atlantic ocean liner cruising between the Seine and the Maison de la Radio. Zebra stripes are the theme tying it all together – in the lobby "gangways", in the fabrics in the rooms, and in the blinds and decoration of the Zebra Square restaurant. Maxims in the long dining room extol the pleasures of life, while the impressive shelves of wine bottles command attention behind the counter. Parisians are in the habit of coming here for the setting, the informal service and the contemporary cuisine. The lounge takes over at night (popular with the smart and beautiful), with its upholstered velvet and comfortable Chesterfield armchairs. The peaceful modern rooms in restful grey tones will accompany you on your journey through the night.

Trocadero Dokhan's

117 r. Lauriston   **Ⓜ** Trocadéro
✉ 75116   **D3**
✆ 0153656699 – **Fax** 0153656688
e-mail welcome@dokhans.com
Web www.dokhans.com

45 rm – ♦€430/510 ♦♦€430/560, ☕€25 – 4 suites

Trocadero Dokhan's

The challenge was to create a luxurious – yet not ostentatious – establishment that would discreetly combine modernity and classic tradition. Mission accomplished at this stylish but absolutely up-to-date hotel a stone's throw from the Place du Trocadéro. The fine 19th century freestone façade is covered in ivy, while sculpted box trees frame the outside steps, shaded by a broad black-and-white striped awning. Inside, it has the charm and elegance of a private mansion, with a circular lobby. The neo-Classical decor – with restored gold-leaf wood panelling – sets the tone of complete freedom in the decor. To create an impression of greater space, the niches were fitted with mirrors in which the round tables, velvet armchairs and warm parquet floors are reflected. In designing the rooms, the decorator also used contrasting tones and materials. For the ultimate in luxury, try the suite conceived as a romantic private pied-à-terre, inviting you to prolong your stay.

Étoile, Trocadéro, Passy, Bois de Boulogne

Sezz

♿ 6 av. Frémiet
✉ 75016
☎ 01 56 75 26 26 – **Fax** 01 56 75 26 16
e-mail mail@hotelsezz.com
Web www.hotelsezz.com

Ⓜ Passy
C2

22 rm – 👨€270/325 👨👩€320/700, ◬€25 – 5 suites

Sezz

Combining an ultramodern concept with a touch of real class is what Christophe Pillet has pulled off after remodelling this fine establishment. It took 18 months of renovations to transform a simple hotel, a magnificent example of Haussmanian architecture, into a temple of chic and functional design. The luxurious grey-toned decor is a minimalist symbiosis with clean lines and seductive curves that puts the grey Portuguese stone in its best light. The rooms are sublime spaces for the enhancement of one's well-being, outrageously comfortable and decorated with a monotony-banishing eye to detail with bold contemporary furniture, glass-partitioned open bathrooms, paintings and photographs picked up at the FIAC show, and sophisticated plasma screens. Two small lounges, a bar area, jacuzzis and steam rooms are also provided for guests. The ultimate luxury: the massages given upon request in a private room.

Regent's Garden

6 r. Pierre-Demours
✉ 75017
℘ 01 45 74 07 30 – **Fax** 01 40 55 01 42
Web www.bestwestern-regents.com

Ⓜ **Ternes**
A3

40 rm – ♦€ 109/279 ♦♦€ 109/279, ☕ €13

Regent's Garden

This superb 19C building has all the roguish charm of the townhouse described in Serge Gainsbourg's song *L'Hôtel Particulier*. The lobby sets the typically Napoleon III tone of the establishment. Its French windows give onto a peaceful and romantic garden, the ideal place to relax or have breakfast - served in the classically 18C dining room in colder weather. The rooms, upstairs, are decorated in different styles (Louis XV and XVI, Voltaire armchairs, cerused wood and Second Empire consoles). They are brightened up with shimmering floral fabrics, and some have canopy beds; the garret rooms on the third floor add a Bohemian touch. The hotel is scheduled for a facelift this year.

Palais des Congrès, Wagram, Ternes, Batignolles

413

Terrass'Hôtel

⫯⫰ 12 r. J. de Maistre
✉ 75018
✆ 0146067285 – **Fax** 0142522911
e-mail reservation@terrass-hotel.com
Web www.terrass-hotel.com

Ⓜ Place de Clichy
A3

85 rm – ⫯€260/290 ⫯⫯€295/340, ⫿€19 – 15 suites

Terrass'Hôtel

The Terrass'Hôtel has a great location in an environment that is both picturesque (at the foot of the Sacré-Cœur hill) and romantic (Montmartre cemetery). The name refers to the terrace at its restaurant, Le Diapason, a real eagle's nest perched on the roof with a view over the whole of Paris from May to September. The rest of the year, you can sample the updated traditional food in the contemporary dining room with clean lines and soft shades of grey before climbing up the steps to the famous basilica. The light and spacious rooms are elegant, with tasteful furniture offsetting the bright and silky fabrics. They offer a range of styles for all tastes, from discreetly classical to more decisively modern. This charming hotel in an unexpected location is only a stone's throw from some of the city's well-known historic places.

Kube

1 passage Ruelle
✉ 75018
✆ 01 42 05 20 00 – **Fax** 01 42 05 21 01
e-mail paris@kubehotel.com
Web www.kubehotel.com

Ⓜ La Chapelle
C3

41 rm – ✝€250 ✝✝€300/750, ☕ €25

Laurent Pons

This building, whose façade is a Historic Monument, is located in a calm little street isolated from the hustle and bustle of the city. Once you cross the threshold, it becomes both private and provocative. The striking concept is high-tech and playful. Fans of new technology are guaranteed to like this hotel with its forty rooms and suites. Those who are fond of the unusual will also enjoy exploring the huge lounge bar with its armchairs covered in synthetic fur, cubic chairs and tables, net curtains hemmed with red fur, and the mirrors and plasma screens covering the walls. In short, it is playful and baroque. Like its extraordinary Ice Kube bar engulfed in 20 tons of ice – an unreal decor where the temperature goes down to minus 5 degrees Centigrade! Black lights, dark walls and fluorescent figures create a different atmosphere in the luminous and distinct rooms with all the modern comforts. It is definitely unusual. But stay here once and you will find that "Kubism" is a state of mind.

Noailles

9 r. Michodière
✉ 75002
01 47 42 92 90 – **Fax** 01 49 24 92 71
e-mail goldentulip.denoailles@wanadoo.fr
Web www.hoteldenoailles.com

Ⓜ Quatre Septembre
B2

A/C SAT VISA AE

59 rm – ♦€ 180/240 ♦♦€ 180/330, ☕ €15 – 2 suites

Noailles

This establishment has that special appeal of certain French hotels with a personal touch. A recent facelift transformed this place, where the classical façade offsets the cutting-edge interior design. The luminous patio-terrace is now the "centre of gravity" for the new interior architecture. Enhanced by a wealth of vegetation, it is the setting for breakfasts, and provides light for the library and side lounges decorated with leather furniture featuring restful, contemporary lines. The jazz cocktail hour on Thursday evenings livens things up in the bar area with a fireplace. Japanese style for the clean and contemporary rooms (also arranged around the patio), and mineral look for the bathrooms. Additional features are the sauna and fitness facilities. The welcoming and enthusiastic staff and the attentive service will guarantee you an extremely pleasant stay here.

Du Petit Moulin

29 r. du Poitou
✉ 75003
☎ 0142741010 – **Fax** 0142741097
e-mail contact@hoteldupetitmoulin.com
Web www.hoteldupetitmoulin.com

Ⓜ St-Sébastien Froissart
C2

17 rm – ▮€ 180/350 ▮▮€ 180/350, ☕ €15

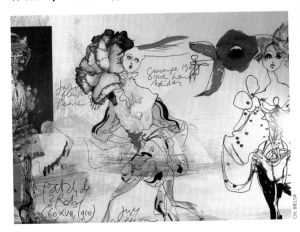

CH. BIELSA

The first clue is a building that housed a bakery not so long ago and has a 1900s front that is a historic monument. It was said to be the oldest bakery in Paris, dating back to Henri IV, where Victor Hugo came to buy his bread.

The second clue is a plain building on the corner of rue de Poitou and rue de Saintonge, connected to the former one and redesigned by the Bastie architecture agency.

The third clue is a famous *couturier* who draws divinely and took pleasure in fulfilling a childhood dream "left behind". He enjoyed building a decor, day after day, in the "colours of the times", creating an atmosphere through volumes and colours rather than merely on paper or through fashion designing.

The answer is the Hôtel du Petit Moulin where Christian Lacroix, who admits he immediately liked the slightly off-kilter perspectives and the maze-like design of the floors, created seventeen different types of ambiance for the seventeen rooms – like seventeen ways of experiencing the Marais!

Le Marais, Beaubourg

Little Palace

🍽 4 r. Salomon de Caus   Ⓜ Réaumur Sébastopol
✉ 75003   **B1**
✆ 0142720815 – **Fax** 0142724581
e-mail info@littlepalacehotel.com
Web www.littlepalacehotel.com

A/C **49 rm** – 🛏€153/218 🛏🛏€172/250, ☕€13 – 4 suites

VISA
MC
AE
DC

Little Palace

With its tiny rooms, the Little Palace lives up to its name. But what a decor! Its cheery Belle Epoque façade across from a small neighbourhood square sets the tone. The boutique hotel decor celebrates 1900s Vienna with huge Klimt reproductions, lilac and white colours, finely carved wood panelling, and stained glass in the breakfast room and pleasant reading room. The same spirit prevails in the restaurant, which tastefully blends retro and contemporary styles. The up-to-date snack menu is prepared by the proprietor himself. The rooms are decorated with angels - the languid women and mythological queens so dear to the Viennese Symbolists. The care taken over the decoration and the quality of the materials make you soon forget the minimalist dimensions. The upper two floors have balconies, a perfect place for enjoying breakfast with a view over the rooftops of Paris. This atypical establishment is the perfect jumping-off point for window-shopping in the Marais.

Bourg Tibourg

19 r. Bourg Tibourg
✉ 75004
☎ 01 42 78 47 39 – **Fax** 01 40 29 07 00
e-mail hotel@bourgtibourg.com
Web www.hotelbourgtibourg.com

Ⓜ Hôtel de Ville
B1

30 rm – ♦€160 ♦♦€220/250, ☕€14

Bourg Tibourg

Île de la Cité, Île St-Louis, St-Paul

This charming little Costes hotel nestled in the heart of the Marais gallantly displays its chic exuberance behind a rather discreet façade. Blending as always "high style and simple ways, the high life and the simple life", and eager to create a "thrilling place", superstar designer Jacques Garcia composed an environment here which is both unique and profuse. The rooms and their astonishing variety of styles reflect the multiple influences which blend into a kaleidoscope of colours and shapes – from Romantic and Baroque to Eastern and neo-Venetian, plunging guests into a world of comfortable exoticism with soft, subtle lighting. Don't expect huge spaces as the ambiance here is decidedly intimate, featuring small, luxuriously furnished rooms with molten-glass mosaics in the bathrooms, wide, flat TV screens and numerous other colourful touches. The hotel lounge is plush and attractive. Don't miss the splendid interior garden designed by Camille Muller.

Villa Mazarin

6 r. des Archives
✉ 75004
✆ 01 53 01 90 90 – **Fax** 01 53 01 90 91
e-mail resa@villamalraux.com
Web www.villamalraux.com

M Hôtel de Ville
B1

26 rm – ♦€130/400 ♦♦€130/400, ⌁€12

Villa Mazarin

The former Villa Malraux, created in 2005, targets a business and international clientele (mainly from across the Atlantic in the latter case), which is rather surprising for an establishment in the heart of the Marais. But all the expense appears to have paid off, and the businessmen have indeed answered the call. The smart decor has been designed in an Empire style subtly reinvented in a more contemporary spirit. The clean lines steer clear of exaggerated displays while featuring refined antique whitewood furniture, some of it original (headboard representing the façade of a temple). Each floor is done in a particular colour; and all the rooms – quite spacious for the neighbourhood – have the same aesthetic, successfully incorporating all the latest hi-tech facilities (flat screens, high-speed Wi-Fi connection, film and satellite channels). The "Wet bars" in every room, which combine a sink, refrigerator and microwave oven in the same unit, are another unusual touch. The hotel is entirely non-smoking.

Caron de Beaumarchais

12 r. Vieille-du-Temple
⊠ 75004
✆ 0142723412 – **Fax** 0142723463
e-mail hotel@carondebeaumarchais.com
Web www.carondebeaumarchais.com

Ⓜ Hôtel de Ville
B2

19 rm – 🛏€125/162 🛏🛏€125/162, ⊇€12

Caron de Beaumarchais

The author of the Barber of Seville and the Marriage of Figaro has lent his name to this amazing haven of aristocratic charm. Being a guest here is more like taking a trip into the past than merely staying at a hotel, for one is transported into an era of pomp and luxury when France's language and culture reigned in Europe (and the rest of the world). The establishment honours the memory of those blessed times with its spectacular 17C interior featuring rooms in noble materials including wood, stone and velvet, Gustavian-style period furniture and really fine exposed beams. Its perfection can be seen in the refinement of details, in the superb prints, old documents on the walls or on a Louis XV writing desk, and in the personalised linens. Most of the rooms give onto a pretty inner courtyard, and the smaller ones on the top floor have a magnificent view of the Right Bank. An exceptional place for an absolutely unforgettable experience.

Île de la Cité, Île St-Louis, St-Paul

Grands Hommes

17 pl. Panthéon
✉ 75005
📞 0146341960 – **Fax** 0143266732
e-mail reservation@hoteldesgrandshommes.com
Web www.hoteldesgrandshommes.com

Ⓜ Luxembourg
B2

31 rm – ¥€185/215 ¥¥€195/255,⌂€12

Jérome D'ALMEIDA

This fine 18th century building is across from the Pantheon, near the Luxembourg Gardens and the Sorbonne. It is no anonymous place, and its name is quite distinctive. André Breton, the father of Surrealism, lived here while writing his manifesto, *Les champs magnétiques*. And it was here that he invented automatic writing with his associate Philippe Soupault.

Sleeping across from the Pantheon, which is visible from all the upper rooms, one inevitably thinks of the famous neighbours resting in peace under the dome, such as Alexandre Dumas, Victor Hugo, Pierre and Marie Curie, André Malraux and Jean Jaurès.

The upper floors look out over the rooftops of Paris and Sacré-Cœur in the distance. Luxury and quiet comfort are the watchwords here, with the refined furniture, Directoire decor – a tribute to Napoleon – and wall hangings in shimmering colours. The environment is also key, featuring morning walks in the Luxembourg Gardens and evening outings in the area, so close to Saint-Germain-des-Prés!

Le Walt

37 av. de La Motte Picquet
✉ 75007
✆ 01 45 51 55 83 – **Fax** 01 47 05 77 59
e-mail lewalt@inwoodhotel.com
Web www.lewaltparis.com

Ⓜ Ecole Militaire
B2

25 rm – ☗€ 260/310 ☗☗€ 280/330, ☕€ 13

Le Walt

A haven of chic and charm a stone's throw from the École Militaire, Le Walt has style, all the modern conveniences, and a touch of imagination too. You couldn't find a better location than this central and relatively quiet spot near the Eiffel Tower, the golden dome of Invalides, UNESCO and the market on rue Cler. The welcoming and admirably restrained painted wood façade conceals a refined and cosy interior. Decorator Paul Sartres, who "wanted to create a young, modern interior that was timeless", has given free rein to his imagination. The warm and intimate rooms feature noble materials and pastel tones in a luminous setting decorated with original works by local artists. Large Renaissance-style portraits serve as head boards for the beds. The patio garden adds a very pleasant landscaped look at breakfast.

Tour Eiffel, École Militaire, Invalides

Pershing Hall

🍴 49 r. P. Charon   Ⓜ George V
✉ 75008   **B3**
📞 0158365800 – **Fax** 0158365801
e-mail info@pershinghall.com
Web www.pershinghall.com

20 rm – ♦€336/420 ♦♦€336/420, 🛏€26 – 6 suites

Pershing Hall

One of the most unusual gardens in Paris is hidden here, where the names of John Pershing and Andrée Putman are closely linked. The former, commander of American forces in France, used this townhouse as his residence during the First World War. The latter, a designer, created the decor when it was turned into a charming hotel.

Nothing has changed on the Empire-style façade. But, inside, the building has been considerably altered over the years. Andrée Putman took on the task of designing the space and the furniture on the five floors of rooms. From the patio, the entire house wraps itself around the surprising open-air garden, which combines hundreds of different varieties of plants, creating an ideal place for relaxing. The elegant and cosy rooms feature luxury with clean lines, lighting effects, and a blend of noble materials and colours. The bathrooms are lined with molten glass mosaics. Works by countless contemporary artists fill the rooms and corridors.

Chambiges Élysées

8 r. Chambiges
⊠ 75008
☏ 0144318383 – **Fax** 0140709551
e-mail reservation@hotelchambiges.com
Web www.hotelchambiges.com

Ⓜ Alma Marceau
B3

26 rm ⌂ – ♦€265/340 ♦♦€265/340 – 8 suites

Chambiges Élysées

Deluxe fabrics, antique consoles and original paintings make up the refined decor at the Chambiges Élysées, where the attention to detail, warm colours and comfortable surroundings are all part of the cosy atmosphere. Facilities include three categories of well-designed rooms – Standard, Deluxe (with a small sitting room, in red, raspberry, yellow or blue) and Suites (caramel, yellow or green) – and a superb 45m² apartment on the top floor. Each of the rooms has its own personality - *toile de Jouy* wallpaper, old lithographs, large mirrors and period furniture. Not to mention the "special touches" which add an extra note of charm to the place, such as the buffet breakfast in a plush and cosy room in shades of red and yellow, bathed in light from the stylish winter garden. In the afternoon, you can relax in the tea room over a cup of tea and a pastry – or get some work done (high-speed Wi-Fi connection).

Le A

4 r. d' Artois
✉ 75008
☎ 0142569999 – **Fax** 0142569990
e-mail hotel-le-a@wanadoo.fr
Web www.paris-hotel-a.com

Ⓜ St-Philippe du Roule

16 rm – †€345/472 ††€345/472, ☕€23 – 10 suites

The essence of this recently opened contemporary hotel can be summed up in two words: "A" as in atypical and artistic. Designed by architect Frédéric Méchiche as a private house illustrating the latest in modernism, the A, hidden behind a classical Haussmann façade, features a highly graphic and totally black-and-white decor. The indoor/outdoor contrast is striking. Far from monotonous, this two-toned environment is dotted with Buren-like stripes (on some of the walls and carpets), designer wengue furniture, comfortable armchairs, orchids placed in slender vases, and stylized lamps. Artist Fabrice Hyber has also invented creative designs for the rooms, the bar and the lounge-library. Luxury and refinement blend together here without ostentation, creating a feeling of discreet elegance. This original venue near the Champs-Élysées was designed for the kind of guest who enjoys staying in cosy and peaceful places with a different touch.

Le 123

123 r. du Faubourg St Honoré

✉ 75008

☎ 0153890123 – **Fax** 0145610907

e-mail hotel.le123@astotel.com

Web www.astotel.com

41 rm – ♦€250/420 ♦♦€298/468, ⊑ €22

Ⓜ St-Philippe du Roule

C2

Le 123

In an area known for its famous fashion designers, it was inevitable that the decor here at 123, created by Philippe Maidenberg, would play the haute couture card. This architect and designer had fun putting together an original display of materials. Grained leather sits side by side with chain mail, while silk blends with velvet, and the wooden bar stools mix in well with the restaurant's leather tables. Your gaze is irresistibly drawn to the monumental chandelier, composed of 3000 Swarovski pendants, while the red crystal sconces create a magical feeling. The staircase, decorated in typical London red brick, leads up to the rooms and suites designed in a contemporary style. Some rooms have cut stone, others have four-poster beds; several of the bathrooms have light oak parquet floors, a view of the starry sky above their zinc roofs, warm Cordovan leather, English wallpaper and tiles, creating a very well-designed blend of styles.

Élysées Céramic

34 av. Wagram
✉ 75008
☎ 0142272030 – **Fax** 0146229583
e-mail info@elysees-ceramic.com
Web www.elysees-ceramic.com

Ⓜ Ternes
A1

57 rm – 🛉€175/185 🛉🛉€200/210, ☕€10

Élysées Céramic

The Belle Epoque era attempted to bring art into even the smallest aspects of everyday life; and that is the spirit in which one should contemplate the façade of the Élysées Céramic and its organic architecture with intertwining forms, glazed stoneware and sculpted stone created by Lavirotte in 1904 – a pure example of the modern style at its most exuberant. The "show" continues into the lobby and lounge area, all in wood, with ceiling mouldings, a fireplace decorated with ceramics, and heavy draperies. The rooms are done in the same Art Nouveau style, but in a more understated way – with silvery lotus flower prints, and furniture and lighting that fit in – to create a restful environment. The modern bathrooms are cleverly laid out. The buffet breakfast is served in a winter garden setting. After that, you have your choice of the shops on the avenue des Ternes, the théâtre de l'Empire, sightseeing on the Champs-Élysées or the peace and quiet of the parc Monceau.

Kléber

7 r. Belloy
✉ 75116
☏ 01 47 23 80 22 – **Fax** 01 49 52 07 20
e-mail kleberhotel@wanadoo.fr
Web www.kleberhotel.com

Ⓜ Boissière
D3

23 rm – ♦ €129/199 ♦♦€139/299, ☕ €14 – 1 suite

G.Corbic/MICHELIN

The charm of the intimate, family-friendly Kléber comes from the talents of its antique-hunting proprietors, who acquired the period furniture, including lacquerware commodes, coffee tables with porphyry tops, fine marquetry in precious wood, velvet draperies with gilded tassles, sideboards covered with motifs, Oriental rugs, luxurious tapestries, richly framed paintings and mirrors, and painted ceramic lamp bases. This is a generous reconstitution of the Baroque spirit of the 18C and 19C. Trompe-l'œil frescoes evoking the Commedia dell'Arte add to the charm. The rooms have fine parquet floors and personal touches. The bathrooms decorated with mosaics have spa baths and hydromassage showers.

Étoile, Trocadéro, Passy, Bois de Boulogne

Bassano

15 r. Bassano
⊠ 75116
✆ 01 47 23 78 23 – **Fax** 01 47 20 41 22
e-mail info@hotel-bassano.com
Web www.hotel-bassano.com

Ⓜ George V
D3

28 rm – ✝€150/260 ✝✝€170/280, ⌧ €18 – 3 suites

G.Corbic/MICHELIN

The Bassanos, a dynasty of painters in the Italian Renaissance, gave their name to this street and the freestone hotel on a corner, strategically located a stone's throw from the Champs-Élysées. The Mediterranean influence is evident from the minute you walk into the hotel, where Provençal colours prevail over Parisian greys. The cosy atmosphere is enhanced by a harmonious blend of colours – with discreet tones in the wood panelling and cerused wood furniture, and brighter shades in the fabrics and cosy armchairs – and the rooms are true havens of peace and quiet. Wrought-iron furnishings adorn the bright and roomy reception area, while the dining room is decorated with large pale wood panels and wall paintings representing bowls full of vegetation. Enjoy a copious breakfast there before heading off to the luxury boutiques and admiring the view from on top of the Arc de Triomphe, or wandering around the immensity of Petit and Grand Palais.

Banville

166 bd Berthier
✉ 75017
☎ 0142677016 – **Fax** 0144404277
e-mail info@hotelbanville.fr
Web www.hotelbanville.fr

Ⓜ Porte de Champerret
B2

38 rm – ♦€150/270 ♦♦€150/380, ☕€18

G.Corbic/MICHELIN

This 1930s building only a few minutes from Étoile houses one of the most charming hotels in the capital. Here, elegance and comfort are the watchwords, and there is a sense of total harmony the minute you enter the lobby, with its grand piano, fireplace and comfortable armchairs. The feeling of airiness and clarity continues as you enter one of the rooms, all with a personal touch. Préludes and Pastourelles, the latest rooms, are very attractive, as are their two neighbours on the eighth (and top) floor, the Appartement de Marie and the Chambre d'Amélie. From their ideally placed terrace, there is a wonderful view of Paris. "It's nice to come to a place where you feel at ease", confides one guest. "Everything here is so easy and designed to help you relax. You are in a real Parisian neighbourhood where you rub shoulders with the local inhabitants, and you adopt their lifestyle and habits", added another guest. Room service, air conditioning, soundproofing, relaxing massage and beauty treatments are some of the features available in the rooms. A luxurious and pleasurable environment.

Palais des Congrès, Wagram, Ternes, Batignolles

Waldorf Arc de Triomphe

36 r. Pierre Demours
⊠ 75017
✆ 0147646767 – **Fax** 0140539134
e-mail arc@hotelswaldorfparis.com
Web www.hotelswaldorfparis.com

45 rm – ♦€ 340/430 ♦♦€ 370/460, ☕€20

Ⓜ Ternes
B3

Palais des Congrès, Wagram, Ternes, Batignolles

Waldorf Arc de Triomphe

This prestigious chain has inaugurated its third Parisian hotel after extensive renovations, and the result is very appealing. Located at a reasonable distance from the place de l'Étoile, it has even preserved a certain peace and quiet far from the hustle and bustle of the Champs Élysées. The range of standard, superior and deluxe rooms in neutral, pleasantly restful tones is elegant and contemporary. The personalized furniture, refined fittings and exquisite taste, down to the tiniest details, go along with the establishment's seamless luxury status. The diligent service and quality of the breakfast, taken in the comfortable cream-coloured dining room, come as no surprise. Everything here has been done to make the guests feel comfortable, including the sauna and steam room awaiting you downstairs where you can unwind after a long day. The height of luxury – the small indoor swimming pool and fitness room are a pleasant alternative to television. Impeccable.

Amour

🍴 8 r. de Navarin Ⓜ Pigalle
✉ 75009 **C1**
☎ 0148783180 – **Fax** 0148741409

📞 **20 rm – ⊤€90 ⊤⊤€120,⌴€10**

VISA
ⓂⒸ
AE

Amour

A description of this place sounds rather like a Prévert poem – photos of Terry Richardson, table football, combed wool on the floor and benches outside where you can sip your cappuccino; as well as ivory Bakelite light switches, rooms with tattooed walls, second-hand books, black moleskin banquettes, a bathtub in the middle of another room, and a hound's-tooth carpet – not to mention the Paris metro tiles and glossy black paint.

With every room designed by a different contemporary artist, the decor is quite head-turning! No two lamps or carpets are alike, nor any two bathrooms decorated in the same style. The bar is unforgettable with its several-yard-long counter and album covers on the walls. In short, it is full of soul. Everyone is talking about this new place near the place Saint-Georges, and the restaurant is always packed. A sweet little hotel that is devilishly attractive.

Opéra, Grands Boulevards

Index of plans

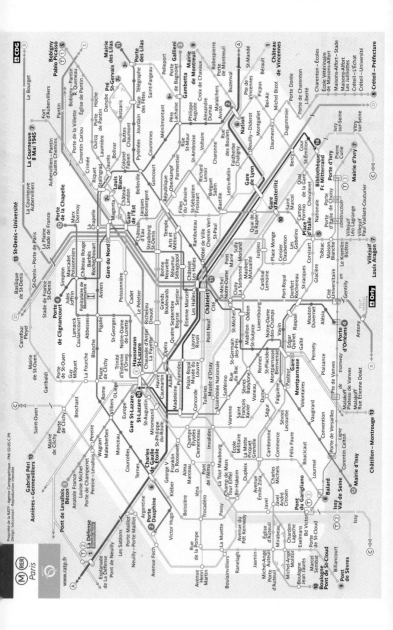

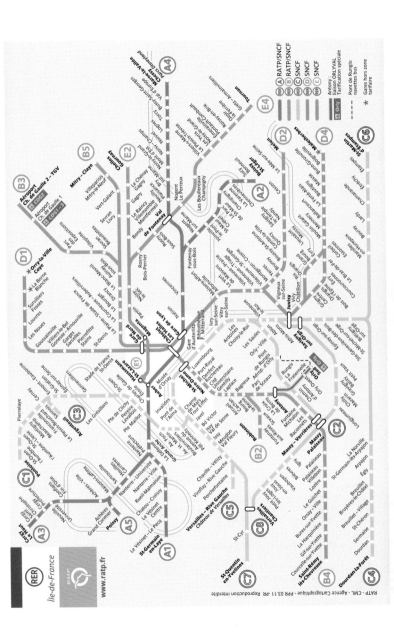

RER MAP **439**

Manufacture française des pneumatiques Michelin

Société en commandite par actions au capital de 304 000 000 EUR.
Place des Carmes-Déchaux – 63 Clermont-Ferrand (France)
R.C.S. Clermont-Fd B 855 200 507

© **Michelin, Propriétaires-Éditeurs**

Dépôt légal février 2007
Printed in France, 02-2007/5.1

Typesetting : APS à Tours
Printing and binding : AUBIN à Ligugé